AF847405

Medical Radiology

Diagnostic Imaging

Series Editors

Hans-Ulrich Kauczor
Paul M. Parizel
Wilfred C. G. Peh

The book series *Medical Radiology – Diagnostic Imaging* provides accurate and up-to-date overviews about the latest advances in the rapidly evolving field of diagnostic imaging and interventional radiology. Each volume is conceived as a practical and clinically useful reference book and is developed under the direction of an experienced editor, who is a world-renowned specialist in the field. Book chapters are written by expert authors in the field and are richly illustrated with high quality figures, tables and graphs. Editors and authors are committed to provide detailed and coherent information in a readily accessible and easy-to-understand format, directly applicable to daily practice.

Medical Radiology – Diagnostic Imaging covers all organ systems and addresses all modern imaging techniques and image-guided treatment modalities, as well as hot topics in management, workflow, and quality and safety issues in radiology and imaging. The judicious choice of relevant topics, the careful selection of expert editors and authors, and the emphasis on providing practically useful information, contribute to the wide appeal and ongoing success of the series. The series is indexed in Scopus.

Fabrice Dedouit • Kathrin Yen
Sarah Heinze
Editors

Forensic Imaging

A Practical Guide

Springer

Editors
Fabrice Dedouit
Service de médecine légale
CHU Rangueil
Toulouse
France

Sarah Heinze
Institute of Forensic and Traffic Medicine
University Hospital Heidelberg
Heidelberg
Germany

Kathrin Yen
Institute of Forensic and Traffic Medicine
University Hospital Heidelberg
Heidelberg
Germany

ISSN 0942-5373 ISSN 2197-4187 (electronic)
Medical Radiology
ISSN 2731-4677 ISSN 2731-4685 (electronic)
Diagnostic Imaging
ISBN 978-3-030-83351-0 ISBN 978-3-030-83352-7 (eBook)
https://doi.org/10.1007/978-3-030-83352-7

© Springer Nature Switzerland AG 2022
This work is subject to copyright. All rights are reserved by the Publisher, whether the whole or part of the material is concerned, specifically the rights of translation, reprinting, reuse of illustrations, recitation, broadcasting, reproduction on microfilms or in any other physical way, and transmission or information storage and retrieval, electronic adaptation, computer software, or by similar or dissimilar methodology now known or hereafter developed.
The use of general descriptive names, registered names, trademarks, service marks, etc. in this publication does not imply, even in the absence of a specific statement, that such names are exempt from the relevant protective laws and regulations and therefore free for general use.
The publisher, the authors, and the editors are safe to assume that the advice and information in this book are believed to be true and accurate at the date of publication. Neither the publisher nor the authors or the editors give a warranty, expressed or implied, with respect to the material contained herein or for any errors or omissions that may have been made. The publisher remains neutral with regard to jurisdictional claims in published maps and institutional affiliations.

This Springer imprint is published by the registered company Springer Nature Switzerland AG
The registered company address is: Gewerbestrasse 11, 6330 Cham, Switzerland

Foreword

Since about 20 years ago forensic post-mortem imaging was developed systematically at first in Bern, then in whole Switzerland and now worldwide. Richard Dirnhofer, the father of "Virtopsy"[1], summarizes the scientific development of post-mortem imaging techniques as follows:

> *It was against the background of rapid technological advances in various imaging techniques, that at the turn of the century, the academic concept of the "Virtopsy" research programme was realized at the University of Bern in Switzerland. The aim of this project has been to develop a minimally invasive autopsy procedure in which evidentially relevant findings are obtained from a corpse predominantly by means of medical imaging methods. Depending on the individual case and the specific issue involved, this leaves, the option open to perform a conventional autopsy to acquire further relevant facts, such as histological, toxicological and bacteriological examinations.*
>
> *The international impact of this idea has been reflected in an exponential increase in scientific publications around the world dealing with forensic radiology. For instance, the recently published study by M. Baglivo et al. showed a tenfold increase in the volume of publications compared to the turn of the millennium, when the "Virtopsy" project started.*
>
> *This academic "hype" in the field of postmortem radiology has had a very positive influence on the attractiveness of radiology for the new generation of academics in forensic medicine.*
>
> *In short, the results of these numerous publications documents that postmortem imaging is not only equal to autopsy in many respects but that this method can even achieve better results than conventional autopsy procedures. This has also called into question the status of conventional autopsy as the "gold standard" for obtaining and recording forensic medical findings.*

At the beginning of the virtopsy project, there was a confrontation between supporters of new developments and the defenders of the classical autopsy. This confrontation has now been resolved due to the success of Forensic Imaging.

Forensic Imaging in living individuals is of course also useful for the forensic examiner in different medicolegal contexts or situations as it is the only way of documenting internal lesions in living persons.

Also in this field post-portem imaging and forensic medicine have been very successful in the last years.

[1]The term "Virtopsy" is a neologism comprising the words "virtual" and "autopsy". It is used for imaging in Forensic Medicine, especially post-mortem imaging (CT, MRT, surface scanning, angiography).

From the beginning on in Bern Forensic Imaging could make its successful way only by the collaboration of experts in forensic medicine together with radiologists.

Richard Dirnhofer always acknowledges the support by the former Professor of Radiology at the University Hospital in Bern, Peter Vock.

Both radiologists and forensic practitioners have to learn their lessons since forensic radiology is a unique subdiscipline and not only an application of imaging in a forensic context.

It has impacts from both disciplines. Classical questions of forensic medicine have to be answered by methods of forensic radiology.

And this is also the approach of this book: Collaboration between forensic medicine and radiology. At least one of the editors is board certified both as expert in forensic medicine and as radiologist.

This book is not an introductory book. It is based on experience and own research in many fields of forensic radiology.

Meanwhile forensic radiology has become a standard method in forensic case assessment and diagnostics. According to the authors, the importance of interdisciplinary research and cooperation will further increase in the near future.

Since forensic imaging profits from new projects and collaborations between forensic medicine, radiology and other associated disciplines, it is nowadays mandatory for the expert in forensic medicine to have beside his own textbook a further one on forensic radiology, just like this one.

The table of contents covers a broad field both from forensic medicine and radiology. For instance:

- Imaging methods
- Analogies and differences between forensic and clinical imaging
- Post-mortem changes
- Normal post-mortem imaging findings in foetuses and children
- Artefacts (Mummification, Adipocere and Artefacts)
- Forensic radiology in trauma cases (blunt, gunshot, sharp wounds)
- Asphyxia
- Child abuse
- Post-mortem CT of charred victims
- Natural death
- Post-mortem imaging in fatal hospital cases after medical interventions

The authors come from several countries and offer an up-to-date view of the various facets of forensic radiology.

It is a pleasure for me to recommend this book not only for practitioners in forensic medicine, but also for radiologists who are beginning to deal with imaging in forensics: to understand the questions addressed in a medicolegal context and being aware of the required proof of evidence of an expert opinion, interpret traumatic alterations which are rarely seen in a clinical context and being aware of post-mortem changes.

Imaging in Forensics has gained its success by the contribution of both disciplines.

It is really amazing how fast this new and unique subdiscipline has developed within the last 20 years: by communication and cooperation between the disciplines radiology and forensic medicine and also between the institutes of forensic medicine in Europe. Forensic Imaging has given our discipline a new and strong scientific direction.

I congratulate the editors and the authors. For me it was a great honour to have been invited to write this foreword. I wish the book a great success.

December 2021

Bonn, Germany
Burkhard Madea

Preface

The rise of Forensic Imaging began around the year 2000 with the increasing use of CT and MRI in post-mortem and later also in living forensic cases and growing research activities in this newly developing field. Now, more than 20 years later, it seems time to present an overview of the many possibilities, benefits and current applications of imaging in a forensic context. The book shall introduce into forensic imaging casework and provide illustrated examples regarding typical forensic issues such as post-mortem alterations, characteristic signs of violence including the highly complex and important topic of child maltreatment, findings following accidents such as drowning or falls from height, specific needs and pitfalls of forensic image reading and more. The currently applied and presented imaging methods range from classical X-rays to CT, MRI, post-mortem angiography, post-processing methods up to 3D surface scanning and 3D printing, most of them fast developing and offering technologies that perfectly support modern forensic case assessment.

Our work does not claim to be an exhaustive textbook that fully covers all details of Forensic Imaging. We however hope it helps gaining interest in this—from a clinical view—still "exotic" field. If it succeeds in bringing both radiologists and forensic experts closer together and motivates to learn more, and maybe even become an active part of the forensic imaging community, it has fully served its objective.

Last but not least we want to cordially thank all the authors for their outstanding contributions and the publisher Springer for excellent work and support throughout the whole creation process of the book.

Toulouse, France — Fabrice Dedouit
Heidelberg, Germany — Sarah Heinze
Heidelberg, Germany — Kathrin Yen

In Memoriam: B. G. Brogdon (1929–2014)

Prof. Byron Gilliam Brogdon—the still undisputed doyen of forensic radiology—called for interdisciplinary collaboration between radiologists and forensic doctors in his 1998 bestseller, Forensic Radiology, "because sharing of interdisciplinary skills and knowledge would expand the scientific horizon."

This note struck a chord in my soul and mind and at the end of the last century prompted me to establish a transdisciplinary research group at the University of Berne to develop a minimally invasive autopsy. The project was named "Virtopsy" and used the imaging methods CT, MRI, surface scanning, and angiography.

In 2001, the first scientific results were presented in Interlaken on the occasion of the DGRM annual conference. Thankfully, Gil Brogdon accepted the invitation to be a keynote speaker. He was accompanied by his charming wife—his "precious" Babs—who supported him all her life as a lecturer for his scientific activities.

In his lecture, Gil Brogdon said with a wink that our project was "nihil novum sub sole." Because just 3 years after the discovery of X-rays, the first corpse was examined radiologically in the USA. Against the background of his stupendous knowledge of the literature, he also let us know that there was already talk of a "forensic autopsy machine" in forensic scientific circles in the early 1990s. And he also referred me to a specific paper by an Israelite working group that made morphological comparisons between computed tomography and autopsy findings. An illustration of his scientific modesty was the additional remark that the head of this working group Y. Donchin was neither a forensic doctor nor a radiologist, but an anesthetist.

Gil Brogdon spontaneously agreed to support our stringent, comprehensive transdisciplinary approach to our project. Above all, he also welcomed our cooperation with his radiological colleague and friend Prof. Peter Vock, Director of the Institute for Diagnostic Radiology, who was the first to succeed in three-dimensional recording of the body using spiral computed tomography. His willingness to provide support then became very concrete when, as a reviewer of our transdisciplinary publications, he promoted and accelerated their acceptance—also in radiological journals.

He found great pleasure in our word creation "Virtopsy." He found this neologism "a conveniently short but descriptive word." He expressed his approval for this in a congratulations when "Virtopsy" was included in

Lexicon for TIME magazine. In his enthusiasm he said in a letter that the term will establish itself like "Kleenex," "Scotchtape," and "Aspirin."

In an email he let me know 2 years before his death "you and your colleagues have advanced the "new horizons" of forensic imaging far beyond my dreams or expectations at the time of that writing. I am grateful that I have lived to see the results." Of course, there was great joy and gratitude in our team.

In beautiful, golden autumn weather, we spent unforgettable days with Gil and his dear wife in the mountains of the Bernese Oberland. I was also able to get to know her warm-hearted and lovable personality. As a nature lover, Gil Brogdon was, he compared the triumvirate "Eiger–Mönch–Jungfrau" with the McKinley Massif in Alaska.

He also told me that his professional career has always been closely related to forensic doctors and pathologists, such as with the competent Medical Examiner R.S. Fisher and LeRoy Riddick was linked. This "look into the neighbor's garden" made many interdisciplinary studies possible for him and never made him a "specialist idiot." And Gil Brogdon was a specialist and generalist in one, a personality with deep and at the same time broad knowledge—also three-dimensional like our new Virtopsy pictures.

His visionary spirit extended beyond the mere forensic use of imaging techniques. He expressed this in his foreword to our atlas "The Virtopsy Approach" with the sentence from "a Virtopsy guided CPC—the classic Clinico-Pathology Conference—could be an intellectually and visually exciting replacement."

As a bridge builder between radiology and the courtroom, B.G. Brogdon honored with numerous awards. For me and my "Virtopsy Team" he bears the epitheton ornans of "the father of postmortem imaging" and "Gil" will always be remembered with gratitude as such.

University of Bern
Bern, Switzerland

Richard Dirnhofer

In Memoriam: H. Vogel (1942–2018)

Dear Ladies and Gentlemen,

Dear Family Vogel,

I consider it a great good fortune that I was able to get to know Professor Vogel already during his time as a senior physician in the Department of Radiology at the University Medical Center Hamburg-Eppendorf in the 1970s—never completely lost contact with him—then "rediscovered" him for our legal medicine activities in the Middle and Far East, and finally was able to bring him back to the UKE after his retirement. Beyond the professional perspectives, a very friendly, trusting, and cordial relationship has developed.

The team at the Institute of Legal Medicine is very grateful to Hermann Vogel for his tireless dedication to forensic radiology at the Institute of Legal Medicine over the past decade. After his very successful professional life as senior consultant with Professor Bücheler at the UKE and then as head of the X-ray department at the Ochsenzoll General Hospital and St. Georg General Hospital, he has demonstrated another scientific flight of fancy with us in legal medicine. In good academic tradition, we honored him with an international scientific symposium on his 75th birthday on July 01, 2017, under the motto "Visions in Postmortem Imaging." Friends, colleagues, and students had gathered. We have summarized the central messages of this scientific symposium in a commemorative publication.

I would like to briefly trace the key points of Professor Vogel's academic curriculum vitae.

Hermann Vogel became a specialist in radiology in 1975. Shortly thereafter, he successfully completed his habilitation in 1977. By the way, we already knew each other personally then. In 1983, he was appointed professor and was then also chief consultant. He became senior hospital physician first at the Ochsenzoll General Hospital and then at the St. Georg General Hospital. Professor Vogel has written numerous scientific papers and also many books. He has been present at countless congresses in Germany and abroad.

From his scientific life, I would like to present very characteristic aspects. From a very early stage, Professor Vogel dealt with topics that are actually more associated with the field of legal medicine, but for which special radiological expertise is extremely relevant and in-depth. This refers to aspects of violence, torture, acts of war—in particular also in connection with physical effects such as sharp force, blunt force, gunshot, or others.

When asked how the topic of violence and torture in X-rays came into his focus, Hermann Vogel always pointed to a visiting professorship in Mexico, young habilitated, end of the 70s. Over there, he had the weekly experiences of Friday night's being terrible. There is alcohol and the: violence. He observed similar patterns elsewhere, but with different weapons and different injuries: for example, in South Africa, also in Zimbabwe, and in many other countries around the world. He then came into contact with the radiologist Brogdon in Alabama/USA, whom he himself called the forefather of forensic radiology. He still wrote his first book on the radiology of violence alone. The second book, he wrote together with Brogdon. This became the standard work.

Vogel scanned almost everything, including border controls, transport vehicles, and intracorporal drug smuggling. Nothing remained hidden. He always saw through things to the core. And he always raised his voice in warning and presented fascinating picture exhibitions! Clear words against oppression, violence, and torture. But also, clear evidence to convict the perpetrators of criminal activities.

Hermann Vogel was a walking encyclopedia. How many languages did he actually understand and speak fluently? He was a Francophile and an Anglophile in equal measure. Actually, he knew and loved the whole world. He always tried to spice up his lectures with introductory pleasantries in the respective national language and he immediately won over many hearts!

And as a matter of course, he always knew about the culture and history as well as the current political situation in the respective corner of this world. His memory was phenomenal. In a positive sense. He forgot nothing. He was like an elephant.

In connection with his special topics, no congress travel was too far or arduous for him. No call for discussion was too one-sided. Just ask internationally, e.g., in the countries bordering the Mediterranean, in the Middle East, but also in Asian countries (e.g., Japan), in Central America, ultimately on all continents—which forensic-radiological-legal-medical expert is best known there. Most of the time, the answer is: Hermann Vogel, the Vogel.

I have particularly fond memories of joint congress trips to the Middle East, e.g., to Syria, Lebanon, and Egypt. There, in recent years unfortunately again terrorist actions and armed conflicts dominated. We walked together through the temples of Baalbek and through Palmyra. We explored the pyramids of Giza and the Sphinx and we sat on the 40th floor of the Cham Hotel in Cairo in the revolving restaurant above the Nile and philosophized about the meaning of life: With a very positive thinking!

I am very glad that my contact with Hermann Vogel never completely broke off. Then, 10 years ago, I was able to win him over—completely—for legal medicine. We have had our computed tomography since 2008, and he became head of this Forensic Radiology special work area. A real success story! Numerous jointly solved difficult criminal cases and especially complex cases from the clinic, e.g., so-called medical malpractice, and then a series of very respectable publications, new books, numerous lectures, congresses, training courses nationally and internationally. Vogel was always present. In any case, I did not perceive any downtime. He communicated his findings and diagnoses from his bedside on the following days after, e.g., heart surgery.

And when he traveled internationally, he diagnosed remotely via email and the cloud. Simply incredible, fantastic, just Vogel! To say it with Gerhard Adam: As a university teacher and scientist a unique specimen! By the way: he also worked in a responsible position for the Hamburg Medical Association and the Health Authority in the field of radiation protection and as head of the medical office until the end!

Vogel was president, honorary member, and corresponding member in various scientific societies. He has received numerous honors. I am particularly proud of this: The German Society of Forensic Medicine awarded him its Science Prize in 2012; for these outstanding, creative scientific achievements in the field of forensic imaging. For achievements that have advanced the entire field of forensic medicine very far.

Now he has left us. From our point of view, much too early. I have always expressed to him the wish that we retire together from active service in legal medicine. This remains a pipe dream. He had just reached top form in that he had largely completed a 500-page standard work on imaging by computed tomography and angiography in deceased persons. It is a great honor and an obligation for us to hand over this book to posterity and to keep his memory alive.

In the words of my grandchildren: Dear Herman Vogel, how wonderful that you were born. How wonderful that we were allowed to be with you and work together.

We will miss you very much!

University of Hamburg
Hamburg, Germany

Klaus Püschel

Contents

Abbreviations

AHT	Abusive head trauma
ALARA	As low as reasonable achievable
AP	anterior-posterior
CA	Contrast agent
CEUS	Contrast-enhanced ultrasound
CI	Confidence interval
CPR	Cardiopulmonary resuscitation
CT	Computed tomography
DECT	Dual-energy computed tomography
ECMO	Extracorporeal membrane oxygenation
ER	Emergency Room
ESPR	European Society of Paediatric Radiology
EVAR	Endovascular aneurysm repair
FEVAR	Fenestrated endovascular aneurysm repair
H&E	Hematoxylin and eosin stain
HU	Hounsfield Unit
ICU	Intensive care unit
IQR	Interquartile range
ISFRI	International Society for Forensic Radiology and Imaging
kV	kilovoltage
LAD	Left anterior descending artery
LCX	Left circumflex artery
LIMA	Left internal mammary artery
MDCT	Multi detector computed tomography
MIA	Minimal invasive autopsy
MinIP	Minimum intensity projection
MIP	Maximum intensity projection
MPMCTA	Multiphase post-mortem CT-angiography
MPR	Multiplanar reformation
MRI	Magnetic resonance imaging
NAT	Non-accidental trauma
NICU	Neonatal intensive care unit
PACS	Picture archiving and communication system
PCI	Percutaneous coronary intervention
PEG	Percutaneous endoscopic gastrostomy
PET	Positron emission tomography
PM	Post-mortem

PMCT	Post-mortem computed tomography
PMCTA	Post-mortem computed tomography angiography
PMI	Post-mortem Imaging
PMMRI	Post-mortem magnetic resonance imaging
RCA	Right coronary artery
RIMA	Right internal mammary artery
RCR	Royal College of Radiologists
SCD	Sudden cardiac death
SCoR	Society and College of Radiographers
SE	Spin echo
SPNBF	Subperiostal new bone formation
SUDI	Sudden unexpected death in infancy
TAVI	Transcatheter aortic valve replacement
TIR	Turbo inversion recovery
TOP	Termination of pregnancy
TSE	Turbo spin echo
UHR	Ultra high resolution
UID	In utero death
US	Ultrasound
VR	Volume rendering
VRT	Volume rendering Technique
WA	Weeks of amenorrhea
WG	Weeks of gestation
WL	Window length
WW	Window width

Forensic Imaging: A New Subspeciality of Radiology

Fabrice Dedouit, Silke Grabherr, Sarah Heinze, Eva Scheurer, and Kathrin Yen

Contents

1 A "Historical" Introduction

Forensic imaging is often represented as a new field emerging from multidisciplinary work and research in forensic medicine and radiology. However, looking back on the interaction between radiology and forensic medicine, it has to be stated that radiology has always been used also for forensic purposes. This collaboration is therefore nearly as old as radiology itself. The year 1895 is important for radiologists because it was the year of the realization of the first radiography by Wilhelm Conrad Röntgen (Brogdon 1964). In fact, the benefit of radiographs to reveal the body's hidden secrets started to be practically used in 1895 in the United States of America, and then in 1896 in England (Brogdon 1998). These first forensic radiographs were used for clinical and post-mortem purposes. Very early, the possibility of localizing gunshot projectiles on X-ray images was highlighted. These are important facts, because they perfectly illustrate the early interaction between two different medical specialities: radiology and forensic pathology. Interestingly, things are not so different today: radiology assists clinical forensic medicine as well as forensic pathology.

F. Dedouit (✉)
Department of Forensic Medicine, Hôpital Rangueil, Toulouse Cedex 9, France
e-mail: dedouit.f@chu-toulouse.fr

S. Grabherr
Institute of Legal Medicine Lausanne-Geneva, Lausanne, Switzerland
e-mail: silke.grabherr@chuv.ch

S. Heinze · K. Yen
Institute of Forensic and Traffic Medicine, University Hospital Heidelberg, Heidelberg, Germany
e-mail: sarah.heinze@med.uni-heidelberg.de; kathrin.yen@med.uni-heidelberg.de

E. Scheurer
Institute of Forensic Medicine, University of Basel, Basel, Switzerland
e-mail: eva.scheurer@bs.ch

© Springer Nature Switzerland AG 2022

F. Dedouit et al. (eds.), *Forensic Imaging*, Medical Radiology Diagnostic Imaging,
https://doi.org/10.1007/978-3-030-83352-7_1

However, one major difference compared to those early experiences is of course that the radiological tools available today have advanced greatly. Those tools permit to document the inside of a human body and to digitalize it in a highly detailed matter. In post-mortem cases, the investigation of those digitalized bodies is often called "virtual autopsy" (Thali et al. 2003) and used as complementary tool to conventional forensic autopsy.

Using radiology on the deceased is not only of interest in forensic imaging. In fact, the amazing potential of radiography is also important for anthropological purposes. Already in 1896, X-rays were used by Koenig in Frankfurt on human and cat mummies and by Holland in Liverpool on bird mummies (Chhem 2008). Without unwrapping the mummies, Koenig was able to distinguish between mature and immature, and human or non-human subjects. Sigerist wrote that "the roentgenological examination moreover has the great advantage in that it permits the investigator to examine bones without destroying them and to inspect mummies without unwrapping them" (Sigerist 1951; Chhem 2008). The interaction between paleopathology, anthropology, archaeo-anthropology is called paleoradiology. Radiology can support anthropologists and archaeo-anthropologists with radiological tools that permit a virtual representation of the subjects or remains studied, which is the basis of the so-called virtual anthropology (Dedouit et al. 2014; Blau et al. 2017).

When we take a look on modern radiological tools in forensic medicine, we should keep in mind what Roentgen said about his work allowing him to discover X-rays: "I did not think … I investigated" (Glasser 1934; Brogdon 1998).

The history of modern forensic imaging began with B.G. Brogdon. The "Forensic radiology" book was one of the first pillars of this new discipline (Brogdon 1998). Of course, since 1998, many books, manuals, and articles have been written, illustrating the successful interaction between radiology and forensic medicine which requires a close collaboration between radiologists and forensic pathologists. In recent years, it was R. Dirnhofer from the Institute of Forensic Medicine in Bern (Switzerland) who founded the groundbreaking "Virtopsy Project" in 2001 together with P. Vock from the Radiology Department (Thali et al. 2009). This project allowed the scientific community in both fields to realize that modern imaging has an amazing potential for forensic medicine and pathology, as it has for clinical medicine and surgery. The diffusion of this work and of course many other research groups around the world contributed to the creation and the further development of the new medical discipline of forensic radiology.

2 The Role of Forensic Imaging in Today's Forensic Medicine

The word "autopsy" is of ancient Greek origin, being the combination of « aφtos » (self) and « opsomei » (to see). It can be translated as "a seeing for oneself" (Di Maio and Di Maio 2001; Knight et al. 2004). Medico-legal autopsy has many aims: reconstruction of the sequence of events and circumstances which preceded and led to death, including premortem diseases, determination of the cause of death, its judicial classification (homicide, suicide, accident, or natural death), precise time of death, and the identification of the deceased (Knight et al. 2004). Forensic work implies many different scientific, medical, and paramedical specialities: forensic pathology, radiology, radiography, but also odontology, anthropology, archaeo-anthropology, pathology, chemistry, toxicology, genetics, entomology, ballistics, biomechanics, etc.. Additionally, forensic imaging is not limited to radiologic methods. It can include many different other technologies like photography, photogrammetry, and the application of 3D surface scanners (Urschler et al. 2012; Grabherr et al. 2017; Rost et al. 2017; Bornik et al. 2018). The latter implicates the participation of engineers and computer scientists for visualization and segmentation tasks and the construction of 3D models and 3D printing casts. The general impact of such techniques, for example, in criminal trials is important.

2.1 Forensic Imaging in Clinical Forensic Medicine

Forensic imaging in living individuals can be useful for the forensic examiner in different medico-legal contexts or situations as it is the only way of documenting internal lesions in living persons (Yen et al. 2007b; Scheurer and Schoelzke 2014; Scheurer 2016; Yen and Krauskopf 2018). Examples for the application of clinical forensic imaging methods include the following issues.

- Living victims of violences or traffic accidents may have undergone radiological exploration (radiographies, CT, MRI …) for medical reasons. In this case, an additional forensic radiological interpretation is useful, as it will focus on the forensic questions and, thus, will be different from the clinical radiological interpretation (Schuh et al. 2013). This will help the forensic examiner, for example, to detect specific traumatic injuries or to interpret the findings according to forensic needs (Malli et al. 2013). Additionally, it is the only way to diagnose internal lesions of high forensic interest like trajectories or depths of stab wounds, gunshot wound channels, or deeper tissue and organ lesions. Interestingly, regarding dating of trauma, and specifically bone trauma, recent works dealing with quantitative MRI yielded promising results (Neumayer et al. 2014; Hassler et al. 2015; Baron et al. 2016a, b; Ogris et al. 2017).
- In some specific situations, namely survived victims after an attempt of strangulation, neck MRI can be useful to detect, e.g., deep soft tissue lesions or deep bloody effusions (Yen et al. 2007b).
- For some victims, it is necessary to obtain a comparison between an injury, e.g., formed bleedings into the skin, and an object, e.g., a shoe (Campana et al. 2016). The aim is to evaluate the match between both elements. In those cases, photogrammetry or 3D surface scanning of the object and the injury are crucial. In some cases, comparison between photogrammetry or 3D surface scanning of the object and a 3D CT model of the bone injury is possible. All data from 3D surface documentation can be merged with other imaging data such as CT or MRI (Urschler et al. 2014; Webb et al. 2015).
- Age assessment in legal procedures (administrative, penal or civil). For this case a specific procedure as presented in the AGFAD ("Arbeitsgemeinschaft für Forensische Altersdiagnostik," i.e., working group for forensic age estimation of the German Society of Forensic Medicine) has been established. Radiographies of the wrist and the teeth may be completed by a CT of the clavicles when the wrist bone maturation is already completed (Schmeling et al. 2006; Wittschieber et al. 2014). Current research, however, indicates that MRI will increasingly replace the radiation-based imaging methods in these cases (Baumann et al. 2015; Urschler et al. 2016; Widek et al. 2019).

2.2 Forensic Imaging in Forensic Pathology

The application of post-mortem forensic imaging has meanwhile shown great benefits regarding the documentation of the body as well as identification (Thali et al. 2009; Grabherr et al. 2016). The most relevant examples are:

- Documentation of the ***normal post-mortem radiological aspects and findings***:
  This part was the first important step into post-mortem imaging permitting a description of the normal semiology of post-mortem radiological images. Indeed, radiological images obtained from a deceased person and those obtained from the living are not the same. Specific knowledge is necessary in order to interpret them correctly, and the consequences of post-mortem changes need to be considered for the radiological interpretation (Dedouit et al. 2006). While in situ magnetic resonance spectroscopy has been investigated for the estimation of the post-mortem interval (Ith et al. 2002, 2011; Scheurer et al. 2005), the

use of forensic imaging methods generally allowed extensive new insights, providing useful information such as a detailed cartography of the distribution of post-mortem gas in a body, or the state of the vascular system after death (Egger et al. 2012; Grabherr et al. 2016; Stumm et al. 2020).

- Documentation of ***lesions and pathology***:
  - Diagnosis of traumatic and other lesions as well as pathologic changes:
    Of soft tissues, bones, organs, and vessels (Yen et al. 2004, 2007a; Anon et al. 2008; Scheurer et al. 2011; Bauer et al. 2020),
- In specifically forensic contexts:
  - determination of trajectories, directions, distances, up to the realization of a complete 3D biometric analysis that can, for example, be important for the analysis of stab wounds and gunshot wounds (Grabherr et al. 2017),
  - characterization of the injury-causing agent,
  - virtual reconstruction of the traumatic event, especially following traffic accidents, by fusions of 3D data as from CT, photogrammetry or 3D surface scanning (Schuh et al. 2013),
  - non-traumatic pathological findings including traumatic and infectious lesions, tumors or arthropathies (Dedouit et al. 2014).
  - Differentiation of non-lethal from lethal lesions, which is important for the determination of the cause of death, being crucial in forensic pathology.
  - Vital reactions, which are also of highest importance for forensic casework.
- Detection of ***foreign bodies*** (in traumatic contexts, e.g., bullets, pellets or for identification purposes prostheses or any surgical material).
- Identification of ***individuals*** (Dedouit et al. 2014; Weiss et al. 2018):
  - It can allow positive identification of an unidentified body without requiring DNA analysis.
  - Identification by the documentation of lesions (which includes the lesions previously described).
  - Comparative identification (comparison of antemortem and post-mortem data).
  - Reconstructive identification (based on the determination and assessment of important anthropological parameters: racial phenotype, age at death, sex, stature).

Today, clinical and post-mortem forensic radiology are subject to ***three main limitations***:

- The first is ***human***, represented by the physician who does the radiological interpretation (radiologist and/or forensic pathologist) and who must own specialized knowledge in clinical and post-mortem forensic imaging (Christe et al. 2009; Scholing et al. 2009). It is strongly recommended that only experienced persons as board-certified forensic pathologists and radiologists with a profound background in forensic radiology perform the reading and interpretation of forensic radiology images. Best case scenario is an interdisciplinary reading.
- The second is ***technical***. One classical mistake in post-mortem forensic imaging is to perform the examination such as post-mortem CT (PMCT) or MRI (PMMRI) according to clinical rules. It is necessary to optimize the imaging parameters according to the forensic needs. It is, for example, possible to scan very thin slices in PMCT, which would not be allowed in a clinical context due to radioprotection rules or to perform PMMRI scans with a duration of several hours.
- The third is the ***financial*** aspect, which is obviously a limit to the worldwide expansion of forensic radiological imaging.
- Not a real "limitation" but an important fact that limits today's application of forensic imaging methods is that imaging is not assigned by the responsible authorities in a relevant number of cases that would benefit from its use. This again is due to financial reasons and a still existing lack of knowledge about the indications and added value of imaging.

3 From Today to the Future

Although there is a broad agreement within the medico-legal community regarding the advantages of forensic radiology, there are still many forensic centers all over the world that do not have access to modern imaging technologies. Hence, in many countries forensic radiology remains far from becoming realistic. In addition, even if it can be used, it must be applied with care, and experts have to know the limits of the radiological tools they use. To further spread forensic imaging, it can help to promote it through specific working groups (e.g., the Technical Working Group Post-mortem Angiography Methods (TWGPAM), focused on post-mortem angiography) or scientific societies such as the International Society of Forensic Imaging (ISFRI) besides the classical national and international societies for radiology and for forensic medicine. The improvement of forensic imaging will also be supported through its inclusion in national official programs dedicated to the professional education of radiologists, radiographers and forensic pathologists and forensic examiners.

Forensic imaging has many advantages complementing the "classical" forensic methods. The most important are the noninvasive in situ diagnostics and visualization also possible in living persons, the possibility of unlimited digital storage, the possibility of image transfer, and finally yet important the fact that new interpretations are always possible on the same basis (Thali et al. 2003; Grabherr et al. 2017).

The development of "virtual autopsies" influences not only forensic but also clinical pathology (Heinemann et al. 2015). The possibility of radiological documentation and getting first insights into the body prior to autopsy changes autopsy practice and the management of the bodies (Grabherr et al. 2018). Consequently, new gold standards regarding forensic imaging procedures and its conjunction to autopsy have to be defined (Grabherr et al. 2018). The spirit of complementarity for post-mortem imaging and classical autopsy with added value for both is a driving force for the further development of forensic imaging methods.

But what about the future of forensic imaging? It has become more and more a standard method in forensic case assessment and diagnostics, specifically in a post-mortem context. In clinical forensic medicine forensic imaging methods are still not routinely applied in forensic case work even though imaging methods are the only possibility to assess internal findings and lesions. However, the forensic assessment and usage of previously obtained clinical imaging data is continuously increasing. Facing this rapidly growing field of forensic expertise the Institute of Forensic and Traffic Medicine in Heidelberg was the first to open a Forensic Radiology Centre (FoRCe) in 2019.

In a technical view, the future promises further developments of imaging tools. First "forensic" insights were already gained by the application of 7 T MRI and photon counting CT at the Institute of Forensic and Traffic Medicine in Heidelberg in cooperation with the German Center of Cancer Research. These latest technical advances not only allow highest image resolution and therefore new insights into the morphology of trauma and other findings but also highlight the additional value of clinical and forensic co-operations.

To the authors' view, the importance of interdisciplinary research and cooperation will further increase in the near future. Forensic imaging will profit from new projects and collaborations between forensic medicine, radiology, and associated disciplines. New applications, for example, using quantitative methods, minimal invasive procedures, or special techniques such as MR spectroscopy will open new diagnostic possibilities. Additionally, machine learning techniques might further advance forensic imaging research and practice in the future. What has been achieved so far will be complemented by the newly established. Forensic imaging will not replace the classical forensic methods, but is a precious contribution that will be a fixed and important part in future forensic medicine.

These are few points among many, which make forensic radiology so unique and so exciting in the medical field.

References

Anon J, Remonda L, Spreng A, Scheurer E, Schroth G, Boesch C, Thali M, Dirnhofer R, Yen K (2008) Traumatic extra-axial hemorrhage: correlation of post-mortem MSCT, MRI, and forensic-pathological findings. J Magn Reson Imaging 28(4):823–836. https://doi.org/10.1002/jmri.21495

Baron K, Neumayer B, Amerstorfer E, Scheurer E, Diwoky C, Stollberger R, Sprenger H, Weinberg AM (2016a) Time-dependent changes in T1 during fracture healing in juvenile rats: a quantitative MR approach. PLoS One 11(11):e0164284. https://doi.org/10.1371/journal.pone.0164284

Baron K, Neumayer B, Widek T, Schick F, Scheicher S, Hassler E, Scheurer E (2016b) Quantitative MR imaging in fracture dating—initial results. Forensic Sci Int 261:61–69. https://doi.org/10.1016/j.forsciint.2016.01.020

Bauer M, Gerlach K, Scheurer E, Lenz C (2020) Analysis of different post mortem assessment methods for cerebral edema. Forensic Sci Int 308:110164. https://doi.org/10.1016/j.forsciint.2020.110164

Baumann P, Widek T, Merkens H, Boldt J, Petrovic A, Urschler M, Kirnbauer B, Jakse N, Scheurer E (2015) Dental age estimation of living persons: comparison of MRI with OPG. Forensic Sci Int 253:76–80. https://doi.org/10.1016/j.forsciint.2015.06.001

Blau S, Ranson D, O'Donnell C (2017) An atlas of skeletal trauma in medico-legal contexts. Academic Press, Oxford

Bornik A, Urschler M, Schmalstieg D, Bischof H, Krauskopf A, Schwark T, Scheurer E, Yen K (2018) Integrated computer-aided forensic case analysis, presentation, and documentation based on multimodal 3D data. Forensic Sci Int 287:12–24. https://doi.org/10.1016/j.forsciint.2018.03.031

Brogdon BG (1964) Wilhelm Conrad Roentgen (1845–1923). Investig Urol 2:200–202

Brogdon BG (1998) Forensic radiology. CRC Press, Boca Raton

Campana L, Breitbeck R, Bauer-Kreuz R, Buck U (2016) 3D documentation and visualization of external injury findings by integration of simple photography in CT/MRI data sets (IprojeCT). Int J Legal Med 130(3):787–797. https://doi.org/10.1007/s00414-015-1274-3

Chhem R (2008) Paleoradiology : imaging mummies and fossils. Springer, Berlin

Christe A, Ross S, Oesterhelweg L, Spendlove D, Bolliger S, Vock P, Thali MJ (2009) Abdominal trauma--sensitivity and specificity of postmortem noncontrast imaging findings compared with autopsy findings. J Trauma 66(5):1302–1307. https://doi.org/10.1097/TA.0b013e31818c1441

Dedouit F, Otal P, Costagliola R, Loubes Lacroix F, Telmon N, Rouge D, Joffre F (2006) Role of modern cross-sectional imaging in thanatology: a pictorial essay. J Radiol 87(6 Pt 1):619–638

Dedouit F, Savall F, Mokrane FZ, Rousseau H, Crubezy E, Rouge D, Telmon N (2014) Virtual anthropology and forensic identification using multidetector CT. Br J Radiol 87(1036):20130468

Di Maio DJ, Di Maio VJM (2001) Forensic pathology, 2nd edn. CRC Press, Boca Raton

Egger C, Bize P, Vaucher P, Mosimann P, Schneider B, Dominguez A, Meuli R, Mangin P, Grabherr S (2012) Distribution of artifactual gas on post-mortem multidetector computed tomography (MDCT). Int J Legal Med 126(1):3–12

Glasser O (1934) Wilhelm Conrad Röntgen and the early history of the roentgen rays, 4th edn. Charles C Thomas, Springfield, IL

Grabherr S, Egger C, Vilarino R, Campana L, Jotterand M, Dedouit F (2017) Modern post-mortem imaging: an update on recent developments. Forensic Sci Res 2(2):52–64. https://doi.org/10.1080/20961790.2017.1330738

Grabherr S, Grimm JM, Heinemann A (2016) Atlas of Postmortem angiography

Grabherr S, Heinemann A, Vogel H, Rutty G, Morgan B, Wozniak K, Dedouit F, Fischer F, Lochner S, Wittig H, Guglielmi G, Eplinius F, Michaud K, Palmiere C, Chevallier C, Mangin P, Grimm JM (2018) Postmortem CT angiography compared with autopsy: a forensic multicenter study. Radiology 288(1):270–276. https://doi.org/10.1148/radiol.2018170559

Hassler EM, Ogris K, Petrovic A, Neumayer B, Widek T, Yen K, Scheurer E (2015) Contrast of artificial subcutaneous hematomas in MRI over time. Int J Legal Med 129(2):317–324. https://doi.org/10.1007/s00414-014-1124-8

Heinemann A, Vogel H, Heller M, Tzikas A, Puschel K (2015) Investigation of medical intervention with fatal outcome: the impact of post-mortem CT and CT angiography. Radiol Med 120(9):835–845. https://doi.org/10.1007/s11547-015-0574-5

Ith M, Bigler P, Scheurer E, Kreis R, Hofmann L, Dirnhofer R, Boesch C (2002) Observation and identification of metabolites emerging during postmortem decomposition of brain tissue by means of in situ 1H-magnetic resonance spectroscopy. Magn Reson Med 48(5):915–920

Ith M, Scheurer E, Kreis R, Thali M, Dirnhofer R, Boesch C (2011) Estimation of the postmortem interval by means of (1)H MRS of decomposing brain tissue: influence of ambient temperature. NMR Biomed 24(7):791–798. https://doi.org/10.1002/nbm.1623

Knight B, Knight BF, Saukko PJ (2004) Knight's forensic pathology, 3rd edn. Arnold, London

Malli N, Ehammer T, Yen K, Scheurer E (2013) Detection and characterization of traumatic scalp injuries for forensic evaluation using computed tomography. Int J Legal Med 127(1):195–200. https://doi.org/10.1007/s00414-012-0690-x

Neumayer B, Hassler E, Petrovic A, Widek T, Ogris K, Scheurer E (2014) Age determination of soft tissue hematomas. NMR Biomed 27(11):1397–1402. https://doi.org/10.1002/nbm.3202

Ogris K, Petrovic A, Scheicher S, Sprenger H, Urschler M, Hassler EM, Yen K, Scheurer E (2017) Detection and volume estimation of artificial hematomas in the subcutaneous fatty tissue: comparison of different MR sequences at 3.0 T. Forensic Sci Med Pathol 13(2):135–144. https://doi.org/10.1007/s12024-017-9847-8

Rost T, Kalberer N, Scheurer E (2017) A user-friendly technical set-up for infrared photography of forensic findings. Forensic Sci Int 278:148–155. https://doi.org/10.1016/j.forsciint.2017.07.001

Scheurer E (2016) Bildgebende Methoden in der klinischen Rechtsmedizin. In: Dirnhofer R, Schick P (eds) Bildgebung in der Rechtsmedizin—Der gläserne Körper als Beweismittel. NWV Verlag GmbH, Wien, pp 41–45

Scheurer E, Ith M, Dietrich D, Kreis R, Husler J, Dirnhofer R, Boesch C (2005) Statistical evaluation of time-dependent metabolite concentrations: estimation of post-mortem intervals based on in situ 1H-MRS of the brain. NMR Biomed 18(3):163–172. https://doi.org/10.1002/nbm.934

Scheurer E, Lovblad KO, Kreis R, Maier SE, Boesch C, Dirnhofer R, Yen K (2011) Forensic application of postmortem diffusion-weighted and diffusion tensor MR imaging of the human brain in situ. AJNR Am J Neuroradiol 32(8):1518–1524. https://doi.org/10.3174/ajnr.A2508

Scheurer E, Schoelzke S (2014) Consent to forensic radiologic examinations by living crime victims. Int J Legal Med 128(2):323–328. https://doi.org/10.1007/s00414-013-0831-x

Schmeling A, Reisinger W, Geserick G, Olze A (2006) Age estimation of unaccompanied minors. Part I. general considerations. Forensic Sci Int 159(Suppl 1):S61–S64

Scholing M, Saltzherr TP, Fung Kon Jin PH, Ponsen KJ, Reitsma JB, Lameris JS, Goslings JC (2009) The value of postmortem computed tomography as an alternative for autopsy in trauma victims: a systematic review. Eur Radiol 19(10):2333–2341. https://doi.org/10.1007/s00330-009-1440-4

Schuh P, Scheurer E, Fritz K, Pavlic M, Hassler E, Rienmuller R, Yen K (2013) Can clinical CT data improve forensic reconstruction? Int J Legal Med 127(3):631–638. https://doi.org/10.1007/s00414-013-0830-y

Sigerist H (1951) A history of medicine. Oxford University Press, New York

Stumm CJ, Wittig H, Kalberer NM, Scheurer E (2020) Histomorphological assessment of isolated abdominal organs after targeted perfusion with the contrast agent Angiofil(R) in postmortem computed tomography angiography. Forensic Sci Int 315:110427. https://doi.org/10.1016/j.forsciint.2020.110427

Thali MJ, Dirnhofer R, Vock P (2009) The virtopsy approach : 3D optical and radiological scanning and reconstruction in forensic medicine. CRC Press/Taylor & Francis, Boca Raton/London

Thali MJ, Yen K, Schweitzer W, Vock P, Boesch C, Ozdoba C, Schroth G, Ith M, Sonnenschein M, Doernhoefer T, Scheurer E, Plattner T, Dirnhofer R (2003) Virtopsy, a new imaging horizon in forensic pathology: virtual autopsy by postmortem multislice computed tomography (MSCT) and magnetic resonance imaging (MRI)--a feasibility study. J Forensic Sci 48(2):386–403

Urschler M, Bornik A, Scheurer E, Yen K, Bischof H, Schmalstieg D (2012) Forensic-case analysis: from 3D imaging to interactive visualization. IEEE Comput Graph Appl 32(4):79–87. https://doi.org/10.1109/MCG.2012.75

Urschler M, Holler J, Bornik A, Paul T, Giretzlehner M, Bischof H, Yen K, Scheurer E (2014) Intuitive presentation of clinical forensic data using anonymous and person-specific 3D reference manikins. Forensic Sci Int 241:155–166. https://doi.org/10.1016/j.forsciint.2014.05.017

Urschler M, Krauskopf A, Widek T, Sorantin E, Ehammer T, Borkenstein M, Yen K, Scheurer E (2016) Applicability of Greulich-Pyle and Tanner-Whitehouse grading methods to MRI when assessing hand bone age in forensic age estimation: a pilot study. Forensic Sci Int 266:281–288. https://doi.org/10.1016/j.forsciint.2016.06.016

Webb BA, Petrovic A, Urschler M, Scheurer E (2015) Assessment of fiducial markers to enable the co-registration of photographs and MRI data. Forensic Sci Int 248:148–153. https://doi.org/10.1016/j.forsciint.2014.12.027

Weiss G, Wittig H, Scheurer E, Ruprecht R, Lenz C (2018) Identification of deceased based on sternal bone computed tomography features. Forensic Sci Int 286:233–238. https://doi.org/10.1016/j.forsciint.2018.03.018

Widek T, Genet P, Merkens H, Boldt J, Petrovic A, Vallis J, Scheurer E (2019) Dental age estimation: the chronology of mineralization and eruption of male third molars with 3T MRI. Forensic Sci Int 297:228–235. https://doi.org/10.1016/j.forsciint.2019.02.019

Wittschieber D, Schulz R, Vieth V, Kuppers M, Bajanowski T, Ramsthaler F, Puschel K, Pfeiffer H, Schmidt S, Schmeling A (2014) The value of substages and thin slices for the assessment of the medial clavicular epiphysis: a prospective multi-center CT study. Forensic Sci Med Pathol 10(2):163–169. https://doi.org/10.1007/s12024-013-9511-x

Yen K, Krauskopf A (2018) Clinical forensic imaging. In: Ferrara SH (ed) P5 medicine and justice. Springer International Publishing, New York, pp 533–544

Yen K, Lovblad KO, Scheurer E, Ozdoba C, Thali MJ, Aghayev E, Jackowski C, Anon J, Frickey N, Zwygart K, Weis J, Dirnhofer R (2007a) Post-mortem forensic neuroimaging: correlation of MSCT and MRI findings with autopsy results. Forensic Sci Int 173(1):21–35. https://doi.org/10.1016/j.forsciint.2007.01.027

Yen K, Vock P, Christe A, Scheurer E, Plattner T, Schon C, Aghayev E, Jackowski C, Beutler V, Thali MJ, Dirnhofer R (2007b) Clinical forensic radiology in strangulation victims: forensic expertise based on magnetic resonance imaging (MRI) findings. Int J Legal Med 121(2):115–123. https://doi.org/10.1007/s00414-006-0121-y

Yen K, Vock P, Tiefenthaler B, Ranner G, Scheurer E, Thali MJ, Zwygart K, Sonnenschein M, Wiltgen M, Dirnhofer R (2004) Virtopsy: forensic traumatology of the subcutaneous fatty tissue; multislice computed tomography (MSCT) and magnetic resonance imaging (MRI) as diagnostic tools. J Forensic Sci 49(4):799–806

Imaging Methods

Anastasia Tsaklakidis

Contents

1 Introduction

Since Wilhelm Conrad Roentgen, born near Remscheid in 1854, discovered X-rays on 8th November 1895 and Sir Godfrey N. Hounsfield, born in the UK 1919, developed the CT scanner in the late 60s, imaging techniques have advanced significantly and have been indispensable in the practice of medicine since decades.

Only few months after Roentgen's discovery of X-radiation, the first forensic X-rays were done to detect bullets inside the human bodies and consequently this discovery could help solving crime cases. Even the first post-mortem angiography is dated in 1896 (Grabherr et al. 2016). Therefore, the advantages of diagnostic radiology and its application in the forensic field have been established and well recognized.

Whereas diagnostic radiology focuses on pathological findings and diseases, forensic radiology further emphasizes on the cause of death and the kind and intensity of injuries. For example, in order to reveal additional findings to classic autopsy or even replace it, post-mortem imaging can be used to detect the impact of external forces applied to the body by an assailant or different foreign objects including weapons. Furthermore, unknown corpses can be identified by comparing antemortem to post-mortem imaging.

In forensic ante-mortem imaging the detailed description of the injuries' localization and morphology is required, including the cutis and the subcutis, which is often ignored in diagnostic radiology due to lower relevance, especially in the emergency room (ER).

A. Tsaklakidis (✉)
Institute of Forensic and Traffic Medicine, University Hospital Heidelberg, Heidelberg, Germany
e-mail: anastasia.tsaklakidis@med.uni-heidelberg.de

© Springer Nature Switzerland AG 2022

F. Dedouit et al. (eds.), *Forensic Imaging*, Medical Radiology Diagnostic Imaging,
https://doi.org/10.1007/978-3-030-83352-7_2

Ante-mortem imaging, mainly performed during the emergency care in hospital, is usually seen first by the diagnostic radiologist who focuses on the relevant diagnoses in the urgent clinical pathological context. Forensic reading is done after the treatment and surgery. Ergo, both situations can mean a loss of information and sometimes important questions can only be answered or the case can only be solved by forensic radiological reevaluation of the initial imaging later on.

Regardless of the cause of death or trauma every forensic radiologic aspects and information can help to reconstruct or investigate a crime and can influence the court ruling.

In addition, forensic imaging and its reevaluation can be necessary to detect malpractice, used in civil conditions like age estimation of immigrants or be performed in special situations like choking or strangulation and screening of siblings of an abused child.

Besides X-ray, CT, Ultrasound and MRI, there are different other imaging techniques and methods that are used worldwide in forensic imaging. Nevertheless, it is especially cross-sectional imaging which allows 3D reconstructions, like the 3D volume rendering technique in different possible opacities, or even the creation of 3D prints to visualize and illustrate the findings, notably even for non-physicians like the police and the court.

Saving the acquired imaging data, e.g., in classic PACS systems (Picture Archiving and Communication System) or on external hard discs, enables the longtime permanent storage of post-mortem imaging like in conventional diagnostic radiology. Moreover, saving the data makes reevaluations and 3D reconstructions and prints possible, even after a long time, and an objective reproductive second forensic analysis can be done if necessary later on.

In contrast to classic diagnostic ante-mortem imaging, which in many countries has to be stored for a specific time, in post-mortem imaging, at least in Germany, there aren't any boundaries by law yet, which obligates the storage of forensic images for a predetermined time. Therefore, the different departments of forensic medicine can decide by themselves how long the acquired imaging should be kept and stored.

2 Technologies

2.1 X-Ray

As at the time of its discovering by Wilhelm C. Roentgen in his laboratory of the Physical Institute of the University of Würzburg in 1885, X-radiation is still produced by thermionic emission at the cathode filaments inside of the X-ray tube. Accelerated electrons of the heated cathode collide and interact with the stationary or rotating positively charged anode. While decelerating the electron energy is released mostly as heat and for a small amount as X-radiation. The number and energy of X-rays depends on the amount of mAs (Milliampere-seconds) and kVp (Kilovoltage peak). The X-ray beam, which leaves the generator passes through the object, if not completely absorbed by it, and is captured by a nowadays often digital detector placed behind the object, where the two-dimensional image, after being converted, is created (Loewenhardt and Müller 2006).

Besides the well-known X-ray of his wife Anna Bertha Ludwig's, hand (Fig. 1), Wilhelm C. Roentgen, while investigating and experimenting with the unknown rays, examined his shotgun among other objects and so the first X-ray of a weapon was obtained. Quickly after his discovery further scientists made X-rays of human beings to detect injuries, even after shotgun trauma (Fig. 2) (Glasser 2013).

Nowadays, diagnostic and forensic X-ray imaging continue to be an inherent part of medicine, for example revealing the extent of

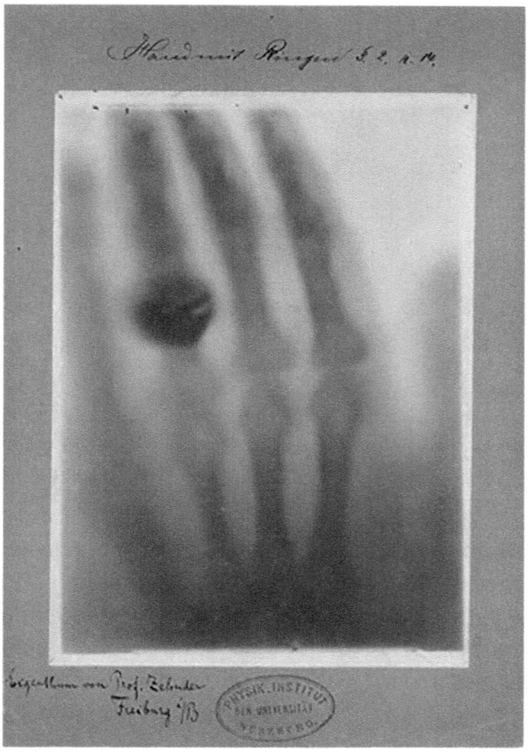

Fig. 1 Hand with rings. X-ray of Anna Bertha Roentgen's hand. (Reprinted by permission from Springer: Springer Nature, Wilhelm Conrad und die Geschichte der Röntgenstrahlen by Otto Glasser © (Jan 1, 1995)

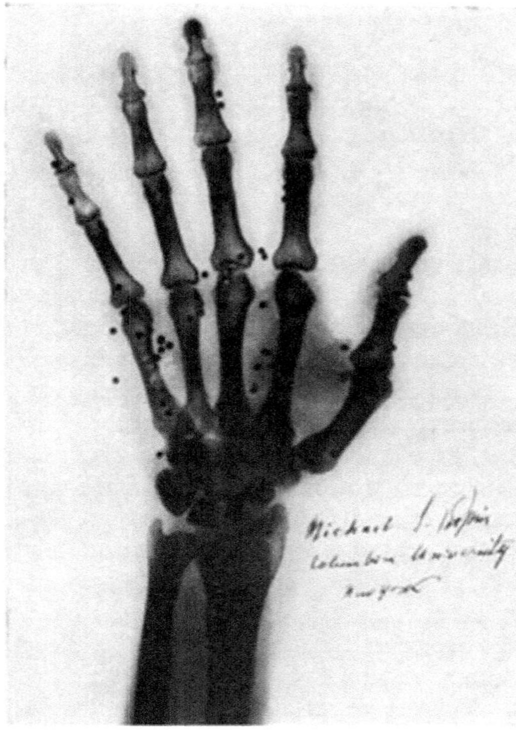

Fig. 2 Hand X-ray after a shotgun injury. Done by M. Pupin in New York in February 1896. (Reprinted by permission from Springer: Springer Nature, Wilhelm Conrad und die Geschichte der Röntgenstrahlen by Otto Glasser © (Jan 1, 1995)

injuries or detecting foreign bodies. Even non-metallic foreign bodies, like wooden splinters, glass or even drugs packed in cling-film and ingested oral (bodypacking) can be seen in X-ray. Furthermore, of course bullets and other metallic objects and fragments following blast and ballistic injuries can be detected by X-ray. X-ray examinations are usually indicated by the treating physicians and if necessary reevaluated by the forensic radiologist.

X-ray imaging is also frequently used in non-medical forensic investigations and settings, like scanning lorries or passangers' luggage at the airport to detect prohibited items.

In cases where child abuse is suspected, a radiographic skeletal survey has to be done in all children under the age of two, whereas the essential performed X-rays may differ slightly from country to country. Some imaging should be repeated after about 10–14 days, while healing fractures may be more recognizable then than on the initial studies. Detecting and dating fractures is one of the most important parts in the reevaluation and estimation of the intensity of child abuse. Furthermore, like mentioned above, the forensic pathologist can require X ray screening of the abused child's younger siblings or X ray imaging of the left hand and the jaw in age estimation programms (Figs. 3 and 4).

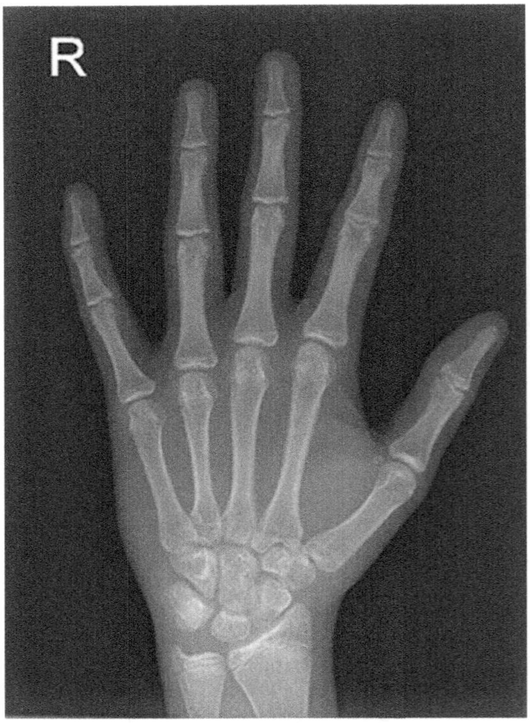

Fig. 3 X-ray of the left hand to analyze the growth plates to estimate the person's age

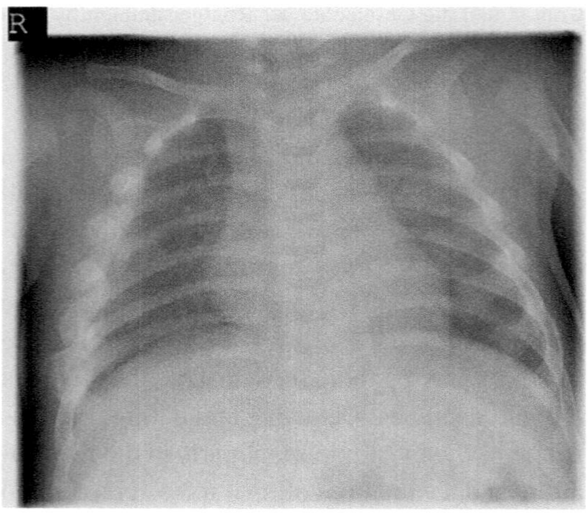

Fig. 4 X-ray of a child's thorax with rib fractures on the right

2.2 Computed Tomography

In 1971 the English electrical engineer Sir Godfrey N. Hounsfield developed the first CT scanner while working for EMI, Ltd. in Hayes,

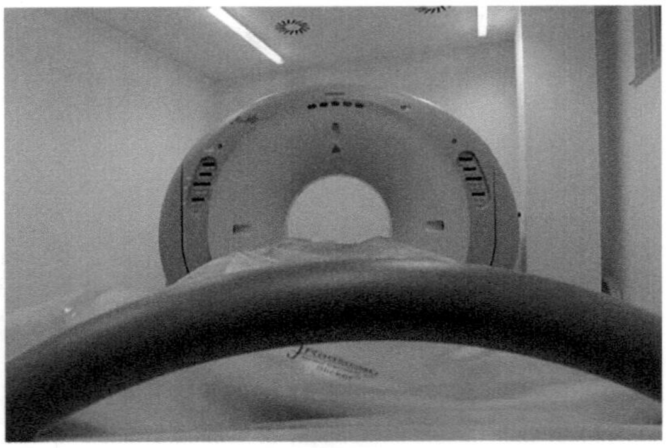

Fig. 5 The current CT scanner used for everyday post-mortem scans at the Heidelberg Forensic Institute (Canon Toshiba Aquilion 16, Department of Anatomy and Cellular Biology, University of Heidelberg)

Middlesex. His prototype was a single detector head scanner and after been successfully tested the first scanner was set up in the Atkinson Morley's Hospital in London. While the concept of a rotating X-ray source around the circular gantry, in which the patient or object is positioned and scanned by an often (since the second generation) fan-shaped X-ray beam with the detector on the opposite side, hasn't changed much, especially the speed, the detector size and shape have improved extremely. While in the early beginning just four slices of 13 mm thickness could be acquired in almost half an hour, nowadays by using multi-slice spiral scanners whole-body scans with micrometers of thickness can be done in seconds with rotation speeds up to over 700 mm/s (Loewenhardt and Müller 2006; Prokop et al. 2006). By using current techniques like Dual Source or Multi-Energy Computed Tomography with different energy levels the scan time and the amount of contrast media can be reduced, and further differentiations of tissues are possible due to different absorption in different energy levels. By additional techniques like iterative reconstruction methods or by using prefilters the radiation dose can be reduced as well (Fig. 5).

2.2.1 Ante-mortem Computed Tomography

Typically, the ante-mortem computed tomography, which is reevaluated under forensic aspects, has been done earlier in an emergency situation, for example after an accident, a fight or a fall from the height. In these classic ER scans the main focus lies on medical relevant injuries. But in forensic imaging it is very important to get a complete captured scan. For example, while doing a CT of the head, often cutis and subcutis of the upper epicranium aren't pictured completely and important forensic findings could be missed. So, to be sure not to withhold any findings accidentally, which could be relevant or even the key finding of a crime, the radiographer or examiner should scan the whole area and keep an eye on the stored reconstructions. At least one of the scans or reconstructions should include everything, and if possible, to support later forensic reevaluation, thin sliced reconstructions of 1 mm or less should be stored in the PACS system precautionary.

Whereas in post-mortem imaging exposure of radiation doesn't play a role, in ante-mortem forensic imaging the ALARA principle (as low as reasonable achievable) has to be obeyed like in conventional diagnostic radiology. There are only few situations in forensic medicine which require a CT examination of an allegedly healthy person. An example is the scan of the sternoclavicular junction of immigrants to evaluate the epiphysis and the probable age of the examined person if the X-ray of the left hand and jaw aren't enough for a final statement (Fig. 6).

2.2.2 Post-mortem Computed Tomography

There aren't many differences to the procedure of scanning a human being ante-mortem or post-mortem but some facts have to be considered. The dead body is brought in a body bag with its identification documentary to the CT-scanner. An employee of the institute has to escort the dead body at any time. If contrast medium is not applied, tissue extraction or biopsies are not needed, the body bag remains closed. In addition, if possible for the scanner and software, programs to reduce metallic artifact can be used. Furthermore, because radiation doesn't play a role in post-mortem imaging, to reduce beam hardening artifacts, the radiation and voltage can be increased. To avoid unnecessary changes of the corpse and hereby possible loss of information but especially due to the corpse's rigidity, often the body remains in its position, which may not be the physiological correct straight one, for the feet-first scan (Fig. 7). After the scout view, the head, the cervical spine and then the body including extremities are scanned. The reconstructions include bone, pulmonary and soft tissue windows in the required slice thickness, but as mentioned to ensure high resolution results and enable the possibility of further reconstructions later on, additional 1 mm reconstructions of every scanned part should be done and stored. 3D volume rendering technique (VRT) and maximum intensity projections (MIP) can be reconstructed later on if needed or required.

Like in the classical ante-mortem scan, you can get more information while using contrast media, but despite that even the native scan can show direct or indirect findings which can lead to the cause of death. The exact localization of foreign bodies or the exact position of multifragmental fractures, typical corticalis blast fractures of burned bodies or the morphology of in-driven fragments can be determined. Furthermore, abnormal gas collections, hemorrhage and subcutaneous hematomas or injuries can be seen native. When contrast media is used and if poisoning can't be ruled out a biopsy and sampling of blood and some organs' content should be done in advance to avoid falsified results.

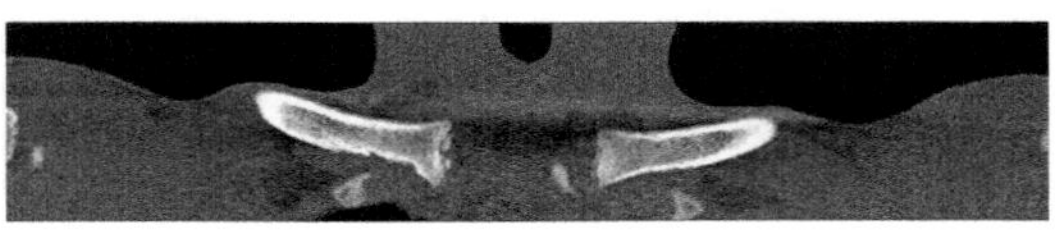

Fig. 6 CT of the clavicular und sternoclavicular junction and the clavicula's growth plate, coronar reconstruction

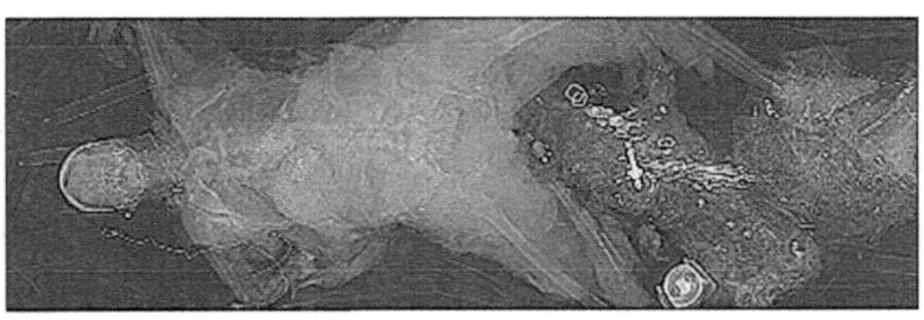

Fig. 7 CT-Scout of a burned corpse in abnormal position with different foreign bodies

After the scan, the corpse is returned back to the department of forensic medicine to initiate the autopsy.

2.3 Magnetic Resonance Imaging (MRI)

In the mid- and late 40s of the last century, nuclear magnetic resonance was discovered among others by Felix Bloch, a Swiss-American physicist who immigrated to the United States during World War II, and Edward Mills Purcell, an American physicist, independently. In 1952 they shared the Nobel Prize for Physics "for their development of new methods for nuclear magnetic precision measurements and discoveries in connection therewith" (NobelPrize.org 2021a).

First nuclear magnetic resonance was used for studies and analyses of atoms and molecules in chemistry. The American physician Raymond Damadian invented the first concept of a MR scan after his researches on the role of the potassium ion in cells using nuclear magnetic resonance. He detected that tumor cells have longer relaxation times in NMR ("Tumor Detection by Nuclear Magnetic Resonance") (Damadian 1971). In the end, it was Sir Peter Mansfield, an English physicist, who received the Nobel prize shared with Paul Lauterbur in Physiology or Medicine in 2003 for their discoveries concerning magnetic resonance imaging (NobelPrize.org 2021b; NobelPrize.org 2021c).

Sir Mansfield started his research while studying science in nuclear magnetic resonance and in 1977, after further studies and inventions, he made first a student's finger and later on his own abdomen visible by using MRI. Before that, Paul Lauterbur, an American chemist, enabled the visualization of liquids by magnetic fields and published his results in the "Nature Science Journal."

The first clinical scanner started in the early 80s, while one single scan took about 5 min (Loewenhardt and Müller 2006). Today, 40 years later, fast clinical MRI Scanners up to 7 T, open and upright MRI, MR spectroscopy or functional MRI exist.

The MRI technique is nowadays a permanent and important part of imaging in clinical and forensic medicine. Often MR imaging in forensic medicine is done like CT imaging in a clinical context and in criminal cases, accidents or malpractice reevaluated by an experienced forensic radiologist if needed. With different sequences and multiplanar acquired images or 3D reconstructions lesions, fragments, small fractures or bleedings can be detected and localized correctly. Fractures and bleedings/hematomas can be classified more detailed and their age can be estimated (Fig. 8). For example, a whole-body scan of infants can be helpful to localize fractures and bone marrow edemas or in strangulation victims it might visualize internal injuries of the neck (Yen et al. 2007).

In contrast to X-ray, CT, or PET scans, MRI does not use radiation and is a non-invasive imaging technique. This technique is based on

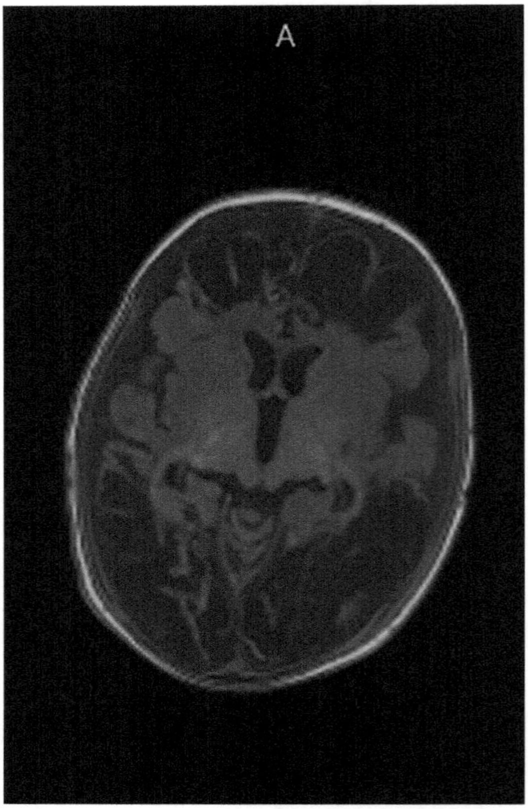

Fig. 8 MRI scan, T1 tra, months after NAHI with extended parenchymal destructions

the fact that different organs and tissues contain different amounts of protons of water and fat, which enables their differentiation. MRI uses a strong magnetic field and magnetic field gradients, which align the bodies' protons. By using short pulsed radio waves additionaly the protons are flipped out of their alignement. Their returning process to their normal spin can be measured and made visible. While combining different sequences with different pulses and attenuations this method is especially suitable to visualize all different kind of soft tissues and of course the neuronal axis. Because of the abscence of radiation it is a useful and harmless method in diagnostic imaging, especially of children or healthy individuals in for example age estimation programs instead of using computed tomography as usual (Fig. 9).

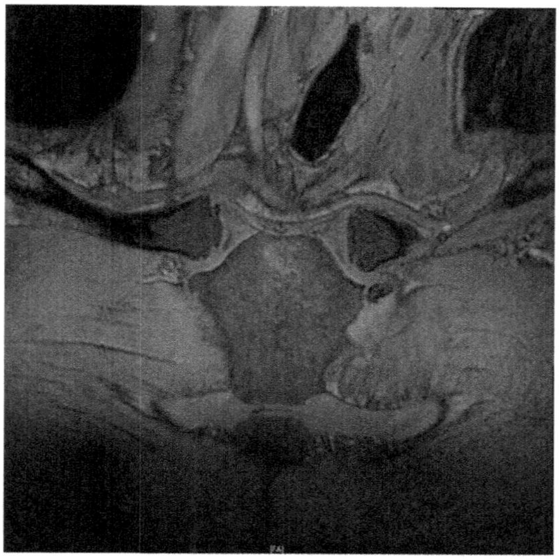

Fig. 9 Coronal MRI Scan, T1, of the sternoclavicular joint, the growth plate is still visible

However, MRI is fundamentally limited by the simple fact of long examination time that necessitates long non-movement phases and the known different contraindications for using this technique in general, like pacemakers, metal, pregnancy etc..

In turn, in post-mortem MR imaging you have to be aware of some differences compared to ante-mortem imaging. Though movement- and breathing or pulsation artifacts do not play a role metallic artifacts can still be a problem, for example, when the history of the corpse is missing and metallic intracorporal objects like metallic splinters or ferromagnetic bullets and projectiles cause unwanted artifacts or even migrate during the scan. Of course, extracorporal metallic objects can cause a reduction of information as well, so if possible, these should be removed before the scan.

Another important fact is that in contrast to ante-mortem imaging heating effects aren't relevant for the corpse itself or for the autopsy, but especially due to the corpse cooling, which can range between 4 and 36 degrees, changes in the relaxation times of the tissues' protons and the tissues' temperature can occur, so its image can change even during the scan, depending on the chosen sequences and duration of the whole scan (Scheurer n.d.).

Furthermore, gas bubbles within the tissue including bone and vessels caused by putrefaction have to be considered in the analysis of the sequences and should not be mistaken for air bubbles due to an injury or inflammation.

MR spectroscopy can be used as well in ante- and in post-mortem imaging to visualize various metabolites and to get further information about postmortal processes or changes, which can be helpful to detect possible underlying diseases.

2.4 Contrast Agents

Different types of contrast agents are available for different kind of imaging in ante-mortem imaging to enhance and differentiate tissues and help specifying pathologies, whether it is the water-soluble iodinated contrast agent used in plain radiography, angiography and ante-mortem computed tomography, the gadolinium contrast agents used in the magnet resonance imaging or the microbubbles used in contrast-enhanced ultrasound (CEUS). Depending on the questions physicians have, they can be used to improve the amount of information about the vessels, tissues, and organs and their pathological findings, but can be helpful in the forensic context as well. For example, injuries, traumatic bleedings, or trauma-associated lesions of parenchyma can be enhanced and shown. Usually, in ante-mortem imaging the diagnostic radiologist or the physician, who is in charge for the patient, decides whether contrast agent is needed or not. In post-mortem imaging the usage of contrast media depends on the settings of the forensic department, but if possible, it can be used in almost every case.

Different facts have to be considered in post-mortem contrast-enhanced imaging. First of all, the absence of blood circulation limits the quantity of different phases and therefore the quantity of information compared to ante-mortem imaging. In post-mortem computed tomography, primarily the vessels can be portrayed by using contrast agents, whereas post-mortem angiography can be as informative as the diagnostic ante-mortem angiography. Nowadays, similar to ante-mortem imaging different post-mortem angiography methods as well as different mixtures of contrast agents are used. Especially the so-called multiphase post-mortem CT angiography (MPMCTA) using an oily based contrast medium is well established. The MPMCTA starts with a native scan, followed by an arterial and venous scan and in the end a dynamic phase can be done. Because of post-mortem putrefaction the permeability of the different tissues and vessels changes and rises. This leads to a diffusion of water-soluble iodinated contrast agents, which are used in ante-mortem imaging, from the vessels in the surrounding tissue if not combined with fluids and agents, which support the intravascular persistence. To reduce this effect special oily based contrast mediums with low viscosity and high radio opacity for post-mortem imaging were invented to increase their intravascular persistence.

But still, different protocols with different water- or oil-based contrast agent solutions or mixtures with polyethylene glycol can be used to perform a post-mortem angiography.

Because of the missing blood flow and circulation, the needed amount of fluid for the injection is different, as well. Usually up to some liters of a mixture of contrast agent and the oily or water-based solution have to be pumped into the vessels mechanically, e.g., with a modified heart lung machine. Often the injection is made via femoral vessels, separately via Arteria and the Vena femoralis. In contrast to ante-mortem imaging during the venous phase, the first applied arterial contrast persists, so in the venous scan both vessel systems are contrasted. Of course, because of the missing blood circulation organic phases or excretion phases aren't possible in post-mortem imaging as they are known in ante-mortem imaging. Furthermore, small vessels can be blocked by clotted blood or extensive arterial calcifications in arteriosclerosis can reduce the results, similar to ante-mortem imaging. On the other hand, because of the simultaneously contrast of arteries and veins, sometimes even more vessels or vascular connections and variations, injuries or malformations can be detected compared to ante-mortem imaging. The evaluation of the scan can take place in the desired window, usually in the vessel, soft tissue, lung, or bone window like in ante-mortem imaging (Grabherr et al. 2016).

2.5 Further Technologies

2.5.1 Photography/Video-Technics

Whether a commercial photo camera or video camera is used, crime scenes, the surface of the ground, of buildings, objects and corpses or injuries can be documented and saved for later analysis. Using photogrammetry it is possible to determine its shape and position indirectly. Therefore, it can be used to reconstruct 3D-models.

2.5.2 3D Surface Scanning

First 3D surface scanning was just used in production and industry. Nowadays different scanners are also used in forensic medicine to scan surfaces and colors of different kind of objects and situations to reconstruct a crime or accident. A corpse, a wound, as a weapon used object (e.g., shoe's profile), vehicles or even whole crime scenes can be scanned and reproduced in a 3D image. These scanners are available in fixed or mobile exemplars. There are different kinds of surface scanners, for example, based on a fringe-pattern or other patterned light system technology (mobile hand scanners) or 3D laser scanner. For example, laser scanning is an interaction of million scans of the object. Measuring the distance, calculating the coordinates and the object's shape, lead to a dot cloud. This dot cloud can be transformed into a 3D image by fusion it with additional panoramic pictures of the object. These additional scans of scenes enable a virtual walk through the scenery or can be merged with cross-sectional imaging for example for further crime reconstructions and correlations of human injuries with forms or damages of objects.

2.5.3 Scintigraphy

Small amounts of radioactive molecules which are attached to agents are applied to make some diseases visible in a gamma scan while using their metabolic activity and accumulation in the affected areas. So, this method can only be used in living individuals. Basically, classic bone scans, using Technetium-99m, can be helpful to detect fractures of different age, an important information when investigating child abuse.

2.5.4 Ultrasound

This technique uses high-frequency sound waves, mostly between 1-18 MHz, to make different types of tissue visible. The higher the frequence, the higher the resolution, but the lower the penetration depth. The ultrasound waves are sent and the tissues' echos are received by the transducer. These echos can be visualized and translated in an image of different amounts of echos to assign the different tissues and organs. Mostly the B-mode (brightness mode) is used. The amplitude of the returned echo signal affects the brightness of it. Doppler ultrasound detects movements of echos and is able to distinguish, whether the echo is moving towards or away from the transducer. To enhance and characterize a lesion, tissue or vessel, contrast agents can be used as well. Though the amount and correctness of the results and findings, whether contrast agent is used or not, depends more on the experience of the examiner than in other imaging techniques. But the absence of radiation, and the fast and easy use, makes it an attractive diagnostic and forensic imaging technique.

2.5.5 Photon-Counting Computed Tomography

Besides the known Computed Tomography technique with energy-integrating detectors, which has become way faster and the resolution incomparably higher compared to its beginning, now a novel technology, the Photon-Counting Computed Tomography, starts to take part in diagnostic and forensic imaging. The Photon-Counting CT is an experimental and early clinical method, which is still researched and investigated in its possibilities. However, by counting every single Photon by a semiconductor detector, usually Cadmium Telluride (CdTe), resolution can be increased to Ultra-High Resolution (UHR), radiation and image noise can be reduced with less loss of information, and even thinner slices are possible. The absorption of an X-ray photon results in the formation of a charge cloud that is transported to the electrodes, so-called pixels, forming the detected signal. If the detector pixels are sufficiently small, the counting of single photons and quantification of their energy becomes possible and the axial and longitudinal spatial resolution can be increased compared to conventional CT systems. Acquisitions with smaller detector pixels lead to noise and dose reduction as well if data is reconstructed to standard resolutions.

Furthermore, similar to the known Computed Tomography with Dual Source Energy, the quantification of X-ray photon energy allows an acquisition of dual- and multi-energy data and consequent spectral data analysis, but within a single scan. In addition, this leads to further advantages like a relevant reduction of administered intravenous contrast media and dose reduction.

Photon-counting technology is expected to be an integral part of diagnostic and forensic imaging allowing for a multitude of exiting new possibilities and applications (Sawall et al. 2020; Klein et al. 2020).

References

Damadian R (1971) Tumor detection by nuclear magnetic resonance. Science 171(3976):1151–1153

Glasser O (2013) Wilhelm Conrad Röntgen und die Geschichte der Röntgenstrahlen. Springer-Verlag, Berlin

Grabherr S, Grimm JM, Heinemann A (2016) Atlas of postmortem angiography. Springer, Cham

Klein L, Dorn S, Amato C, Heinze S, Uhrig M, Schlemmer HP et al (2020) Effects of detector sampling on noise reduction in clinical photon-counting whole-body computed tomography. Investig Radiol 55(2):111–119

Loewenhardt B, Müller E (2006) Bildgebende diagnostik: technik–anatomie–pathologie, Heidelberg

NobelPrize.org (2021a) The Nobel prize in physics 1952: NobelPrize.org. Available from: https://www.nobelprize.org/prizes/physics/1952/summary/

NobelPrize.org (2021b) Paul C. Lauterbur—facts: Nobel Media AB 2021. Available from: https://www.nobelprize.org/prizes/medicine/2003/lauterbur/facts/

NobelPrize.org (2021c) Sir Peter Mansfield—facts. Nobel Media AB 2021. Available from: https://www.nobelprize.org/prizes/medicine/2003/mansfield/facts/

Prokop M, Galanski M, Schaefer-Prokop C (2006) Ganzkörper-computertomographie: spiral-und multislice-CT. Georg Thieme Verlag, New York

Sawall S, Klein L, Amato C, Wehrse E, Dorn S, Maier J et al (2020) Iodine contrast-to-noise ratio improvement at unit dose and contrast media volume reduction in whole-body photon-counting CT. Eur J Radiol 126:108909

Scheurer E (n.d.) Neuro MRI at the End (Necropsy) Forensic/Research Indications

Yen K, Vock P, Christe A, Scheurer E, Plattner T, Schön C et al (2007) Clinical forensic radiology in strangulation victims: forensic expertise based on magnetic resonance imaging (MRI) findings. Int J Legal Med 121(2):115–123

What Can the Clinical Radiologist Learn from Forensic Imaging? Analogies and Differences Between Forensic and Clinical Imaging

Sarah Heinze and Fabrice Dedouit

Contents

Abstract

There are huge differences between interpretating radiological images from a forensic point of view versus a clinical point of view. Additionally, in post-mortem imaging post-mortem changes and typical signs have to be kept in mind and recognized on the images for correct interpretation.

The differences between clinical and forensic radiology as well as topics one radiologist can learn from the other are discussed in this chapter.

S. Heinze (✉)
Institute of Forensic and Traffic Medicine, University Hospital Heidelberg, Heidelberg, Germany
e-mail: sarah.heinze@med.uni-heidelberg.de

F. Dedouit
Department of Forensic Medicine, Hôpital Rangueil, Toulouse, France

© Springer Nature Switzerland AG 2022

F. Dedouit et al. (eds.), *Forensic Imaging*, Medical Radiology Diagnostic Imaging,
https://doi.org/10.1007/978-3-030-83352-7_3

1 Introduction

Clinical and forensic radiology are different. Forensic imaging includes different advanced digital imaging methods than clinical radiology, e.g., 3D surface scan, photogrammetry, and photography (Grabherr et al. 2017). Additional knowledge is needed to read the images correctly. This applies for clinical forensic as well as for post-mortem forensic imaging (Yen et al. 2007; O'Donnell and Woodford 2008; Flach et al. 2014; Heinze et al. 2019; Christe et al. 2010). Clinical radiologists without any or with occasional experience in post-mortem imaging are at risk not to describe important findings or to misinterpret findings.

Because of the differences between the two subjects, the clinical radiologist can learn many things from the forensic radiologist and vice versa to improve the quality of work. Furthermore, specific knowledge is necessary for the correct description and interpretation of radiological images under forensic perceptive.

2 Different Reason to Perform an Examination

In clinical radiology images are produced to help a patient in this moment or to find out what kind of disease the physician is dealing with or if a therapy (e.g., cancer treatment) is effective. Hence, the clinical radiologist determines current events and is working for the future of the patient. On the other hand, looking mostly into the past the forensic radiologist aims at determining the cause and manner of injuries or death, identifying the deceased and finding out what happened to the patient as well as reconstructing the event/crime. For that, forensic perspective focuses additionally on other aspects of the injuries, which are of minor relevance in the clinical context (such as bruises), or on the description of non-life-threatening, even smallest and discrete injuries. Especially minor injuries of the skin and the subcutaneous fat tissue might not be described in clinical cases routinely. These injuries, however, might be the most useful ones to reconstruct an event or an accident (Fig. 1a–d) (Yen et al. 2004). In concomitant with autopsy results, different types and different sites of injuries complete the puzzles and tell the story.

Conclusively, forensic radiologists investigate the past events to build up scenarios to find out how death, trauma or accidents occurred and to reconstruct a crime scene. They search for the manner and cause of death. Additionally, they work for the future in front of court to present findings. For the patient, forensic analysis is important when it comes to a court proceeding where imaging evidence increasingly plays a major role. Forensic imaging helps to clarify what has happened to a person. By this it also helps to prevent the (surviving) victim and others from further violence - e.g. in a proven child maltreatment case, when the child is removed from its violent environment.

3 Distinguishing the Description and Interpretation in Radiological Reports

Often the description and the interpretation of findings in radiological reports are mixed in the daily routine of clinical radiology. It is not surprising to find a report with only one paragraph. The description or the interpretation has been filled out and the second slot is left blank. Like any other forensic expert opinion, the two parts should be imperatively and strictly separated in forensic imaging reports. This might take some time but is an excellent possibility to reconsider and check the diagnosis. In post-mortem forensic cases it helps to determine the cause and manner of death. Furthermore, legal considerations should be always beard in mind (see below). Therefore, it is necessary to work on these clinical forensic and post-mortem forensic cases as an interdisciplinary unit and interpret the findings from the forensic as well as the radiological point of view.

4 Usage of Easy, Understandable Language Without Any Medical Terms

The forensic radiologist should describe his or her findings in native language without any foreign (medical) terminology. In most countries the official language in court proceedings is the

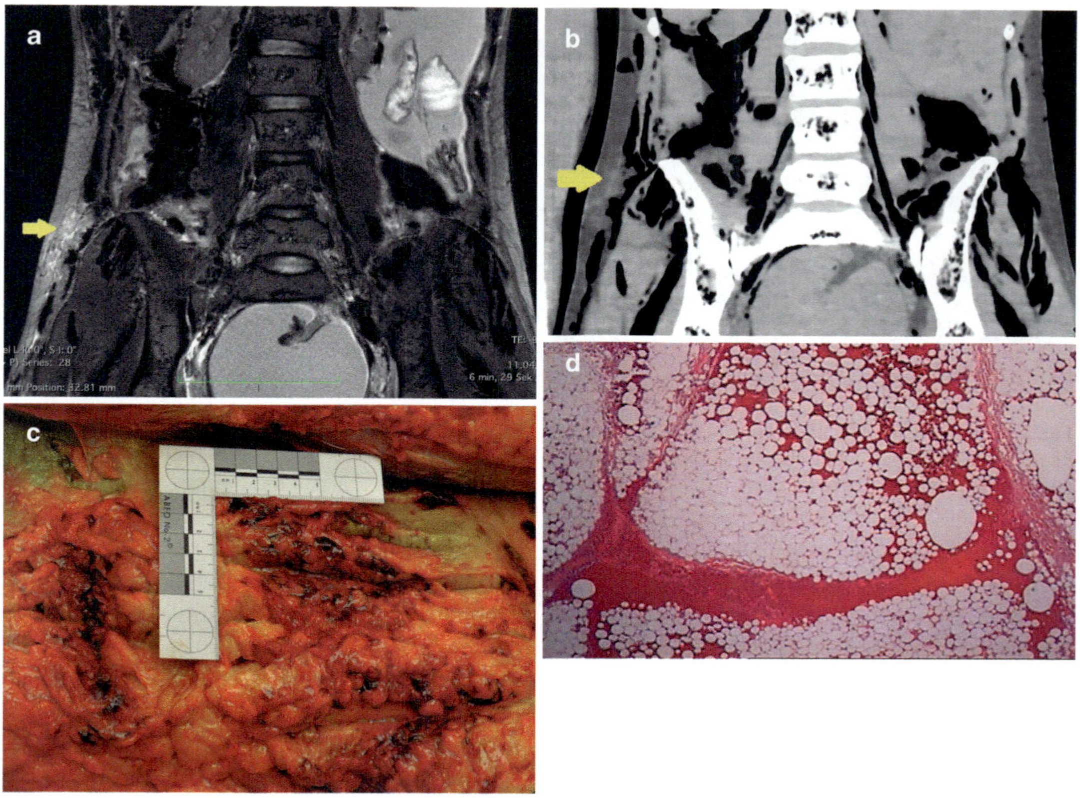

Fig. 1 (**a**) Post-mortem MRI, T2 TSE sequence (turbo spin echo) in the coronal plane of the lower part of the abdomen. Despite putrefaction artifacts damage of the subcutaneous fatty tissue caused by blunt force trauma of the right sight is visible (arrow). (**b**) Post-mortem CT MPR reconstruction in the coronal plane of the lower part of the abdomen. In correlation to the MRI, damage of the subcutaneous fatty tissue of the right sight is detectable (arrow). (**c**) Autopsy clipping of the radiological seen subcutaneous fatty tissue damage. (**d**) Subcutaneous fatty tissue (H&E × 40), morphologically stage II (contusion) of fatty tissue damage (Yen et al. 2004)

native language of the respective country. The described context must be understandable for the laymen. Patient communication skills might profit from the usage of an easier language with more explanations of the findings than the usage of (for the patient) foreign medical terms.

5 Receiving Specific Questions

In Forensic Imaging the radiologist must receive specific questions with the imaging request from the forensic pathologist, who knows the specifities of the case, to be able to give correct and/or required answers for the case in question. Otherwise, certain post processing reconstructions which might be necessary in certain cases or special algorithms for certain injuries might be missing. One example is the high-resolution CT scan of the larynx in cases of suspected strangulation. Furthermore, 3D visualization or even an animation might help to present the case in court or can be used to explain the mechanism in the classroom.

Different working groups are preparing standardized forensic imaging protocols for post-mortem CT scans as well as for clinical forensic imaging. Furthermore, the working group of forensic imaging of the German Society of Legal Medicine is working on establishing standardized reporting forms, to optimize the output of forensic CT scans.

In daily radiological routine, patients are often transferred to the radiology department with the request for a region imaging, however, without clear questions for the clinical radiologist to be

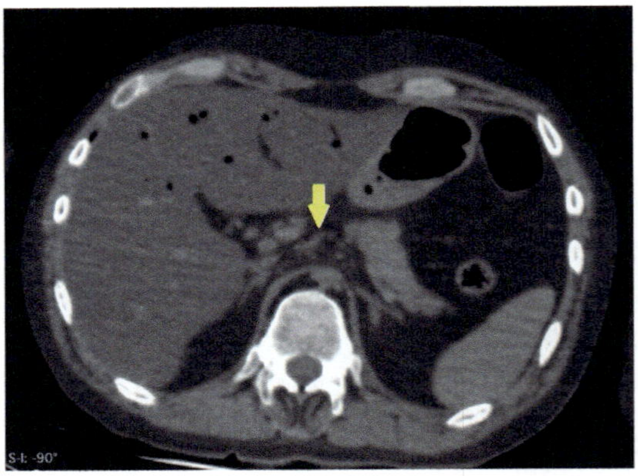

Fig. 2 Post-mortem CT MPR reconstruction in the axial plane of the upper part of the abdomen. Typical post mortal collapsed vena cava inferior (arrow)

answered. This results in some insufficient examinations or takes the radiologist a huge amount of time to contact the referring physician. Such suboptimal conditions are catastrophic in forensic imaging.

Nevertheless, both clinical and forensic radiologists have to exclude or include differential diagnoses in their opinion and need certain information to plan a correct and useful examination. Therefore, the forensic requirements should find their way into daily clinical routine.

6 Optimization of Protocols on the Deceased for the Living

Post-mortem imaging includes certain specific findings which are unknown to the clinical radiologist or even appear as a sign of medical condition, e.g., a collapsed inferior vena cava in post-mortem CT (Fig. 2) (Flach et al. 2014; Gascho et al. 2018). As mentioned above, these signs have to be learned before starting to read post-mortem images. Nevertheless, because of the non-existing motion artifacts like breathing artifacts, and the possibility to use radiation without worrying about radiation sickness or tumor induction in the deceased, it is possible to optimize different protocols on the deceased and later to apply them in living patients, e.g., radiation reduction in pediatrics.

7 Morphology

In cases where post-mortem imaging is initiated and an autopsy is performed, direct comparison between radiological images and injuries or diseases, revealed during autopsy, is possible and gives great opportunities for learning and understanding to both, the forensic and clinical radiologist. Even detailed comparisons between images, gross anatomy, and histology are possible (Fig. 3a–d). From extensive diseases to small changes in the human body, which might give a hint to a certain illness or injury, the skills to recognize these changes by the radiologist can be trained using also the autopsy results and findings.

In Forensic Radiology one must inspect every single detail, even those details which might sometimes appear clinically irrelevant. The morphology of the injuries must be described and might be used for the reconstruction of the event, that led to the injuries or for the interpretation of the severity of an incident.

8 Increase of Knowledge in Inflicted Trauma

In post-mortem radiology, forensic radiologists have to interpret distinct injuries and diseases more detailed than medical radiology peers. Forensic radiology provides deeper and novel knowledge about inflicted trauma which enables a better understanding of clinical mechanisms and possible dangerous consequences that should be considered by the attending physician for the patient's safety, e.g., after vehicle accidents, falls from high, blunt force or sharp force trauma, and even gunshot wounds (GSW) (Figs. 4 and 5; see Chap. 7).

Typically, reconstructions of gunshot wounds or stab wounds by the forensic radiologist might help the clinical radiologist to give the surgeons a quick and reliable description of the bullet path and injured structures for preparation of the operation. To our knowledge, this is otherwise only described in combat radiology (Folio 2010). In Forensic Radiology the reconstructions of the

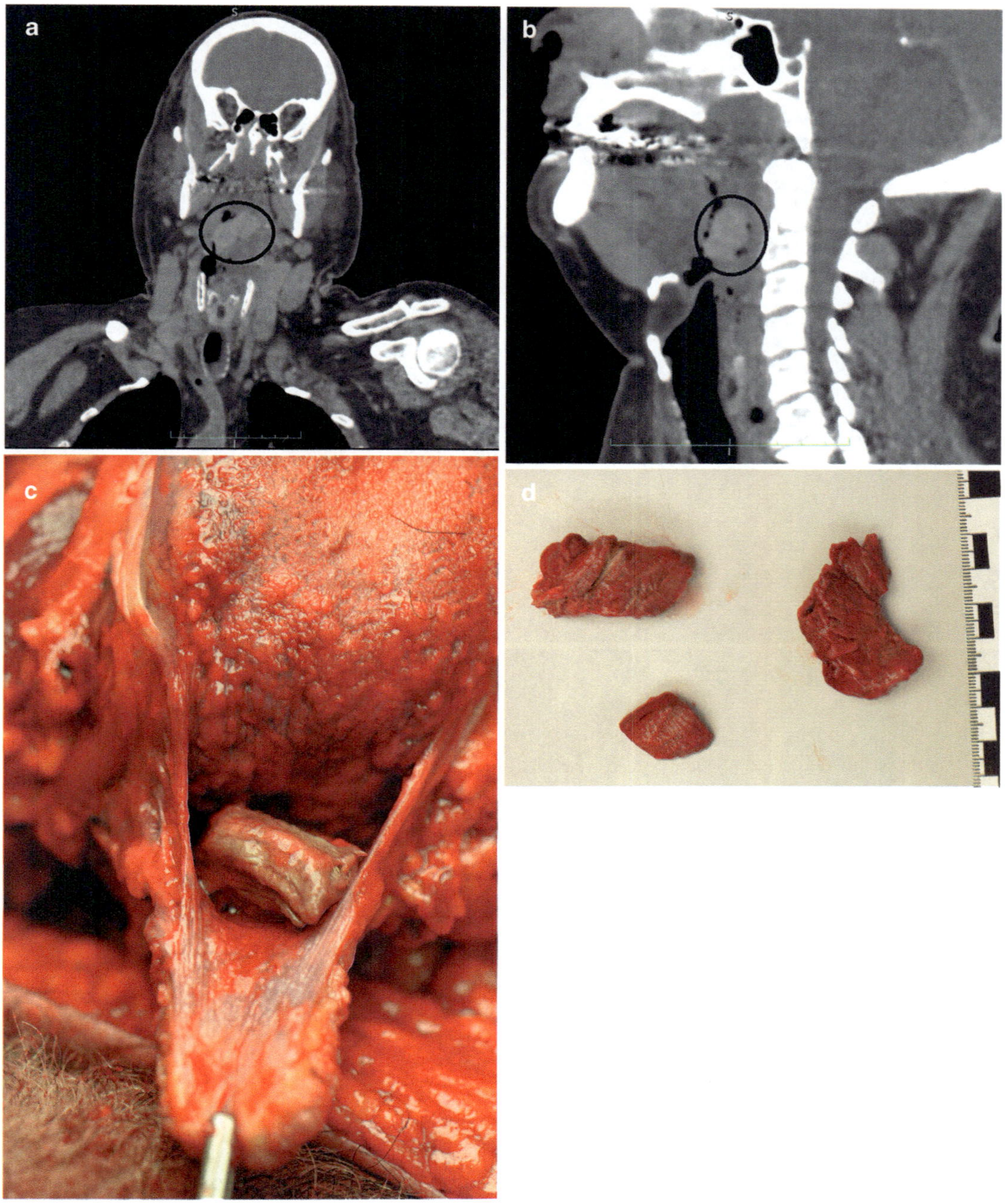

Fig. 3 (**a**) Post-mortem CT MPR reconstruction in oblique coronal plane of the neck and upper part of the chest. The bolus, which consisted of meat, is displayed as hyperdense structure definable (black circle). (**b**) Post-mortem CT MPR reconstruction of the same case in oblique sagittal plane of the neck and upper part of the chest. The bolus clogs the entrance of the trachea (black circle). (**c**) Position of the bolus during autopsy. (**d**) Extracted bolus. The measurements correspond to the radiological size of the bolus

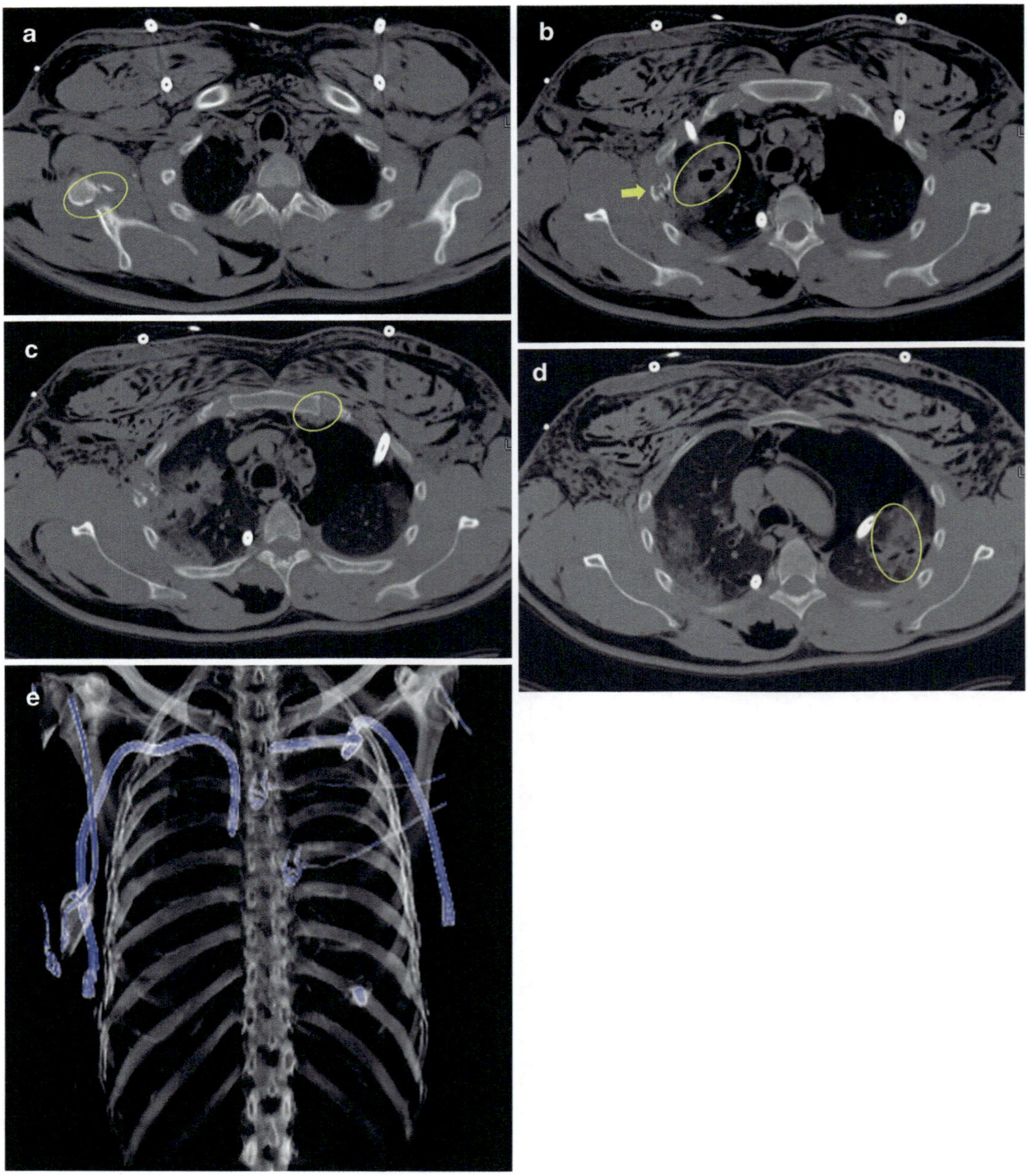

Fig. 4 Clinical CT scan of a GSW victim. Reconstruction of the trajectory: (**a**) entrance through the right scapula (circle), (**b**) fracture of the right third rip (narrow decreasing angle) (arrow), causing an injury of the right lung (right back side to the medial front) (circle), (**c**) causing a fracture of the sternum at the contralateral side (circle), and (**d**) ricochets through the left lung (circle) further down to its (**e**) resting place (height of the tenth left rib)

wounds help to determine if the injuries are life-threatening as well as to reconstruct the event.

Another area of expertise of the forensic radiologist is domestic violence and child abuse. These cases must be recognized. Signs ridden and a course of action interdisciplinary decided. The findings have to be written down as a conclusive report and to be presented in front of court.

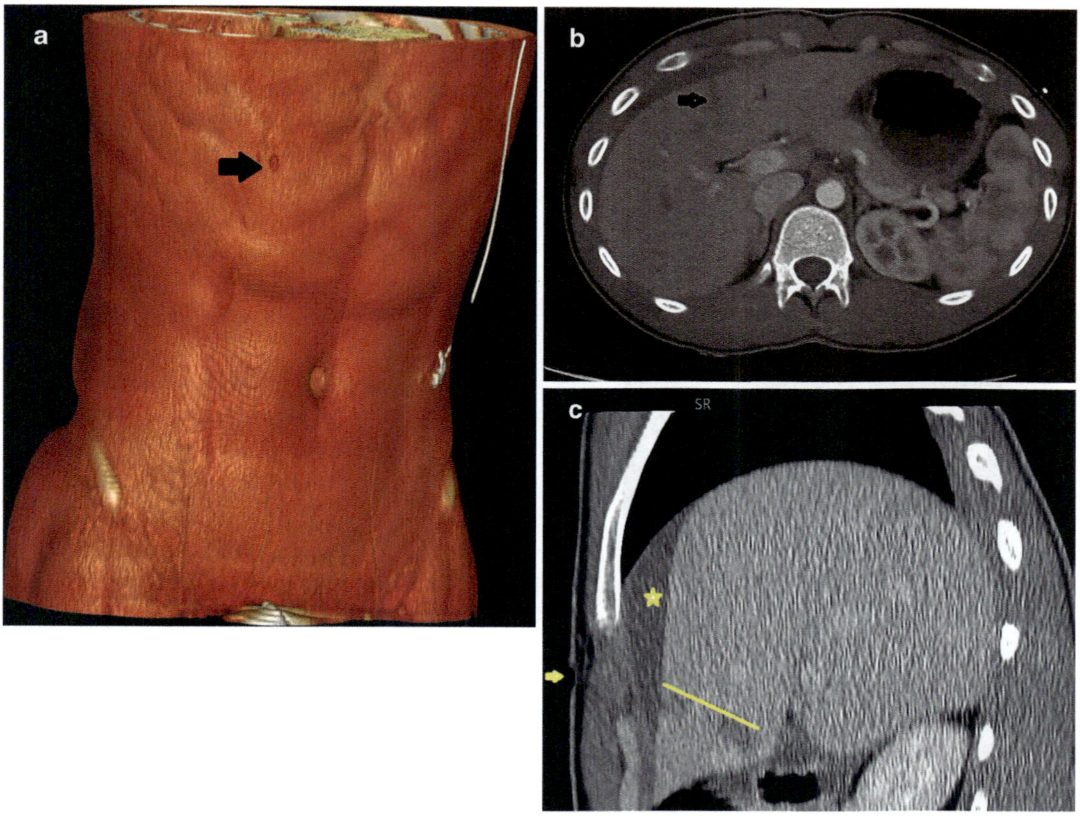

Fig. 5 Clinical CT scan of the abdomen after sharp force trauma. (**a**) Surface reconstruction with visible skin defect (arrow), (**b**) abdominal CT axial plane with trajectory in the liver (black arrow), (**c**) sagittal plane of the same case with skin defect (yellow arrow), perihepatic hematoma (asterix), and trajectory in a decreasing angle (line)

9 Different Point of View of Injuries and their "Consequences"

As mentioned above the reason to perform an examination differs between forensic and clinical radiologists. The detection of injuries should be congruent. But the interpretation and the emphasis of the interpretation and consequences are different. For example, in a case of a traffic vehicle accident a patient receives a trauma CT scan and multiple rib fractures are diagnosed. The clinical radiologist has to consider the instability of the thorax and the patient has to be sent to the intermediate care unit or to ICU (depending on the country and the hospital), whereas the forensic radiologist searches for the seatbelt sign in the subcutaneous tissue to get information if the patient was the driver or passenger of the vehicle (Fig. 6). Another example would be an abdominal stab wound. The clinical radiologist needs information like which organs

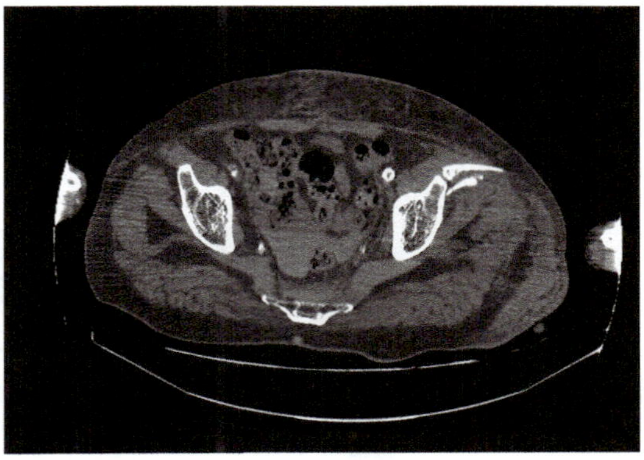

Fig. 6 Post-mortem CT axial plane of the lower abdomen. Imbibition of the subcutaneous fatty tissue (seatbelt sign)

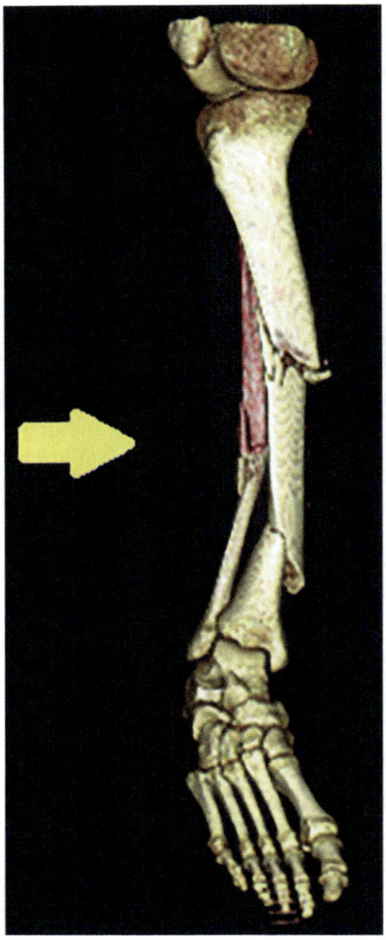

Fig. 7 Clinical CT VRT of the right lower leg. Person found unconscious at the side of the street. The first police investigations considered a fall from height. The CT scan revealed the impact side at the lower leg (arrow). Hit and run

are injured, if there is an active bleeding, etc., while the forensic radiologist is additionally interested in the wound track, the depth, the course, the structures nearby the wound channel (information if the event was life-threatening), and in the reconstruction of the event.

In cases of unconscious patients a whole-body trauma CT scan might reveal information about the incident that led to admission and therefore to further police investigations or to the closing of a case file. For example, an unconscious patient is found on or near a road. Was the person dumped there or hit by a car or suffered an acute incident due to an underlying disease (Fig. 7). Another important fact is the differentiation between a head trauma as a result of a fall versus one as a result of blunt force by a third party. The forensic radiologist has not only to look at the fracture system but also to look for a contre-coup as a sign of the fall to be able to distinguish between the incidents (Figs. 8a, b and 9).

10 Dating Injury: Wound Healing, Fracture Healing

In forensic medicine dating of injuries and wound healing have been subject of interest since early decades. During the last few years the interpretation of fractures and hematomas has been researched especially using MRI (Kruger et al. 1999; Neumayer et al. 2013; Baron et al. 2016).

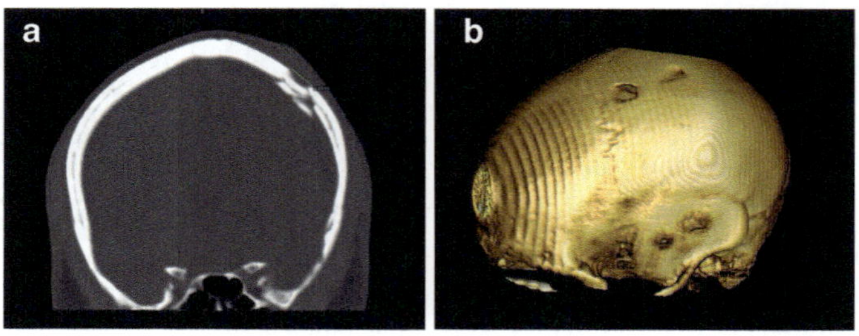

Fig. 8 (**a**) Clinical CT of the head. Coronal plane of clinical images with an impact fracture. Note the suboptimal windowing caused by only available soft tissue windows. Person found unconscious at the bottom of the stairs. Suspected fall. The CT scan revealed two impacts to the head above the head brim by an angular object, e.g., a hammer. (**b**) VRT of the same case. Suboptimal imaging caused by high slice thickness. Note that not the whole cranium has been scanned in this clinical setting. Important information of other soft tissue injuries and even fractures might be lost. Clearly visible corners of the impact fractures

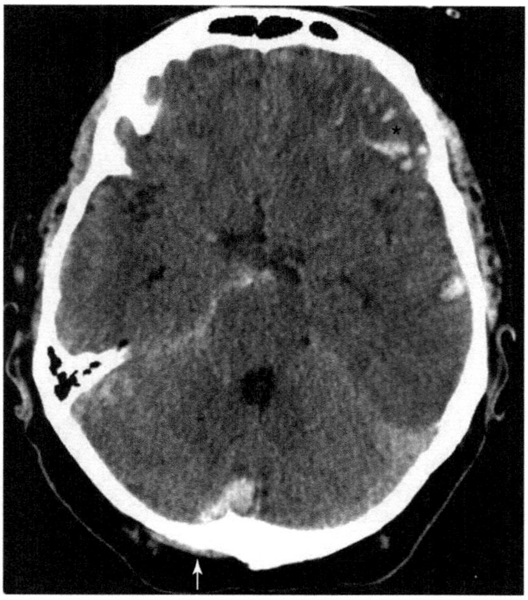

Fig. 9 Clinical CT axial plane of the head. Coup (arrow) and Contre-coup (asterix)

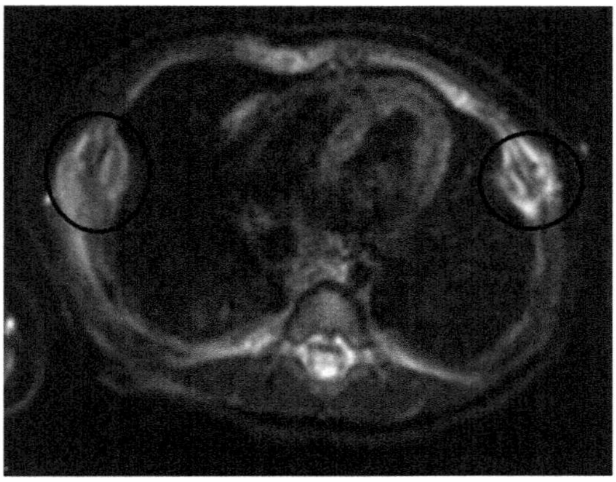

Fig. 10 Clinical MRI, T2 TSE (turbo spin echo) sequence in the axial plane of the thorax. Rib fractures at both sides. The hyperintense signal is brighter on the left sight. The callous formation less pronounced. Child abuse case with different events

This knowledge helps not only in the clinical setting to better understand the fracture or even to determine its age in cases of child abuse, but also to understand the phases of healing and its appearance on the image sequences (Fig. 10). The knowledge of fracture dating/healing from the forensic radiologist might be very useful to the clinical radiologist. Orthopedic surgeons as well as their patients might benefit from a more detailed and accurate diagnosis of fracture healing. It will be easier to define the proper time a person can be allowed to put weight on a fracture or a desmorrhexis.

Another example is the forensic knowledge of subdural fluid collections.

In abusive head trauma (AHT) the existence of subdural hematomas, an age determination of these liquid collections, as well as the estimation of the quantity of blood are of extreme importance to the forensic radiologist. Accordingly, neomembranes, blood clots, and ruptured bridging veins especially lollipop signs (also called tadpole sign; bridging vein that terminates in a blood clot) have to be described (Hahnemann et al. 2015; Choudhary et al. 2015, 2018). Spinal imaging is additionally recommended (Choudhary et al. 2018). In MRI, depending on different sequences and the appearance of blood collections or blood clots (not the subdural fluid collection itself), a time interval might be established (Bradford et al. 2013; Siesswerda-Hoogendoorn et al. 2014; Wittschieber et al. 2019). Furthermore, one of the differential diagnoses of a heterogenous hypo- and hyperdense subdural fluid collection is an acute on chronic subdural hematoma, which gives hints for two or more hemorrhagic events (Wittschieber et al. 2019) (Fig. 11a–c).

11 Legal Considerations and the Obligations of the Radiologist

Most books dedicated to child abuse and torture have special chapters which discuss different legal matters like legal consent, documentation and medical records, reporting statutes and practical issues for the radiologist. Nevertheless, the clinical radiologist has to keep in mind that not only the mentioned cases, but also a lot of other incidents like blunt and sharp force trauma, vehicle accidents, etc. might become law cases. Therefore, the radiologist should be aware that he/she and the case records might become the subject of a court order.

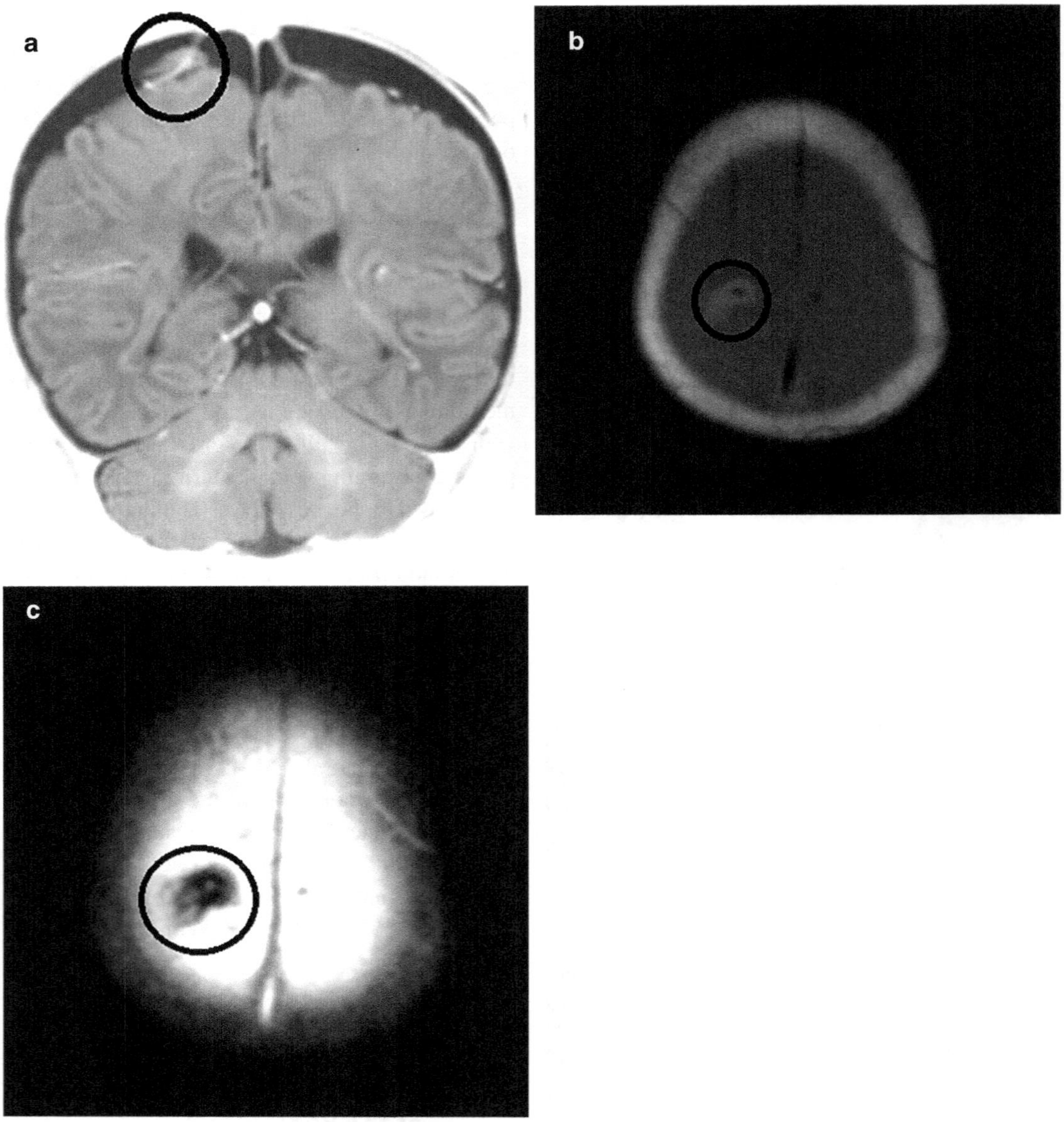

Fig. 11 (**a**) Clinical MRI T1 TIR (turbo inversion recovery) in the coronal plane of the head. Bridging vein thrombosis (Tadpole sign) in the right parietal region (black circle). (**b**) MRI T1 SE (spin echo) in the axial plane of the head. Round- to oval-shaped blood clot in the right parietal region (incomplete Tadpole sign ("body"); black circle). (**c**) MRI T2*-weighted gradient echo in the axial plane of the head (same case as (**b**)). Round- to oval-shaped blood clot in the right parietal region (incomplete Tadpole sign ("body"); black circle)

Especially after writing a radiological report on blunt or sharp trauma cases, gunshot injuries, child abuse, or domestic violence cases, these files might become part of a legal investigation. The images might be used for a second forensic radiological reading to reconstruct trajectories, angles and depth of stab wounds, impact sides of blunt force trauma, and so on.

As mentioned above, one typical forensic question is, the determination if an injury is life-threatening or not. Furthermore, forensic radiologists have to establish a timeline of the events/the wound age. Most times only time periods can be given and compared to the anamnestic information of the case. Therefore, one should be careful in describing these injuries in detail or in giving information on the reconstruction of an event, if one has not the experience/knowledge of forensic imaging, and forensic radiology should be performed and interpreted interdisciplinary by a radiologist and a forensic pathologist.

References

Baron K, Neumayer B, Widek T et al (2016) Quantitative MR imaging in fracture dating—initial results. Forensic Sci Int 261:61–69

Bradford R, Choudhary AK, Dias MK (2013) Serial neuroimaging in infants with abusive head trauma: timing abusive injuries. J Neurosurg Pediatr 12:110–119

Choudhary AK, Bradford R, Dias MK et al (2015) Venous injury in abusive head trauma. Pediatr Radiol 45:1803–1813

Choudhary AK, Servaes S, Slovis TL et al (2018) Consensus statement on abusive head trauma in infants and young children. Pediatr Radiol 45:1048–1065

Christe A, Flach P, Ross S, Spendlove D, Bollinger S, Vock P, Thali MJ (2010) Clinical radiology and postmortem imaging (Virtopsy) are not the same: specific and unspecific postmortem signs. Legal Med 12:215–222

Flach PM, Gascho D, Schweitzer W et al (2014) Imaging in forensic radiology: an illustrated guide for postmortem computed tomography technique and protocols. Forensic Sci Med Pathol 10:583–606

Flach PM, Thali MJ, Germerott T (2014) Times have changed! Forensic radiology—a new challenge for radiology and forensic pathology. AJR Am J Roentgenol 202:325–334

Folio LR (2010) Combat radiology. Diagnostic imaging of blast and ballistic injuries, 1st edn. Springer, Heidelberg

Gascho D, Thali MJ, Niemann T (2018) Post-mortem computed tomography: technical principles and recommended parameter settings for high-resolution imaging. Am J Forensic Med Pathol 39:30–37

Grabherr S, Egger C, Vilarino R et al (2017) Modern post-mortem imaging: an update on recent developments. Forensic Sci Res 2:52–64

Hahnemann ML, Kinner S, Schweiger B et al (2015) Imaging of bridging vein thrombosis in infants with abusive head trauma: the “tadpole sign”. Eur Radiol 25:299–305

Heinze S, Hettler L, Breitmeier D et al (2019) Befundung postmortaler thorakaler Röntgenbilder—Fachärzte für Rechtsmedizin und Radiologie im Vergleich. Arch Kriminol 243:28–38

Kruger K, Heindel W, Burger C et al (1999) The MR tomographic imaging of uncomplicated secondary fracture healing exemplified by the distal radius fracture. RoFo 170:262–268

Neumayer B, Hassler E, Petrovic A et al (2013) Age determination of soft tissue hematomas. NMR Biomed 27:1397–1402

O’Donnell C, Woodford N (2008) Post-mortem radiology—a new sub-speciality? Clin Radiol 63:1189–1194

Siesswerda-Hoogendoorn T, Postema FAM, Verbaa D et al (2014) Age determination of subdural hematomas with CT and MRI: a systematic review. Eur J Radiol 83:1257–1268

Wittschieber D, Karger B, Pfeiffer H et al (2019) Understanding subdural collections in pediatric abusive head trauma. Am J Neuroradiol 40:388–395

Yen K, Lövblad KO, Scheurer E et al (2007) Post-mortem forensic neuroimaging: correlation of MSCT and MRI findings with autopsy results. Forensic Sci Int 173:21–35

Yen K, Vock P, Tiefenthaler B et al (2004) Virtopsy: forensic traumatology of the subcutaneous fatty tissue; multislice computed tomography (MSCT) and magnetic resonance imaging (MRI) as diagnostic tools. J Forensic Sci 49:799–806

Part I

Typical Normal Post-mortem Findings

Post-mortem Changes

Florian Fischer

Contents

The interpretation of post-mortem and clinical imaging is significantly different because of post-mortem changes. Those findings that result initially because of the cessation of circulation and biochemical physiological processes and later on due to the process of putrefaction alter the images substantially. Besides livores, mostly gas accumulations represent those post-mortem changes. These changes are influenced by premortal changes, like resuscitation efforts, mechanical ventilation, sepsis and hyperbaric environment and post-mortem changes like putrefaction. Knowledge of these findings is mandatory for any post-mortem forensic diagnostic, as they do not occur regularly in clinical casework, if they occur clinically at all.

F. Fischer (✉)
Institut für Rechtsmedizin der Universität, München, Germany
e-mail: florian.fischer@med.uni.muenchen.de

1 Livores

Being a sign of death, livores can be seen on post-mortem CT as relatively homogenous higher attenuation in dependent areas of organs and in subcutaneous fatty tissue. Gravity dictates the accumulation of blood, which usually itself shows around 60 HU, towards the lower areas of the body. Therefore the position of the body influences where internal and external livores result. There is only a poor understanding of the time dependency of inner livores at this time, despite extensive experience and regular use to roughly estimate the time

© Springer Nature Switzerland AG 2022

F. Dedouit et al. (eds.), *Forensic Imaging*, Medical Radiology Diagnostic Imaging,
https://doi.org/10.1007/978-3-030-83352-7_4

since death by external livores. The attenuation values have not been proved to be useful to graduate the livores, which likely is due to interference with relatively radiopaque muscle tissue and the lack of studies in the very early post-mortem interval. Basically one might assume that the mechanism is the same, so in approximately the first 6 h after death also inner livores can rearrange due to altered positioning. In this interval increasing attenuation in the CT shows inner livores. The ability to rearrange decreases gradually over time and generally after approximately 12 h no significant rearrangement would be expected. As inner livores might be closer to great vessels, it seems not unreasonable, that this time window might be larger. At least great vessels in independent areas usually show a high attenuation and retain their anatomic shape, whereas great central vessels (especially veins) tend to collapse due to the redistribution of blood. Anyway, inner livores can also give clues to rearrangements of a body by only partial or not fitting to the position of the body. In that way they need to be reported on every basic PMCT. Usually sedimentation levels can be seen in the dependent parts of the lungs, the heart, the spleen, the liver but also in dependent parts of soft tissue, especially subcutaneous fatty tissue. The lungs often show the most easily recognizable inner livores due to the good contrast within that organ. Often artifacts coming from the humerus in regular position with arms beside the body interfere with the dependent areas in a supine position. Pathological processes that go along with enhanced radiopacity are the main differential diagnoses, such as pneumonia, atelectasis, and aspiration (Figs. 1, 2, 3, and 4).

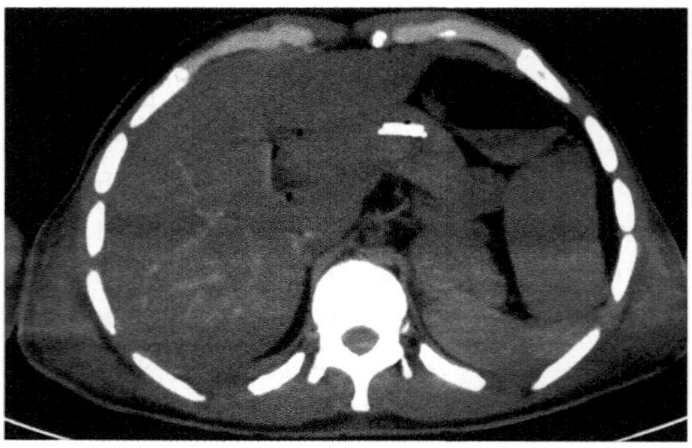

Fig. 1 Post-mortem axial CT-image of the liver congestion in dependent parts, male 19

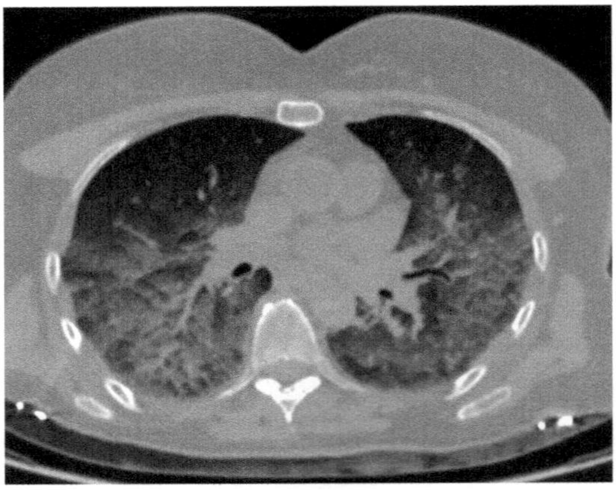

Fig. 2 Post-mortem axial CT-image of inner livores of the lungs, female 58y

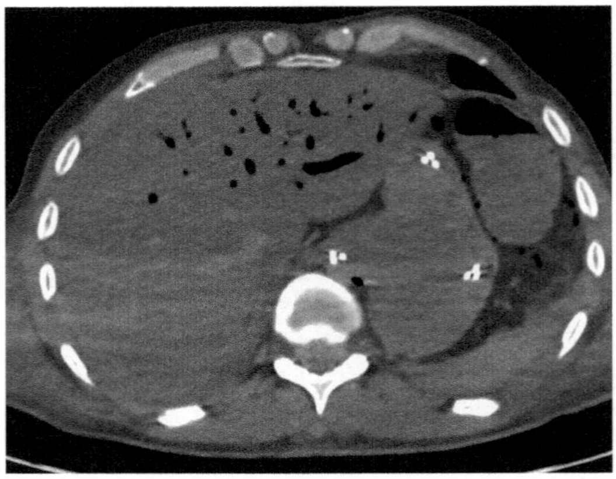

Fig. 3 Post-mortem axial CT-image of the liver, Gas Grade II, male 64y

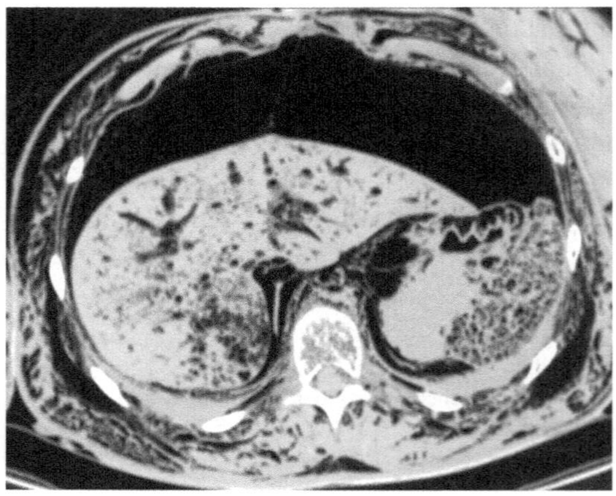

Fig. 4 Post-mortem axial CT-image, extensive gas by putrefaction

2 Rigor Mortis

Rigor does not show a pronounced or proven change in PMCT (Levy et al. 2010). However it can complicate positioning for a proper PMCT.

3 Gas

CT cannot distinguish between different kinds of gas. The attenuation of the ambient air is used during its calibration process. Therefore, when referring to gas, it is unclear what kind of gas is represented by very low attenuation of around −1024 HU. Nitrogen and carbon dioxide and oxygen have been described—analyzed by gas-chromatography-mass-spectrometry (GC-MS), also several organic gases produced by bacteria while putrefaction as methane. Gas can enter the body or is produced within the body. When it enters the body via non-physiological ways, it is often caused by some kind of trauma. Also bodies that underwent resuscitative efforts persistently show more gas in the big vessels than without the "trauma" of ventilation and chest compressions (Bernaldo de Quirós et al. 2013).

The sensitivity and sensibility of PMCT for gas accumulations in the body is by far superior to conventional autopsy, because at autopsy gas can usually not be seen and most of the gas is found in areas where it cannot be assessed by destructive methods. Also mechanical effects of gas, like tension pneumothorax with a midline shift, are detected easier and earlier on PMCT. Small changes, like tiny bubbles due to putrefaction, are not accessible by autopsy at all. CT shows low to very low attenuation levels consistent with the calibration of a clinical CT, where "air" shows −1024 HU. Therefore, the diagnosis of gas is fairly easy to make because of the excellent contrast it provides. Numbers above are usually caused by the partial volume effect, which comes into play with bubbles smaller than the available minimal voxel size. Nonetheless the lungs present a good example of the possible range of HU in gas-dominated areas. Attempts to use gas as contrast agent have been made, but have not proved universally applicable.

The pattern of gas distribution is due to gravitational effects, gas having low density, and anatomical structures that cause accumulations of bubbles. The origin of gas bubbles in the early post-mortem stages, up to 29 h, remains unclear. In this phase—without trauma—gas accumulates in the liver veins and partly in the portal vein, the latter possibly originating in the gastrointestinal tract, since clinically bowels necrosis is connected to portal vein gas. In the first 24 h usually no large amount of gas is to be expected in the hepatic arteries.

It is obvious that the main problem is the differentiation of putrefaction and gas embolism. After 1–2 days post-mortem, depending on the temperature and usually referred to room temperature, putrefaction produces significantly gas, which then is found in the soft tissue and parenchyma of the solid organs. However, so far there has not been shown a reliable, usable relationship between the post-mortem interval and the gas distribution (Okumura et al. 2017). Nevertheless, there seems to be a fairly constant time pattern (Sapienza et al. 2017). Primarily the right heart cavities and the liver show first signs of gas accumulation (Fischer et al. 2011). This has to be kept in mind for the diagnosis of gas embolism. The abdominal vessels of the digestive system are the next likely area to contain gas (Jackowski et al. 2007; Fischer et al. 2012).

To deal with the differentiation of putrefaction-related gas and diagnostically relevant gas, the radiological-alteration index (RA-Index) has been proposed by Egger et al. (Egger et al. 2012). The index ranges from 0 to 100, indicating no gas (0) to gas in every tissue (100). Four grades, 0 to III, representing no gas, one to a few gas bubbles, partly gas filled, and completely filled with gas, respectively, are used. The grades are converted into a coefficient weighed score to add up as the RA-Index.

Table 1 Radiological-alteration Index (RA-Index) (Egger et al. 2012)

Site	Grade (score)
Heart cavities	I (1), II (8), III (17)
Liver parenchyma and vessels	I (1), II (5), III (20)
Left innominate vein	I (5), II (15), III (15)
Abdominal aorta	I (8), II (8), III (8)

Site	Grade (score)
Kidney parenchyma	I (0), II (7), III (7)
Vertebra L3	I (5), II (10), III (25)
Subcutaneous pectoral tissues	I (8), II (8), III (8)
RA-Index	Sum of scores (0–100)

This method allows a grading of the post-mortem changes by gas. It is reasonable to give the RA-Index as baseline when diagnosing gas accumulations in the body that are relevant for the forensic diagnosis. For example, isolated gas in the right heart is indicative for air embolism, when the index indicates no further relevant alteration. This is also applicable in traumatic cases, thus highlighting the superior diagnostic capability of PMCT for diagnostically relevant gases in the human body. The almost regular presence of gas in the cardiovascular system after CPR might also illustrate the importance of reporting those diagnoses with a proper reference. The significance and origin of resuscitation associated gas accumulations remains to be discussed, whereas it might show interesting aspects for the diagnosis of the applied resucitative method.

In summary, gases are easily recognizable in post-mortem CT, the origin can be traumatic, due to putrefaction and likely to the redistribution of gases in the digestive system. A low overall alteration index suggests trauma; therefore gases should always be considered as hint for traumatic diagnoses.

4 Putrefaction Liquids

With ongoing decay, fluids accumulate in the body cavity as cells break and interstitial and intracellular liquids leak. This may simulate pleural and abdominal effusions. Normally those effusions tend to show HU slightly above water and can be easily differentiated from blood and bloody liquids.

5 Temperature

Whereas CT is considered to be independent from temperature changes above 0 °C and only freezing results in significant changes, the physical properties measured in MRI are quite temperature sensitive. It has been demonstrated fairly impressive that contrast diminishes with falling temperature. It is recommended to perform post-mortem MRI at temperatures above 10 °C body core temperature and use temperature corrected scan-parameters (Ruder et al. 2012).

6 Brain

PM-Changes in the brain happen in a short period of time, complicating the image-based diagnosis. The brain in PMCT loses its gray-white matter differentiation rapidly. The attenuation of the gray matter falls and rises in white matter. It is thought that the brain takes up water, resulting in a mild post-mortem edema. There is no evidence that this influences signs of intracranial pressure, as the main anatomic changes are based on intravital processes. Studies using MRI and diffusion weighted imaging (DWI) have reported that diffusion processes seem to be lowest around 19 h post-mortem and are comparable to those of ischemic strokes (Schmidt et al. 2012). There are some implications that the diffusion is closely linked to the post-mortem interval (Scheurer et al. 2011).

7 Vessels

Being one of the most relevant areas of clinical radiology, post-mortem changes in vessels can be considered as minor, compared to other organs. Only bone and skin seem to be less affected.

The diameter of the aorta shrinks after death at all levels; it becomes oval in the descending and abdominal segments. Compared to the diameter of living patients this effect is pronounced in younger patients and less visible in older individuals (Takahashi et al. 2013). The age difference is understood as effect of the common loss of elasticity and of arteriosclerosis, it is readily comprehensible in conventional autopsy. The loss of blood pressure, redistribution of blood into the depending smaller vessels, becoming livores, and loss of water into the interstitium explain the volume loosing effect.

As in living individuals the diameter is bigger in aged individuals. The contrast of the wall is enhanced, likely due to the contraction of elastic fibers, and can be described as hyperattenuating aortic wall (Shiotani et al. 2002). The loss of motion artifacts may add to the elevated contrast, but this could be considered a very common observation in post-mortem CT. In fatal hemorrhages the shrinkage is also visible in other great vessels, like the pulmonary arteries (Aghayev et al. 2006). Remarkable is the fact that post-mortem CT-Angiography is feasible for long post-mortem intervals, only limited by obvious tissue destruction (Franckenberg et al. 2015). The vascular system shows a significant resilience against putrefaction and whereas the decomposition of inner organs is advanced, it is still possible to obtain diagnostically valuable angiographies.

In summary, a profound knowledge of autoptic post-mortem changes is necessary to interpret post-mortem imaging, especially to set a context with clinical findings. The time since death and the grade of alteration are important to document as basis for the interpretation of those images. Nevertheless PMCT can help decisively to facilitate autopsy procedures and findings in decaying bodies.

References

Aghayev E, Sonnenschein M, Jackowski C et al (2006) Postmortem radiology of fatal hemorrhage: measurements of cross-sectional areas of major blood vessels and volumes of aorta and spleen on MDCT and volumes of heart chambers on MRI. AJR Am J Roentgenol 187:209–215

Bernaldo de Quirós Y, González-Díaz O, Møllerløkken A et al (2013) Differentiation at autopsy between in vivo gas embolism and putrefaction using gas composition analysis. Int J Legal Med 127:437–445

Egger C, Vaucher P, Doenz F, Palmiere C, Mangin P, Grabherr S (2012) Development and validation of a postmortem radiological alteration index: the RA-index. Int J Legal Med 126:559–566. https://link-springer-com.emedien.ub.uni-muenchen.de/article/10.1007/s00414-012-0686-6#citeas

Fischer F, Grimm J, Kirchhoff C, Reiser MF, Graw M, Kirchhoff S (2012) Postmortem 24-h interval computed tomography findings on intrahepatic gas development and changes of liver parenchyma radiopacity. Forensic Sci Int 214:118–123

Fischer F, Urschler M, Kirchhoff S, Ehammer T, Herzog P. Systematic approach to liver gas volume and distribution in post-mortem CT by computer aided density analysis. 8th International Symposium Advances in Legal Medicine (ISALM) combined with the 90th Annual Conference of the German Society of Legal Medicine 2011

Franckenberg S, Flach PM, Gascho D, Thali MJ, Ross SG (2015) Postmortem computed tomography-angiography (PMCTA) in decomposed bodies ÔÇô a feasibility study. J Forensic Radiol Imaging 3:226–234

Jackowski C, Sonnenschein M, Thali MJ et al (2007) Intrahepatic gas at postmortem computed tomography: forensic experience as a potential guide for in vivo trauma imaging. J Trauma 62:979–988

Levy AD, Harcke HT, Mallak CT (2010) Postmortem Imaging. Am J Forensic Med Pathol 31:12–17

Okumura M, Usumoto Y, Tsuji A, Kudo K, Ikeda N (2017) Analysis of postmortem changes in internal organs and gases using computed tomography data. Leg Med (Tokyo) 25:11–15

Ruder TD, Hatch GM, Siegenthaler L et al (2012) The influence of body temperature on image contrast in post mortem MRI. Eur J Radiol 81:1366–1370

Sapienza D, Bottari A, Gualniera P, Asmundo A, Perri F, Gaeta M (2017) Post mortem CT of intrahepatic gas distribution in twenty-seven victims of a flood: patterns and timing. Leg Med (Tokyo) 29:18–21. http://www.sciencedirect.com/science/article/pii/S134462231730319X

Scheurer E, Lovblad K-O, Kreis R et al (2011) Forensic application of postmortem diffusion-weighted and diffusion tensor MR imaging of the human brain in situ. AJNR Am J Neuroradiol 32:1518–1524

Schmidt TM, Fischer R, Acar S et al (2012) DWI of the brain: Postmortal DWI of the brain in comparison with in vivo data. Forensic Sci Int 220:180–183. http://www.sciencedirect.com/science/article/pii/S0379073812000989

Shiotani S, Kohno M, Ohashi N et al (2002) Hyperattenuating aortic wall on postmortem computed tomography (PMCT). Radiat Med 20:201–206

Takahashi N, Higuchi T, Hirose Y, Yamanouchi H, Takatsuka H, Funayama K (2013) Changes in aortic shape and diameters after death: comparison of early postmortem computed tomography with antemortem computed tomography. Forensic Sci Int 225:27–31

Normal Post-mortem Imaging Findings in Foetuses and Children

Mathilde Ducloyer, Ana Carballeira-Alvarez, Lucile Tuchtan, Clémence Delteil, Marie-Dominique Piercecchi-Marti, Guillaume Gorincour, and Olivier Prodhomme

Contents

M. Ducloyer (✉)
Department of Radiology, Nantes University Hospital, Nantes, France

Department of Forensic Medicine, Nantes University Hospital, Nantes, France
e-mail: mathilde.ducloyer@chu-nantes.fr

A. Carballeira-Alvarez
Department of Radiology, Marseille University Hospital, Marseille, France

L. Tuchtan · C. Delteil · M.-D. Piercecchi-Marti
Department of Forensic Medicine, Marseille University Hospital, Marseille, France

O. Prodhomme
Department of Pediatric Radiology, Montpellier University Hospital, Montpellier, France

G. Gorincour
ELSAN, Clinique Bouchard, Marseille, France

© Springer Nature Switzerland AG 2022
F. Dedouit et al. (eds.), *Forensic Imaging*, Medical Radiology Diagnostic Imaging,
https://doi.org/10.1007/978-3-030-83352-7_5

1 Introduction

The first step for learning post-mortem imaging (PMI) is definitely the identification of «normal» post-mortem findings, and thus the ability to differentiate them from abnormal findings which will correlate to a specific cause of death. These normal aspects depend primarily on the type of examination (Computed tomography (CT) mainly, Magnetic resonance Imaging (MRI) and ultrasound (US) for foetuses), the age of the deceased, the interval between death and imaging and consequently on the environmental setting of the corpse during this interval.

Post-mortem imaging in foetuses and children is one of the most meaningful issues in this field. The reasons for performing post-mortem imaging are multiple (Wright 2004; Sarda-Quarello et al. 2015; Arthurs et al. 2017; Tuchtan et al. 2018): to explore the cause of in utero foetal demise, to avoid a recurrence in a future pregnancy, to detect traumatic injury as arguments for homicide in a sudden unexpected death, or to help the forensic pathologist to diagnose vitality and viability in a newborn. Though, a child is not a miniature adult. Specific semiology and anatomic and physiological particularities have to be known by the forensic radiologist: the different stages of development in foetuses and children, the malformation diseases, the artefacts due to cardiopulmonary resuscitation, the specificities of traumatic bone injuries.

In this chapter we will describe and illustrate the prominent post-mortem findings by age category and by imaging modality.

2 Foetuses

2.1 Objective

The occurrence of a fetal death always arises questioning, surprise and grief, both for the future parents and for the medical staff who take care of them after this loss. The main objective of post-mortem investigations in this context is to determine the cause of death, sometimes already suspected by in utero fetal imaging. The causes and circumstances of fetal deaths are generally devoid of forensic issue, as death can occur spontaneously (in utero fetal death (IUD)) or after the parents' decision to terminate the pregnancy (termination of pregnancy, TOP). The etiologies can actually be classified in 3 main types: malformation, vascular diseases, mostly due to placental conditions, and infections.

To this day, standard autopsy remains the gold standard for providing the necessary elements for diagnosis (Prodhomme et al. 2015a, b). Despite the importance of determining the cause of death to help parents in their mourning process, the proportion of parents refusing an autopsy has been rising for several years (Wright 2004). Proposing alternative solutions is consequently a priority, especially as the number of fetopathologists decreases and their availability is not always and everywhere guaranteed. Fetal post-mortem imaging is responding to this challenge, thanks to modern technical progress, to the development of specific training related to post-mortem imaging and the jump of scientific research in this field (Cain et al. 2014).

Post-mortem imaging will also be a precious tool to estimate the gestational age of the foetuses and newborns. Many morphometric parameters can be used: measurement of the long bones (femur, humerus, tibia) (Fazekas and Kósa 1978; Piercecchi-Marti et al. 2002; Carneiro et al. 2016), detection of secondary ossification centres of the limbs, especially the knee (Adair and Scammon 1921; Gentili et al. 1984), or evaluation of cerebral gyration (Garel et al. 2003). Measurements of cephalic and/or abdominal perimeters can be performed, following measurements realized in clinical practice, but they must be cautiously interpreted on account of the post-mortem changes (e.g. dehydration) or delivery conditions (head and body moulding due to passage through the genital tract).

In the field of foetal and perinatal imaging, differences of appearance between stillborn and liveborn babies are also important to be known and will be thereafter detailed.

2.2 Radiographs (Calder and Offiah 2015)

2.2.1 Technique

Plain radiographs with two orthogonal views, anteroposterior (AP) and lateral views (Fig. 1), of the whole skeleton are useful to depict growth retardation, evaluate bone maturation and search for occult bone dysplasia. This technique has the best spatial resolution of all PMI. It explains its usefulness in PMI of foetuses, especially in the smallest ones. In older foetuses, additionally AP and lateral plain radiographs of the skull are recommended particular attention at extremities' position is necessary to have them in AP incidence on at least one radiograph. The length of the femoral bone is compared to the abacus to evaluate foetal growth and/or to suspect a bone dysplasia. The presence or absence of the ossification centres of the pelvic, the tarsal bones and of the knee give an estimation of bone maturation of the foetus. Attentive study of bones morphology can detect some clue anomalies for the diagnosis of a bone dysplasia (Fig. 2) or a polymalformative syndrome with skeletal involvement. Sometimes abnormal calcifications can be depicted in cartilages, spine, peritoneum cavity or brain (Fig. 3).

2.2.2 Normal Post-mortem Findings

Figure 1 shows that bone maturation and the length of the femoral bone are in concordance with the gestational age. There are twelve pairs of ribs. Nasal bones are seen in lateral view and semicircular canals are visible from 20 WG. The bone shape of all bones is normal. No abnormal calcification can be seen.

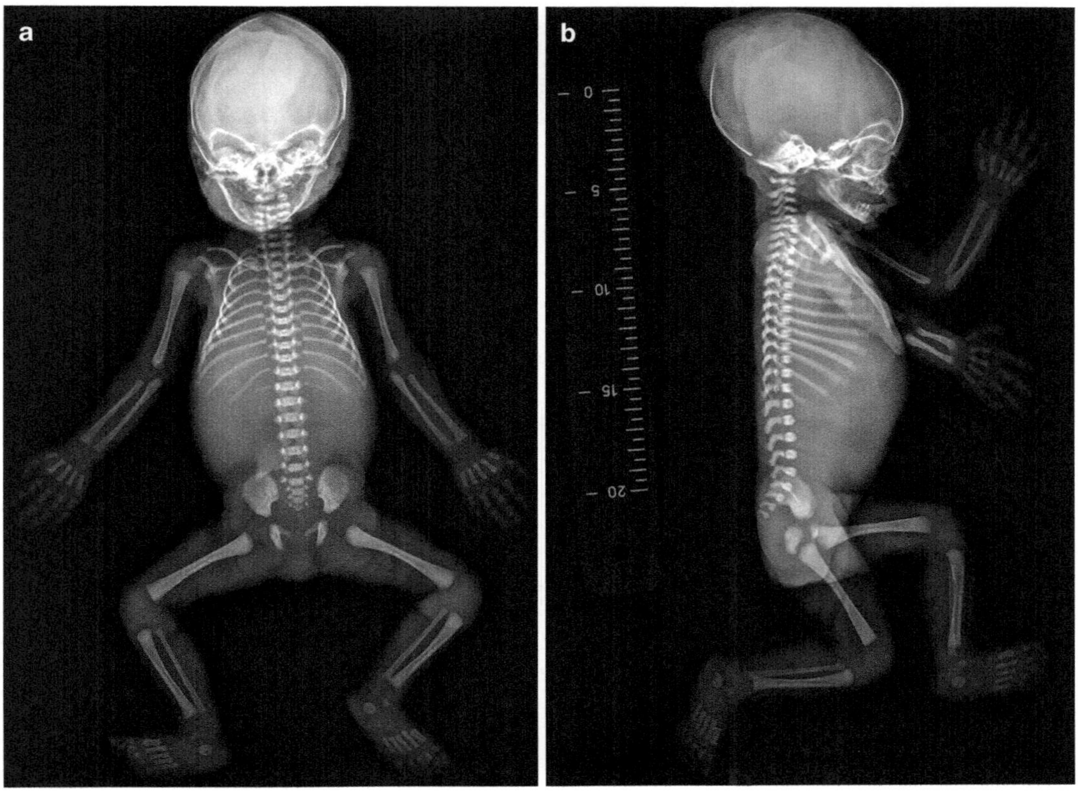

Fig. 1 X-ray, anteroposterior (**a**) and lateral (**b**) incidences, in a foetus of 32 WG (in utero foetal death). Normal foetal skeleton. See also text above

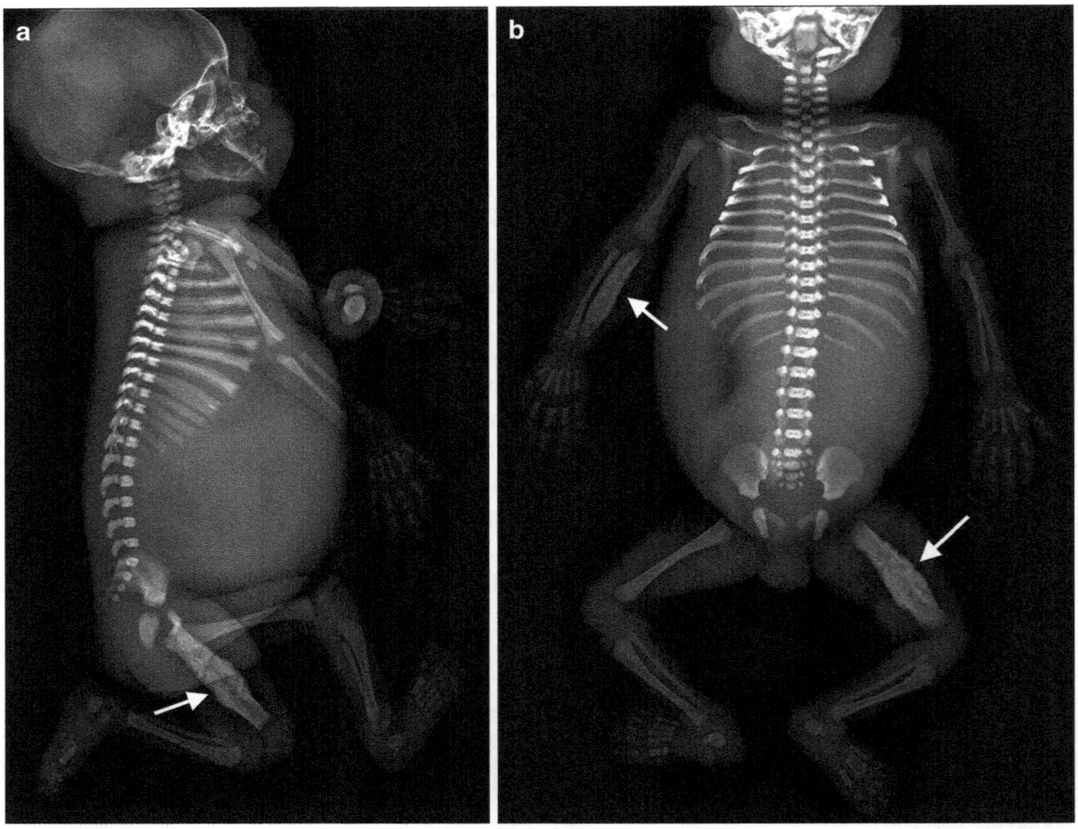

Fig. 2 X-ray, lateral (**a**) and anteroposterior (**b**) view of a foetus at 31 WG after termination of pregnancy for hydrops foetalis. Post-mortem diagnosis of skeletal malformations of Caffey disease, involving the right ulna and the left femur (arrows)

2.3 Ultrasound (Prodhomme et al. 2015a)

2.3.1 Technique

Ultrasonography (US) presents the advantage of being easily available and quick to realize (Prodhomme et al. 2015b). The small size of the body allows for an exhaustive study of internal organs (Prodhomme et al. 2015a). Even if contrast resolution may be poorer than in living patients, the image resolution remains fully satisfactory. However, the radiologist must be aware that the absence of blood circulation may change the acoustic properties of the organs, wich may not be corrected by usual clinical devices. Abdominal exploration may only be limited by the expansion of intestinal gas (Charlier et al. 2013). The use of a high-frequency linear or convex probe is essential, as in living children. The younger the foetus is, the better the US exam is in comparison to MRI.

2.3.2 Normal Post-mortem Findings

2.3.2.1 Brain and Spine

The study of the central nervous system (brain and spine) can be achieved following the modality of exploration in living children (Prodhomme et al. 2015a). The anterior fontanelle allows for an easy approach of the brain, as transfontanellar ultrasound in neonates, with a micro-convex probe and/or a high frequency linear probe (≥12 MHz) (Fig. 4). The cerebellum and posterior fossa will be better analysed by a posterior view through parieto- and temporo-occipital sutures (Fig. 5). The two orbits and eyeballs are, for evident reasons, easier to be explored in the usual planes, and ultrasound can provide precise biometric and morphological information (Fig. 6). The spinal cord can be followed along its entire length, with a good image resolution, using a high frequency linear probe; the body lying in

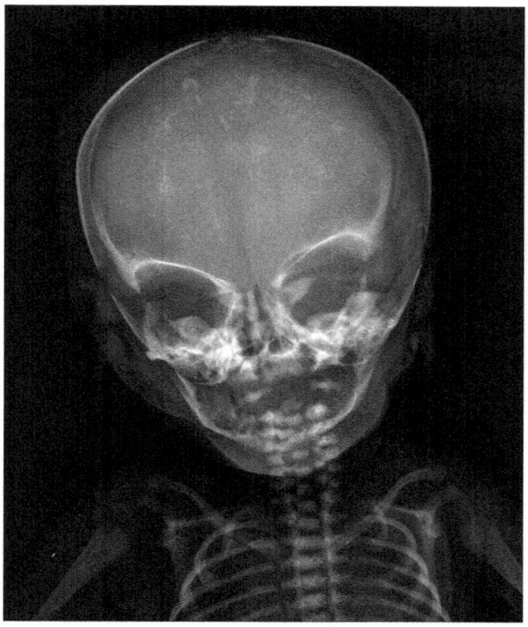

Fig. 3 X-ray, anteroposterior view of the skull after unexpected neonatal death. Unknown polymalformative syndrome with multiple brain calcifications

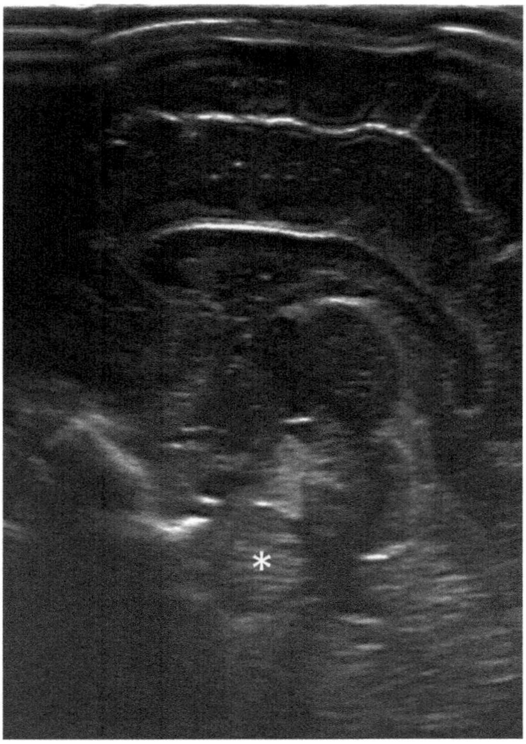

Fig. 4 Ultrasound, sagittal view of the brain with linear probe (12 MHz) in a foetus at 34 WG (in utero foetal demise). Normal corpus callosum and posterior fossa, annular protuberance (asterisk)

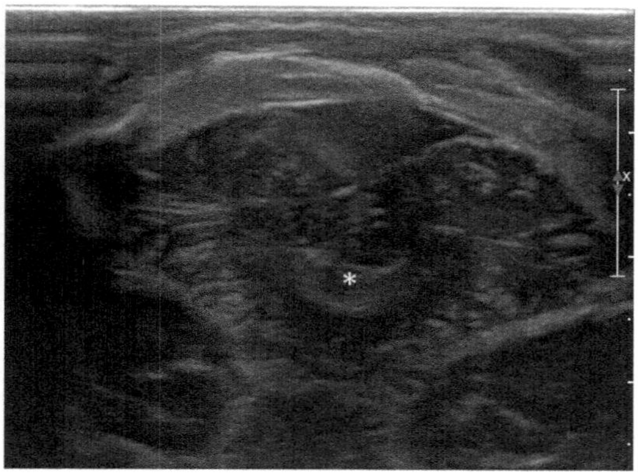

Fig. 5 Ultrasound, axial view of the cerebellum with linear probe (12 MHz) in a foetus at 32 WG (in utero foetal demise). The two hemispheres of the cerebellum and the fourth ventricle (asterisk) are clearly visible

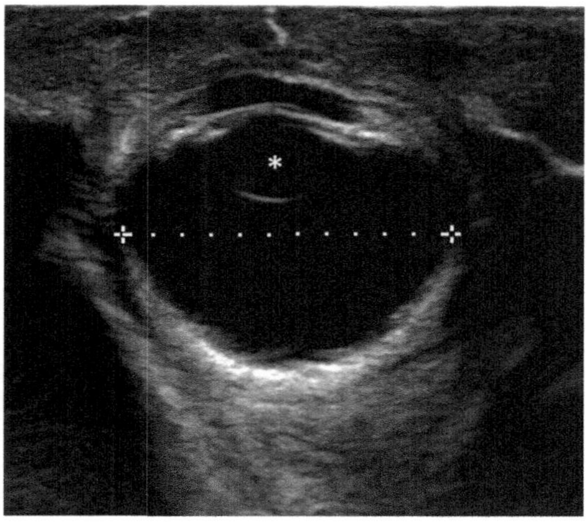

Fig. 6 Ultrasound, axial view of the left eye of a foetus at 34 WG (termination of pregnancy). The lens is visible (asterisk) and the ocular ball can be measured

prone position (Fig. 7). Even if the vertebrae can be examined in detail, plain radiographs are more reliable.

2.3.2.2 Chest

At chest level, an axial and sagittal scan provides a high-performance analysis of almost all the contents of the chest (Prodhomme et al. 2015a). Starting with a cervical scan, the trachea can be evaluated, often filled with liquids; the continuity of the esophagus can be assessed, from the upper esophagus to the gastroesophageal junction. Segmentation, fissures and parenchyma of both

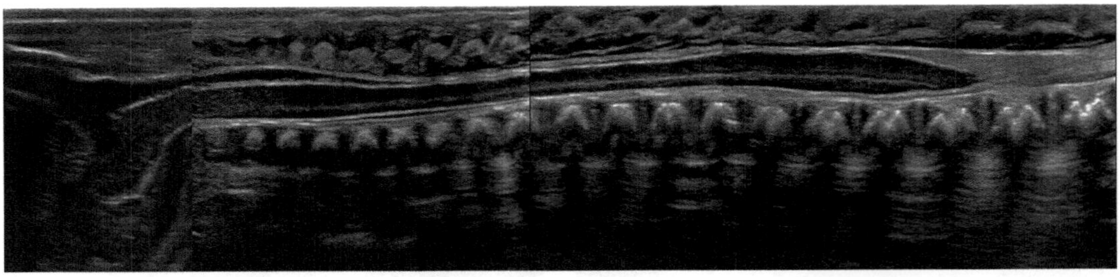

Fig. 7 Ultrasound, sagittal view of the spinal cord with linear probe (12 MHz) in a 30 WG foetus (termination of pregnancy). Foetus in prone position; normal spinal cord resulting from the addition of four images from posterior fossa to cauda equina

unaerated lungs are rather easy to explore, especially when a pleural effusion, considered as a normal post-mortem change, is associated (Fig. 8). A single sagittal scan allows to analyse the lungs, the diaphragmatic cupula and the liver/spleen, all the more easily as the size of the body is small (Fig. 8). Conversely, the heart and great vessels may be challenging to describe, due to a low contrast of the middle mediastinum and post-mortem intravascular clots and blood sedimentation in the heart cavities. Depending on the experience of the radiologist and the term of the pregnancy, some anatomical disposition may be more difficult to see and describe, such as the atrioventricular and ventriculo-arterial connections, the aortic arch or the pulmonary artery. The evaluation of the thymus will be facilitated by a poor ossification of the sternum, which allows for a complete description of its size and echogenicity (Fig. 9) (Prodhomme et al. 2015a).

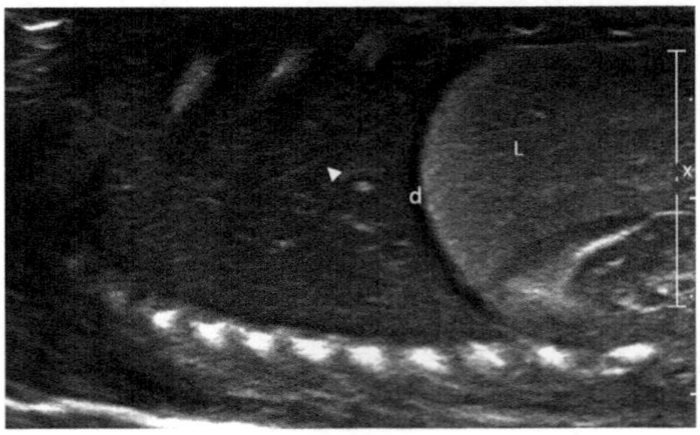

Fig. 8 Ultrasound, sagittal view of the chest in a foetus at 16 WG (in utero foetal demise). View of the left lung with the unique fissure (white arrow head); left diaphragm (d) is well seen with the sagittal view between the left lung and the left lobe of the liver (L)

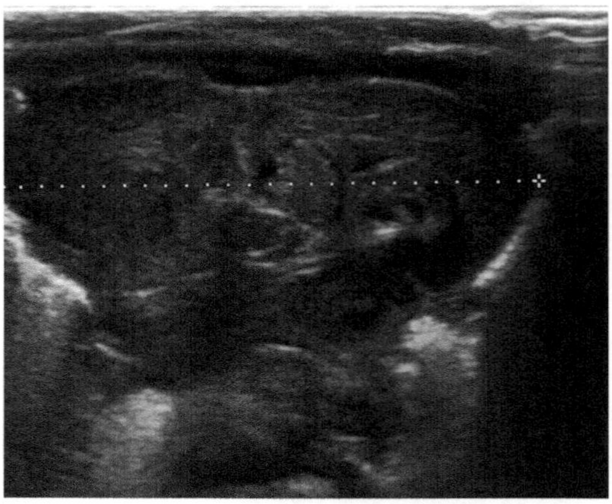

Fig. 9 Ultrasound, axial view of the chest with linear probe (12 MHz) in a foetus at 34 WG (in utero foetal demise). Axial view of the thymus (axial diameter)

2.3.2.3 Abdomen

In the abdominal area, the entire liver parenchyma can be analyzed, as well as the gallbladder and the spleen (Prodhomme et al. 2015a). It is important, however, to be aware of the limitation of ultrasound to study the pancreas, the retroperitoneum, and the digestive vessels (including mesenteric vessels), due to a poor contrast resolution and intravascular blood stasis. On the opposite, a major part of the digestive tractus, from the pylorus to the anal canal, can be explored (wall, content, caliber). Distinction between colon and small bowel will be facilitate by the hypoechoic aspect of the meconium which fills the lumen of the colon.

While great vessels of the retroperitoneum are difficult to analyse, the kidneys and adrenals remain easy to study exhaustively with adequate probes. A prone position will be helpful for a posterior approach, especially for later-term fetuses.

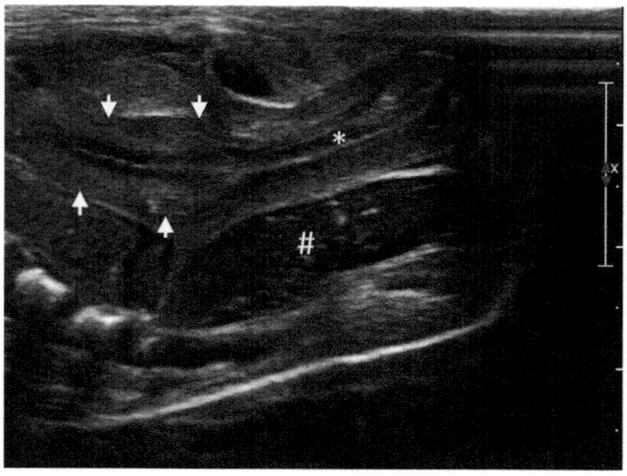

Fig. 10 Ultrasound, sagittal view with linear probe (12 MHz) of the pelvis cavity in a foetus at 35 WH (termination of pregnancy). The uterus (white arrows) and the vagina (asterisk) and in the back the rectum and the distal sigmoid with meconial content (hash sign)

In females, the internal genital tract (uterus and sometimes vagina) can be explored by a sagittal scan, eventually associated with a perineal scan (Fig. 10). Ovaries are rarely seen.

In conclusion, the contribution of post-mortem ultrasound is summarised by a satisfactory contrast and image resolution in small bodies, potentialized by the absence of air in chest and abdomen. More, US offers the possibility of percutaneous echo guided biopsies, especially when an autopsy is refused by the parents (Furness et al. 1989; Fariña et al. 2002). It allows to provide good-quality samples, guided by the abnormalities that may be seen and/or by the clinical ante-mortem history (Fig. 11).

On the contrary, the presence of gas in the lungs and digestive tract, sometimes increased and spread by putrefaction, will remain a major limitation of ultrasound in adults and children born alive (Charlier et al. 2013).

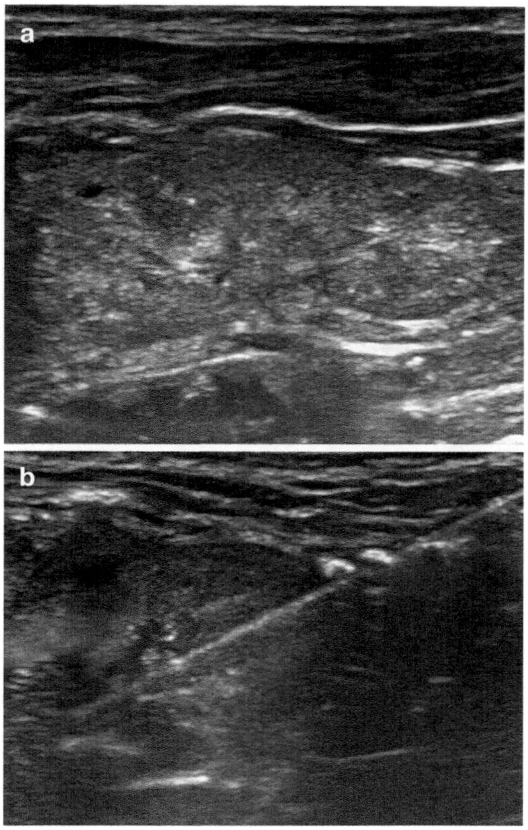

Fig. 11 Ultrasound, sagittal views with linear probe (12 MHz). Example of Microinvasive autopsy with targeted sampling. A boy presented perinatal death at 2 days of life with terminal renal failure after a twin pregnancy. The medical history was marked by a maternal antecedent of renal transplantation and familial history of renal transplantations. The twin brother had no symptoms. Imaging showed (**a**) bilateral hypoplastic kidney (22 × 8 mm) without hyperechoic parenchyma differentiation. Parents refused conventional autopsy but gave consent for post-mortem imaging and targeted biopsies (**b**). The material of biopsies was unfortunately non-contributive but *PAX2* mutation was found after genetic screening

2.4 Opacifications

2.4.1 Technique

In case of TOP for complex malformations, it would be useful to perform an opacification to confirm prenatal findings and to help the foetopathologist in areas of complex dissection. The best example of the usefulness of post-mortem opacification is cloacal malformations. The dissection of the pelvic/perineal region is difficult and opacification of bladder, colpos and digestive tract (sigmoid colon and rectum) can allow a better comprehension of these complex malformations (Fig. 12). This technique is a real-time exam, so when the contrast media enhance a new cavity by a fistula, the communication pathways between urinary, genital and digestive tracts can be easily assessed. Natural orifices can be catheterized but also some internal cavities or vessels using echoguided catheterization. This technique is performed in very few cases and only in pathological situations. A vascular (arterial) opacification was performed in one only case to explore a complex vascular malformation of the lower limb with an echoguided catheterization of the aorta (Fig. 13). In this case, the opacification did not give more information for the diagnosis.

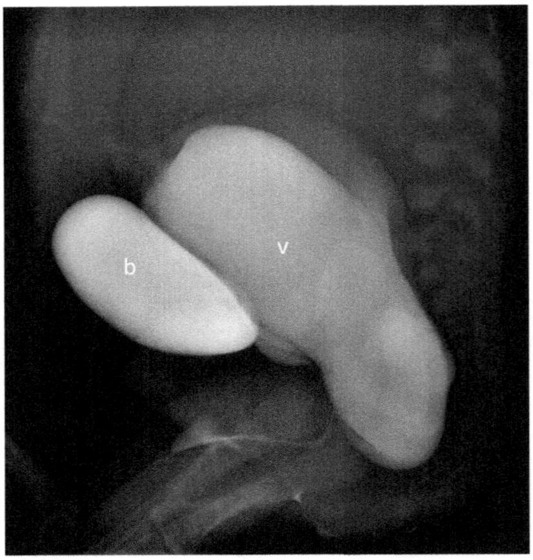

Fig. 12 X-ray, sagittal incidence with opacification of the pelvis in a foetus at 28 WG (termination of pregnancy). Urogenital sinus catheterization with dilated (hydro)-colpos: dilated vaginal cavity (v) and bladder (**b**) in a case of cloacal malformation (rectovaginal fistula, not illustrated)

2.5 Magnetic Resonance Imaging

2.5.1 Technique

Post-mortem MRI is increasingly used as a support of conventional autopsy in foetuses, despite its accessibility is lower than CT (Addison et al. 2014; Norman et al. 2016). It provides a high contrast resolution whole-body imaging and is particularly efficient for the detection of central nervous system diseases (Arthurs et al. 2015). The Technical protocol can include T1- and T2-weighted whole-body sequences, with dedicated sequences on brain and spine. The spatial resolution of MRI is very helpful for second and third trimester foetuses but can be limited in foetuses of less than 15 WA, contrarily to US (Norman et al. 2016).

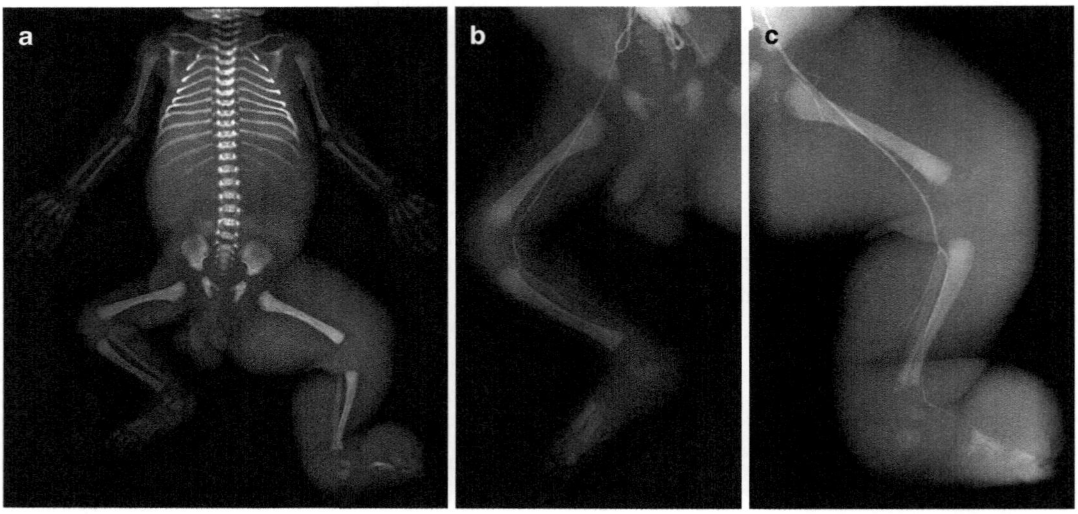

Fig. 13 X-ray, coronal incidence with vascular opacification, in a foetus at 38 WG (termination of pregnancy). Experimental angiography of the arterial vascularization, after US guided puncture of the aorta, in a case of severe vascular malformation of the left lower limb; (**a**) AP plain radiograph. (**b**) arterial angiography of the normal right lower limb. (**c**) arterial angiography of the abnormal left lower limb. No anatomical abnormality of the arterial system of the left lower limb was found

2.5.2 Normal Post-mortem Findings

Maceration is a particular putrefaction statement, due to aseptic lysis, in case of delayed delivery following in utero foetal death. It is clinically characterized by the alteration of the skin, which turns into red or velvet colour and epidermolysis. Internal changes susceptible to be seen on MRI are pleural and abdominal effusion, skull deformation, collapse of the ocular globes, and abdominal and sometimes thoracic organs shifting. It is fundamental to be aware of the clinical context, i.e. TOP vs. IUD, to not misinterpret artefacts due to foeticide, e.g. gas in heart cavities.

2.5.2.1 Brain (Prayer et al. 2006; Arthurs et al. 2015; Barkovich and Barkovich 2019) (Fig. 14)

Evaluation of the cerebral structure is quite similar as in living foetuses and newborn. The cortical gyration gradually becomes more complex as the gestational age progresses. We can cite as example the appearance of the sylvian fissure and the central sulcus (respectively 16 and 26 WA) as possible points of reference to evaluate the neurological development. Accuracy of MRI is very high to diagnose and quantify intraventricular haemorrhages. It may however be limited in small foetuses (<24 WA) to detect some congenital brain malformations.

2.5.2.2 Chest (Arthurs et al. 2014; Barber et al. 2015) (Fig. 15)

Lungs in stillborn children appear in isosignal in T1- and T2-weighted sequences but maceration can lead to aera of hyposignal. Blood stasis is commonly observed with a fluid-fluid level in heart cavities particular attention should be paid to analyze the heart and detect heart congenital diseases.

2.5.2.3 Abdomen

Examination of the abdominal content aims to describe solid organs malformations, especially of the urological tractus. Large and small bowel can be distended; meconium appears in hypersignal in T1-weighted sequences.

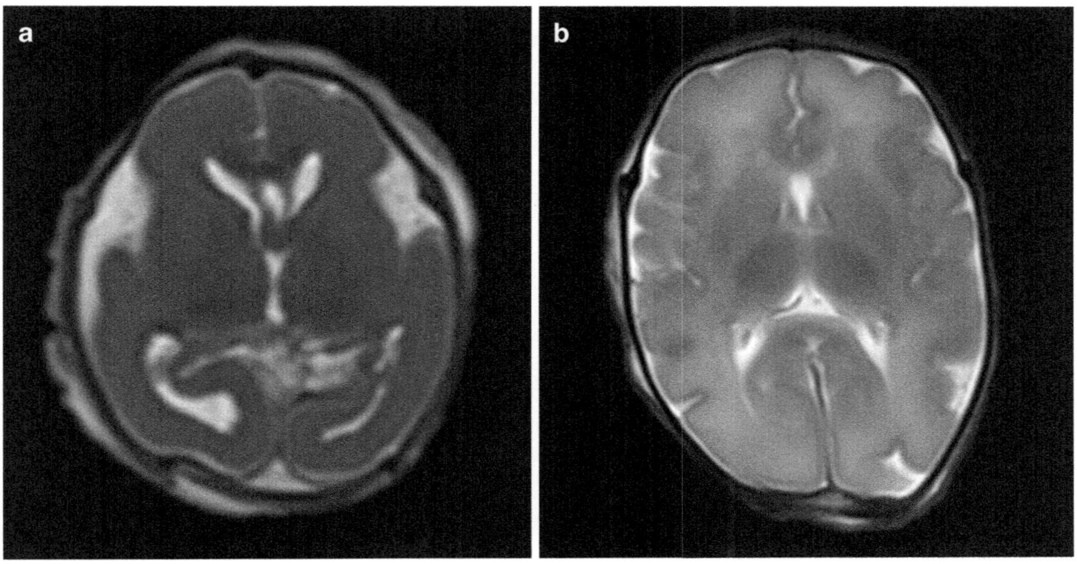

Fig. 14 (**a**) MRI, axial view, T2-weighted sequence (T2 CISS 3D) on the brain of a foetus at 24 WG. Foetal brain; incomplete gyration of the cerebral cortex with the outline of the sylvian fissure; volume of the ventricles is important, regarding to the total cerebral volume. (**b**) MRI, axial view, T2-weighted sequence on the brain of a foetus at 30 WG. Foetal brain; brain maturation is advanced with an increase of the number and the depth of the sulci and a decrease of the ventricle volume. Grey matter becomes more distinguishable from white matter

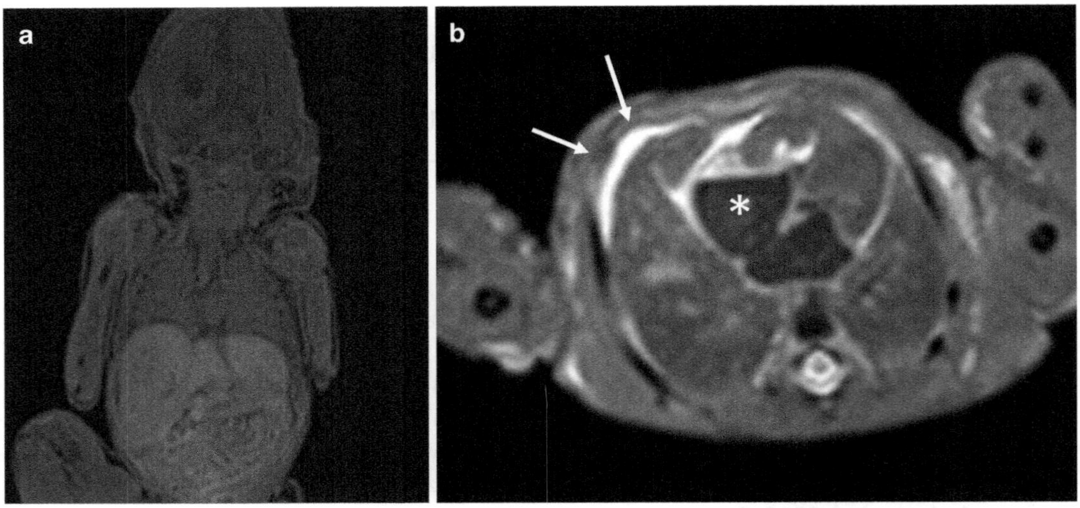

Fig. 15 (**a**) MRI, coronal view of the chest, T1-weighted sequence of a stillborn foetus at 24 WG. Normal appearance in isosignal of the condensed and unaerated lungs of a stillborn foetus. (**b**) MRI, axial view of the chest, T2-weighted sequence, of a stillborn foetus at 30 WG. Normal appearance of the thorax, with a scarce pleural effusion in hypersignal (arrow), blood stagnation leading to a blood level in the heart in hyposignal (asterisk) and unaerated lungs in isosignal in a foetus who did not breath

2.6 Computed Tomography (CT), CT Angiography, Post-mortem micro-CT and High Field MRI

Post-mortem CT is part of the routinely diagnostic arsenal in PMI. However, its role in foetopathology remains limited, mainly due to an insufficient spatial resolution (Shelmerdine et al. 2020; Kang et al. 2020). Micro-CT could be an interesting alternative to minimize this inconvenience (Hutchinson et al. 2018). PMCT is particularly relevant for detecting skeleton diseases or malformation or for defining the gestational age by the measurement of the long bones. But it is widely supplanted by MRI for the study of organs and soft tissues. Post-mortem CT Angiography (PMCTA) is a complementary technique developed in few centres. Different techniques have been described (Votino et al. 2012; Sarda-Quarello et al. 2015, 2016). Injection of the contrast medium can be performed in the umbilical vessels after catheterization or directly in the heart. Different types of contrast media have been used, such as a conventional iodine contrast, which may be diluted up to 50%, or mixture of iodine contrast with oily liquid. Injection greatly helps for the study of the heart, but also the vascular system (Votino et al. 2012). The main limitation of this technique is the presence of post-mortem intravascular coagulation, the difficulty of catheterization of umbilical vessels and the extravasation of contrast medium (Sarda-Quarello et al. 2016).

To date, post-mortem micro-CT and high field MRI are new tools only used in research programmes, to study very young foetuses and/or for ex vivo study of the organs (Hutchinson et al. 2018; Sandrini et al. 2019; Shelmerdine et al. 2020).

3 Children

3.1 General Considerations

Post imaging in children is performed in three main circumstances (Fleming et al. 2004;

Adamsbaum and Rey-Salmon 2013; Sieswerda-Hoogendoorn et al. 2014):

- To investigate sudden unexpected death in infancy (SUDI), usually concerning children under 2 years, who die during sleep,
- To explore a natural or traumatic death which occurs in a school age child,
- To explore a death in infancy suspected of resulting from child maltreatment.

In these contexts, PMI provides a first exhaustive evaluation of possible traumatic soft tissue and organ injuries, as CT and radiographs are excellent for the detection of bones injuries. It also assists the forensic pathologist in the gross and microscopic examination and sometimes allows to complete external examination when the autopsy is refused by parents (Wright 2004).

Concerning SUDI, post-mortem investigations are usually performed very shortly after death and following a specific protocol (Haute Autorité de Santé 2007; Sonnemans et al. 2018). Signs of putrefaction such as gas in vessels and soft tissue will most of the time be absent. Specific artefacts related to resuscitation procedures (intubation, intraosseous catheter, venous line) and sampling (lumbar puncture, intracardiac puncture, suprapubic catheterization) must however be known. It is consequently important to know what type of resuscitation was performed and what type of specimens were taken before imaging.

3.2 Radiographs

X-ray of the whole skeleton is currently recommended to be systematically performed to explore SUDI in France. The aim of these radiographs is to detect traumatic bone injuries, as a sign of child abuse. It must include, as for living children, X-ray of the skull (anterior-posterior and lateral), of the thorax, with four incidences (anterior-posterior, lateral right and left oblique incidences), lumbar spine (anterior-posterior) and pelvic bones (anterior-posterior and lateral), long bones of the limbs (anterior-posterior), segment by segment, with possible adjunction of a lateral incidence on the knees and ankles. The obtention of optimal incidences can be difficult when rigor mortis is established, especially for the hands. Considering its high spatial resolution, X-ray remains the gold standard for the detection of metaphyseal fractures and fractures of the extremities. However, X-ray is less effective for the detection of ribs and skull fractures (Shelmerdine et al. 2018). The study of the skeleton needs to be exhaustive, to find traumatic injuries such as fractures, periosteal appositions, and soft tissue infiltration. Each bone must be detailed attentively, to seek bone malformation, evocative of constitutional bone disease and to evaluate mineralization and bone maturation.

3.3 Computed Tomography

3.3.1 Technique

Images acquisition must be performed from vertex to toes. A separate head acquisition can be added. As an example, CT parameters can be set as follows: Voltage, 120–140 kV; Tension 300 mAs or modulated, Slice thickness 1 mm max. Reconstructions need to include soft-tissue filter, bone filter on the whole acquisition and lung filter on the chest. Volume rendering reconstructions and/or MIP reformatting can be processed for a rapid analysis of the skeleton (Fig. 16).

3.3.2 Non-specific Findings

Multiple post-mortem artefacts and non-specific findings can be described and must be known to not misinterpret them as a possible cause of death (Proisy et al. 2015).

3.3.2.1 Brain (Bardainne et al. 1996; Sieswerda-Hoogendoorn et al. 2015)

As for adults, the intracranial venous sinuses are spontaneously hyperdense (Fig. 17). They may make the detection of intracranial bleeding

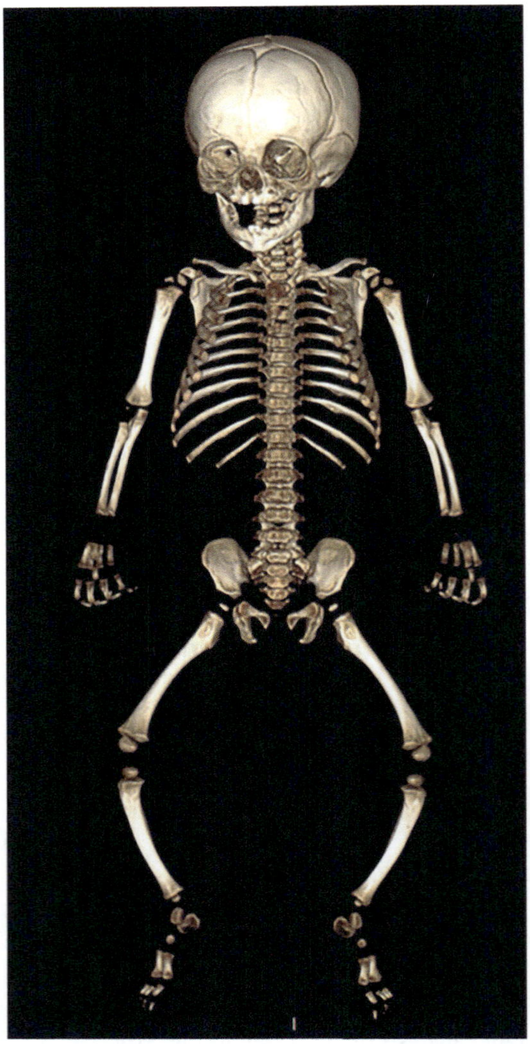

Fig. 16 Unenhanced PMCT, frontal view, in a 5-month-old girl (sudden unexpected death). Example of whole-body volume rendering reconstruction of the skeleton

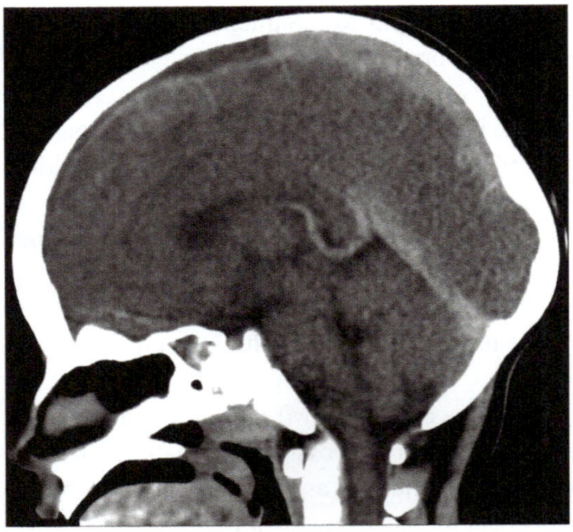

Fig. 17 Unenhanced PMCT, sagittal view of the brain in a 5-month-old boy (sudden unexpected death). Normal imaging of the brain, with spontaneous density of the intracranial sinuses

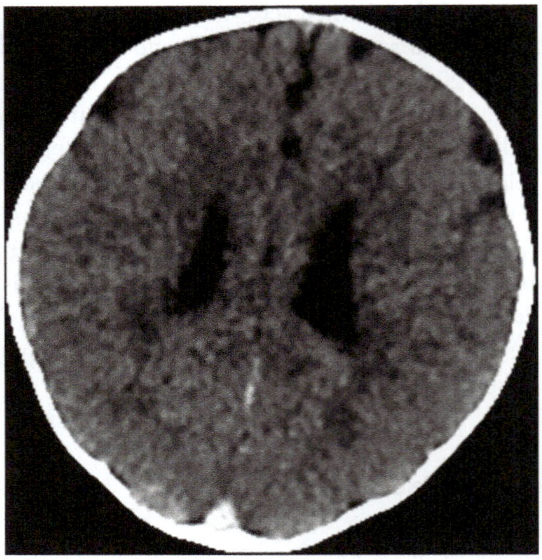

Fig. 18 Unenhanced PMCT, axial view of the brain in a girl of 3 months (sudden unexpected death). Normal imaging of the brain; poor myelinization of the white matter increases contrast between grey and white matter

uneasy, especially when cerebral oedema is important. The difference between white and grey matter is dulled, with a lesser degree than in adults, because of the poor myelinization of the white matter (Fig. 18).

3.3.2.2 Chest

A hyperdense fluid-fluid level is usually observed in cardiac cavities and large mediastinal vessels, related to stasis of the blood and post-mortem coagulation (Fig. 19). The other normal post-mortem findings of the chest are: hyperdensity of the aortic wall, calcification of the ligamentum arteriosum (Fig. 20), collapsed inferior vena cava, and gas in the lower oesophagus. The presence of gas in the pericardium or the mediastinum and/or hemopericardia must be correlated to intracardiac blood puncture and/or resuscitation. The thymus, which may be sometimes prominent, should not be interpreted as hemopericardium.

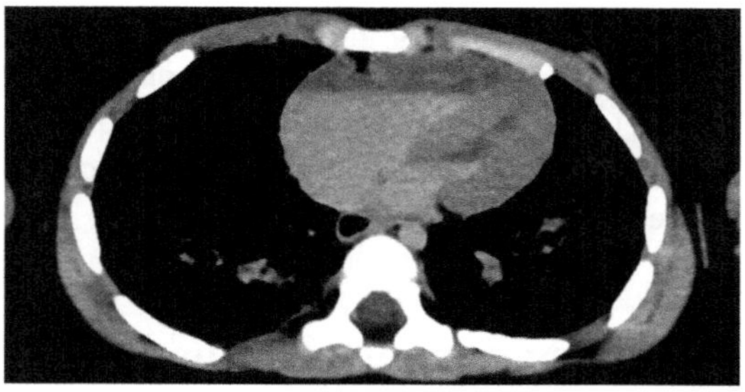

Fig. 19 Unenhanced PMCT (soft tissue window), axial view of the chest in a 4-month-old girl (sudden unexpected death). Normal imaging of the heart, with a fluid-fluid level within the heart cavities, due to blood stagnation

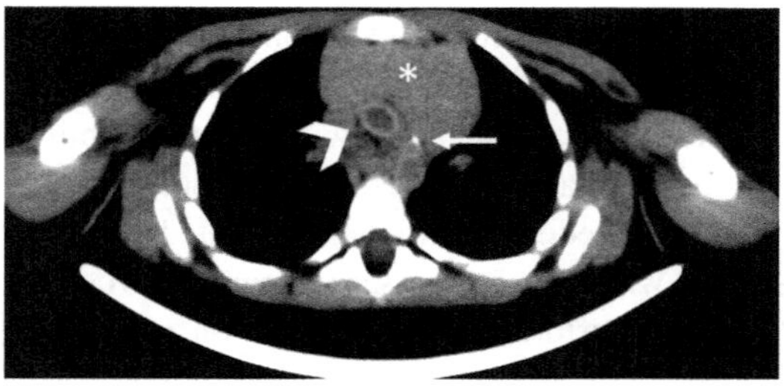

Fig. 20 Unenhanced PMCT (soft tissue window), axial view of the chest in a 5-month-old boy (sudden unexpected death). Normal thoracic findings, with the thymus (asterisk), hyperdensity of the aortic wall (arrow head) and calcification of the ligamentum arteriosum (arrow)

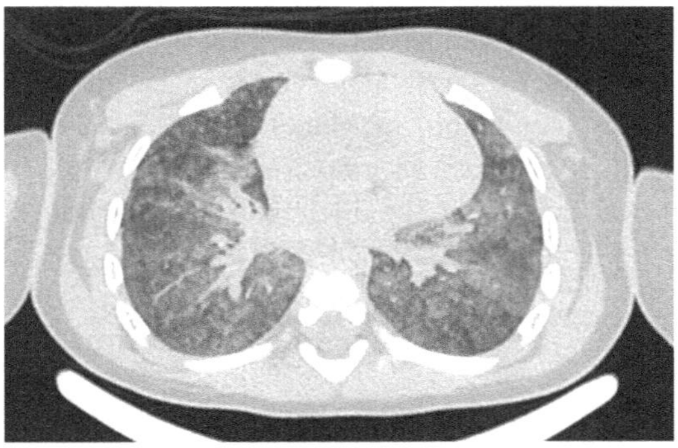

Fig. 21 Unenhanced PMCT (lung window), axial view on the chest in a 5-month-old boy (sudden unexpected death). Normal imaging of the lungs with unspecific diffuse ground-glass opacities

The tracheobronchial tree is very often filled with gastric fluid, due to post-mortem mobilization and/or oro-tracheal intubation (Knight 1975; Shiotani et al. 2004). Diffuse and bilateral ground-glass opacities are almost constant (Fig. 21). Consolidations of the lungs are frequent, and sometimes extensive, with no specific significance (Fig. 22).

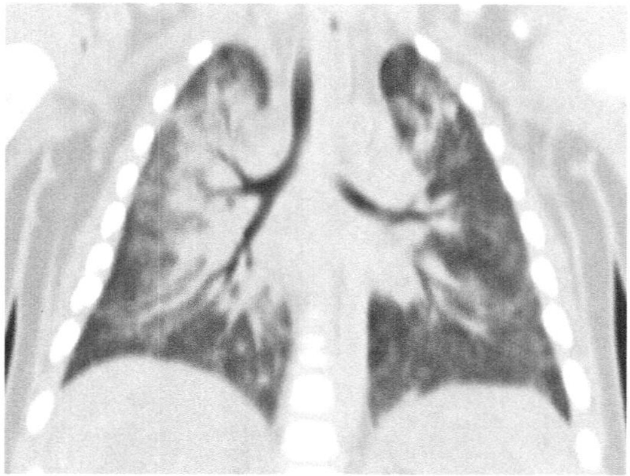

Fig. 22 Unenhanced PMCT (lung window), coronal view of the chest in a 5-month-old boy (sudden unexpected death). Unspecific bilateral peribronchovascular consolidations

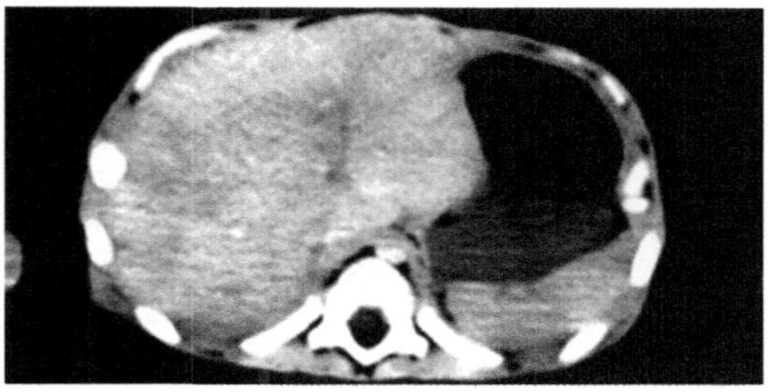

Fig. 23 Unenhanced PMCT (soft tissue window), axial view of the abdomen, in a 4-month-old boy (sudden unexpected death). Heterogenous density of the liver; periportal oedema is frequently observed

3.3.2.3 Abdomen-Pelvis

Analysis of the abdominal solid organs is difficult by the low fat content of the abdominal cavity. Decreasing the width of the window of Hounsfield Unit (HU) can help to increase the contrast between organs. The parenchyma of the liver is usually heterogeneous, related to perfusion trouble and periportal oedema (Fig. 23). The density of the liver is higher than that of the kidneys, resulting in a hepatorenal gradient (Fig. 24). Inversion of this gradient can be a sign of fat accumulation in the liver and a possible metabolic disease. Changes in the vascular system include hyperdensity of the portal, hepatic and umbilical veins, and possible calcification of the umbilical arteries. Distension of stomach and

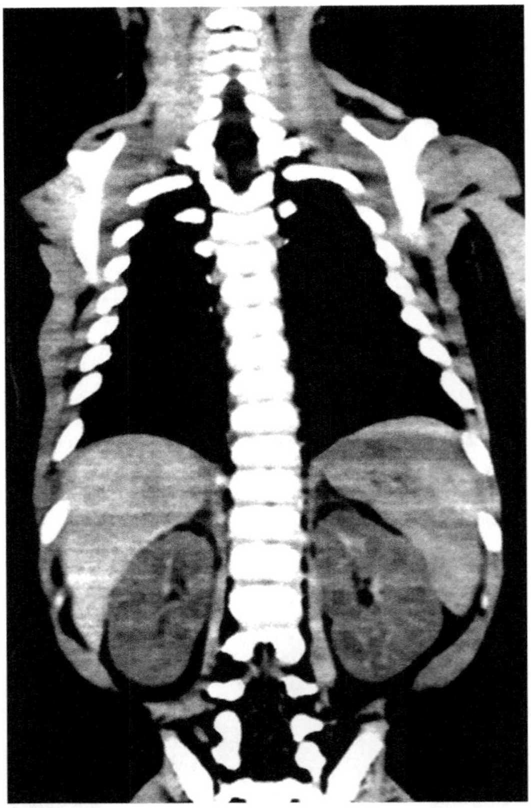

Fig. 24 Unenhanced PMCT (soft tissue filter), coronal view of the abdomen in a 6-month-old boy (sudden unexpected death). Hepatorenal gradient, with a higher density of the liver and the spleen. Inversion of this gradient can help for the detection of fat accumulation in the liver

bowel with gas is variable but more marked as ventilation was prolonged during cardiopulmonary resuscitation (CPR).

Cardiac puncture, lumbar puncture and suprapubic catheterization can be responsible for bubbles of gas, respectively, in the upper part of the abdomen, in the medullary canal and in/around the bladder.

3.3.2.4 Skeleton

Normal findings include the presence of gas and sometimes even fracture of the anterior tibial spines consecutive to an intraosseous line procedure. Deformation of the anterior parts of the ribs (called "buckle fracture") are sometimes observed (Fig. 25). Physiological periosteal appositions of the long bones (tibia, femur, humerus) are possible during the first weeks of life, up to 6 months. They are typically thin, regular, bilateral and symmetric (Kwon et al. 2002) (Fig. 26). Besides, Wormian bones are frequent during the first months of life and should not be interpreted as skull fractures. They are frequently multiple and located on both sides of the occipital suture (Idriz et al. 2015) (Fig. 27).

3.4 Magnetic Resonance Imaging

3.4.1 Technique (Norman et al. 2016) (Fig. 28)

Different acquisition protocols and sequence parameters can be used. Brain exploration must contain at least one 2D T2-weighted acquisition (for example, short-tau inversion recovery, STIR) which may be completed by a 3D T1-weighted sequence, eventually with susceptibility-weighted imaging (SWI) for detection of intracranial bleeding. Diffusion-weighted imaging (DWI) will be less necessary, especially when the time for performing the acquisition imaging is short. Exploration of the body will include high-resolution 3D T2-weighted and a 3D T1-weighted sequences. Cardiac exploration can be based on high-resolution isotropic T2-weighted sequence centred on the heart, such as a 3D CISS sequence. The spinal cord can benefit from dedicated sequences, such as sagittal 2D T1- and T2-weighted sequences. On a case-by-case basis, In-Phase/Out-Phase sequences can be added if fat accumulation of the liver is suspected. Evaluation of organ volumes is also feasible in MRI, thanks to the high soft tissue contrast (Prodhomme et al. 2012).

3.4.2 Normal Post-mortem Findings

3.4.2.1 Brain (Arthurs et al. 2015)

MRI provides a high-resolution imaging of cerebral content. Cerebral oedema is usually observed in the form of diminution of ventricles volume and less visibility of cortical sulci. Such as in CT, differentiation between grey and white matter may be difficult in T1- or T2-weighted sequences (Fig. 28). Stasis of the blood in intracranial veins results in a hypointense signal on T2 sequences, especially in GE sequences (Fig. 29). Detection of rupture of the bridging veins is very challenging in PMI because of taphonomic thrombosis of all bridging veins after death.

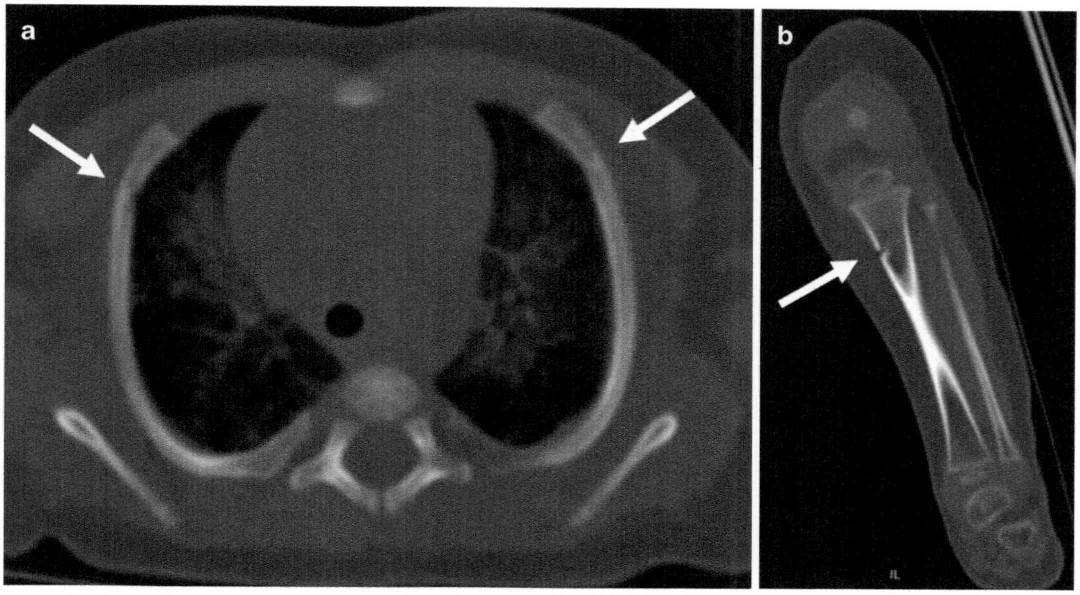

Fig. 25 (**a**) Unenhanced PMCT (bone window), axial view on the chest in a 1-month-old boy (sudden unexpected death). "Buckle fractures" (arrows) of the anterior part of the ribs, after external cardiac massage. (**b**) Unenhanced PMCT (bone window), coronal view of the chest in an 8-month-old boy (sudden unexpected death). Focal fracture of the anterior tibial spine, due to attempt of intraosseous catheter placement (arrow)

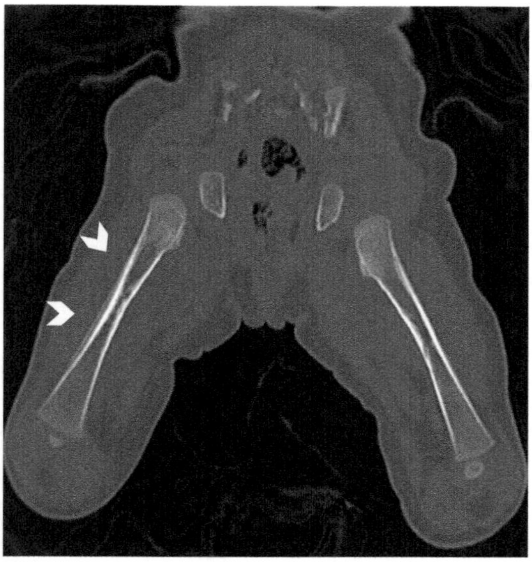

Fig. 26 Unenhanced PMCT (bone window), coronal view of the lower limbs in a 6-week-old girl (sudden unexpected death). Linear and regular physiologic periosteal apposition of the right femur (arrow head)

3.4.2.2 Chest (Arthurs et al. 2014)

In the same way as CT, the appearance of the lungs is very variable and the major part of the changes can't be reliably interpreted (Thayyil et al. 2013). A fluid-fluid level hyper-/isointense in T2 sequences is frequently observed in heart cavities, due to blood sedimentation (Fig. 30). Gas in cardiac cavities and vessels appears hypointense on T1 and T2 sequences. MRI is more sensitive to detect pleural and/or pericardium effusion in T2w sequences than in CT scan (Fig. 31).

3.4.2.3 Abdomen and Pelvis

MRI allows a better distinction of the abdominal content. Organomegaly can easily be evaluated by the measurement of organ size. The liver appears hypointense on T1-weighted sequences. Intraperitoneal effusion will be easy to detect as it appears hyperintense on T2-weighted sequences (Fig. 32). Meconium is usually hyperintense in T1.

3.4.2.4 Skeleton

STIRw sequences are very sensitive to depict abnormal soft-tissues infiltration such as subcutaneous perfusion diffusion in the leg because of tibial puncture. Its high sensitivity will help the reader to focus on the adjacent bone, looking for traumatic injuries.

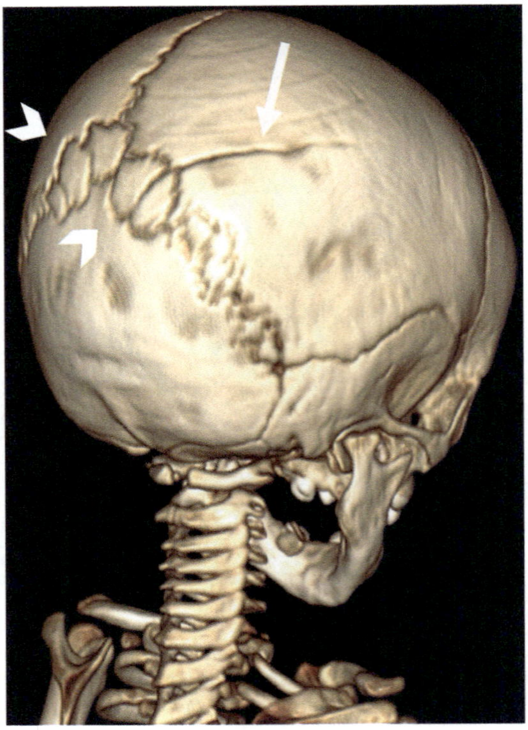

Fig. 27 Unenhanced PMCT, volume rendering reconstructions of the skull in an 8-month-old boy (suspected sudden unexpected death revealing shaken-baby syndrome with head impact). Posterior view of the skull showing Wormian bones (head arrow) and a right parietal fracture (arrow)

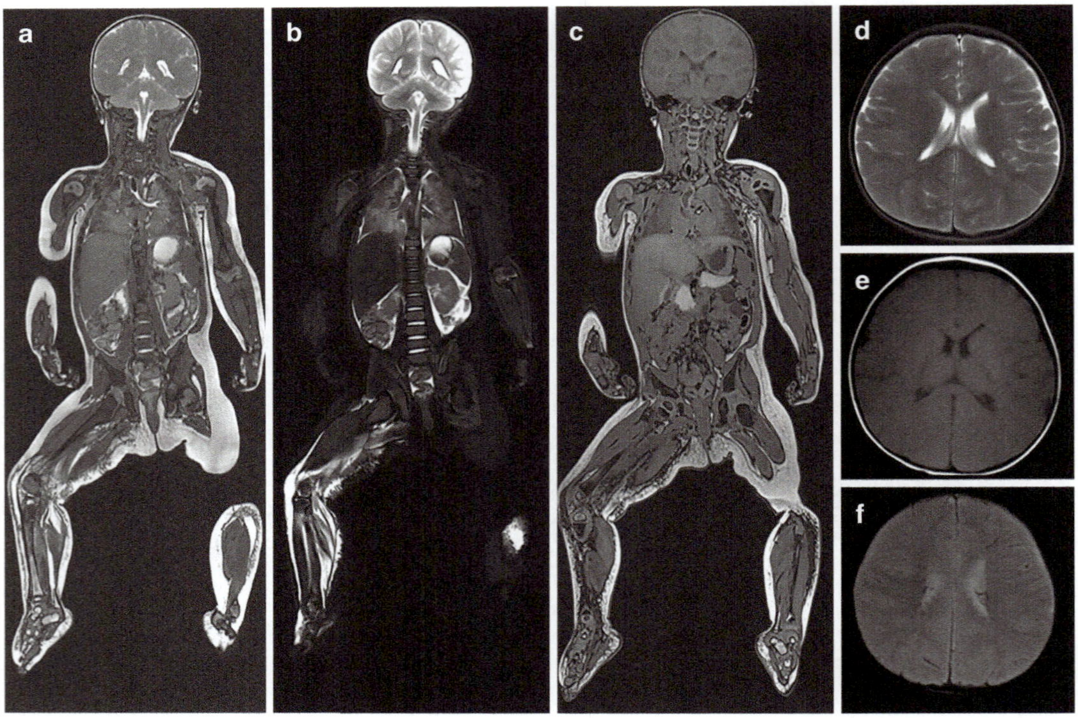

Fig. 28 PMMRI, coronal view, (**a**) T2-weighted sequence, (**b**) STIR sequence and (**c**) T1-weighted sequence; axial view of the brain in (**d**) T2-weighted sequence, (**f**) T2 Gradient Echo-weighted sequence and (**e**) T1-weighted sequence. Normal post-mortem MRI in a 1-year-old male infant with sudden unexpected death

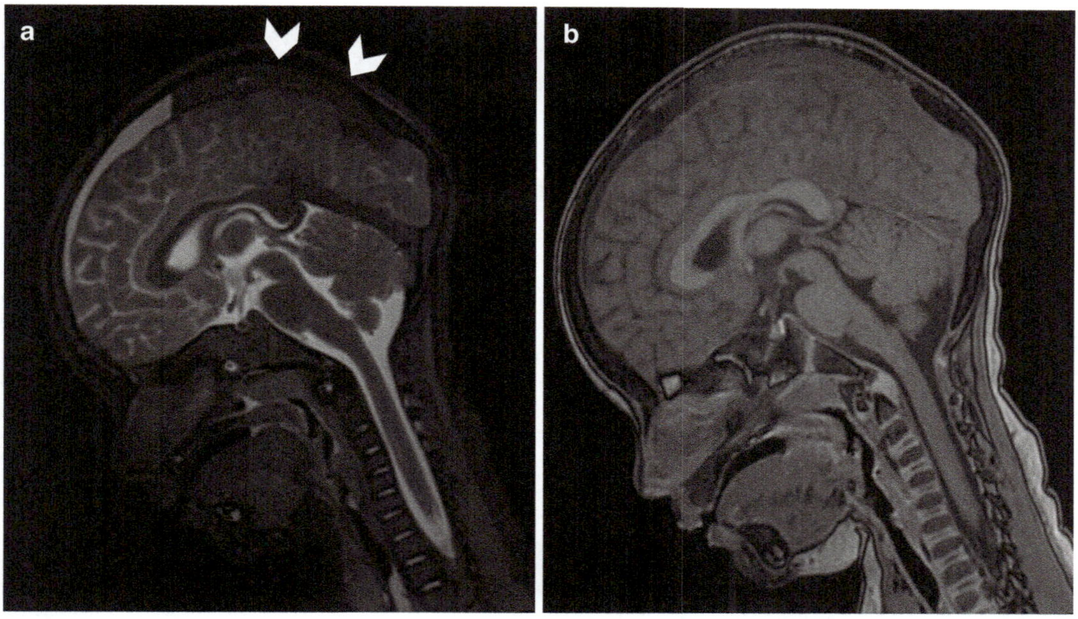

Fig. 29 PMMRI, sagittal view, (**a**) T2-weighted and (**b**) T1-weighted sequence of the brain in a 1-year-old boy. Normal imaging of the brain showing normal hypointense signal of the intracranial venous sinuses (arrow)

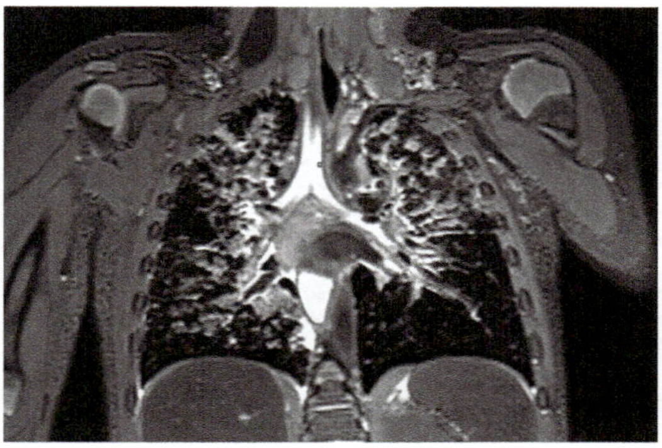

Fig. 30 PMMRI, coronal view, T2-weighted sequence on the chest in a 10-month-old boy (sudden unexpected death). Fulfilling of the tracheobronchial tree by hyperintense digestive fluid, considered as a normal phenomenon due to passive post-mortem mobilization and/or cardio-pulmonary resuscitation. Isointense unspecific bilateral consolidation, in contrast with the absence of signal of the aerated lungs

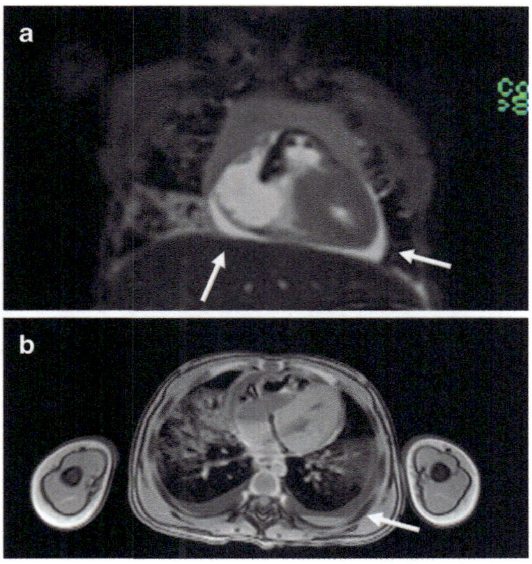

Fig. 31 (**a**) PMMRI, coronal view, T2-weighted sequence of the thorax in a 1-year-old boy. Hyperintense signal of pericardial effusion (arrows). (**b**) MRI, axial view, T1-weighted sequence of the thorax in a 1-year-old boy. Haemothorax: fluid-fluid level within a bilateral thoracic effusion

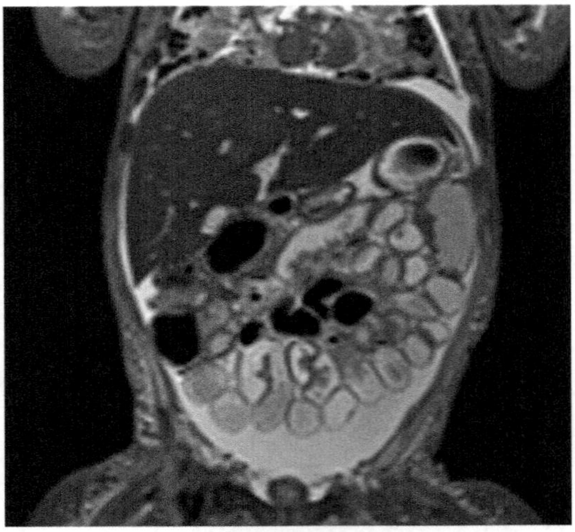

Fig. 32 PMMRI, coronal view, T2-w sequence of the abdomen. Diffuse hyperintense intraperitoneal effusion

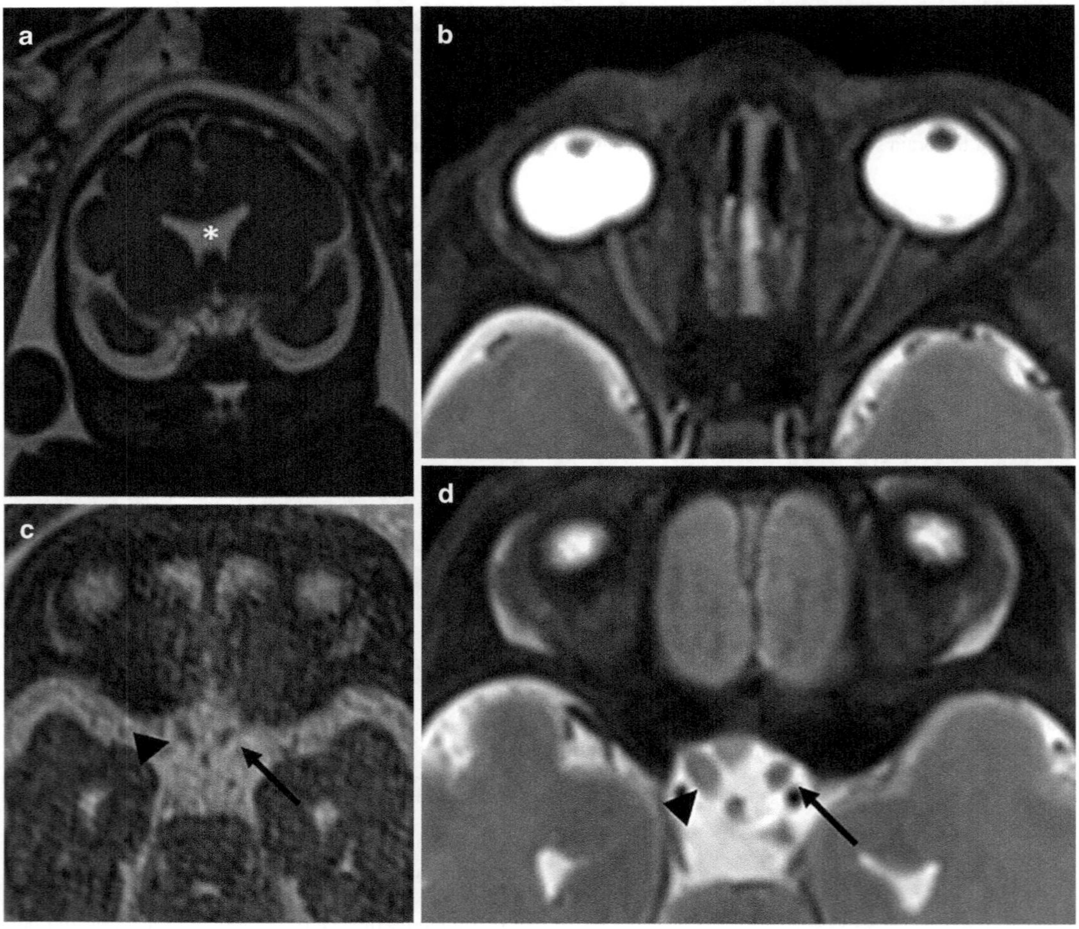

Fig. 33 (**a**) and (**c**) Antemortem MRI in (**a**) coronal view and (**c**) axial view in T2-weighted sequences of the brain. (**b**) and (**d**) PMMRI, axial view in T2-weighted sequences of the brain of a foetus at 34 WG (termination of pregnancy). A case of prenatal (**a, c**) and post-mortem correlation (**b, d**) in a septo-optic dysplasia (**a**: septal cavity agenesis (asterisk)) with hypoplasia of the left optical nerve, of intra-orbital (**b**) and pre-chiasmatic (**c, d**) parts (left: black arrows, right: black arrowheads)

4 Illustrated Pathological Examples

- Foetus
  Example of a septo-optic dysplasia, ante natal diagnosed, lead to termination of pregnancy at 34 WG (Fig. 33).
- Children
  - 8-week-old male infant who deceased suddenly. A whole-body post-mortem MRI was performed, which showed left subdural haematoma, clots in the dural sac and diffuse cerebral oedema, confirmed by autopsy, conducting to the diagnosis of shaken-baby syndrome (Fig. 34).
  - 5-year-old boy deceased after suffering from acute abdominal pain and vomiting. He was operated in the previous year for acute appendicitis. Clinical examination found signs of dehydration (ringed eyes, wrinkled skin, sleepiness). Post-mortem imaging showed dilatation of the bowels, with a transition flat bowel–dilated bowel in the right iliac fossa. Peritoneal adhesion was confirmed by the autopsy (Fig. 35).

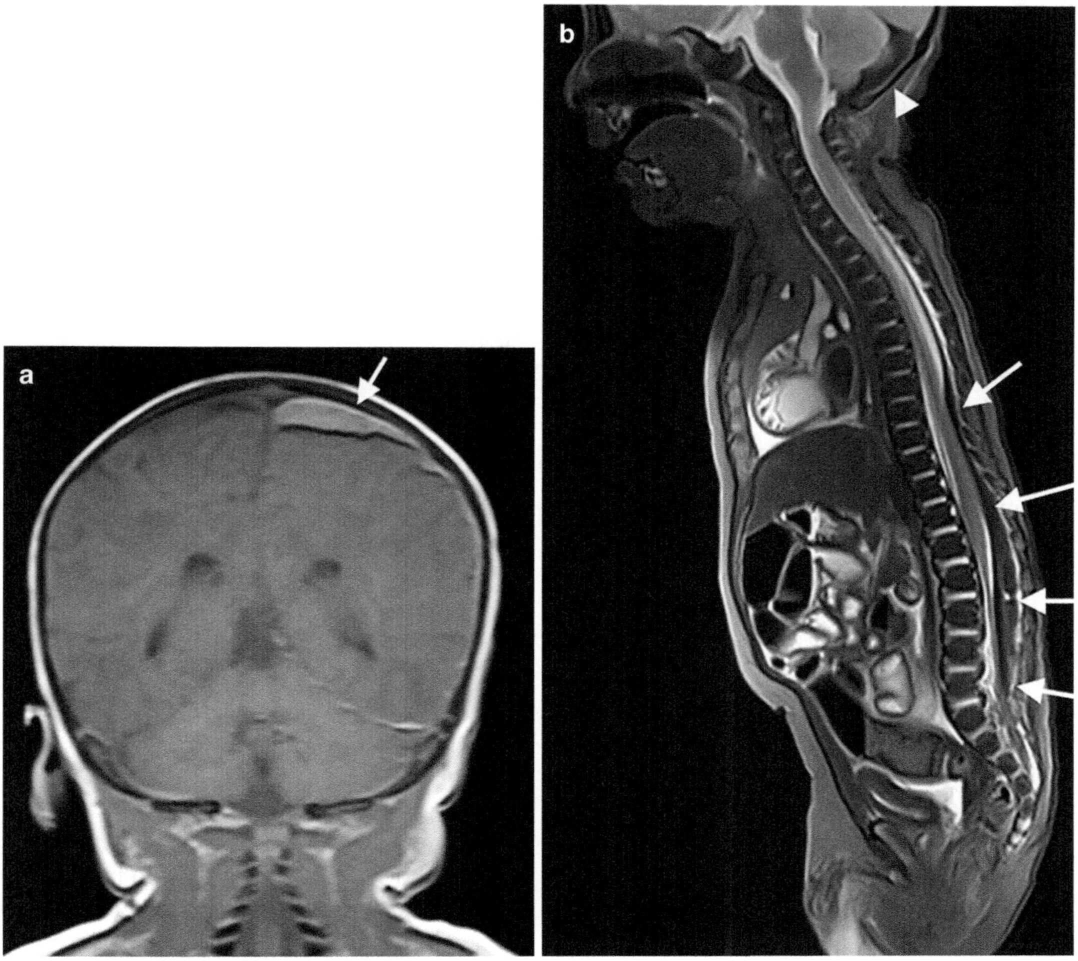

Fig. 34 (**a**) PMMRI, coronal view, T1 weighted sequence of the brain in an 8 weeks old boy, who died of shaken baby syndrome. Left subdural hematoma of the convexity. Hyperintense in T1 sequences (white arrow) (**b**) PMMRI, sagittal view, T2 weighted sequence of the spine of the same child. Clots in the dural sac (white arrows) and subdural hematoma in the posterior fossa (white arrow head)

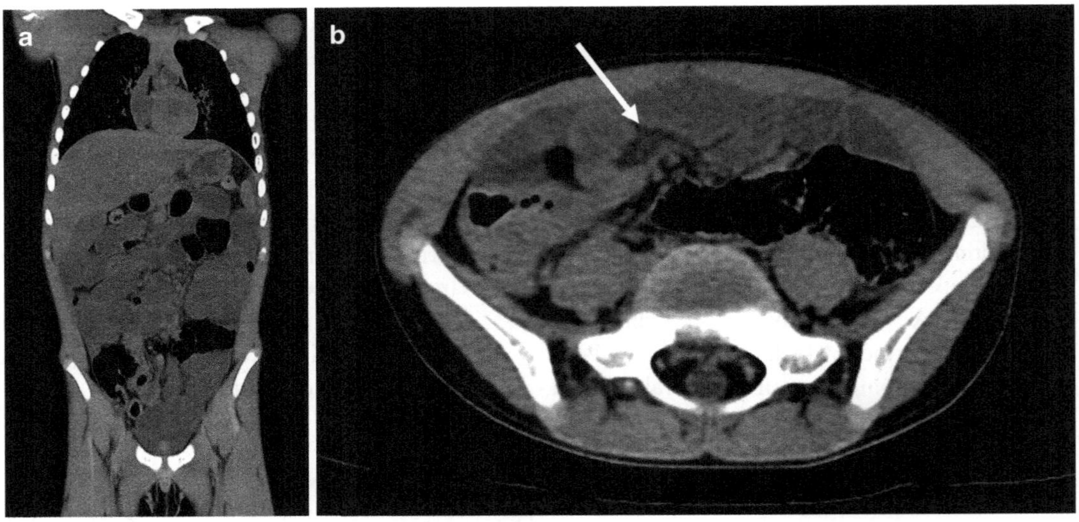

Fig. 35 Unenhanced PMCT (soft tissue). (**a**) axial and (**b**) coronal view of the abdomen, in a 5-year-old boy who presented sudden death after abdominal pain and vomiting. Distension of the bowels, filled with air and fluid, with a transition zone between flat and dilated bowel in the right iliac fossa (arrow). Autopsy confirmed the peritoneal adhesion, responsible for acute bowel occlusion

- particularities of neonaticide

Neonaticide is defined as the killing of a newborn during its first 24 hours of life, most often by the mother in the setting of hidden or denied pregnancy. A CT scan and an autopsy should always be done in this situation to answer three questions:

– Are there any signs of inflicted trauma?
– Was the child viable?
– Is the newborn considered stillborn or liveborn?

The answer to this last question is of paramount importance, shifting the "neonate" from the status of a foetus to the status of a living child with legal existence. It is brought by highlighting the occurrence of breathing after birth. It is thus very important to know if cardiopulmonary resuscitation was performed. The main radiological signs of ante-mortem breathing are (Ducloyer et al. 2019): the presence of gas in both lungs, proved by lung density measurement and visible in chest VR reconstructions; the presence of gas in bowel, especially if present beyond the duodeno-jejunal junction. We illustrate this specific situation with images of a stillborn foetus of 30 WG who presented unaerated, white lungs, with no aeration of the bowel (Fig. 36). On the opposite, The figure 37 illustrates the case of a 41 WG girl, who was found in a plastic bag after his mother was

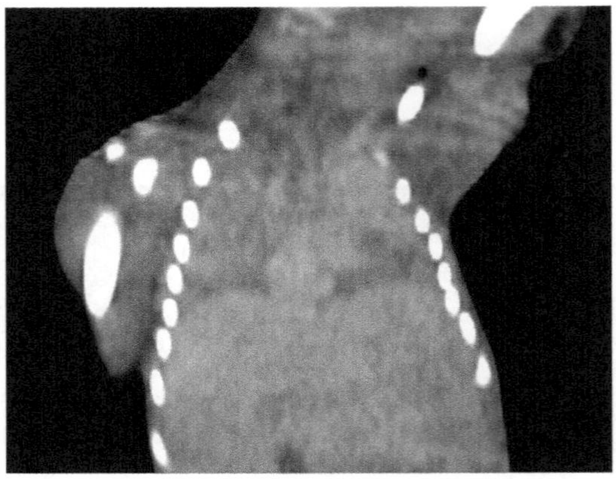

Fig. 36 Unenhanced PMCT (soft tissue window), coronal view of the chest in a stillborn foetus at 30 WA, in a context of delivering after concealed pregnancy. Both lungs are dense and unventilated. Gas is present in the stomach but the bowel is fulfilled with liquid

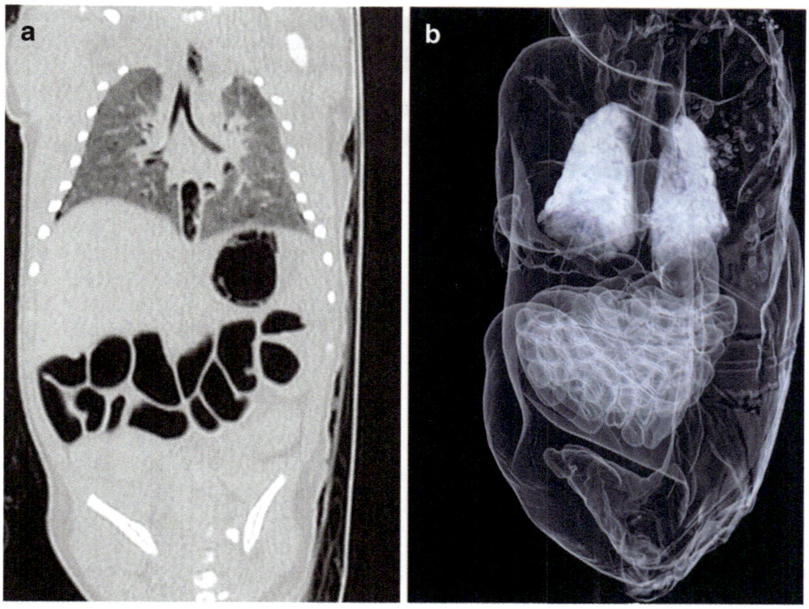

Fig. 37 (**a**) Unenhanced PMCT (lung window), coronal view of the chest in a liveborn female at 41 WG, in a case of neonaticide. Diffuse ground-glass opacities, aeration of the tracheobronchial tree and important aeration of almost all the small bowel. (**b**) Unenhanced PMCT, volume rendering reconstruction, coronal view of the whole body. Three-dimensional reconstructions are a useful tool, with a high sensitivity, to highlight the presence of gas within both lungs and the bowel

admitted to hospital for genital haemorrhage. PMCT showed aeration of both lungs, presenting diffuse ground-glass opacities and gas within the major part of the bowel (Fig. 37).

5 Conclusion

All PMI techniques are complementary: X-ray has the best spatial resolution and thus is useful for the analysis of small and/or thin bone structures; ultrasound with high-frequency probes is very interesting in young foetuses without ingested or inhaled air and few ossified structures; CT is superior for complex 3D bone structures like thorax and skull and for detection and analysis of gas structures but has poor soft tissues contrast; and last, MRI has the best soft tissue contrast including brain, abdominal cavity, muscles and subcutaneous fat, but is less useful for calcified structures (such as ossified bone) and hollow organs. Performing and interpreting post-mortem imaging requires specific paediatric skills about normal foetal growth, birth and child growth. The enventuality of infanticide must be kept in mind, especially in newborns and children. The development of post-mortem imaging in foetuses and children is the essential preliminary step for the generalization of "mini-invasive autopsy" which may allow for targeted sampling guided by imaging (Hutchinson et al. 2019; Hailu et al. 2020; Herath & Herath 2020; Hyde et al. 2020). Pursuing researches is necessary to precise indications and limitations of this new type of post-mortem investigation and how it can be applied in children and foetuses.

References

Adair FL, Scammon RE (1921) A study of the ossification centers of the wrist, knee and ankle at birth, with particular reference to the physical development and maturity of the newborn. Am J Obstet Gynecol 2:35–60

Adamsbaum C, Rey-Salmon C (2013) Maltraitance chez l'enfant. Médecine Sciences Publications-Lavoisier, Paris

Addison S, Arthurs OJ, Thayyil S (2014) Post-mortem MRI as an alternative to non-forensic autopsy in foetuses and children: from research into clinical practice. Br J Radiol 87:20130621

Arthurs OJ, Hutchinson JC, Sebire NJ (2017) Current issues in postmortem imaging of perinatal and forensic childhood deaths. Forensic Sci Med Pathol 13:58–66

Arthurs OJ, Thayyil S, Pauliah SS et al (2015) Diagnostic accuracy and limitations of post-mortem MRI for neurological abnormalities in fetuses and children. Clin Radiol 70:872–880

Arthurs OJ, Thayyil S, Magnetic Resonance Imaging Autopsy Study (MaRIAS) Collaborative Group et al (2014) Diagnostic accuracy of post-mortem MRI for thoracic abnormalities in fetuses and children. Eur Radiol 24:2876–2884

Barber JL, Sebire NJ, Chitty LS, Taylor AM, Arthurs OJ (2015) Lung aeration on post-mortem magnetic resonance imaging is a useful marker of live birth versus stillbirth. Int J Legal Med 129:531–536

Bardainne M, Rolland Y, Tréguier C, Claeyssen-Rolland V, Dagorne M, Broussine L, Jouan H, Roussey M (1996) Contribution du scanner crânien post-mortem à l'étude de la mort subite du nourrisson. Arch Pédiatrie 3:661–667

Barkovich MJ, Barkovich AJ (2019) MR imaging of normal brain development. Neuroimaging Clin N Am 29:325–337

Cain MA, Guidi CB, Steffensen T, Whiteman VE, Gilbert-Barness E, Johnson DR (2014) Postmortem ultrasonography of the macerated Fetus complements autopsy following in utero fetal demise. Pediatr Dev Pathol 17:217–220

Calder AD, Offiah AC (2015) Foetal radiography for suspected skeletal dysplasia: technique, normal appearances, diagnostic approach. Pediatr Radiol 45:536–548

Carneiro C, Curate F, Cunha E (2016) A method for estimating gestational age of fetal remains based on long bone lengths. Int J Legal Med 130:1333–1341

Charlier P, Chaillot P-F, Watier L, Ménétrier M, Carlier R, Cavard S, Hervé C, de la Grandmaison GL, Huynh-Charlier I (2013) Is post-mortem ultrasonography a useful tool for forensic purposes? Med Sci Law 53:227–234

Ducloyer M, Tuchtan L, Delteil C, Piercecchi M-D, David A, Visseaux G, Bouvet R, Gorincour G, Clement R (2019) Lung density measurement in postmortem computed tomography: a new tool to assess immediate neonatal breath in suspected neonaticides. Int J Legal Med. https://doi.org/10.1007/s00414-019-02103-3

Fariña J, Millana C, Fdez-Aceñero JM, Furió V, Aragoncillo P, Martín VG, Buencuerpo J (2002) Ultrasonographic autopsy (echopsy): a new autopsy technique. Virchows Arch 440:635–639

Fazekas IG, Kósa F (1978) Forensic fetal osteology. Akadémiai Kiadó, Budapest

Fleming PJ, Blair PS, Sidebotham PD, Hayler T (2004) Investigating sudden unexpected deaths in infancy and childhood and caring for bereaved families: an integrated multiagency approach. BMJ 328:331–334

Furness ME, Weckert RC, Parker SA, Knowles S (1989) Ultrasound in the perinatal necropsy. J Med Genet 26:368–372

Garel C, Elmaleh M, Chantrel E, Sebag G, Brisse H (2003) Fetal MRI: normal gestational landmarks for cerebral biometry, gyration and myelination. Childs Nerv Syst 19:422–425

Gentili P, Trasimeni A, Giorlandino C (1984) Fetal ossification centers as predictors of gestational age in normal and abnormal pregnancies. J Ultrasound Med 3:193–197

Hailu R, Desta T, Bekuretsion Y et al (2020) Minimally invasive tissue sampling in preterm deaths: a validation study. Glob Pediatr Health 7:2333794X20953263

Haute Autorité de Santé (2007) Prise en charge en cas de mort inattendue du nourrisson (moins de 2 ans)

Herath JC, Herath SO (2020) Is it time for targeted and minimally invasive post-mortem examination using total body computed tomography in a medicolegal autopsy? Forensic Sci Med Pathol. https://doi.org/10.1007/s12024-020-00279-4

Hutchinson JC, Kang X, Shelmerdine SC, Segers V, Lombardi CM, Cannie MM, Sebire NJ, Jani JC, Arthurs OJ (2018) Postmortem microfocus computed tomography for early gestation fetuses: a validation study against conventional autopsy. Am J Obstet Gynecol 218:445.e1–445.e12

Hutchinson C, Shelmerdine SC, Lewis C, Parmenter J, Simcock IC, Ward L, Ashworth MT, Chitty LS, Arthurs OJ, Sebire NJ (2019) Feasibility and experience of the MinImAL procedure: minimally invasive perinatal and paediatric autopsies with laparoscopically assisted tissue sampling: laparoscopic autopsy. Ultrasound Obstet Gynecol. https://doi.org/10.1002/uog.20211

Hyde G, Rummery R, Whitby EH, Bloor J, Raghavan A, Cohen MC (2020) Benefits and limitations of the minimally invasive Postmortem: a review of an innovative service development. Pediatr Dev Pathol 23:431–437

Idriz S, Patel JH, Ameli Renani S, Allan R, Vlahos I (2015) CT of Normal developmental and variant anatomy of the pediatric skull: distinguishing trauma from normality. Radiographics 35:1585–1601

Kang X, Carlin A, Cannie MM, Sanchez TC, Jani JC (2020) Fetal postmortem imaging: an overview of current techniques and future perspectives. Am J Obstet Gynecol 223:493–515

Knight BH (1975) The significance of the postmortem discovery of gastric contents in the air passages. Forensic Sci 6:229–234

Kwon DS, Spevak MR, Fletcher K, Kleinman PK (2002) Physiologic subperiosteal new bone formation: prevalence, distribution, and thickness in neonates and infants. Am J Roentgenol 179:985–988

Norman W, Jawad N, Jones R, Taylor AM, Arthurs OJ (2016) Perinatal and paediatric post-mortem magnetic resonance imaging (PMMR): sequences and technique. Br J Radiol 89:20151028

Sonnemans LJP, Vester MEM, Kolsteren EEM, Erwich JJHM, Nikkels PGJ, Kint PAM, van Rijn RR, Klein WM, Dutch Post-mortem Imaging Guideline Group (2018) Dutch guideline for clinical foetal-neonatal and paediatric post-mortem radiology, including a review of literature. Eur J Pediatr 177:791–803

Piercecchi-Marti M-D, Adalian P, Bourliere-Najean B, Gouvernet J, Maczel M, Dutour O, Leonetti G (2002) Validation of a radiographic method to establish new fetal growth standards: radio-anatomical correlation. J Forensic Sci 47:328–331

Prayer D, Kasprian G, Krampl E, Ulm B, Witzani L, Prayer L, Brugger PC (2006) MRI of normal fetal brain development. Eur J Radiol 57:199–216

Prodhomme O, Baud C, Saguintaah M, Béchard-Sevette N, Bolivar J, David S, Taleb-Arrada I, Couture A (2015a) Principles of fetal postmortem ultrasound: a personal review. J Forensic Radiol Imaging 3:12–15

Prodhomme O, Baud C, Saguintaah M, Béchard-Sevette N, Bolivar J, David S, Taleb-Arrada I, Couture A (2015b) Comparison of postmortem ultrasound and x-ray with autopsy in fetal death: retrospective study of 169 cases. J Forensic Radiol Imaging 3:120–130

Prodhomme O, Seguret F, Martrille L, Pidoux O, Cambonie G, Couture A, Rouleau C (2012) Organ volume measurements: comparison between MRI and autopsy findings in infants following sudden unexpected death. Arch Dis Child Fetal Neonatal Ed 97:F434–F438

Proisy M, Loget P, Bouvet R, Roussey M, Pelé F, Rozel C, Treguier C, Darnault P, Bruneau B (2015) Non-specific post-mortem modifications on whole-body post-mortem computed tomography in sudden unexpected death in infancy. J Forensic Radiol Imaging 3:16–23

Sandrini C, Rossetti L, Zambelli V et al (2019) Accuracy of micro-computed tomography in post-mortem evaluation of Fetal congenital heart disease. Comparison between post-mortem micro-CT and conventional autopsy. Front Pediatr. https://doi.org/10.3389/fped.2019.00092

Sarda-Quarello L, Bartoli C, Laurent P-E, Torrents J, Piercecchi-Marti M-D, Sigaudy S, Ariey-Bonnet D, Gorincour G (2016) Whole body perinatal postmortem CT angiography. Diagn Interv Imaging 97:121–124

Sarda-Quarello L, Tuchtan L, Bartoli C, Bourlière-Najean B, Petit P, Sigaudy S, Piercecchi-Marti M-D, Gorincour G (2015) Imagerie post-mortem périnatale: état des lieux, point de vue et perspectives, échographiques en particulier. Gynécol Obstét Fertil 43:612–615

Sarda-Quarello L, Tuchtan L, Torrents J, Piercecchi-Marti M-D, Bartoli C, Laurent P-E, Bourlière-Najean B, Petit P, Quarello E, Gorincour G (2015) Perinatal death: is there a place for post-mortem angio-CT? J Forensic Radiol Imaging 3:1–4

Shelmerdine SC, Hutchinson JC, Arthurs OJ, Sebire NJ (2020) Latest developments in post-mortem foetal imaging. Prenat Diagn 40:28–37

Shelmerdine SC, Langan D, Hutchinson JC et al (2018) Chest radiographs versus CT for the detection of rib fractures in children (DRIFT): a diagnostic accuracy observational study. Lancet Child Adolesc Health 2:802–811

Shiotani S, Kohno M, Ohashi N, Yamazaki K, Nakayama H, Watanabe K, Oyake Y, Itai Y (2004) Non-traumatic postmortem computed tomographic (PMCT) findings of the lung. Forensic Sci Int 139:39–48

Sieswerda-Hoogendoorn T, Beenen LFM, van Rijn RR (2015) Normal cranial postmortem CT findings in children. Forensic Sci Int 246:43–49

Sieswerda-Hoogendoorn T, Soerdjbalie-Maikoe V, de Bakker H, van Rijn RR (2014) Postmortem CT compared to autopsy in children; concordance in a forensic setting. Int J Legal Med 128:957–965

Thayyil S, Sebire NJ, Chitty LS et al (2013) Post-mortem MRI versus conventional autopsy in fetuses and children: a prospective validation study. Lancet 382:223–233

Tuchtan L, Lesieur E, Bartoli C, Delteil C, Sarda-Quarello L, Torrents J, Sigaudy S, Piercecchi M-D, Gorincour G (2018) Diagnosis of congenital abnormalities with post-mortem ultrasound in perinatal death. Diagn Interv Imaging 99:143–149

Votino C, Cannie M, Segers V, Dobrescu O, Dessy H, Gallo V, Cos T, Damry N, Jani J (2012) Virtual autopsy by computed tomographic angiography of the fetal heart: a feasibility study. Ultrasound Obstet Gynecol 39:679–684

Wright C (2004) Investigating perinatal death: a review of the options when autopsy consent is refused. Arch Dis Child Fetal Neonatal Ed 89:F285–F288

Miscellaneous: Mummification, Adipocere, and Artefacts

Holger Wittig and Eva Scheurer

Contents

Abstract

The investigation of bodies in various states of decomposition and preservation is a common task in forensic medicine. While dissection of a mummified body isn't impossible, it more or less leads to destruction of the sample. Since mummies are often of special scientific interest, destructive forms of investigation are preferably avoided. Computed tomography (CT) has become the number one choice for non-destructive examination. Through the medium of CT, we'll illustrate some examples of mummification as well as formation of adipocere. Note that in this chapter the term "artefact" refers to objects formed by humans, including physical pieces of evidence, e.g. body packing.

H. Wittig (✉) · E. Scheurer
Institut für Rechtsmedizin der Universität Basel, Gesundheits Departement Basel-Stadt, Basel, Switzerland
e-mail: holger.wittig@bs.ch; eva.scheurer@bs.ch

1 Mummification

The process of mummification can be defined as the preservation of human or animal soft tissues by either incidence or intention. Exposure of a corpse to very low humidity, cold or certain chemicals interrupts, as a rule, further decay by loss of water. Natural mummification processes are exsiccation, ice- and salt-mummies as well as bog bodies. Intentionally mummified bodies, well known having come from ancient Egyptian burial rituals, have also been found elsewhere around the world. Many of them are of special scientific interest.

Computed tomography (CT) has evolved into a valuable, non-invasive tool for mummy research since its first application in 1979 (Harwood-Nash 1979) and remains the method of choice for examining mummies. However, mummies are heterogenous objects, when it comes to their investigation. Villa and Lynnerup (2012) performed CT scans of several kinds of body preservation (bog bodies, mummies from hot and cold dry environments, archaeological bones, cremated bones, fossil animal bones and forensic

© Springer Nature Switzerland AG 2022
F. Dedouit et al. (eds.), *Forensic Imaging*, Medical Radiology Diagnostic Imaging,
https://doi.org/10.1007/978-3-030-83352-7_6

cases) and compared them with each other. One of the results of this study was an enormous range of Hounsfield units within, and between, different kinds of mummification.

There is a great variety in the preservation of soft tissues between different mummies. Roughly speaking every state of preservation is possible. On rare occasions internal organs and fine soft tissue structures are really well preserved, for instance the Llullaillaco mummies (Previgliano et al. 2003) or the mummy of Rosalia Lombardo (Panzer et al. 2013). But more often we'll find more or less decay of the soft tissues as a result of taphonomic processes.

Since CT scanning is based on X-rays, dense material like bone is generally easy to visualize. Therefore, skeletal structures may be visualized to assess them morphologically and measure them (Lynnerup 2007). Bog bodies are an exception of this rule because of the demineralization due to the acidic environment in peat bogs (Pestka et al. 2010). Structures with a high collagen content dry out but might still be intact. Desiccation yields a shrinkage of the soft tissue. Sydler et al. (2015) calculated for various kinds of mummification a shrinking rate from fresh to mummified soft tissue between 73 and 82% on average. Panzer et al. (2015) introduced a scoring system for the assessment of soft tissue preservation to facilitate quantitative comparison of mummies. Due to their checklist a standardized and systematic assessment and documentation of soft tissue preservation of human mummies, that underwent whole-body CT, becomes possible.

Lynnerup (2007) precised the soft tissue findings of natural mummies. Tissues with high collagen content and fibrous tissues such as muscle fascia and ligaments and tendons may be still intact. Furthermore, different forensic relevant structures of the throat, such as thyroid cartilage and vocal cords, might be preserved. In the body cavities of desiccated and intact mummies the internal organs are mostly shrunken. Additionally to the lungs in the thoracic cavity, the pleura can be defined. Lung diseases like infections or tuberculosis or tumors can be identified (Lynnerup 2007). In the abdominal cavity the liver is often identifiable and remnants of gut contents and coprolites might be found. The thin-walled gastrointestinal tract is often decayed completely. The inner genitalia are rarely recognizable. Regarding the head, the brain may shrink but undergo adipocerous change. This may result in an excellent morphological preservation of the brain as shown in Fig. 9. As for the eyes, the watercontaining parts like the aqueous humour will have dried out, but the bulbar structures themelves are often well preserved.

In opposition to the aforesaid artificial mummies often show an evisceration of internal organs. A special challenge is the presentation of those alterations due to the mummification process. Large defects in the anterior skull base, the middle portion of the cribriform plate, are common findings at the head (Gupta et al. 2008). Internal organs of the trunk were removed via an abdominal incision or tansperineal. The cranial cavity of excerebrated individuals often shows the presence of resin. Packing of the abdomen and pelvis with linen is largely aimed at restoring natural shape to an eviscerated body. Thoracic packing does not serve this purpose, but is not uncommon (Wade and Nelson 2013). Due to post-processing of the images, soft-tissue details, diagenetically modified tissues as well as structural details can be presented more clearly or if neccesary segmented image by image (Lynnerup 2007). Volume-rendering algorithms might help to show hair, including facial hair, as well as overlying linens, which also can be virtually removed. Using post-processing possibilities a mummy can be virtually unwrapped. This unwrapping without any destruction of the actual mummy, offers obvious advantages over standard anatomic dissection (Hoffman et al. 2002).

One way to increase the differentiation of mummified soft tissues is the opportunity to perform both CT scan and autopsy of mummified bodies. This is not a problem with regard to mummies investigated within routine forensic casework (see Fig. 4). But the investigation of ancient human remains should always take some ethical considerations into account, in particular the issue of appropriateness versus invasiveness (Kreissl Lonfat et al. 2015). The dissection of mummies has become rare since CT is the method of choice for examining mummies. Dedouit et al. (2010) compared CT examination and autopsy results of a frozen mummy with each other. Findings of the convetional autopsy correlated with findings of CT-imaging and vice versa. Additionally, each technique revelaed findings which were missed by the other one. The working group concluded, that whole-body CT imaging and appropriate post-processing techniques are indispensable tools in the multidisziplinary investigation of mummies (Dedouit 2010). Colleter et al. (2018) performed for the first time an angiography of a mummy. According to them, the autopsy in combination with unenhanced as well as enhanced CT-imaging allowed a complete description of evisceration process, and confirmed the absence of vascular pathologies like atherosclerosis or traumatic lesions due to the embalmment process. The combination of both techniques was mandatory to collect and archive this information (Colleter 2018).

Conventional single-source CT suffers from low soft tissue differentiation, especially in postmortem imaging of cases with lost moisture content, like desiccated mummies. Hence, there is an increased interest in novel imaging techniques such as dual-energy computed tomography (DECT). In general, DECT offers more specific tissue characterization than conventional single-source CT and could improve the assessment of diseases for palaeopathological investigations (Johnson et al. 2007; Wanek et al. 2011). A further increase in spatial resolution will offer the introduction of flat panel CT scanners (Gupta et al. 2008) as well as phase-contrast CT (Romell et al. 2018) to the investigation of mummified tissue.

Having been granted permission by the Museum of Cultures in Basel, Switzerland, the authors CT scanned an Inca child mummy (collection number IVc 2813) (Fig. 1) in collaboration with the Natural History Museum (Basel, Switzerland) and the Reiss-Engelhorn-Museen (Mannheim, Germany).

The investigation revealed the mummified remains of a child, aged between 7 and 8 years, with evidence of neurofibromatosis type 1 (Panzer et al. 2017). The most remarkable result, from a forensic point of view, was evidence of fatal peri-mortem violence—see below. Maximum intensity projection image of the chest (Fig. 2) showed the transection of the second to sixth rib on the right side, as well as a linear cut through the first, intercostal space. Inside the chest cavity, well preserved lungs and vessels could be made out. The aortic arch and their out-

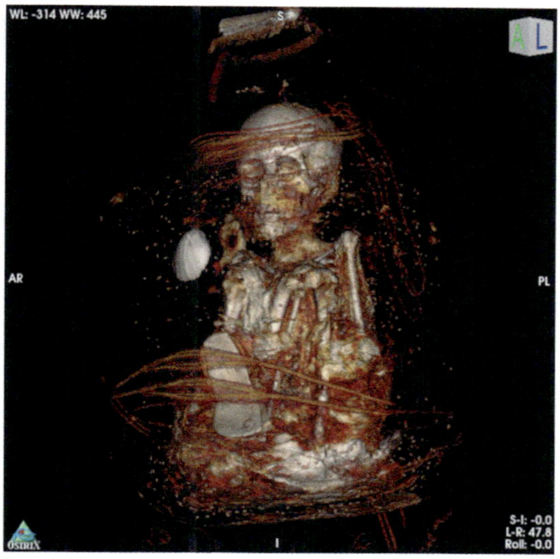

Fig. 1 Semitransparent 3D reconstruction of the CT scan of an Inca mummy bundle (Coll. No IVc 2813, Museum of Cultures Basel). Note the soles of a pair of sandals in front of the legs

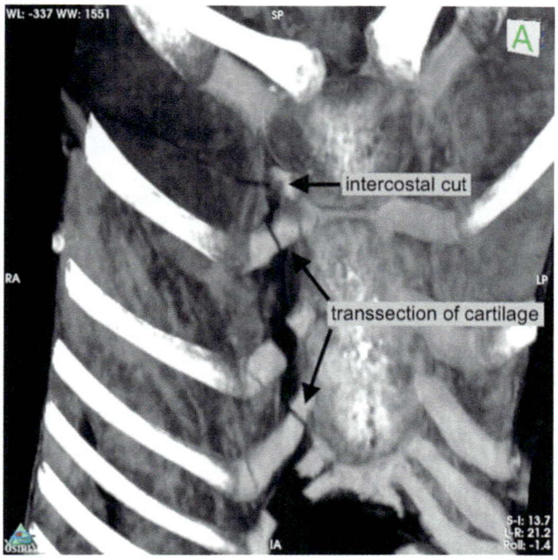

Fig. 2 Maximum intensity projection of the separated chest wall. Linear transections of the rib cartilages and the first intercostal space indicate impact via sharp force

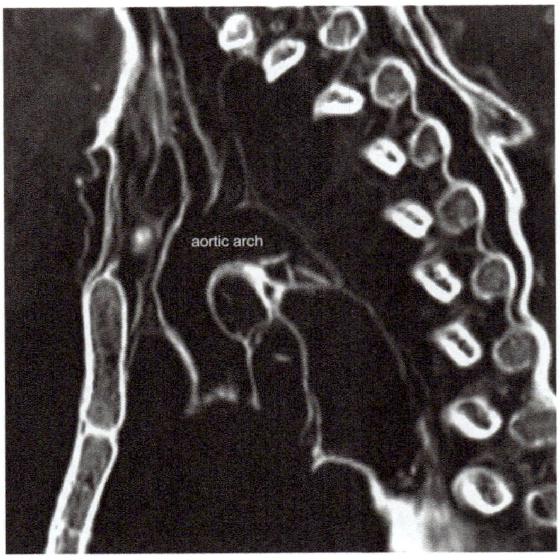

Fig. 3 Sagittal MPR view through the chest. The aortic arch with its first two outflows is clearly detectable—the void below the level of the aortic valve indicates an evisceration of the heart

Fig. 4 Mummified body of a man after approximately 1 year post-mortem interval

flows are clearly detectable (Fig. 3). However, there is a void below the level of the aortic valve, in the area where the heart is expected, indicating an evisceration of the heart. Due to a good preservation of the soft tissues, a large defect of the abdominal wall could be detected. The liver was displaced and a clear indication of the presence of faeces outside of the abdomen was found. The thoracic and abdominal incisions would seem to be the result of an act of violence, apparently by means of a sharp weapon. The exact circumstances of the injuries, especially of those to the chest and abdomen, were not clear. Hypotheses include war, battle, murder, and accident. However, human sacrifice should also be considered (Eeckhout and Owens 2008).

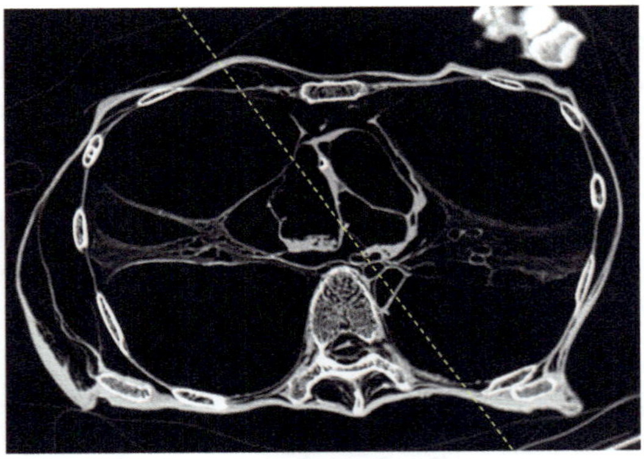

Fig. 5 CT scan of the chest shows well-preserved heart and lungs, even the heart chambers can be distinguished from each other. Note the calcification of a coronary artery. The dotted line marks the oblique image plane of Fig. 6

In addition to the archaeological mummies, human bodies in various states and stages of decay and mummification are also investigated within routine forensic casework. Figure 4 shows an image from a case involving the mummified body of 68-year-old man who had lived an isolated life without social contacts. He was found after having lain dead for 1 year on the floor of his kitchen. Over the last decade we have investigated several cases of mummified bodies, but this was by far the best preserved (Figs. 5 and 6). Cause and manner of death remain unclear; however, calcification of coronary arteries (Fig. 5) indicate possible heart failure.

2 Adipocere

The formation of adipocere (saponification or grave wax) is a result of anaerobic bacterial hydrolysis of fat in tissues to free fatty acids, with the unsaturated fatty acids (e.g. oleic acid) converted to saturated fatty acids, e.g. palmitic acid (Gill-King 1997; Takatori 2001). Its formation replaces the putrefactive stage when the body lies

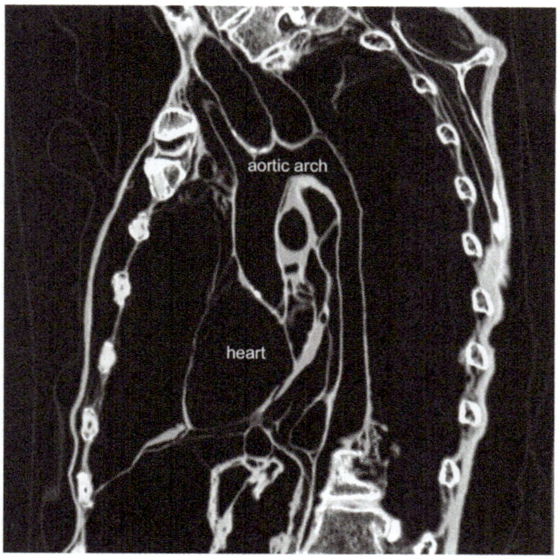

Fig. 6 Oblique image plane through the chest. In contrast to Fig. 3 (the Inca child mummy) clear heart structures can be seen below the level of the aortic valve

buried under wet and oxygen-free conditions or submerged in water (Kumar et al. 2009). Due to the chemical process of saponification, several elements in the environment, such as calcium from soil, may react with cleaved fatty acids to form salts of fatty acids.

While the computed tomography of adipocere bodies has not yet been systematically investigated, several case reports have been published on the subject (Bohnert et al. 1998; Jackowski et al. 2005). Bohnert described Hounsfield units in the range of mixed fatty tissue or less (see Table 1). However, a broad range of Hounsfield units have been reported in the literature.

The Institute of Forensic Medicine in Basel holds two objects with formation of adipocere in its collection: a head (Fig. 7, coll. No. P0012) and a liver (Fig. 8, coll. No. P0013).

The objects were investigated with CT under conditions listed below. The objects were scanned with a tube voltage of 130 kV and 80 kV, respectively. CT images were reconstructed using edge-enhancing kernels.

Inside the skull a shrunken brain could be seen (Fig. 9), with well-identifiable structures, cerebral lobes and cerebral sulci and gyri. Even the cortex of the brain and the white matter could be distinguished from each other. The preservation of the brain is a known phenomenon and has been previously depicted in the literature (Previgliano

Table 1 Hounsfield ranges of adipocere

Study	Tissue	HU ranges
(Bohnert et al. 1998) (three cases)	C1: Orbita C2: Orbita C1: Brain, grey matter C1: Brain, white matter C3: Brain, central	+68 to −100 HU −395 to −597 HU −32 to −81 HU Approx. −130 HU +6 to +15 HU
(Jackowski et al. 2005)		No comment on HU
(Levy et al. 2010)		"Low attenuation appearance on MDCT"
(Altinoz et al. 2014)	Brain	Average of 450 HU
This study	Brain Liver Skin	−80 to +80 HU −800 to −650 HU −650 to −350 HU

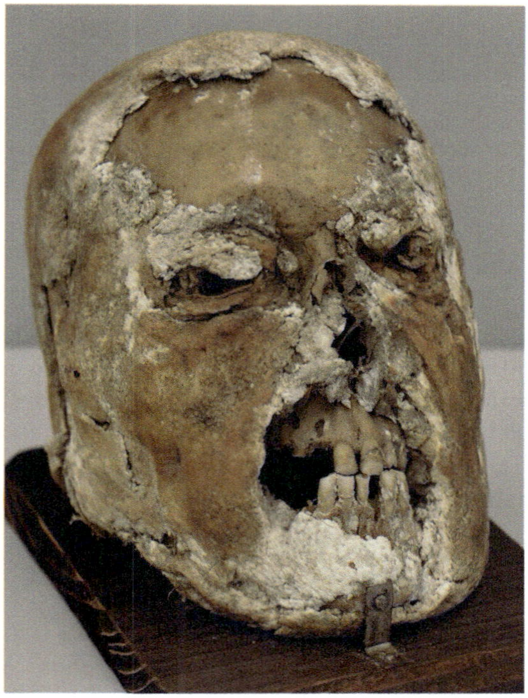

Fig. 7 Investigated adipocere object (P0012-skull) from the collection of the Institute of Forensic Medicine Basel

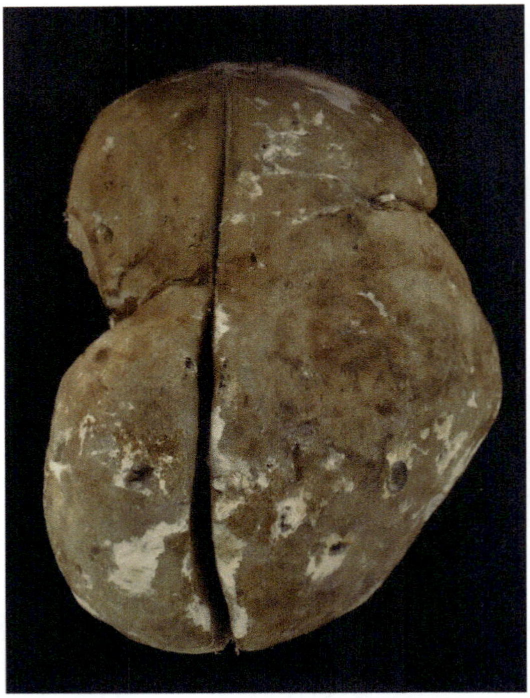

Fig. 8 Investigated adipocere object (P0013 liver) from the collection of the Institute of Forensic Medicine Basel

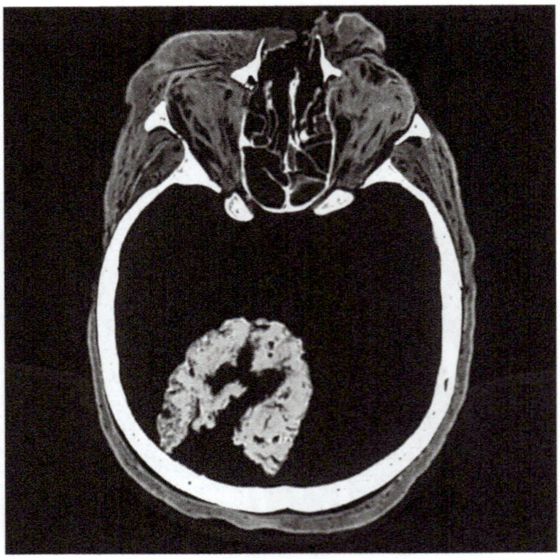

Fig. 9 Head with adipocere. CT 80 kV, WL/WW −500/1400, slab thickness 0.75 mm. The brain is shrunken, white and grey matter can be distinguished from each other

et al. 2003; Papageorgopoulou et al. 2010; Altinoz et al. 2014).

The liver (Figs. 8 and 10) showed a relative homogenous parenchyma with a range of −800 to −650 HU. An outer layer or bark of 3–4 mm exhibits a higher density. Inside the parenchyma, the different vessel systems—portal and hepatic veins—can be clearly distinguished from each other (Fig. 10).

3 Artefacts

In this section the term "artefact" refers to objects formed by humans, including physical pieces of evidence, e.g. body packing. A CT scan offers the possibility to find foreign bodies inside a human body as well as to investigate objects. Gostner (Gostner et al. 2013) investigated various materials in order to identify foreign objects inside mummies using their X-ray structure and Hounsfield units. While shape and size are easily detectable, the material often remains unclear.

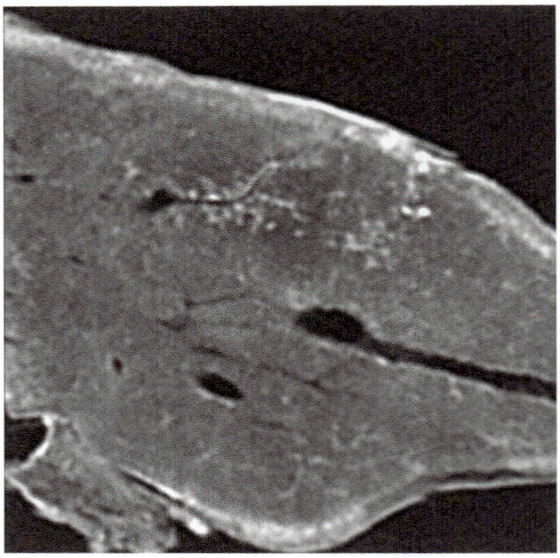

Fig. 10 Adipocere-liver. CT 130 kV, B80s, WL/WW −700/800, slab thickness 1.5 mm MIP. Note an outer bark with elevated density

Figure 11 shows a CT scan of a slab of insulating foam used in montages assembled by a mentally disordered man. He mounted life-sized pictures of women on boards of insulating foam,

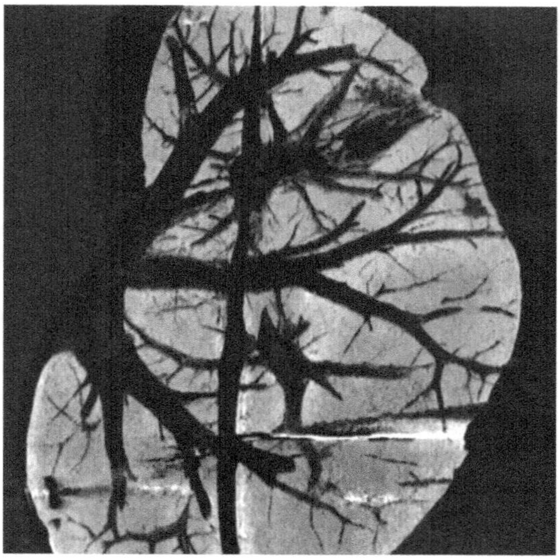

Fig. 11 MinIP, 20 mm, WL/WW −900/450, well preserved internal structures of the liver, portal venous system and hepatic veins

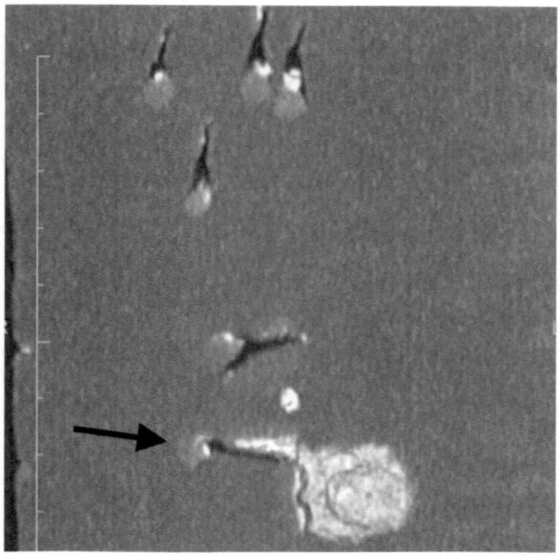

Fig. 12 4 mm MIP of insulating foam just below the surface, WL/WW −950/170. Grouped stab wounds and densification from blunt force. The arrow marks the damage shown on Fig. 13

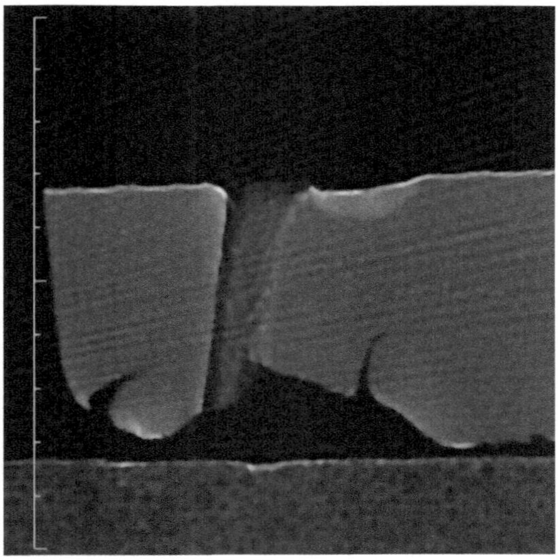

Fig. 13 1.5 mm slab showing the inner structure of the indicated stab wound. The shape of a knife profile edge can be made out. The object was placed on a Styrofoam board

after which he attacked the pictures with different tools and weapons. The man staged several crime scenes, such as murder and rape cases, in forests as well as in residential areas. The Institute of Forensic Medicine in Basel was asked to support a profiler in determining the weapons used (Fig. 12).

Insulating foam is a material of very high radiolucency. We quantified the Hounsfield units of this material to be as low as −963 ± 15 HU, nearly invisible in routine CT scans. Best results were obtained using a low voltage (80 kV) and a high convolution kernel, such as H80s. The elasticity of the material is low and the exposure to different kinds of force resulted in well-defined damage within the material. Clear examples could be seen of different kinds of stab wounds as well as densification zones resulting from blunt force.

One of the most forensically relevant foreign objects inside human bodies, besides projectiles, are drug containers such as those used in cases of body packing. Recent studies have attempted to distinguish between different kinds of drugs or different concentrations of drugs (Leschka et al. 2013; Grimm et al. 2014). While results indicated that this may be possible, the procedure has not as yet been introduced into clinical routine.

Drug containers typically appear as ovoid shape of the size displayed in Fig. 14.

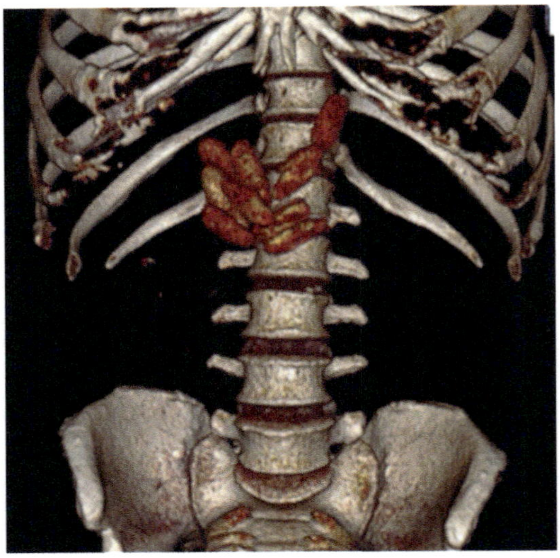

Fig. 14 Typical ovoid drug containers inside the stomach of a suspect. 3D reconstruction of a clinical low dose CT

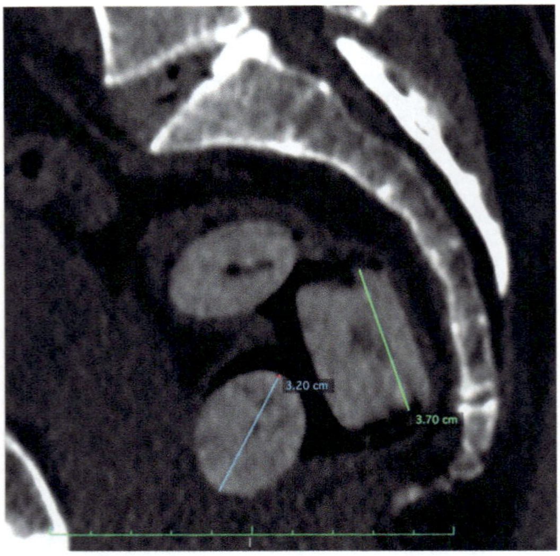

Fig. 15 Foreign bodies inside the rectum of a suspect. Instead of drugs the containers held folded and furled banknotes

Appearances can, however, be deceiving. Figure 15 depicts some foreign bodies inside the rectum of a male suspect. While the size and shape are typical of drug containers, there are some minor differences. The edges were not rounded but flat and tubular air cavities could be identified inside the containers. Upon police investigation, these objects proved to be folded and furled banknotes.

References

Altinoz MA, Ince B, Sav A, Dincer A, Cengiz S, Mercan S, Yazici Z, Bilgen MN (2014) Human brains found in a fire-affected 4000-years old bronze age tumulus layer rich in soil alkalines and boron in Kutahya, Western Anatolia. Homo 65(1):33–50. https://doi.org/10.1016/j.jchb.2013.08.005

Bohnert M, Schmialek A, Faller-Marquardt M, Buitrago-Tellez C, Pollak S (1998) Umwandlung des Gehirns und der Gesichtsweichteile in Leichenlipid–morphologische und radiologische Befunde. Rechtsmedizin 8(4):135–140

Colleter R, Dedouit F, Duchesne S, Gerard P, Dercle L, Poilpre P, Gendrot V, Rousseau H, Crubezy E, Telmon N, Mokrane FZ (2018) Study of a seventeenth-century French artificial mummy: autopsical, native, and contrast-injected CT investigations. Int J Legal Med 132(5):1405–1413. https://doi.org/10.1007/s00414-018-1830-8

Dedouit F, Geraut A, Baranov V, Ludes B, Rouge D, Telmon N, Crubezy E (2010) Virtual and macroscopical studies of mummies--differences or complementarity? Report of a natural frozen Siberian mummy. Forensic Sci Int 200 (1–3):e7–13. https://doi.org/10.1016/j.forsciint.2010.03.028

Eeckhout P, Owens LS (2008) Human sacrifice at Pachacamac. Lat Am Antiq:375–398

Gill-King H (1997) Chemical and ultrastructural aspects of decomposition. In: Sorg MH, Haglund WD (eds) Forensic taphonomy: the postmortem fate of human remains. CRC Press, Boca Raton, pp 93–108

Gostner P, Bonelli M, Pernter P, Graefen A, Zink A (2013) New radiological approach for analysis and identification of foreign objects in ancient and historic mummies. J Archaeol Sci 40(2):1003–1011

Grimm J, Wudy R, Ziegeler E, Wirth S, Uhl M, Reiser MF, Scherr M (2014) Differentiation of heroin and cocaine using dual-energy CT—an experimental study. Int J Legal Med 128(3):475–482

Gupta R, Markowitz Y, Berman L, Chapman P (2008) High-resolution imaging of an ancient Egyptian mummified head: new insights into the mummification process. Am J Neuroradiol 29(4):705–713. https://doi.org/10.3174/ajnr.A0909

Harwood-Nash DC (1979) Computed tomography of ancient Egyptian mummies. J Comput Assist Tomogr 3(6):768–773.

Hoffman H, Torres WE, Ernst RD (2002) Paleoradiology: advanced CT in the evaluation of nine Egyptian mummies. Radiographics 22(2):377–385. https://doi.org/10.1148/radiographics.22.2.g02mr13377

Jackowski C, Thali M, Sonnenschein M, Aghayev E, Yen K, Dirnhofer R (2005) Adipocere in postmortem imaging using multislice computed tomography (MSCT) and magnetic resonance imaging (MRI). Am J Forensic Med Pathol 26(4):360–364. https://doi.org/10.1097/01.paf.0000188091.11225.38

Johnson TRC, Krauß B, Sedlmair M, Grasruck M, Bruder H, Morhard D, Fink C, Weckbach S, Lenhard M, Schmidt B, Flohr T, Reiser MF, Becker CR (2007) Material differentiation by dual energy CT: initial experience. Eur Radiol 17(6):1510–1517. https://doi.org/10.1007/s00330-006-0517-6

Kreissl Lonfat BM, Kaufmann IM, Rühli F (2015) A code of ethics for evidence-based research with ancient human remains. Anat Rec 298(6):1175–1181. https://doi.org/10.1002/ar.23126

Kumar TM, Monteiro FN, Bhagavath P, Bakkannavar SM (2009) Early adipocere formation: a case report and review of literature. J Forensic Legal Med 16(8):475–477

Leschka S, Fornaro J, Laberke P, Blum S, Hatem A, Niederer I, Meile C, Hibbeln D, Hausmann R, Wildermuth S (2013) Differentiation of cocaine from heroine body packs by computed tomography: impact of different tube voltages and the dual-energy index. J Forensic Radiol Imaging 1(2):46–50

Levy AD, Harcke HT, Mallak CT (2010) Postmortem imaging: MDCT features of postmortem change and decomposition. Am J Forensic Med Pathol 31(1):12–17. https://doi.org/10.1097/PAF.0b013e3181c65e1a

Lynnerup N (2007) Mummies. Am J Phys Anthropol Suppl 45:162–190. https://doi.org/10.1002/ajpa.20728

Panzer S, Gill-Frerking H, Rosendahl W, Zink AR, Piombino-Mascali D (2013) Multidetector CT investigation of the mummy of Rosalia Lombardo (1918–1920). Ann Anat 195(5):401–408. https://doi.org/10.1016/j.aanat.2013.03.009

Panzer S, Mc Coy MR, Hitzl W, Piombino-Mascali D, Jankauskas R, Zink AR, Augat P (2015) Checklist and scoring system for the assessment of soft tissue preservation in CT examinations of human mummies. PLoS One 10(8):e0133364. https://doi.org/10.1371/journal.pone.0133364

Panzer S, Wittig H, Zesch S, Rosendahl W, Blache S, Muller-Gerbl M, Hotz G (2017) Evidence of neurofibromatosis type 1 in a multi-morbid Inca child mummy: a paleoradiological investigation using computed tomography. PLoS One 12(4):e0175000. https://doi.org/10.1371/journal.pone.0175000

Papageorgopoulou C, Rentsch K, Raghavan M, Hofmann MI, Colacicco G, Gallien V, Bianucci R, Ruhli F (2010) Preservation of cell structures in a medieval infant brain: a paleohistological, paleogenetic, radiological and physico-chemical study. NeuroImage 50(3):893–901. https://doi.org/10.1016/j.neuroimage.2010.01.029

Pestka JM, Barvencik F, Beil FT, Marshall RP, Jopp E, Schilling AF, Bauerochse A, Fansa M, Püschel K, Amling M (2010) Skeletal analysis and comparison of bog bodies from northern European peat bogs. Naturwissenschaften 97(4):393–402. https://doi.org/10.1007/s00114-010-0653-3

Previgliano CH, Ceruti C, Reinhard J, Araoz FA, Diez JG (2003) Radiologic evaluation of the Llullaillaco mummies. AJR Am J Roentgenol 181(6):1473–1479. https://doi.org/10.2214/ajr.181.6.1811473

Romell J, Vagberg W, Romell M, Haggman S, Ikram S, Hertz HM (2018) Soft-tissue imaging in a human mummy: propagation-based phase-contrast CT. Radiology 289(3):670–676. https://doi.org/10.1148/radiol.2018180945

Sydler C, Ohrstrom L, Rosendahl W, Woitek U, Ruhli F (2015) CT-based assessment of relative soft-tissue alteration in different types of ancient mummies. Anat Rec (Hoboken) 298(6):1162–1174. https://doi.org/10.1002/ar.23144

Takatori T (2001) The mechanism of human adipocere formation. Leg Med (Tokyo) 3(4):193–204. https://doi.org/10.1016/s1344-6223(01)00036-0

Villa C, Lynnerup N (2012) Hounsfield Units ranges in CT-scans of bog bodies and mummies. Anthropol Anz 69(2):127–145. https://doi.org/10.1127/0003-5548/2012/0139

Wade AD, Nelson AJ (2013) Evisceration and excerebration in the Egyptian mummification tradition. J Archaeol Sci 40(12):4198–4206. https://doi.org/10.1016/j.jas.2013.06.017

Wanek J, Szekely G, Ruhli F (2011) X-ray absorption-based imaging and its limitations in the differentiation of ancient mummified tissue. Skelet Radiol 40(5): 595–601. https://doi.org/10.1007/s00256-010-1035-9

Part II

Examples for Typical Traumatic Forensic Cases

Blunt Force, Gunshot, and Sharp Force Injuries

Krzysztof Jerzy Woźniak, Artur Moskała,
Piotr Kluza, and Ewa Rzepecka-Woźniak

Contents

1 Introduction

In recent years PMCT proved to be a valuable tool in post-mortem forensic diagnostics from the very start of the usage of this procedure of post-mortem examination (Scholing et al. 2009; Thali et al. 2009, 2011; Grabherr et al. 2017). PMCT as a relatively inexpensive and easy-to-access method is recommended for widening post-mortem forensic examination in every investigated case; such way of examination gives the opportunity of very spectacular results especially in cases referring to violent deaths due to a variety of mechanical injuries (Fig. 1).

It helps to locate areas of injured tissues, collections of gas (air) and fluid (blood), as well as a location of foreign, mostly metallic, objects. It makes post-mortem examination more comprehensive and detailed, enables to plan the course of conventional autopsy examination being more efficient. In addition, it gives the possibility to document findings and to present them in a way that will be more easily comprehended by people without (forensic) medical knowledge. PMCT nowadays becomes an irreplaceable tool in everyday forensic practice. It is important to remember, though, that this is not a method of examination universally sufficient at different

K. J. Woźniak (✉) · A. Moskała · P. Kluza
E. Rzepecka-Woźniak
Jagiellonian University Medical College, Faculty of Medicine, Department of Forensic Medicine, Kraków, Poland
e-mail: krzys.wozniak@uj.edu.pl

© Springer Nature Switzerland AG 2022

F. Dedouit et al. (eds.), *Forensic Imaging*, Medical Radiology Diagnostic Imaging,
https://doi.org/10.1007/978-3-030-83352-7_7

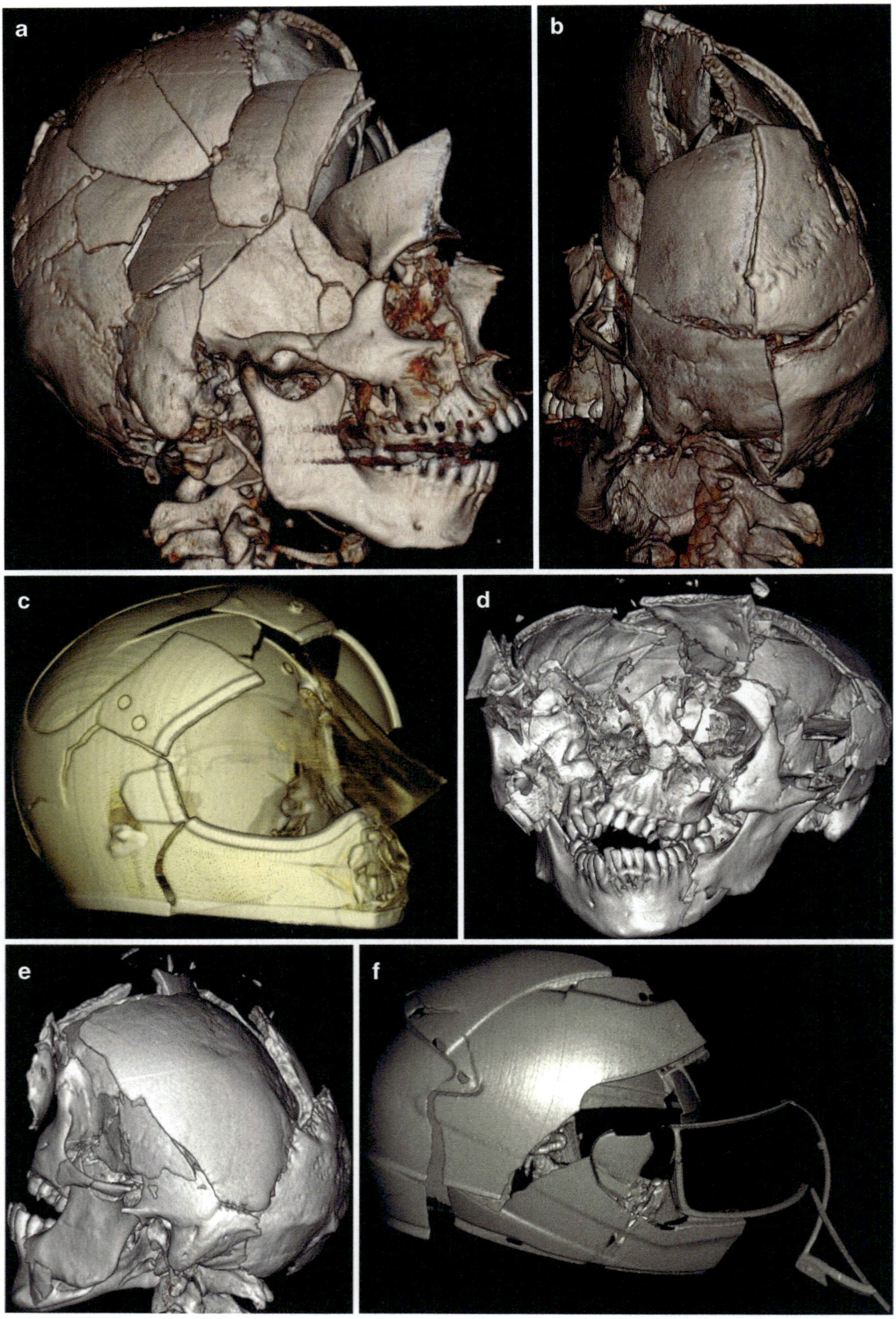

Fig. 1 Volume rendering technique (VRT) reconstructions based on unenhanced PMCT in two cases of motorcyclists—compression of the skull with excerebration: case 1, the skull—seen in the right lateral (**a**) and left posterior (**b**) view, corresponding helmet (**c**); case 2, the skull—seen in the anterior (**d**) and left posterior (**e**) view, corresponding helmet (**f**)

aspects of changes due to trauma. Diagnostic capabilities of unenhanced PMCT regarding external changes, soft tissues, and parenchyma of internal organs might be limited, especially in cases with alteration due to post-mortem putrefaction processes (Egger et al. 2012).

2 External Changes

Excoriations and/ or petechial hemorrhages, as obviously expected, are impossible to be positively shown as the result of PMCT. Quite similarly, due to no/ slight differences in HU units, especially small blood suffusions of soft tissues may be in a considerable number hard to be shown without application of additional techniques. Larger areas of bruising and/or gas spaces at the location of an external injury may make it better to be discerned. Wounds in the variety of possible kinds (ruptures/lacerations, cuts, stabbings, firearm injuries) may be found—localized and visualized; however, due to resolution of PMCT examination, we cannot expect evidence of more detailed features, but for example 3D reconstruction, has shown to be useful especially in combination with other techniques of post-mortem imaging (e.g., 3D laser scanning) (Fig. 2).

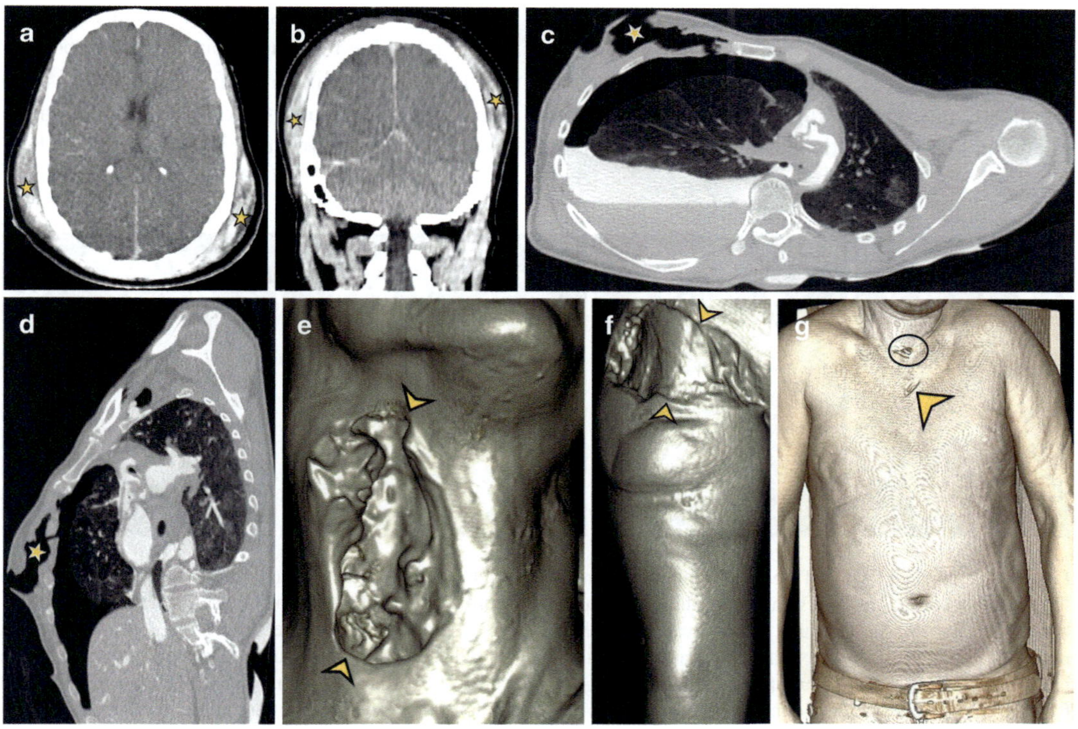

Fig. 2 External changes: unenhanced PMCT scans—axial (**a**) and coronal (**b**) reconstructions of the head showing bilateral bruisings and swelling (stars) of soft tissues areas neighboring the site of a fracture (invisible in these images); MPMCTA—axial oblique (**c**) and sagittal oblique (**d**) reconstructions of the thorax—anterior right stab wound (star) leading to the right pleural cavity—note the presence of gas (air), blood (posteriorly), and oily liquid contrast medium (CA); (**e**) VRT reconstruction of the surface of the neck, anterior view—overlapping incisive/stab wounds (arrowheads); (**f**) VRT reconstruction, anterolateral view of the surface of the right hip and thigh—a lacerated wound (arrowheads) of a teenage pedestrian hit by a car; (**g**) VRT reconstruction of the surface of the trunk, anterior view: a stab wound (yellow arrowhead) located in the middle of the thorax, note the presence of a button (encircled) above the wound and the belt: the corpse was examined in a plastic bag without removal of clothing

In everyday practice, PMCT examination of the corpse may be performed even without opening the transportation plastic bag. However, this may cause problems with successful diagnosis of external findings due to the presence of elements of clothing (especially when wet) or fluids (blood). Additionally, changes located at the back (and sides) of the body may be invisible for evaluation due to pressured tissues against the scan table. It may be necessary to remove clothing as well as to reposition the corpse during examination. This has to be done interdisciplinary with the forensic pathologist. Regarding multiphase PMCT angiography, it is recommended to perform imaging after the external examination of the body.

3 Internal Changes

Results of PMCT acquisition of a victim of violent death may be used for preliminary evaluation of changes due to a critical event, especially when aimed at regions accessible with considerable difficulties during conventional autopsy examination (i.e., splanchnocranium, cranio-cervical junction, cervical spine, the whole spine—especially processes, including transverse processes of the lumbar spine, the pelvis, scapulas, bones of extremities—especially epiphyses). It is much easier to diagnose injuries previously detected at CT scanning as well as find lodged foreign bodies using 3D reconstructions than during a blind search of conventional internal examination.

Even soft tissue and internal organs injuries may be visible, especially when there is a combination of ruptured organs with a presence of gas/fluid. Internal organ injuries may be better visible especially at locations with local HU differences (i.e., the brain, lungs) (Christe et al. 2009; Juźwik et al. 2019).

PMCT evaluation is not only used for locating changes due to trauma, but it is an important tool for the visualization of the pattern of injuries leading to the assessment of the mechanism having caused the trauma. By the shape of bro-

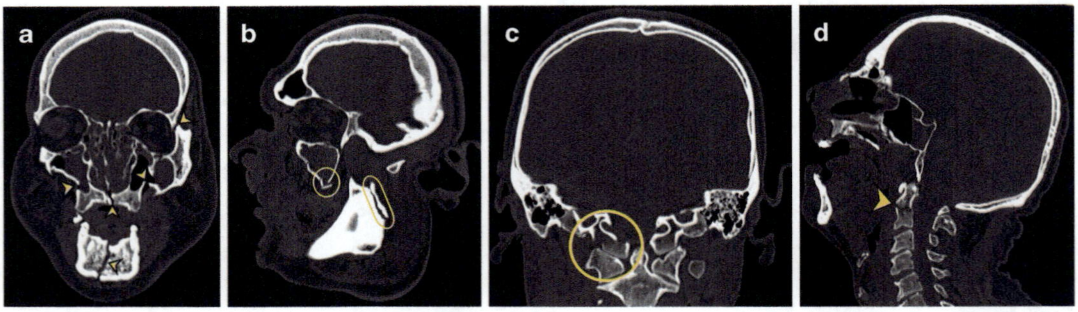

Fig. 3 Unenhanced PMCT. Thick MIP reconstructions of the skull in a coronal (**a**) and sagittal (**b**) plane—fractured bones of the viscerocranium (arrowheads/encircled), including the wall of the maxillary sinus and the mandible; (**c**) coronal reconstruction of the skull—showing the fracture of the right occipital condyle (encircled); sagittal reconstructions of the skull and cervical spine—(**d**) fracture of the axis (arrowhead) and (**e**) displacement (arrowhead) between the cervical vertebrae C2 and C3; (**f**) VRT reconstruction of the skull and the cervical spine, left lateral view—break in the continuity of the upper cervical spine (encircled); (**g**) thick MIP reconstruction in a sagittal plane of the spine—break in the continuity (encircled) of the upper thoracic part; (**h**) thick MIP reconstruction in a coronal plane of the lumbar spine—fracture of the transverse processes L5 on the right and L1–L4 on the left (arrowheads); (**i**) thick MIP reconstruction of the broken scapula (arrowheads); (**j**) thick MIP reconstruction in an axial plane of the lower part of the fractured pelvis (arrowheads); (**k**) thick MIP reconstruction of the distal part of the right femur: fracture of the medial condyle (encircled); (**l**) thick MIP reconstruction in a coronal plane of bones at the knee region: bilateral tibial fractures (yellow arrowheads); (**m**) thick MIP reconstruction of the foot—fractured calcaneus (arrowheads) in a case of a fall from height

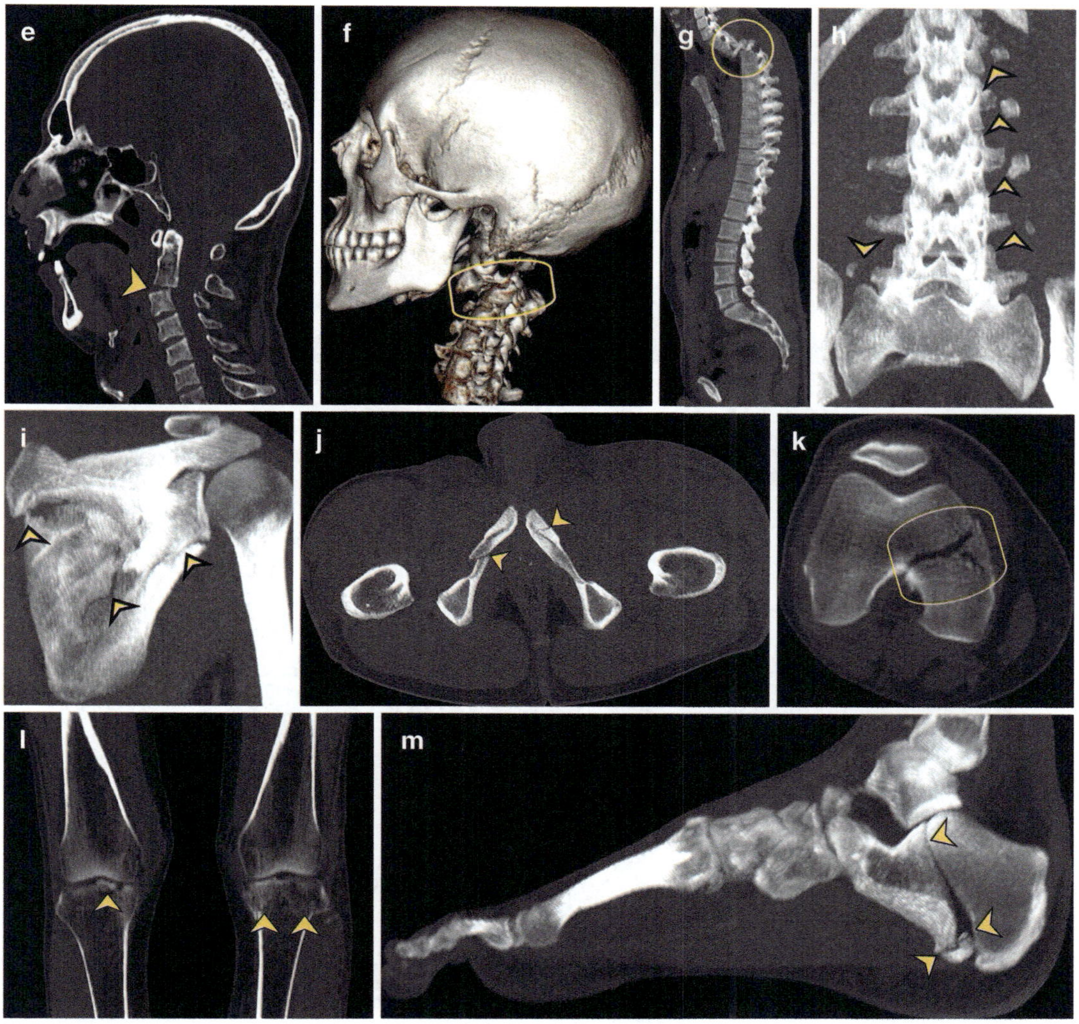

Fig. 3 (continued)

ken bones (especially when we evaluate multi-local changes) some may narrow different hypotheses regarding the course of the critical event (Moskała et al. 2016; Moskała et al. 2017; Blau et al. 2017) (Figs. 3, 4, and 5).

4 Blunt Force Trauma

It is often easy to detect compartments filled with gas or fluid that occurred as a result of blunt trauma (e.g., intracranial bleeding, gas

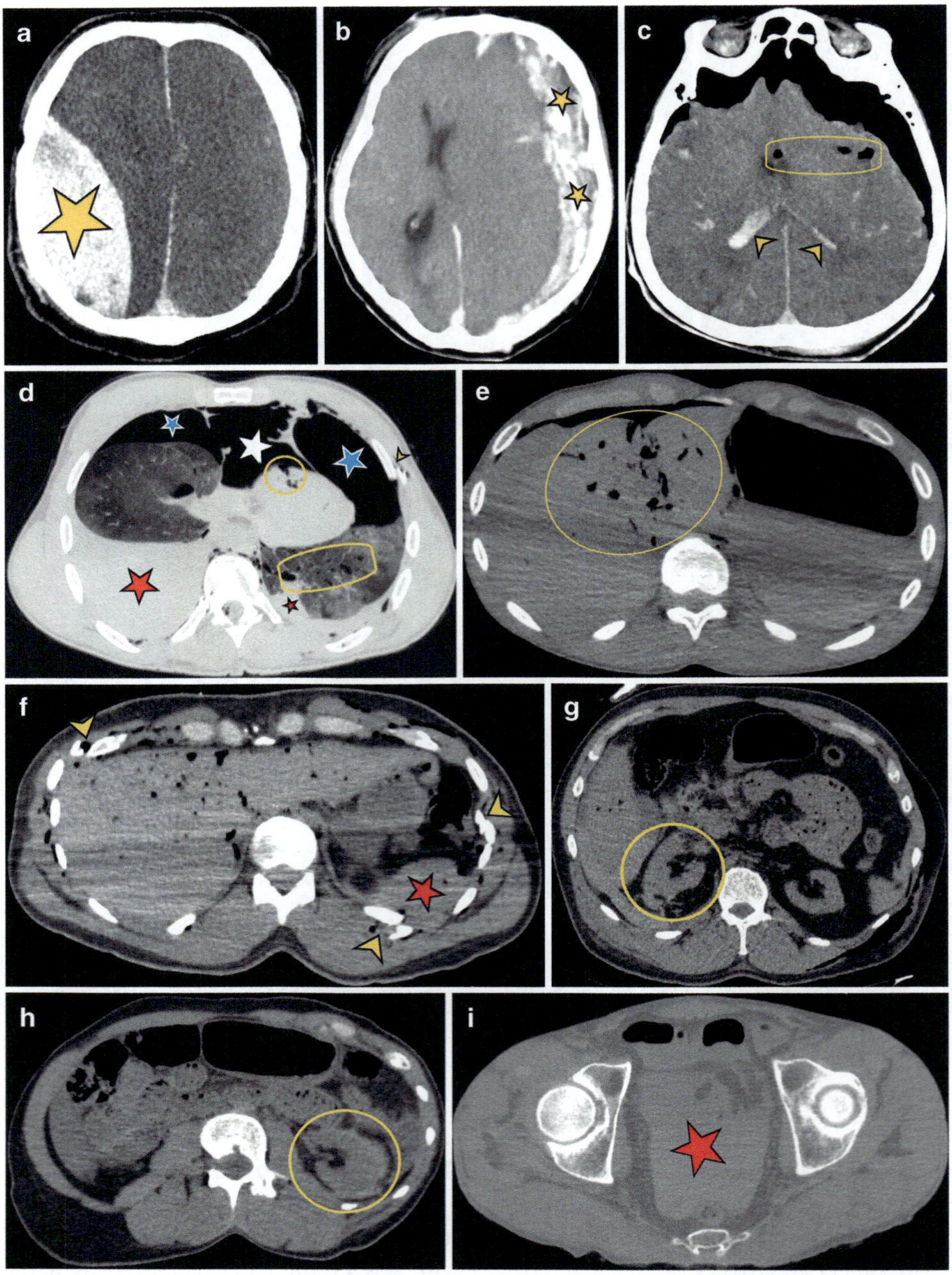

Fig. 4 Axial unenhanced PMCT images of the head: (**a**) right epidural hematoma (star), cerebral edema, (**b**) left-sided subdural hematoma (stars), cerebral edema, (**c**) subarachnoid and intraventricular (arrowheads) blood, intracranial gas ("collapsed brain") and intracerebral gas (encircled) may suggest brain laceration; axial images of the trunk: (**d**) thorax at the level of the heart and lungs: ruptured pericardial sac (white star) and the heart (encircled), contused and lacerated (encircled) left lung, gas (blue stars) and blood (red stars), fractured left rib (arrowhead); (**e**) thorax at the level of the liver—focal accumulation of gas (encircled) suggests the rupture of the liver; (**f**) thorax at the level of the liver and spleen (red star)—both organs fragmented, fractured ribs (arrowheads); axial images of the trunk at the level of the kidneys: blood suffusions of the right kidney (**g**) and at the vicinity of the left kidney (**h**)—both encircled; (**i**) lower part of the pelvis: blood (red star) inside the peritoneal cavity; (**j**) coronal image of the upper part of the trunk: due to compression of the thorax with ruptures of both sides of the diaphragm, abdominal organs are displaced (arrowheads); (**k**) MIP reconstruction of the skull, a lateral view showing a lodged projectile (encircled) and small debris (encircled)

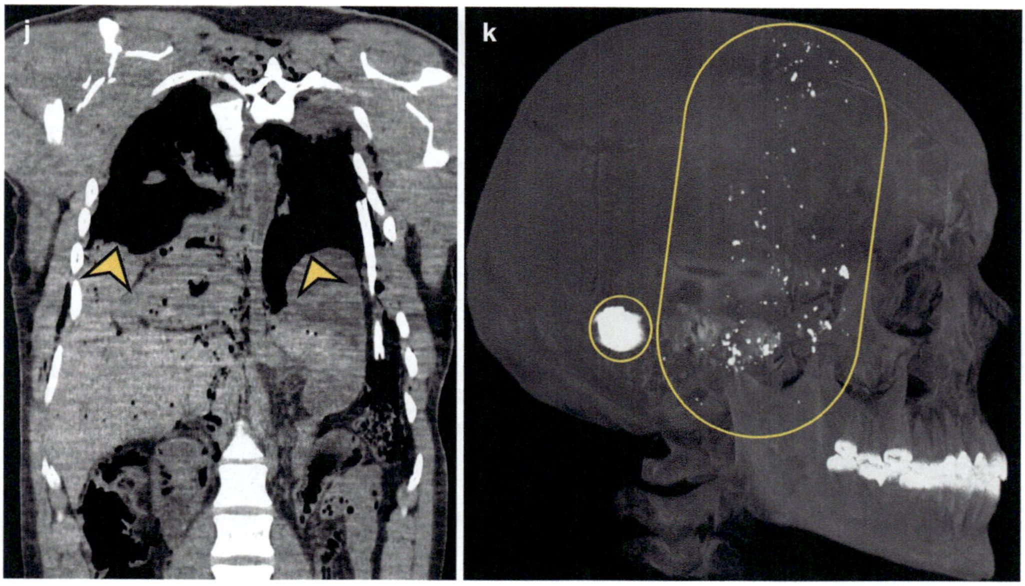

Fig. 4 (continued)

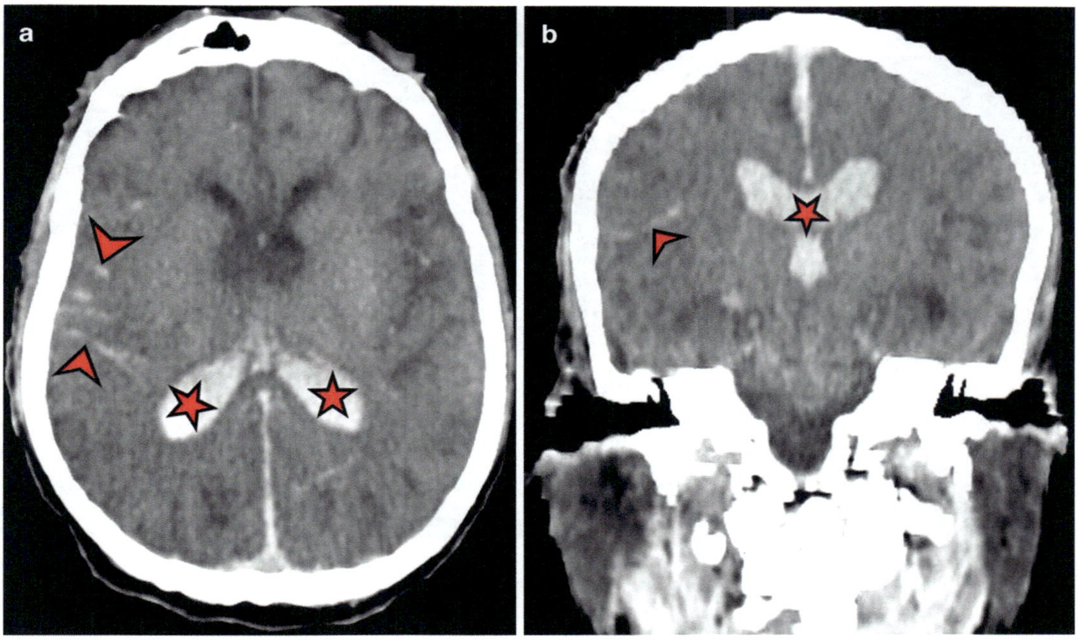

Fig. 5 Unenhanced PMCT. Axial (**a**) and coronal (**b**) reconstructions of the head showing ventricular (stars) and subarachnoid (arrowheads) blood; (**c**) axial image of the thorax—gas (star) inside the right side of the heart in a case of severe blunt injury of the head; axial reconstructions of the trunk: (**d**) upper part of the thorax—gas (blue stars) and blood (red stars) in both pleural cavities, subcutaneous emphysema (green stars), (**e**) thorax at the level of the heart and lungs—gas (blue stars) and blood (red stars) in both pleural cavities, subcutaneous emphysema (green stars), a broken rib (encircled), (**f**) trunk at the level of the lumbar spine—intensified subcutaneous emphysema (green stars), bilateral gas and blood in the pleural cavities; axial (**g**) and coronal (**h**) images of the trunk—tension pneumothorax (diamonds)

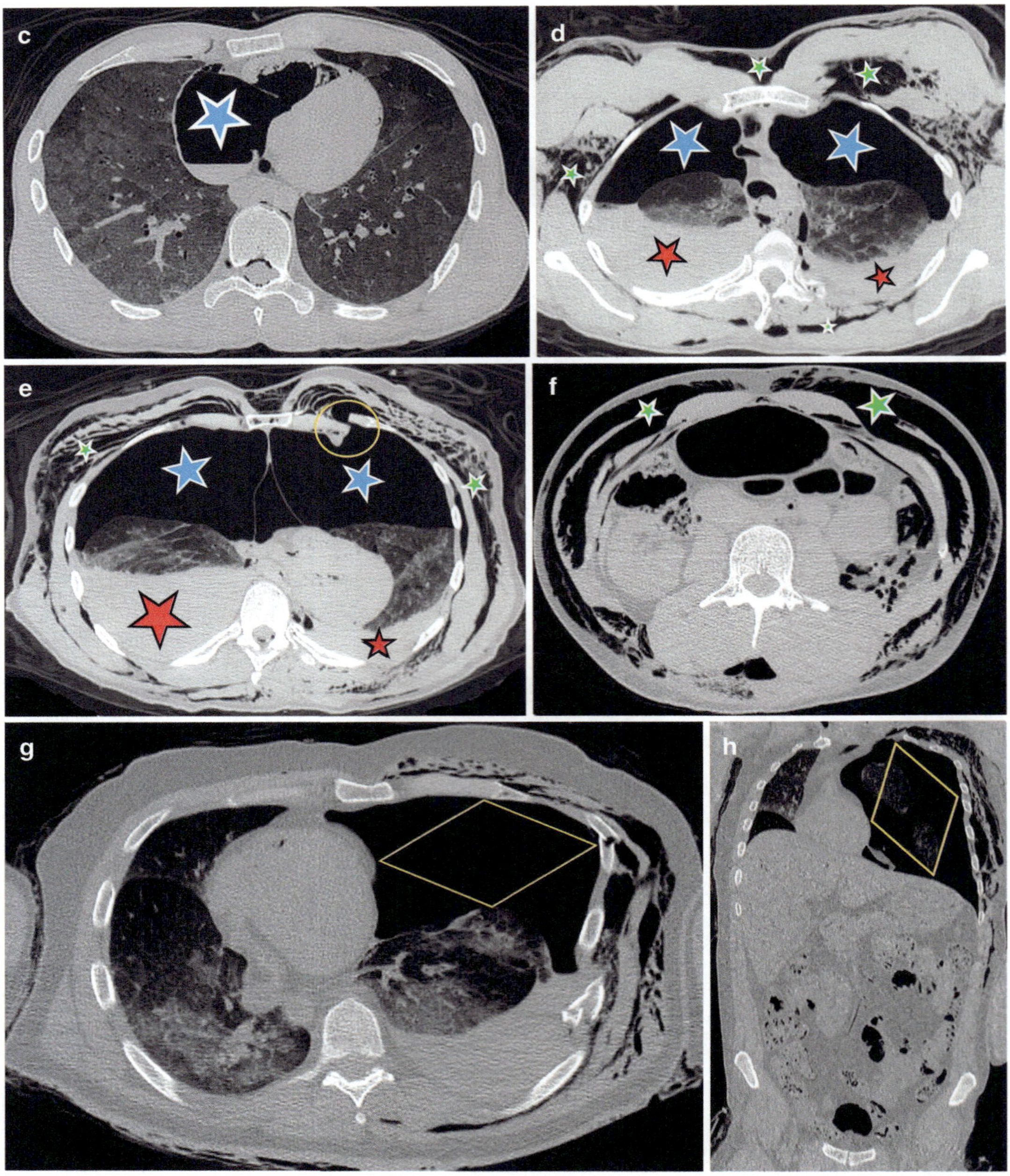

Fig. 5 (continued)

inside the skull, pneumothorax, air embolism) (Lopatin et al. 2019). In many cases the pattern of changes due to a severe traumatic episode are numerous, giving a quite obvious image of injuries leading to death. However, we have to be aware of the fact that even very obvious injuries, easy to find during forensic conventional internal examination, may be problematic to be interpreted unambiguously at the PMCT evaluation. Especially (non-displaced) broken ribs (Schulze et al. 2013) and the broken spine may pose difficulties—even a break of continuity of the spine may be obscured by the position of the body during PMCT acquisition, additionally "fixed" by rigor mortis. Vice versa: due to "wedged" broken elements we may encounter diagnostic problems during conventional autopsy examination even in cases of very well visible fractures of the spine in PMCT imaging (Figs. 6, 7, 8, 9, 10, 11, and 12).

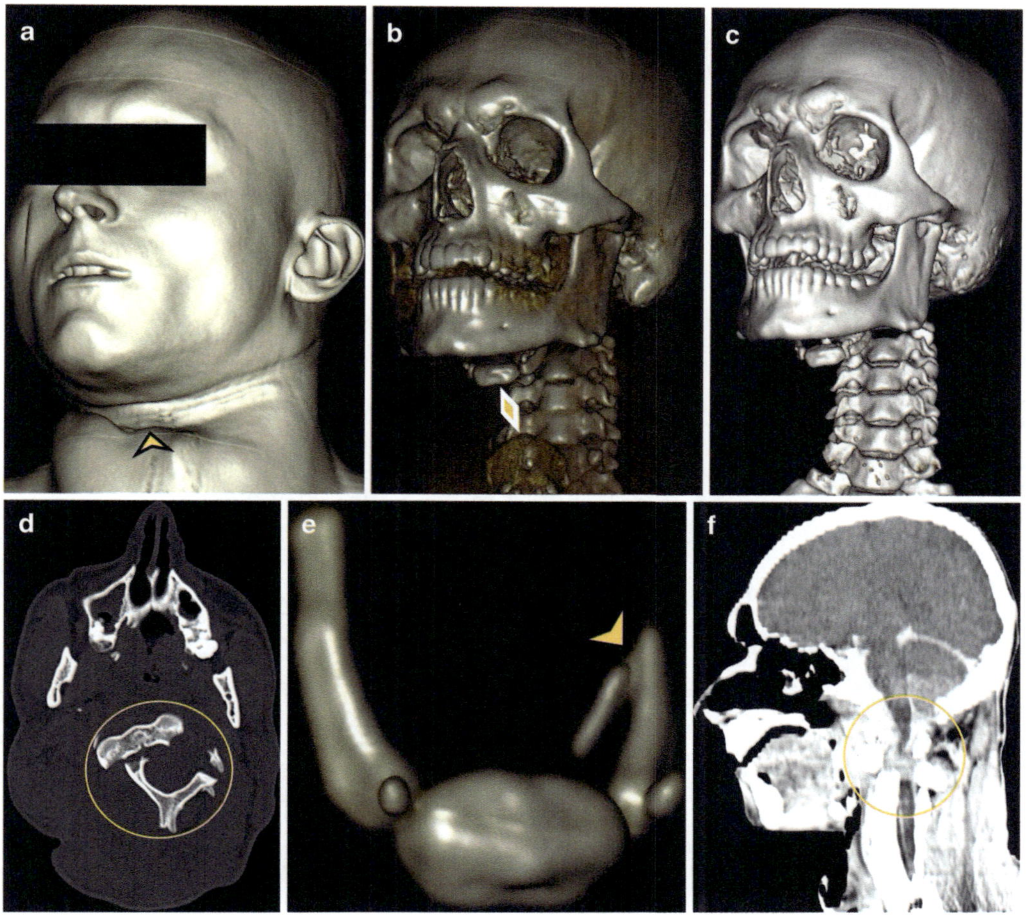

Fig. 6 A case of hanging combined with a jump from height, unenhanced PMCT. VRT reconstructions of: (**a**) the surface of the head and neck—note the presence of the ligature mark (arrowhead), (**b**) bones and cartilages of the head and neck—note a considerable long distance between the hyoid bone and the thyroid cartilage (diamond), (**c**) the position of the cervical spine in relation to the head shows its displacement; (**d**) thick MIP reconstruction in an axial oblique plane of the head and neck: fractured axis (encircled)—"Hangman's fracture"; (**e**) VRT reconstruction of the hyoid bone, anterior superior view—fracture of the left greater horn (arrowhead); (**f**) sagittal reconstruction of the head and neck—note the complete break in continuity (encircled) of the upper part of the spine and the spinal cord

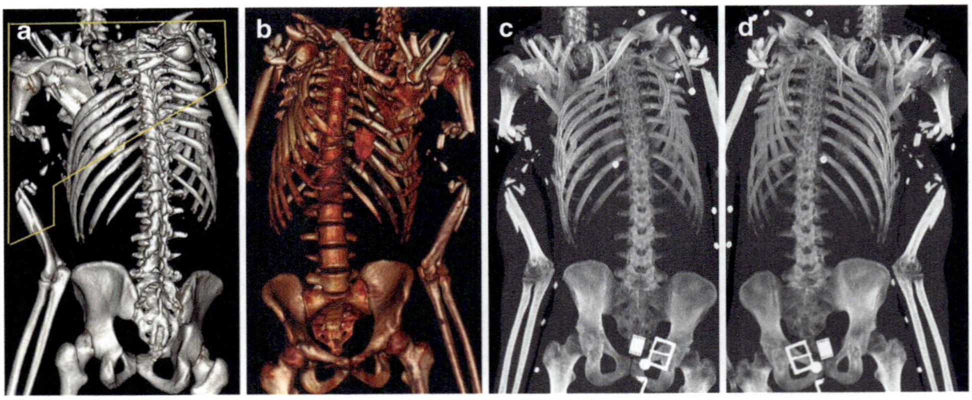

Fig. 7 A victim of run over by the train: complete break in continuity of bones of the upper part of the chest and arms (polygon selection). VRT reconstruction of the bones of the trunk and (partially included in the field of view during acquisition) upper limbs: posterior (**a**) and anterior (**b**) view; MIP reconstruction: posterior (**c**) and anterior (**d**) view—note numerous buttons and elements of the belt, proving that the corpse was examined without removal of clothing. Unenhanced PMCT

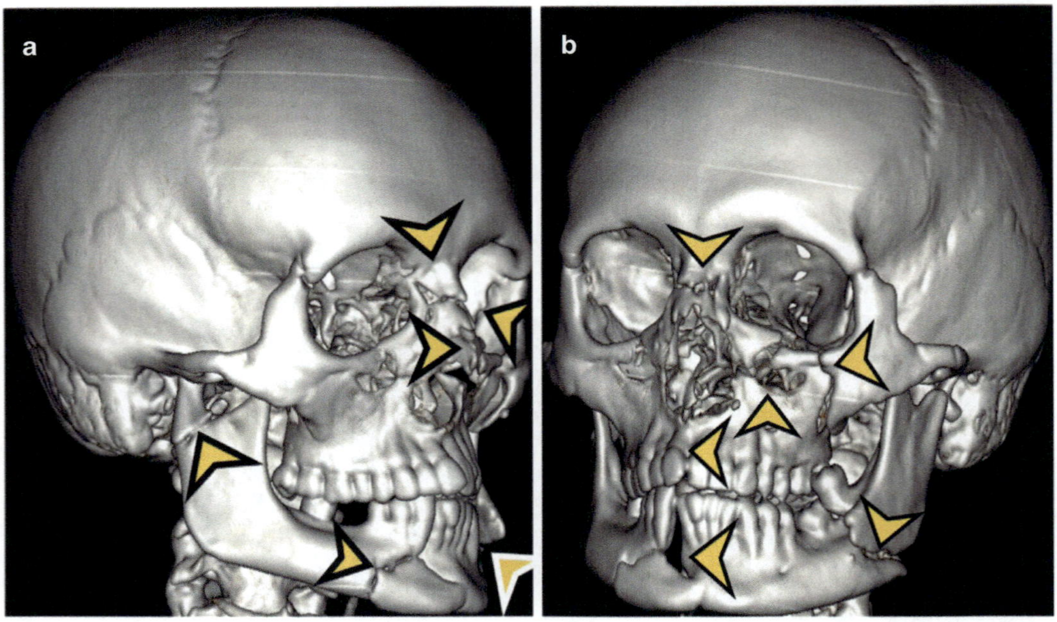

Fig. 8 A victim of a fall from height, unenhanced PMCT. VRT reconstructions of the skull—right anterior (**a**) and left anterior (**b**) view—note multiple fractures of the viscerocranium (arrowheads); bones of the trunk after digital removal of scapulas—anterior (**c**) and posterior (**d**) view—note the break in the continuity of the sternum (encircled), fractured ribs (mostly at the right side), broken transverse processes (encircled) of the lumbar spine; fractured femurs (encircled)—anterior (**e**) and posterior (**f**) view

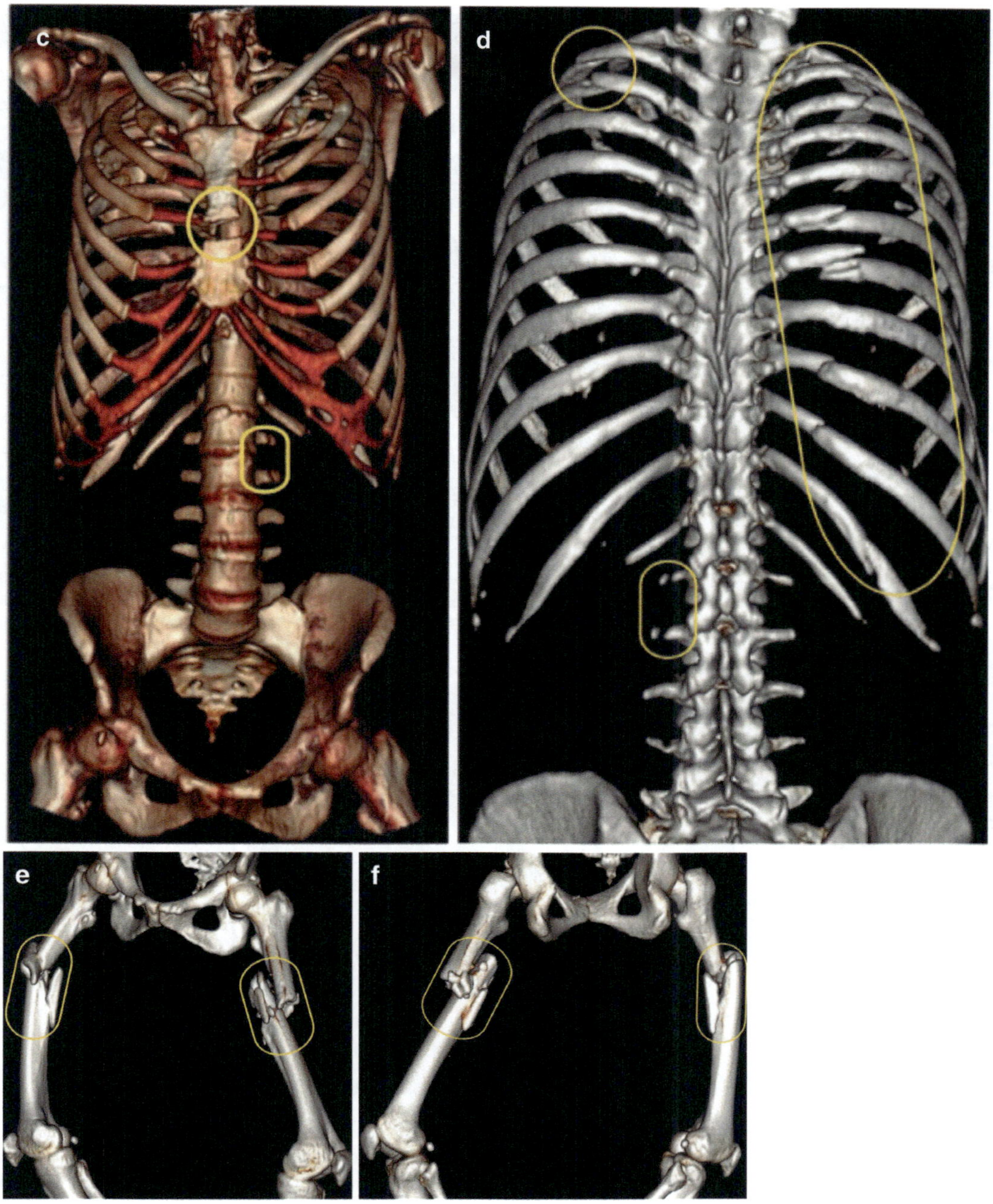

Fig. 8 (continued)

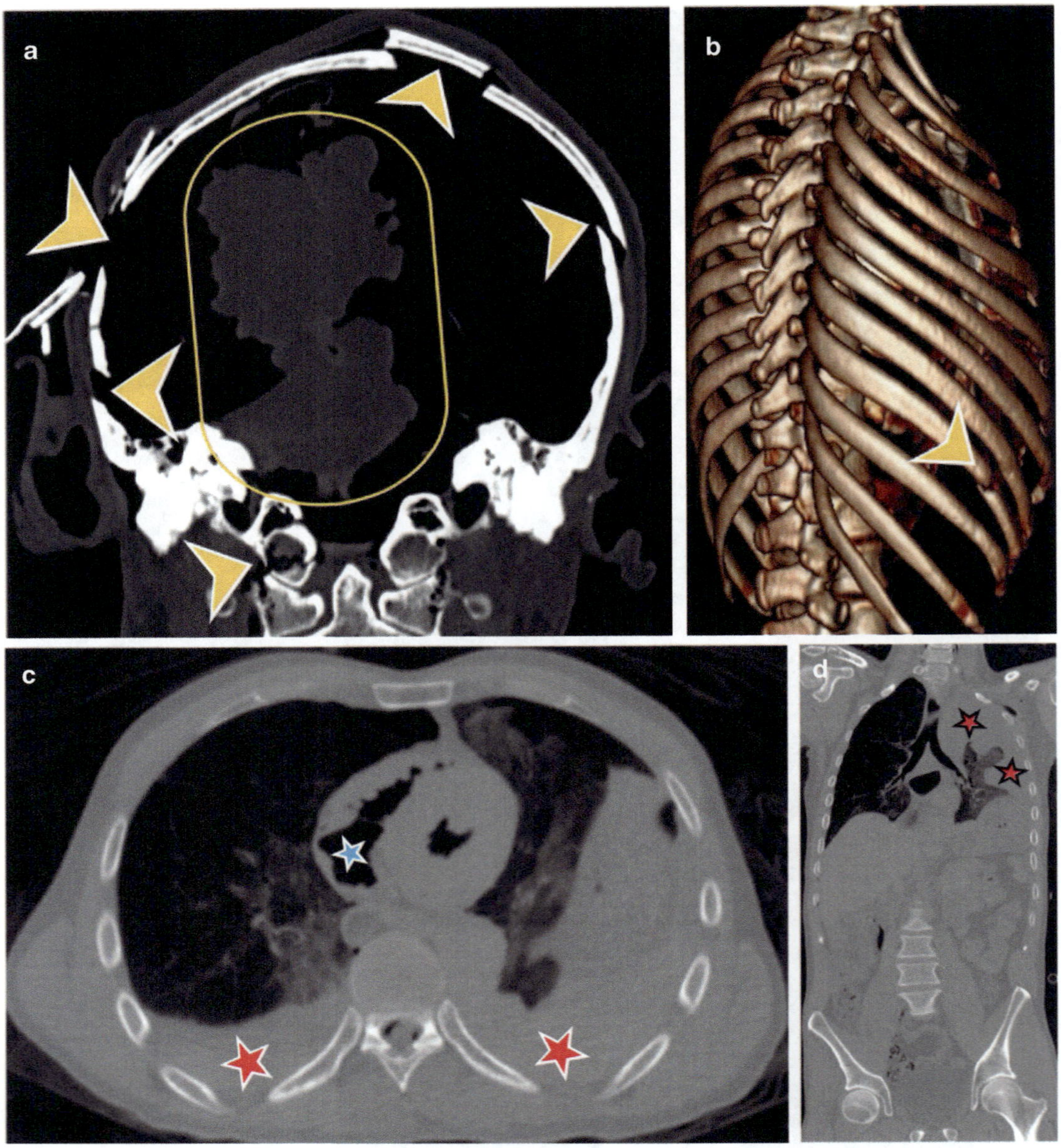

Fig. 9 A pedestrian run over by a motor vehicle, unenhanced PMCT: (**a**) coronal reconstruction of the head—fragmentation of the calvarium (arrowheads), fracture of the right occipital condyles (arrowhead), partial excerebration (encircled); (**b**) VRT reconstruction of the bones of the chest after digital removal of the scapulas—fractured ribs at the lower right (arrowhead); axial (**c**) and coronal (**d**) reconstructions of the trunk—bilateral blood (red stars), mostly to the left, gas (blue star) in the right part of the heart; (**e**) VRT reconstruction of the bones of the lower limbs (excluding the distal part of the left limb)—left posterior view; (**f**) VRT reconstruction of the bones of the distal part of the left limb, posterior view—both parts of the left limb preserved continuity by soft tissues only—locations of broken bones are encircled

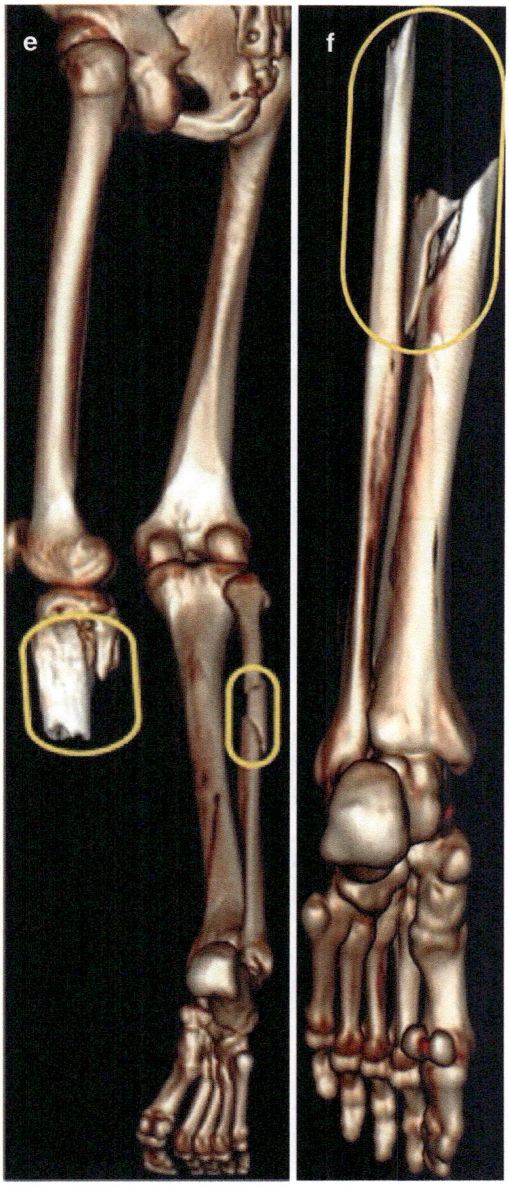

Fig. 9 (continued)

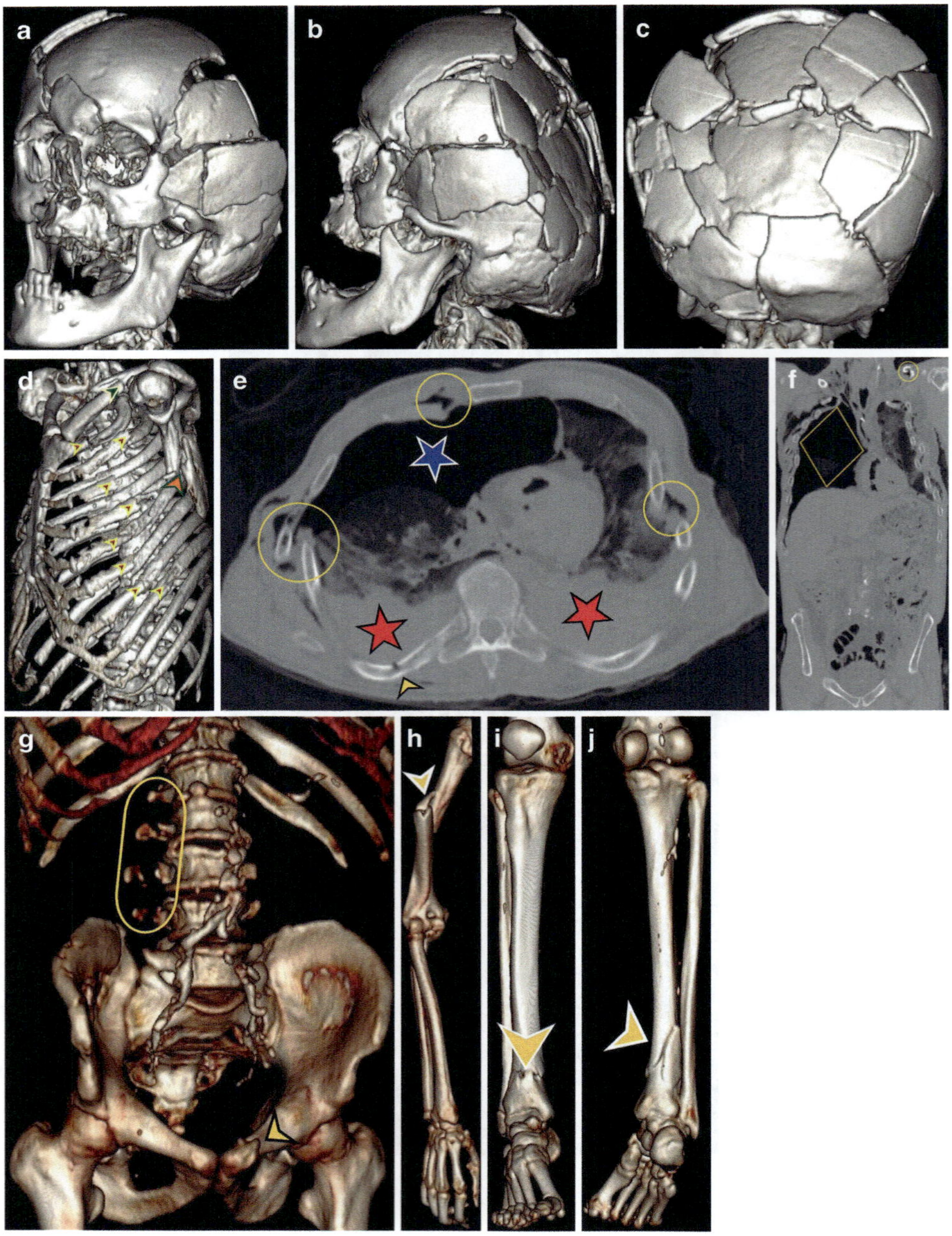

Fig. 10 Unenhanced PMCT. Although the pattern of fractures of the skull may suggest a victim of a fall from height—this is a case of a pedestrian run over by a motor vehicle: VRT reconstruction of the skull—left anterior (**a**), left (**b**) and posterior (**c**) view; (**d**) VRT reconstruction of the thorax—left anterior view—multiple fractures of the ribs (arrowheads), left clavicle (green arrowhead) and scapula (dark yellow arrowhead); (**e**) axial reconstruction of the thorax—gas (blue star) in the right pleural cavity, blood (red stars) on both sides, broken (arrowhead) and displaced (encircled) ribs; (**f**) coronal reconstruction of the trunk—broken left clavicle (encircled), tension pneumothorax (diamond) on the right side; (**g**) VRT reconstruction of the lumbar spine and pelvis—anterior (slightly right) view—note broken transverse processes (encircled) on the right side and the fracture of the left pubic bone (arrowhead), additionally visible are the calcified aorta and iliac arteries; (**h**) VRT reconstruction of the right upper limb—fracture of the humerus (arrowhead); VRT reconstruction of the bones of the distal part of the right lower limb—anterior (**i**) and posterior (**j**) view—fracture of the tibia at the distal part of the shaft (arrowheads)

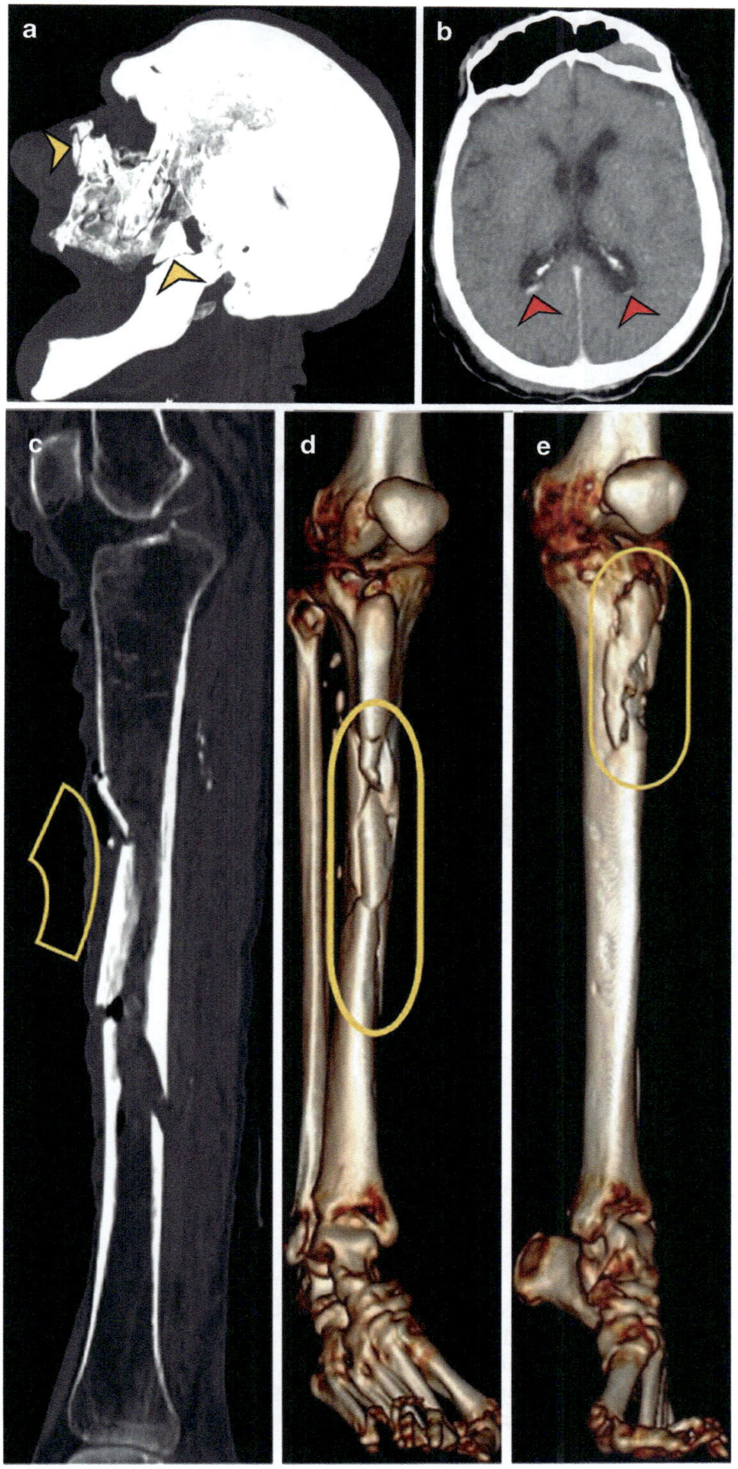

Fig. 11 A victim of assault with the use of blunt objects (unenhanced PMCT): (**a**) thick MIP reconstruction of the head in a sagittal plane—fracture of the mandible and nasal bones (arrowheads); (**b**) axial image of the head—traces of blood (red arrowheads) inside the ventricles of the brain; (**c**) MIP reconstruction of the right tibia — multiple fractures of its shaft, an arched shape symbolizes the weapon of crime; VRT reconstructions, anterior view of the right (**d**) and left (**e**) shank and foot—bone indentation (encircled) caused by a blunt weapon

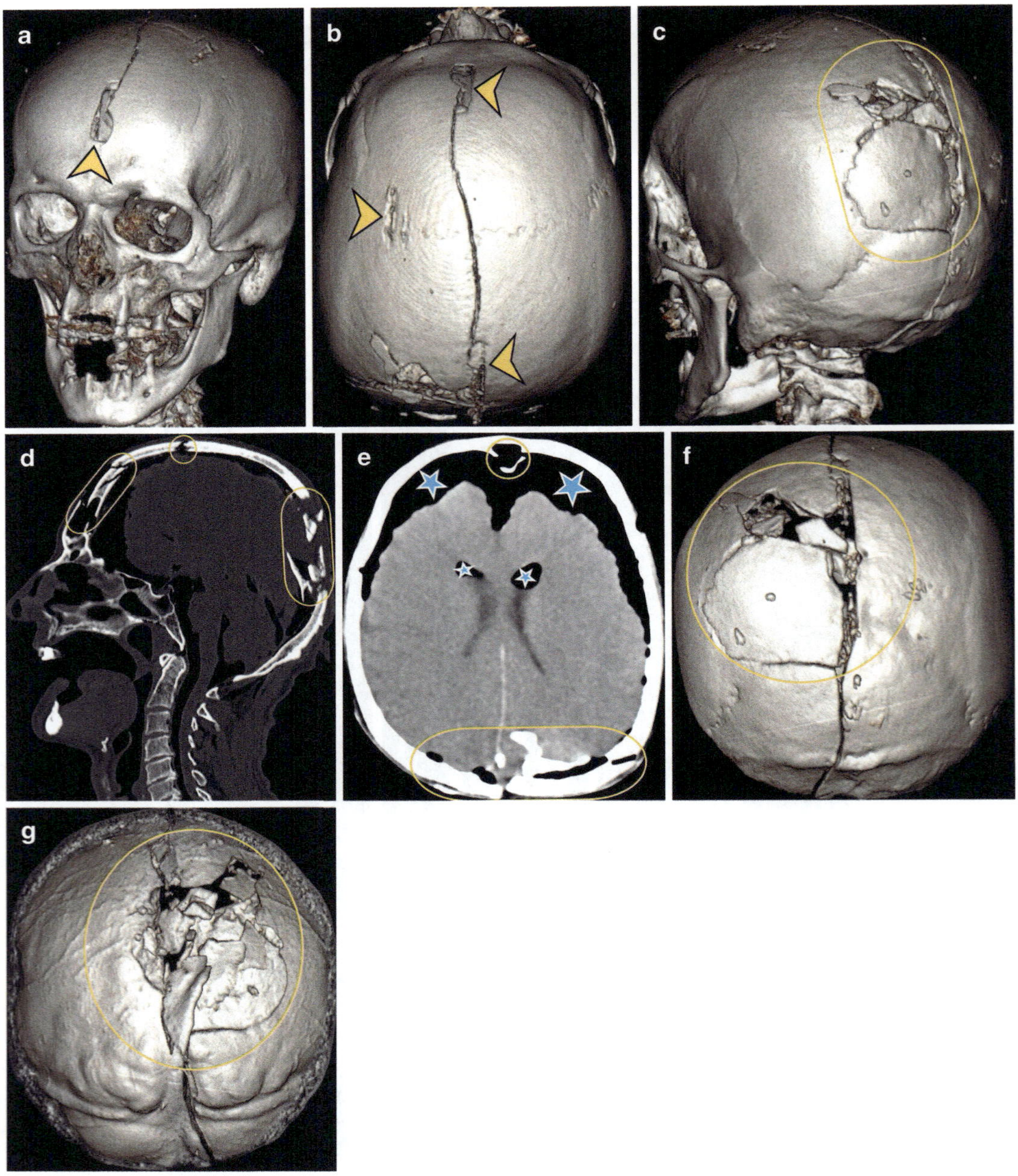

Fig. 12 Unenhanced PMCT. A homicide case—use of the blade and other parts of an axe. VRT reconstruction of the skull: left anterior (**a**), superior (**b**), and left posterior (**c**) view; sagittal (**d**) and axial (**e**) reconstruction of the head—fractured bones of the skull of the anterior, upper, and posterior part (arrowheads/encircled), gas (small blue stars) inside the ventricles of the brain, intracranial gas (blue stars); VRT reconstruction of the most injured (encircled) posterior part of the calvarium, view from the outside (**f**) and inside (**g**); be informed that in this case presence of gas inside the heart was proven—as shown in Fig. 5c

5 Firearm Injuries

Unenhanced PMCT examination may give sufficient data for the reconstruction of the track of a projectile in almost all cases of penetrating/ perforating injuries of the skull, especially in cases of a singular shot (Kirchhoff et al., 2016). It is in many cases quite easy to find the location of the external (entrance) wound, broken bones—both primary and secondary fractures, finally the presence of gas and/ or fluid and foreign body particles (including small pieces of the fragmented bullet) inside the brain. The direction of the bevelling of skull bones helps in the differentiation of the entrance (internal bevelling) from the exit wound (external bevelling). Even in cases of intraoral shooting or with the location of the entrance wound below the mandible, they may be evaluated quite well.

Injuries referring to the chest may be more complicated. However, with the possible apparent location of the external wound and bone injuries (sternum, ribs and the spine), the success of evaluation is to be expected.

Another problem refers to the gunshot wounds located in the abdomen and extremities. It may happen, that the structures of soft tissues are the only ones injured. However, application of PMCTA may give chances for additional pieces of evidence for a successful reconstruction of the injury track(s) (Grabherr et al. 2016). If subcutaneous space filled with contrast medium is seen,

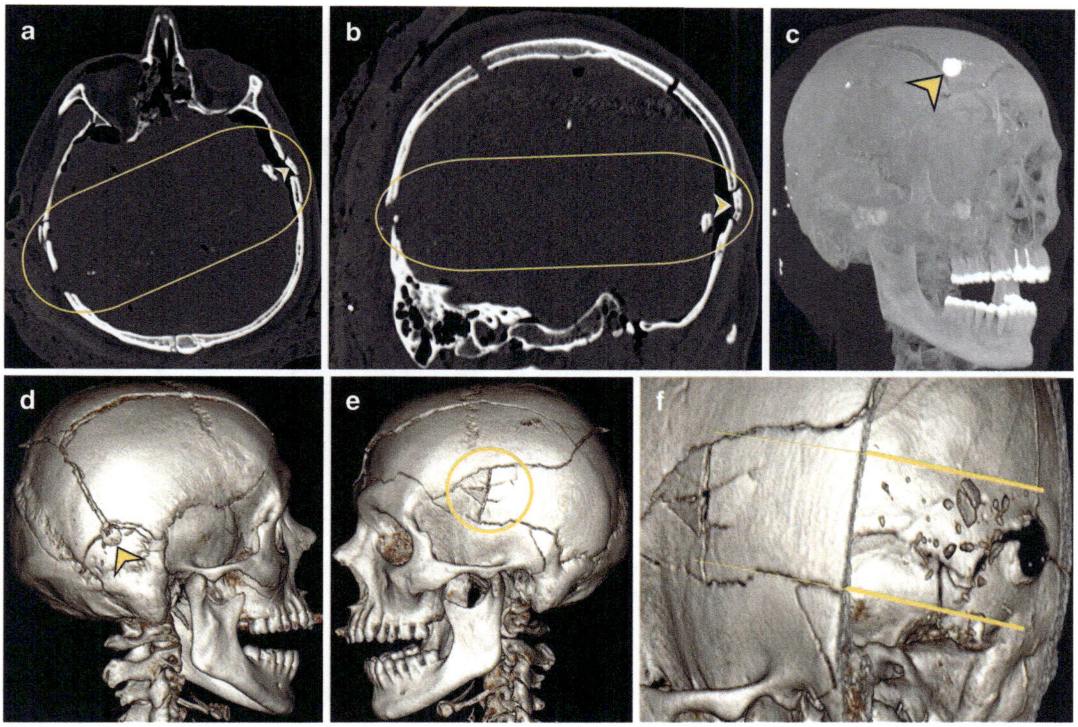

Fig. 13 A penetrating firearm injury of the head: thin MPR reconstructions in an axial (**a**) and coronal (**b**) plane, showing apparently the track from the right to the left (encircled), with deflection (arrowhead) of the projectile; Unenhanced PMCT. (**c**) MIP reconstruction showing a black powder gun bullet (arrowhead) lodged inside the skull; VRT reconstruction—the right (**d**) and left (**e**) lateral view—the entrance wound on the right side (arrowhead). Note the area of deflection of the bullet on the left side (encircled) with a pattern of fractures (**f**) VRT reconstruction of the skull after digital removal of the posterior part of the skull, left posterior view, showing the location of the entrance wound from the inside and the area of deflection of the projectile from the outside (marked with lines)

it may be treated as evidence of the shot from the immediate vicinity. In unenhanced PMCT small metallic particles marking the vicinity of the location of the entrance wound and the wound channel (Figs. 13, 14, 15, 16, 17, and 18).

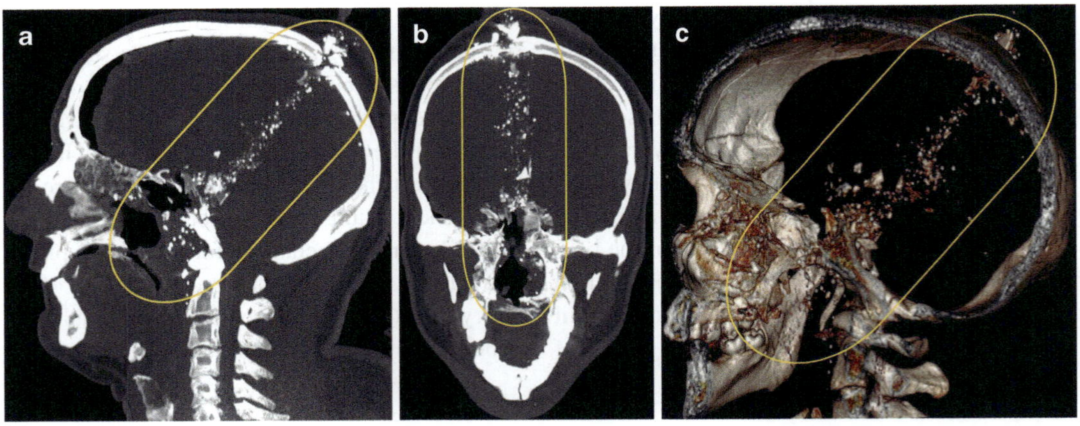

Fig. 14 Unenhanced PMCT. A suicidal intraoral shooting: the track of the bullet with numerous small particles (encircled): thick MIP reconstruction of the head and neck in a sagittal (**a**) and axial oblique (**b**) plane; (**c**) VRT reconstruction of the skull after digital removal of both sides of the skull, left lateral view

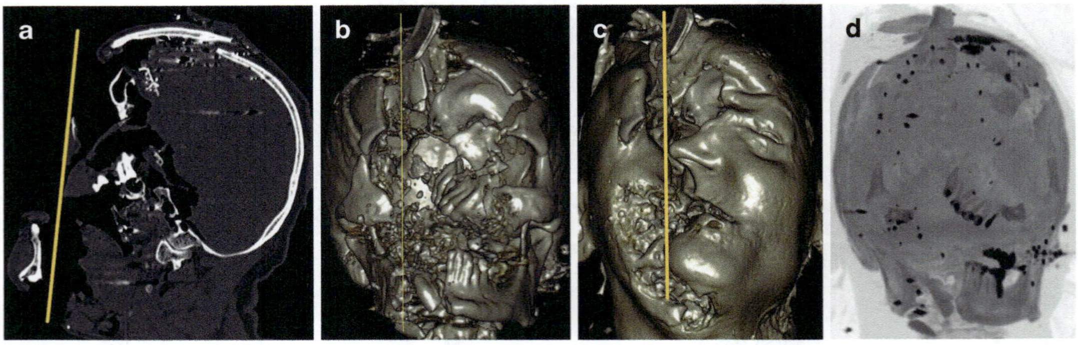

Fig. 15 Unenhanced PMCT. A victim of firearm injuries due to a shotgun, singular submandibular shot: the line shows the track of the injury: (**a**) sagittal oblique reconstruction; VRT reconstructions—anterior view of the skull (**b**) and the head (**c**); (**d**) MIP reconstruction revealing pellets as well as the fragmentation of the skull with displacement of bones

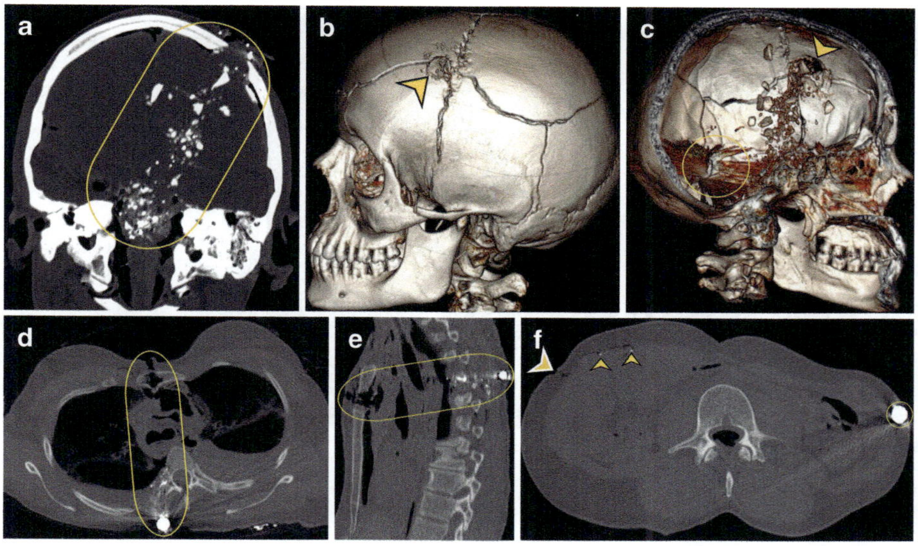

Fig. 16 A female victim of homicide—multiple shots (unenhanced PMCT): (**a**) thick MIP reconstruction of the head in a coronal plane, note numerous particles at the location of the track (encircled); VRT reconstruction of the skull—left lateral, slightly superior view (**b**)—the location of the entrance hole (arrowhead); right lateral view after digital removal of the right side of the skull (**c**)—the location of the entrance (arrowhead) and lodged bullet (encircled); axial (**d**) and sagittal (**e**) reconstruction of the thorax—the entrance wound in the middle of the anterior part of the chest, injury of the sternum, the bullet is lodged at the back side, the track is encircled; (**f**) axial oblique reconstruction of the lower part of the trunk (at the level of the lumbar spine), the entrance wound at the right side (yellow arrowhead), two small particles—foreign bodies (small arrowheads), the bullet is lodged at the opposite side (encircled)

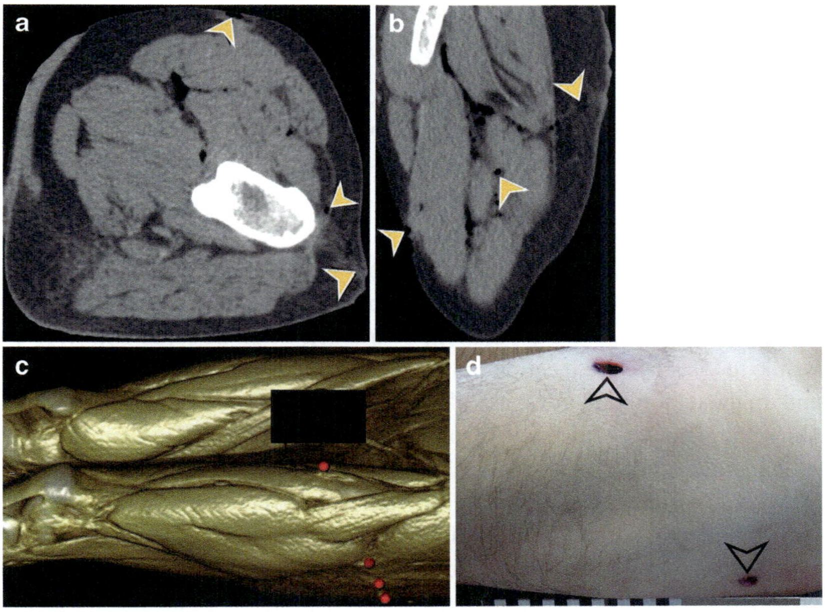

Fig. 17 A perforating gunshot injury of the left thigh (unenhanced PMCT): (**a**)–(**b**) oblique reconstructions of the proximal part of the left thigh—yellow arrowheads are showing locations of a missing part of the skin and a small number of areas with accumulation of gas and traces of blood, determining the location of the injury track; (**c**) VRT reconstruction of musculature of both thighs, left anterior view—red dots put at locations of a missing part of the skin, areas of small gas accumulation and traces of blood; (**d**) for comparison—an autopsy photograph of the left thigh with both the entrance and exit wounds (arrowheads)

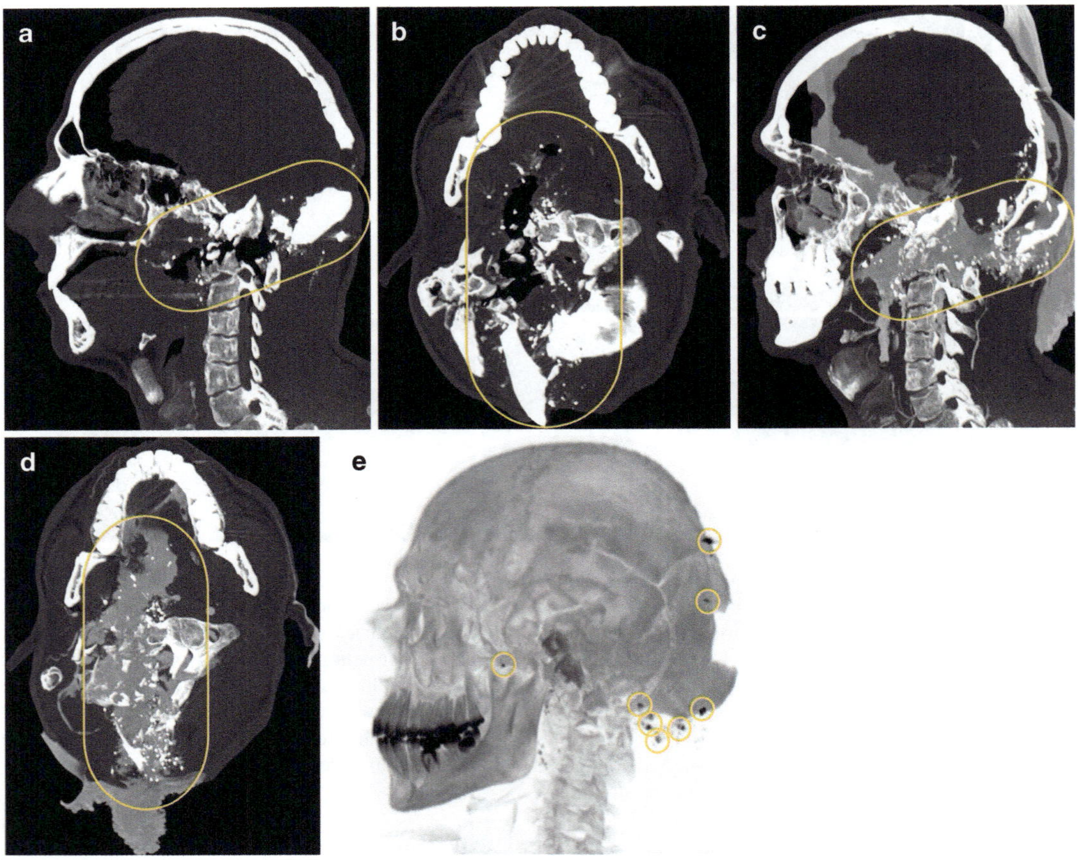

Fig. 18 Unenhanced PMCT. A victim of intraoral shooting: thick MIP sagittal (**a**) and axial oblique (**b**) reconstructions showing the track (encircled) of the projectile—note the presence of numerous contrasting small particles and gas spaces; thick MIP sagittal (**c**) and axial oblique (**d**) reconstructions showing the same areas (encircled) after CA administration; (**e**) MIP reconstruction showing small contrasting particles (encircled) and fragmented bones of the skull and the upper cervical spine

6 Sharp Force Injuries

With the use of unenhanced PMCT examination, it may be possible to visualize the location of the external wound. In the majority of cases, it is also possible to show the damage of internal organs due to sharp trauma (blood (Zech et al. 2014), gas accumulation) without visualization of particular injuries. Such information is sometimes insufficient for the reconstruction of the injury track. For this purpose application of PMCTA is therefore recommended—the authors find cases of sharp force injuries as one of the most indicated ones for the administration of contrast medium in post-mortem imaging (Moskała et al. 2012; Grabherr et al. 2016, 2018). In rare cases a broken fragment of the used weapon can be found left inside a body, which may be visible during PMCT evaluation. This might give the opportunity to locate and secure such a piece of evidence during conventional autopsy. In cases when a tool is left inside a body (Ebner et al. 2014), by performing PMCT before removal of the object, we can get perfect visualization of its location and its relation to important internal organs (Figs. 19, 20, and 21).

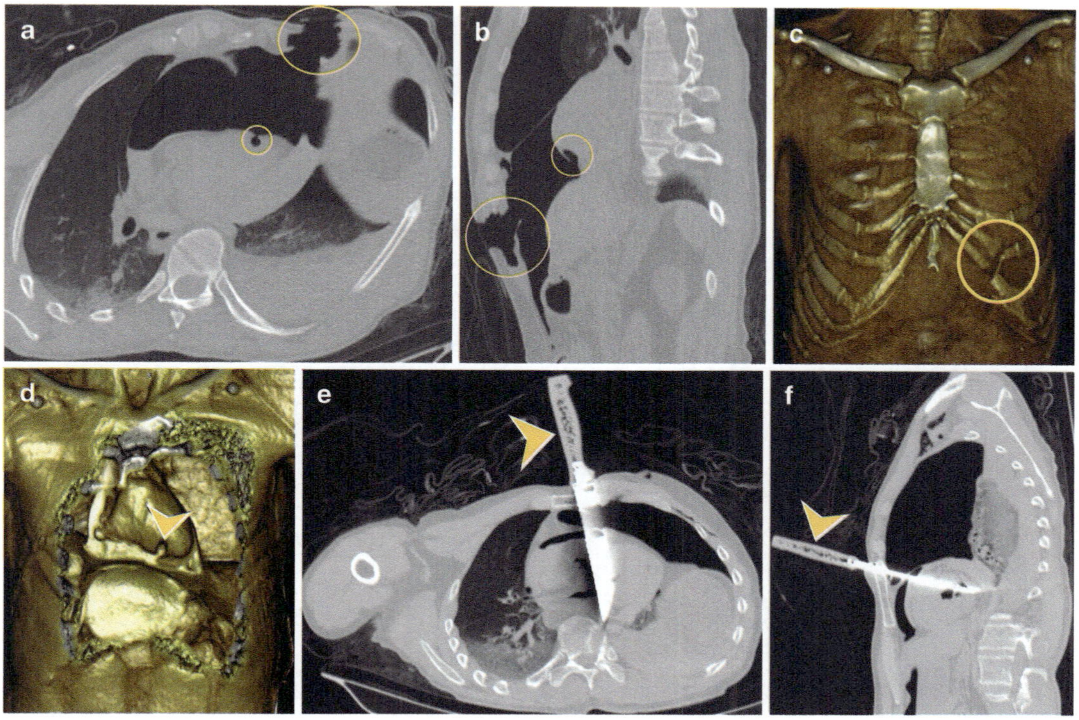

Fig. 19 Two cases of sharp force injuries (unenhanced PMCT): (1) axial oblique (**a**) and sagittal (**b**) reconstructions of the thorax showing injuries of the anterior wall of the chest and the heart (both encircled), gas inside the pericardial sac and the left pleural cavity (in this location combined with blood); VRT reconstructions: (**c**) anterior view of the bones and cartilages of the chest—note that two cartilages of the left ribs are cut (encircled); (**d**) after digital removal of the anterior part of the wall of the chest—note a deep injury of the heart near the apical area (arrowhead); (2) axial oblique (**e**) and sagittal oblique (**f**) reconstructions showing the location of the blade of the knife inside the heart, the handle is marked by arrowheads

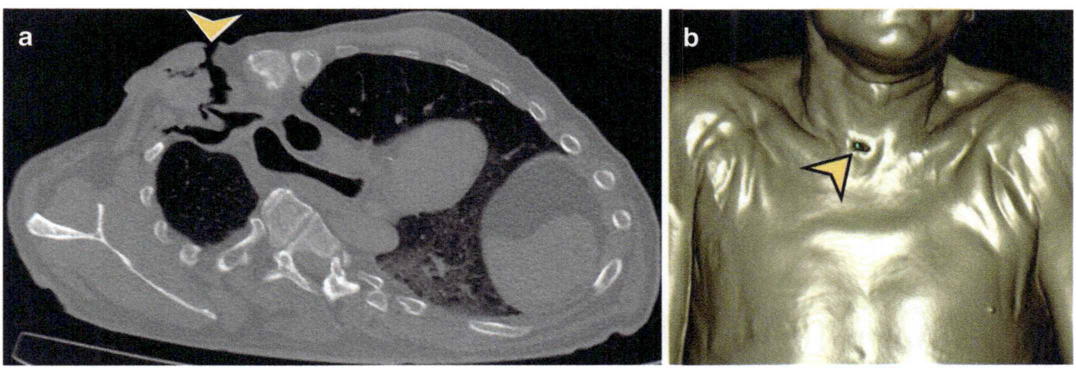

Fig. 20 A singular stab wound with injury of the right common carotid artery (unenhanced PMCT): (**a**) axial oblique reconstruction of the neck and thorax showing the track of the injury at the anterior part (arrowhead); (**b**) VRT reconstruction of the surface of the body, anterior view—showing the location of the wound (arrowhead); coronal oblique (**c, e**) and sagittal (**d**) reconstructions—note hollow arteries (blue stars) containing gas; axial oblique (**f**) and sagittal oblique (**g**) reconstructions showing the area of injury (yellow line) after CA administration (arterial phase); (**h**) VRT reconstruction of thoracic arteries, anterior view, showing the CA extravasation (arrowhead) at the initial part of the right common carotid artery

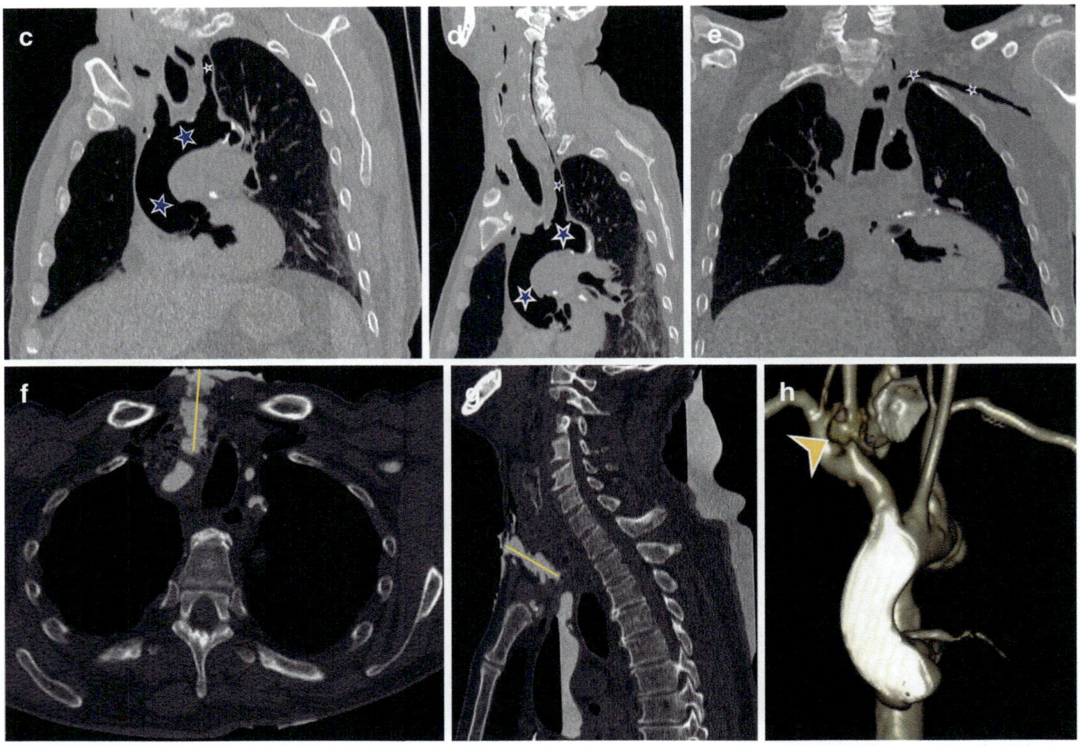

Fig. 20 (continued)

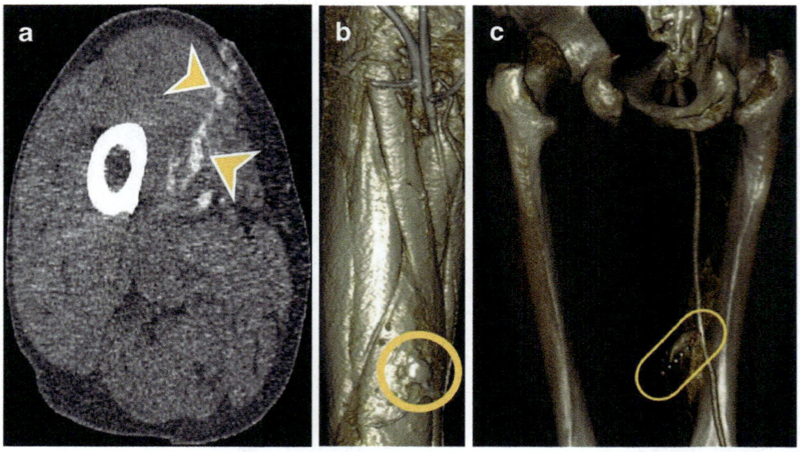

Fig. 21 A singular stab wound of the right thigh, PMCTA examination: (**a**) thin MPR reconstruction in an axial oblique plane showing the track (arrowheads) of the injury after CA administration (arterial phase); (**b**) VRT reconstruction of the muscles of the right thigh—note CA extravasation at the distal part of the thigh (encircled) catheters at the initial part; (**c**) VRT reconstruction based on PMCTA acquisition—arterial phase, posterior (slight left) view—the right femoral artery and the location of the track of the injury (color dots—encircled) are visible

7 Summary

As illustrated, PMCT can perfectly be used for the evaluation of bone fractures, identification of spaces of accumulation of fluid or gas as well as the location of foreign, specifically metallic, objects. As for external changes and soft tissues the use of PMCT is sometimes limited due to problems with body positioning and HU resolution. In cases of blunt force trauma, firearms, and sharp force injuries, application of PMCT has substantial impact on the quality of the post-mortem examination, and it helps with better documentation and presentation of findings. Furthermore, the administration of contrast medium can further increase diagnostic opportunities.

Acknowledgments Foundation of the PMCT Laboratory of the Chair and Department of Forensic Medicine of the Jagiellonian University Medical College was supported by the European Regional Development Fund through Regional Operational Programme Małopolskie Voivodeship programming period 2007–2013.

The authors' PMCT and PMCTA research was approved by the appropriate University Bioethics Committee (KBET/225/B/2012, 1072.6120.10.2017).

References

Blau S, Ranson D, O'Donnell C (2017) An atlas of skeletal trauma in medico-legal contexts. Academic Press, Oxford

Christe A, Ross S, Oesterhelweg L, Spendlove D, Bolliger S, Vock P, Thali MJ (2009) Abdominal trauma—sensitivity and specificity of postmortem noncontrast imaging findings compared with autopsy findings. J Trauma 66(5):1302–1307. https://doi.org/10.1097/TA.0b013e31818c1441

Ebner L, Flach PM, Schumann K, Gascho D, Ruder T, Christe A, Thali M, Ampanozi G (2014) The tip of the tip of the knife: stab sequence reconstruction using postmortem CT in a homicide case. J Forensic Radiol Imaging 2:205–209. https://doi.org/10.1016/j.jofri.2014.08.002

Egger C, Vaucher P, Doenz F, Palmiere C, Mangin P, Grabherr S (2012) Development and validation of a postmortem radiological alteration index: the RA-index. Int J Legal Med 126(4):559–566. https://doi.org/10.1007/s00414-012-0686-6

Grabherr S, Egger C, Vilarino R, Campana L, Jotterand M, Dedouit F (2017) Modern post-mortem imaging: an update on recent developments. Forensic Sci Res 2(2):52–64. https://doi.org/10.1080/20961790.2017.1330738

Grabherr S, Grimm JM, Heinemann A (2016) Atlas of postmortem angiography. Springer, Cham

Grabherr S, Heinemann A, Vogel H, Rutty G, Morgan B, Wozniak KJ, Dedouit F, Fischer F, Lochner S, Wittig H, Guglielmi G, Eplinius F, Michaud K, Palmiere C, Chevallier C, Mangin P, Grimm JM (2018) Postmortem CT angiography compared with autopsy: a forensic multicenter study. Radiology 288(1):270–276. https://doi.org/10.1148/radiol.2018170559

Juźwik E, Moskała A, Woźniak KJ, Kopacz P (2019) Evaluation of usefulness of post-mortem computed tomography in the diagnosis of abdominal parenchymal organ injuries compared to medicolegal autopsy findings. Arch Med Sadowej Kryminol 69(1–2):40–55. https://doi.org/10.5114/amsik.2019.89235

Kirchhoff SM, Scaparra EF, Grimm J, Scherr M, Graw M, Reiser MF, Peschel O (2016) Postmortem computed tomography (PMCT) and autopsy in deadly gunshot wounds—a comparative study. Int J Legal Med 130(3):819–826. https://doi.org/10.1007/s00414-015-1225-z

Lopatin O, Moskała A, Woźniak KJ, Bolechała F (2019) Analysis of cases of traumatic pneumothorax—conclusions based on post-mortem CT examinations for routine autopsy diagnostics. Arch Med Sadowej Kryminol 69(1–2):56–69. https://doi.org/10.5114/amsik.2019.89236

Moskała A, Woźniak KJ, Kluza P, Bolechała F, Rzepecka-Woźniak E, Kołodziej J, Latacz K (2012) [Validity of post-mortem computed tomography angiography (PMCTA) in medico-legal diagnostic management of stab and incised wounds]. Arch Med Sadowej Kryminol. 62 (4):315–326. Polish

Moskała A, Woźniak KJ, Kluza P, Romaszko K, Lopatin O (2016) The importance of post-mortem computed tomography (PMCT) in confrontation with conventional forensic autopsy of victims of motorcycle accidents. Leg Med (Tokyo) 18:25–30. https://doi.org/10.1016/j.legalmed.2015.11.005

Moskała A, Woźniak KJ, Kluza P, Romaszko K, Lopatin O (2017) Usefulness of post mortem computed tomography versus conventional forensic autopsy of road accident victims (drivers and passengers). Arch Med Sadowej Kryminol 67(2):91–103. https://doi.org/10.5114/amsik.2017.71451

Scholing M, Saltzherr TP, Fung Kon Jin PH, Ponsen KJ, Reitsma JB, Lameris JS, Goslings JC (2009) The value of postmortem computed tomography as an alternative for autopsy in trauma victims: a systematic review. Eur Radiol 19(10):2333–2341. https://doi.org/10.1007/s00330-009-1440-4

Schulze C, Hoppe H, Schweitzer W, Schwendener N, Grabherr S, Jackowski C (2013) Rib fractures at postmortem computed tomography (PMCT) validated against the autopsy. Forensic Sci Int 233(1–3):90–98. https://doi.org/10.1016/j.forsciint.2013.08.025

Thali MJ, Dirnhofer R, Vock P (2009) The virtopsy approach. 3D optical and radiological scanning and reconstruction in forensic medicine. CRC Press, Boca Raton

Thali MJ, Viner MD, Brogdon BG (2011) Brogdon's forensic radiology, 2nd edn. CRC Press, Boca Raton

Zech W-D, Jackowski C, Buetikofer Y, Kara L (2014) Characterization and differentiation of body fluids, putrefaction fluid, and blood using Hounsfield unit in postmortem CT. Int J Legal Med 128(5):795–802. https://doi.org/10.1007/s00414-014-1030-0

Asphyxia

Pia Genet and Coraline Egger

Contents

1 Introduction

Asphyxia is defined as an oxygen deficiency, which leads to hypoxic and ischemic lesions of the brain and/or to death (Spitz 2006). Asphyxia can be divided into mechanical or atmospheric asphyxia. Mechanical asphyxia can be caused by obstructive and restrictive triggers which cause an oxygen deficiency by interfering with the delivery and/or the uptake of the oxygen. Obstructive triggers can be, e.g., strangulation or hanging, leading to an obstruction of the vessels of the neck and/or the airways, or an occlusion of the airways by aspiration of liquids, e.g., drowning or a foreign body. Restrictive triggers are instead associated to an interference of the

P. Genet (✉)
University Centre of Legal Medicine, Lausanne, Switzerland

University Centre of Legal Medicine, Geneva, Switzerland

CURML, Unité d'imagerie et anthropologie forensiques, Lausanne, Switzerland
e-mail: pia.genet@chuv.ch, PiaPatricia.Baumann@hcuge.ch

C. Egger
University Centre of Legal Medicine, Geneva, Switzerland

CURML, Unité d'imagerie et anthropologie forensiques, Geneva, Switzerland
e-mail: coraline.egger@hcuge.ch

© Springer Nature Switzerland AG 2022
F. Dedouit et al. (eds.), *Forensic Imaging*, Medical Radiology Diagnostic Imaging,
https://doi.org/10.1007/978-3-030-83352-7_8

thoracic movements, e.g., by a compression of the thoracic cage, burking, positional asphyxia, a trauma leading to rib fractures, etc.. Paralysis of the respiratory muscles, which impede a regular respiration and the assimilation of oxygen, can also result in asphyxia. Pneumo- or hemothorax can also have an influence on the respiratory movements and lead to an asphyxia (Brinkmann 2004).

Atmospheric asphyxia is related to an oxygen deficit in the air, e.g., big heights in the mountains, or to a problem which has an impact on the transportation of oxygen in the blood, e.g., intoxication of carbon monoxide or another gas (Brinkmann 2004).

Cases of asphyxia are common and play an important role in forensic routine (DiMaio and DiMaio 2001; Brinkmann 2004; Saukko and Knight 2004; Azmak 2006; Spitz 2006). As radiological methods, especially Multi Detector Computed Tomography (MDCT) and Magnetic Resonance Imaging (MRI), are gaining in importance in the forensic field, those methods are getting more and more involved in the process of managing forensic cases correlated to asphyxia (Dirnhofer et al. 2009; Thali et al. 2010; Grabherr et al. 2017). Combined with a conventional forensic autopsy those methods permit to explore a forensic case related to asphyxia in detail in analyzing the soft tissues and the skeleton. As these radiological methods are applied before starting the autopsy, they have the big advantage to be able to "guide" the forensic pathologist during his examination (Poulsen and Simonsen 2007). This permits the physician to be attentive to certain findings which otherwise could have been missed.

In this chapter, we will discuss the advantages of using radiological methods as MDCT and MRI in cases of asphyxia and explain their additional value to a conventional forensic autopsy. Furthermore, we will explain their benefit in handling forensic cases in the living correlated to asphyxia, e.g., survived strangulation victims.

MDCT is the best radiological technique to analyze the skeleton and to detect bone fractures (Peschel et al. 2013; Jalalzadeh et al. 2015; Schmitt-Sody et al. 2016). MDCT permits to perform 2D- and 3D reconstructions, which allow evaluating the soft tissues and the skeletal system in a three-dimensional way. However, MDCT is not the method of choice to analyze the soft tissues. Although an injection of contrast medium in the vessels permits to increase the sensitivity of the examination, small infiltrations and hemorrhages can be missed (Jeffery 2010; Chevallier et al. 2013). This is the reason why this technique should, especially in asphyxia cases related to strangulation and hanging, be combined with MRI. MRI is nowadays the radiological gold standard for the evaluation of the soft tissues and allows identifying also small infiltrations and hemorrhages in the neck muscles, lymph nodes, or salivary glands (Yen et al. 2005; Gascho et al. 2019). Moreover, it is the radiological technique of choice to explore the brain tissue, permitting to identify lesions caused by hypoxia and anoxia (Groenendaal and de Vries 2017).

In this chapter, we will explain several findings which can be found in MDCT and MRI in the different types of asphyxia. As asphyxia related to an atmospheric cause (e.g., big height, intoxication with a gas, which affects the transport of oxygen) does not leave specific, objective signs in the tissues, the organs or the skeleton, which could be found during the conventional forensic autopsy, and as restrictive triggers of mechanical asphyxia are in most of the cases related to trauma, we decided to focus on the types of asphyxia which are caused by obstructive triggers, as strangulation, hanging, obstruction of the airways, and drowning.

2 Hanging and Strangulation

2.1 In the Living

In cases of survived hanging or strangulation forensic imaging tools can be useful (Aneesh et al. 2002; Kalita et al. 2002; Plattner et al. 2005; Zabel et al. 2005; Matsuyama et al. 2006; Yen et al. 2007; Christe et al. 2009, 2010; Bruguier et al. 2019). Typical clinical findings in cases of strangulation and survived hanging are petechial hemorrhages of the skin and the conjunctives, hematomas, bruises, abrasions, or a strangulation mark on the skin. In the living the clinical examination is limited to the findings on the skin and doesn't permit to evaluate the soft tissues (fatty subcutaneous and muscle tissues) of the neck and the submandibular region, as the laryngeal skeleton, the hyoid bone, and the vocal cords. MDCT and MRI can be used to detect hemorrhagic infiltration and edema in the soft tissues (Fig. 1) and fractures of the bone structures of the neck. The aim of the use of those techniques is the assessment of all the lesions of the brain and neck and to analyze the different anatomical structures. It has to be indicated that hypoxic and ischemic lesions of the brain can result as a consequence of prolonged strangulation or hanging. To detect those brain lesions, MRI is the technique of choice (Hori et al. 1991; Miyamoto and Auer 2000; Imamura et al. 2010; Groenendaal and de Vries 2017) (Fig. 2).

In survived strangulation or hanging victims, dissections of the carotid artery, complicated by thrombosis and embolism, can occur. Nowadays such vascular lesions can be identified by an Angio-MDCT and/or a MRI (Kiani and Simes 2000; Malek et al. 2000; Vilke and Chan 2011; Sethi et al. 2012).

If no clinical treatment is necessary and the imaging aim is only of forensic purpose (lesions assessment), MRI should be used, as it's the only technique which does not use radiation.

2.2 In Post-mortem

Typical autopsy findings in cases of strangulation and hanging are findings on the skin of the neck and the conjunctives (petechia, hematomas, bruises, abrasions, strangulation mark),

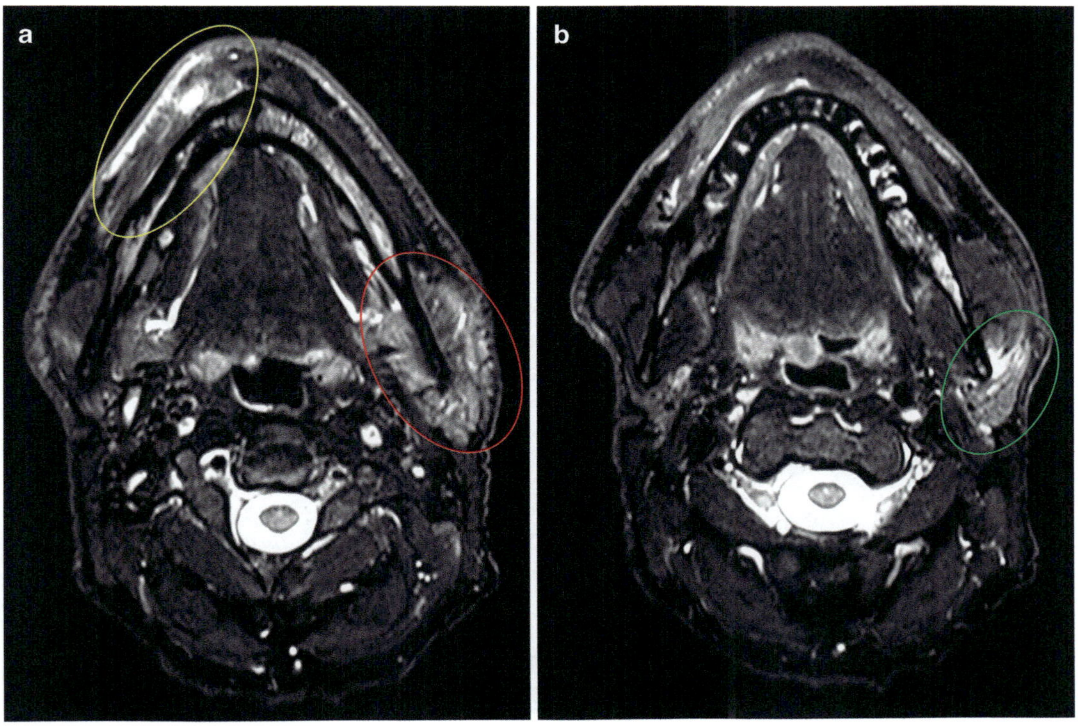

Fig. 1 Clinical MRI in 2D T2 FAT SAT with axial view of the neck in a victim of survived strangulation with visualization of an infiltration of the soft tissues of the right side of the chin (yellow circle, **a**) and the left mandibular angle (red circle, **a**), and a myo-aponeurotic disinsertion of the left masseter muscle (green circle, **b**)

hemorrhagic infiltrations of the soft tissues of the neck (fatty tissues, muscles, pharyngeal and laryngeal mucosae, salivary glands, lymph nodes) and of the periosteum of the clavicles, fractures of the hyoid bone, the laryngeal skeleton (thyroid, cricoid, and arytenoid cartilages) and the cervical vertebral spine, vascular lesions (signs of Amussat and Otto), sub-pleural petechia (Tardieu spots) and hemorrhagic infiltrations of the vertebral disc and/or ligaments of the thoracic-lumbar vertebras in cases of hanging (sign of Simon). As most of the typical findings, which can be found during the conventional autopsy, are located in the soft tissues (fatty tissue and muscles) and the laryngeal skeleton, the use of MDCT and MRI is indicated (Yen et al. 2005; Garetier et al. 2017; Gascho et al. 2019). In addition, the application of those two methods permits to exclude other causes of death, e.g., traumatic lesions or lesions related to the use of firearms, and the search for intra-corporal foreign bodies.

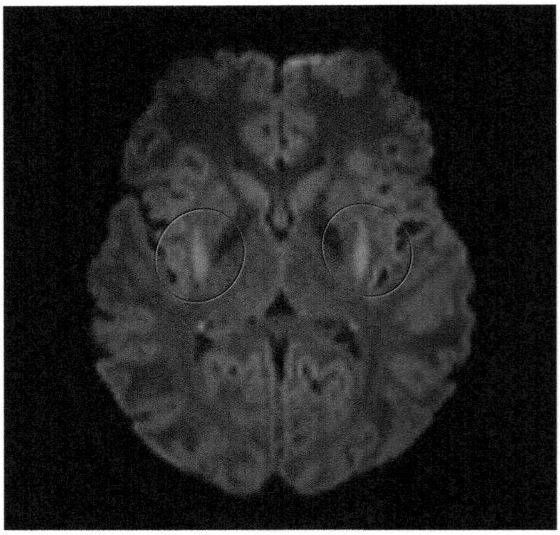

Fig. 2 Clinical MRI in 2D T2 DIXON Water with axial view of the brain in a victim of survived strangulation with visualization of a restriction of the diffusion of the posterior part of the external capsule on both sides (red circles)

For the evaluation of the soft tissues of the neck (fatty and muscle tissue, mucosae) the radiological technique of choice is MRI (Yen et al. 2005; Gascho et al. 2019). Hemorrhagic infiltration as well as edema can be found in the subcutaneous fatty tissue and the muscles of the neck (Fig. 3), the salivary glands, the lymph nodes, and the pharyngo-laryngeal mucosa as in the ligaments of the vertebral cervical spine. However, depending on the size, hemorrhagic infiltrations of the soft tissue can also be found with MDCT. Concerning the analysis of the bone

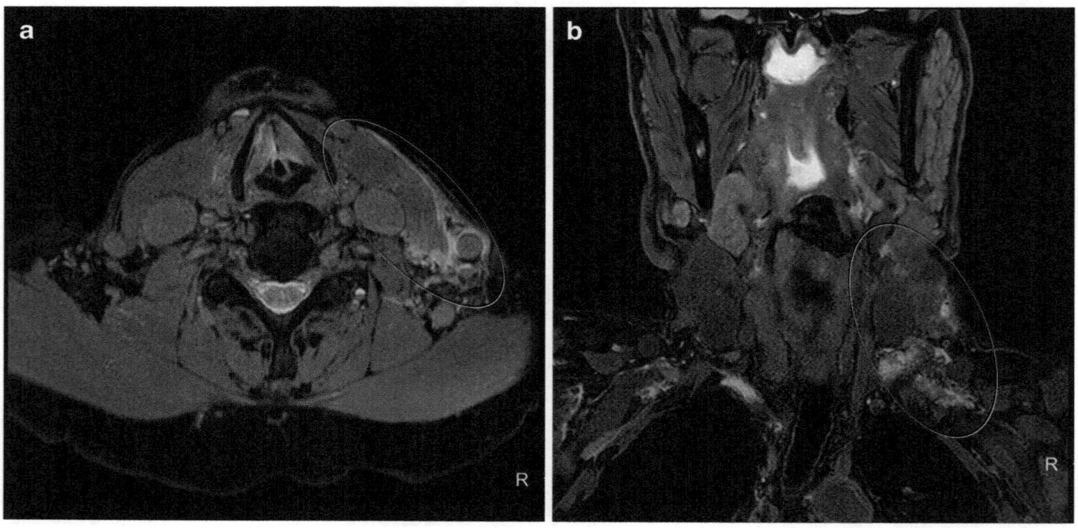

Fig. 3 Post-mortem MRI in 2D T2 DIXON Water with axial (**a**) and coronal (**b**) view of the neck in a case of hanging: infiltrations of the soft tissues of the lower third of the neck (red circles)

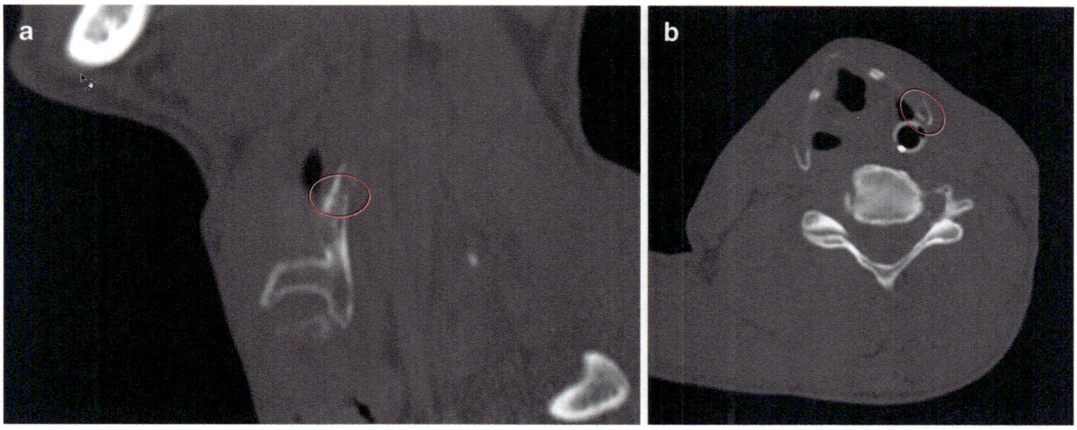

Fig. 4 Post-mortem CT-scan with sagittal (**a**) and axial (**b**) view of the skeleton of the neck in a case of hanging: fracture of the thyroid cartilage on the left side (red circle)

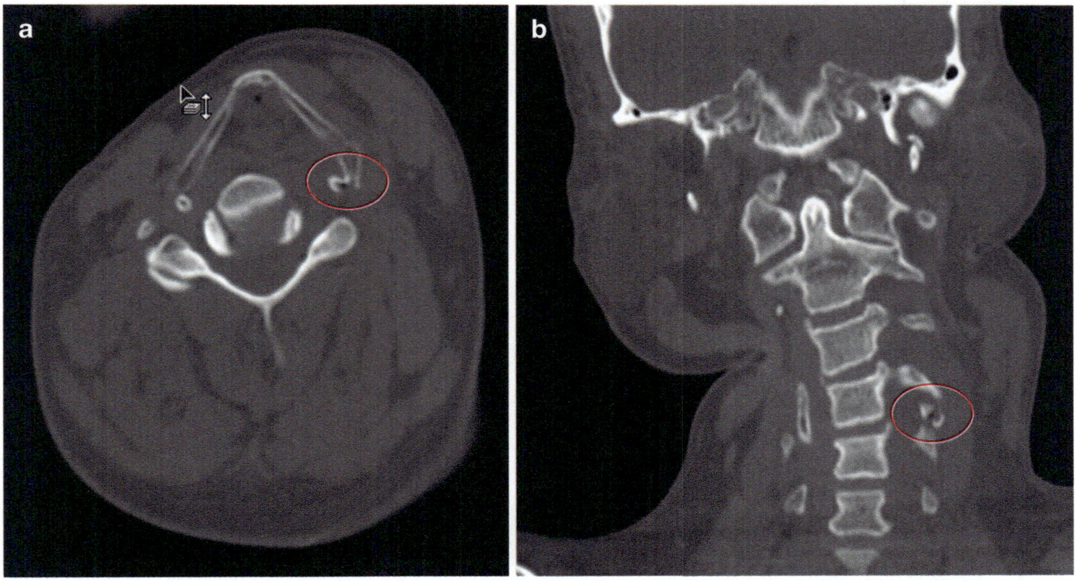

Fig. 5 Post-mortem CT-scan with axial (**a**) and coronal (**b**) view of the skeleton of the neck in a case of hanging: fracture of the thyroid cartilage on the left side (red circles)

structures located in the neck region (hyoid bone, cervical vertebras) and the cartilaginous structures of the larynx (thyroid, cricoid, and arytenoid cartilages) MDCT is the best technique (Poulsen and Simonsen 2007; Kempter et al. 2009; Jeffery 2010; Chevallier et al. 2013; Maiese et al. 2014) (Figs. 4 and 5). However, evaluation of the laryngeal skeleton in MRI permits to visualize fractures too (Ruder et al. 2013) (Fig. 6). Moreover, MRI allows visualizing edema of the soft tissues situated next to a fracture as also bone edema itself. However, it has to be kept in mind that small fractures of the bone and lesions of the cartilage can be missed in MDCT as in MRI (Matsuyama et al. 2006). Indeed, they can be shown only by a detailed anatomical dissection of the hyoid bone and the thyroid, cricoid, and arytenoid cartilages.

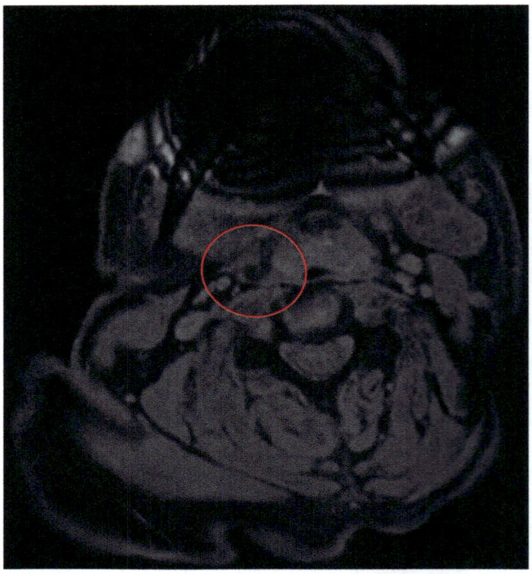

Fig. 6 Post-mortem MRI in 2D T1 DIXON Water with axial view of the neck in a case of hanging: fracture of the right great horn of the hyoid bone (red circle).

3D reconstructions of the laryngeal skeleton performed by MDCT can be used in court to visualize the lesions to someone who hasn't anatomical knowledge (Fig. 7). Furthermore, 3D reconstructions of the skin done by MDCT scan can be useful to identify the strangulation tool and to illustrate its position and/or the strangulation mark (Peschel et al. 2013).

Vascular lesions of the intima of the carotid artery and the jugular vein can be detected by MRI, depending however on their size; small intima tears can only be made visible by a detailed anatomical dissection.

However it's important to underline that not all typical signs of hanging and strangulation can be visualized by using forensic imaging tools (MDCT, MRI), such as findings which are located on the skin (petechia, bruises, abrasions) or others, as Tardieu spots and/or slight hemorrhagic infiltrations of the vertebral disc and of the ligaments.

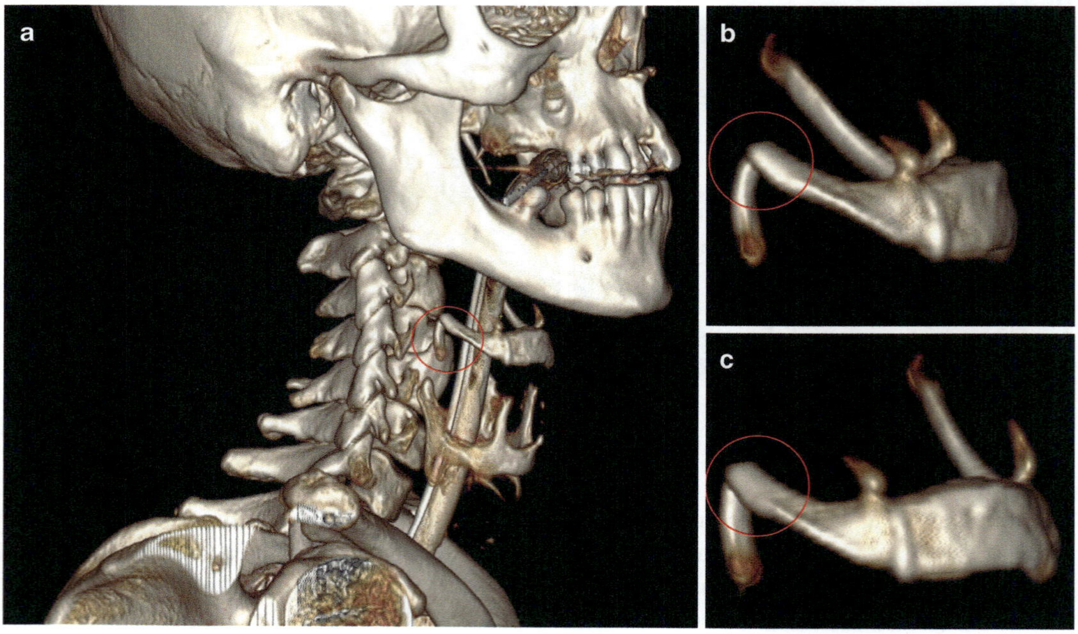

Fig. 7 3D reconstructions of a post-mortem CT-scan with visualization of the right side of the skeleton of the neck (**a**) and the hyoid bone from the right side (**b**) and the antero-right side (**c**) in a case of hanging with visualization of a fracture of the right great horn (red circles)

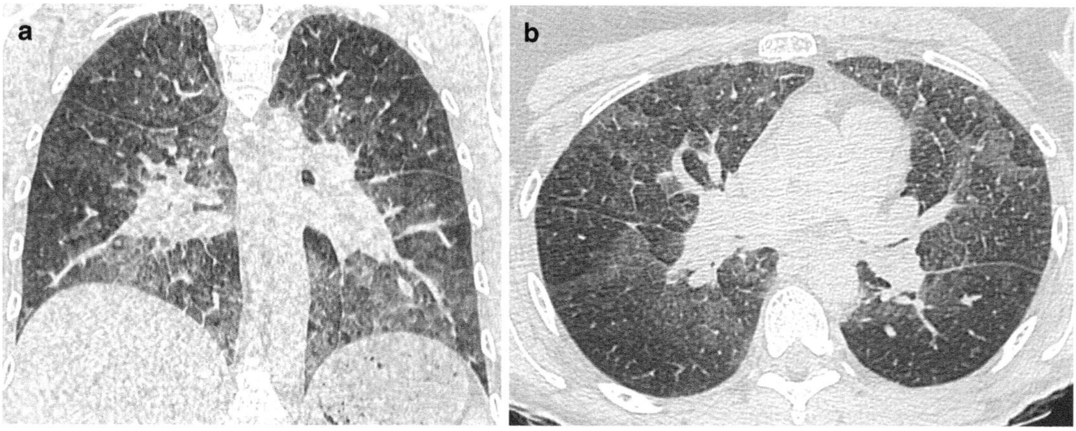

Fig. 8 Post-mortem CT-scan with coronal (**a**) and axial (**b**) view of the lung parenchyma of a victim of drowning with visualization of diffuse ground glass opacities, thickening of the inter-alveolar walls and overdistension of the lungs with almost overlapping on the anterior middle line (**b**)

3 Drowning

3.1 In the Living

In case of survived drowning the clinicians will evaluate if the near drowning is associated with a trauma, an intoxication, a convulsive crisis, or hypothermia. In case of trauma they will perform a MDCT in order to detect potential internal lesions, e.g., fractures, bleedings, etc. If the victim aspirated a big quantity of water, they may perform a MDCT of the thorax to evaluate the lungs. In cases of suspicion of hypoxic or ischemic lesions of the brain, MRI can be conducted.

3.2 In Post-mortem

In forensics, drowning is a diagnosis of exclusion. However the forensic pathologist will search for some specific signs which will support the diagnosis of drowning in the absence of another cause of death (natural, intoxication, etc.). The specific signs are foam protruding from the respiratory orifices, associated to frothy liquid in the airways, 3-phase sedimentation of the gastric content (sign of Wydler), overdistension of the lungs with overlapping anteriorly, associated to an emphysema aquosum in freshwater drowning and to an edema in salt-water drowning. Sub-pleural hemorrhages (Paltauf's spots), liquid in the paranasal-sinus, and hemorrhagic infiltrations of the mastoid cells and the neck, trunk, and upper extremities muscles are also described (Brinkmann 2004).

By using forensic imaging tools, especially MDCT, some of those signs can be found (Gluecker et al. 1999; Levy et al. 2007; Christe et al. 2008, 2010; Ambrosetti et al. 2012; Kawasumi et al. 2012, 2013; Van Hoyweghen et al. 2012; Raux et al. 2014). In MDCT frothy liquid can be seen in the airways (oral cavity, trachea, bronchi) as well as diffuse ground glass opacities in the pulmonary parenchyma associated with a thickening of the inter-alveolar walls (Fig. 8). However in freshwater drowning the overdistension of the lungs with overlapping on the middle line is more specific than the other signs. Moreover a liquid level can be observed in the paranasal sinuses and the stomach.

4 Obstruction of the Airways

An obstruction of the airways can be provocated by an external obstruction of the mouth and the nose as by a foreign body situated in the oral cavity, the larynx, the trachea, and the bronchia. An external obstruction of the mouth and the nose can be caused by, e.g., soft covering, hands, or other objects. Usually this form of obstruction doesn't leave specific forensic signs. At the external examination of the body abrasions or bruises can be detected on the skin of the face and the neck and during autopsy small hemorrhages can be seen in the soft tissues (mucosa of the oral cavity, subcutaneous fatty and muscle tissue of the face and the neck). As those findings are difficult to detect or not visible with radiological techniques, as MDCT and MRI, their contribution in these cases is limited (Oesterhelweg et al. 2009). However, small hemorrhagic infiltrations in the soft tissues will be rather visible with MRI than with MDCT.

In cases of obstruction of the superior and/or inferior airways by a foreign body, the foreign body may, depending on its manner and size, be visible with MDCT and/or MRI (Fig. 9). This is important as it permits to determine the exact location, the size, and the degree of expansion of the foreign body before manipulation of the body.

An acute pulmonary emphysema, associated to a foamy liquid, can be detected during autopsy in cases of external obstruction of the airways and respiratory orifices as also in cases of obstruction of the airways by a foreign body (bolus). This acute pulmonary emphysema can be also visible by MDCT (overdistension of the lungs with overlapping on the middle line, foamy liquid in the oral cavity, the larynx and the airways).

5 Compression of the Thoracic Cage

In cases of asphyxia related to a compression of the thoracic cage (e.g., car, train, or airplane accidents, crushes by big and hard objects, compression in a crowd), intensive congestion of the skin and the soft tissues (subcutaneous fatty and muscle tissue of the upper part of the body), associated to petechiae on the skin and hemorrhages of the soft tissues, can be observed. Rib or sternal fractures can be also detected.

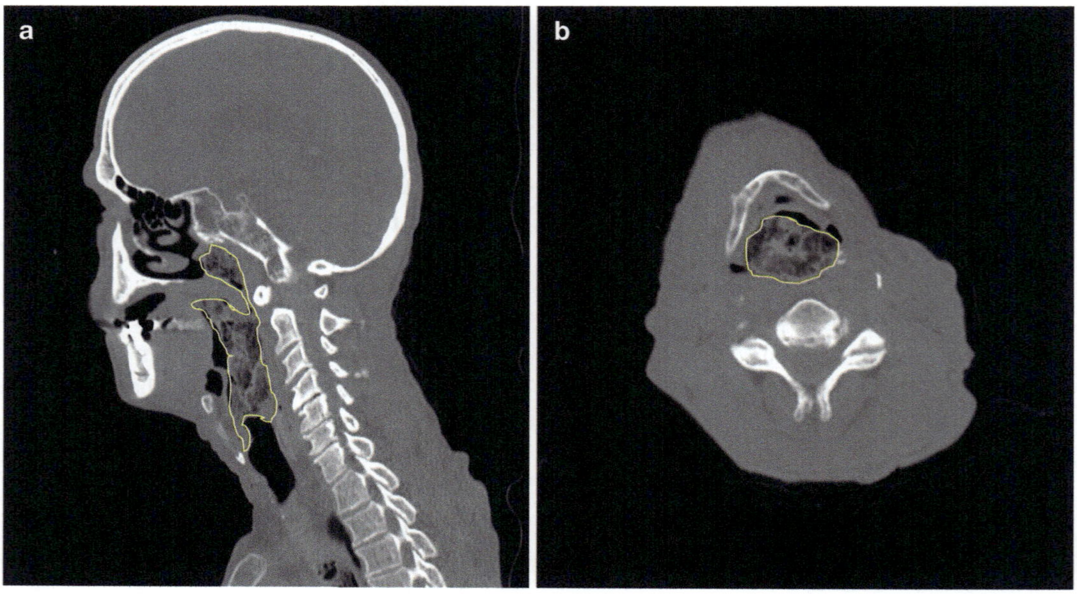

Fig. 9 Post-mortem CT-scan with sagittal (**a**) and axial (**b**) view of the neck of a corps presenting an obstruction of the superior and/or inferior airways by a foreign body (yellow marks)

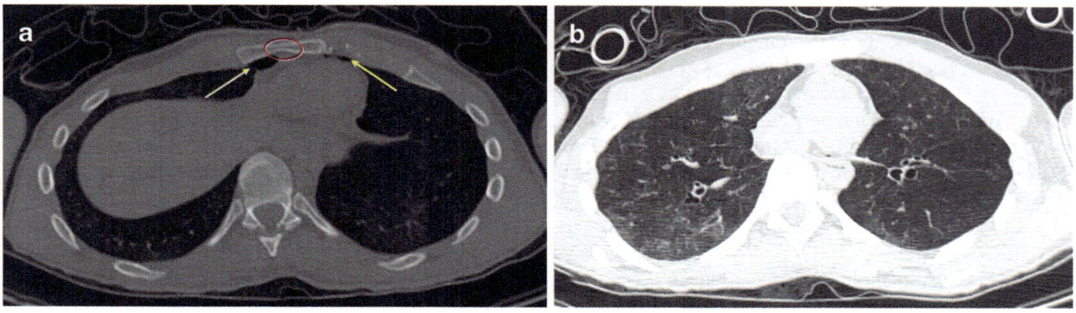

Fig. 10 Post-mortem CT-scan with axial view of the skeleton of the thoracic cage (**a**) and the lung parenchyma (**b**) of a victim of thoracic compression with visualization of a fracture of the corticalis of the sternum (red circle), a small pneumothorax on both sides (yellow arrows) and an overdistension of the lungs with almost overlapping on the anterior middle line (**b**)

The contribution of MDCT and MRI in this cases is limited like in cases of obstruction of the airways; however large hemorrhagic infiltrations of the soft tissues can be found, especially by MRI. A compression of the thoracic cage, associated with traumatic lesions, like rib or sternum fractures can be visualized by MDCT (Fig. 10 (a) Moreover, overdistension of the lungs with overlapping on the middle line (Fig. 10 (b) and contusion of the lung parenchyma may be visible by MDCT and MRI. Hemo- and pneumothorax are also detectable by radiological methods and may give an idea on their degree of expansion and their consequence on the cardio-respiratory system (compression and shift of the mediastinum, the heart, and the lungs).

6 Conclusion

Asphyxia plays an important role in forensic medicine. Despite the increasing importance of forensic imaging in the routine of forensic pathologists, the gold standard in cases of asphyxia remains the external and internal examination of the corpses and the forensic clinical examination of the victims. However forensic imaging techniques like MDCT and MRI may contribute to the investigation and documentation of the cases. MDCT is the best method to detect and to complete the overview of skeletal lesions. MRI instead is the technique of choice to evaluate the soft tissues. Both techniques can guide the forensic pathologist during autopsy or complete the examination in the living.

References

Ambrosetti MC, Barbiani C, El-Dalati G, Pellini E, Raniero D, De Salvia A, Pozzi MR (2012) Virtual autopsy using multislice computed tomography in forensic medical diagnosis of drowning. Radiol Med 118:679–687

Aneesh B, Singhal M, Topcuoglu A, Koroshetz WJ (2002) Diffusion MRI in three types of anoxic encephalopathy. J Neurol Sci 196:37–40

Azmak D (2006) "Asphyxial deaths". A retrospective study and review of the literature. Am J Forensic Med Pathol 27(2):134–144

Brinkmann B (2004) Ersticken. In: Brinkmann B, Madea B (eds) Handbuch gerichtliche Medizin. Springer, New York, pp 699–796

Bruguier C, Genet P, Zerlauth J-B, Dédouit F, Grimm J, Meuli R, Fracasso T, Grabherr S (2019) Neck-MRI experience for investigation of survived strangulation victims. Forensic Sci Res 5(2):113–118

Chevallier C, Doenz F, Vaucher P, Palmiere C, Dominguez A, Binaghi S, Mangin P, Grabherr S (2013) Postmortem computed tomography angiography vs. conventional autopsy: advantages and inconveniences of each method. Int J Legal Med 127:981–989

Christe A, Aghayev E, Jackowski C, Thali MJ, Vock P (2008) Drowning post mortem imaging findings by computed tomography. Eur Radiol 18:283–290

Christe A, Flach P, Ross S, Spendlove D, Bolliger S, Vock P, Thali MJ (2010) Clinical radiology and postmortem imaging (Virtopsy) are not the same: specific and unspecific post-mortem signs. Leg Med (Tokyo) 12:215–222

Christe A, Oesterhelweg L, Ross S, Spendlove D, Bolliger S, Vock P, Thali MJ (2010) Can MRI of the neck com-

pete with clinical findings in assessing danger to life for survivors of manual strangulation? A statistical analysis. Leg Med (Tokyo) 12(5):228–232
Christe A, Thoeny H, Ross S, Spendlove D, Tshering D, Bolliger S, Grabherr S, Thali MJ, Vock P, Oesterhelweg L (2009) Life-threatening versus non-life-threatening manual strangulation: are there appropriate criteria for MR imaging of the neck? Eur Radiol 19(8):1882–1889
DiMaio VJ, DiMaio D (2001) Asphyxia. In: Geberth VJ (ed) Forensic pathology, 2nd edn. CRC Press, Boca Raton, FL, pp 229–277
Dirnhofer R, Thali M, Vock P (2009) The virtopsy approach: 3D optical and radiological scanning and reconstruction in forensic medicine. CRC Press, Boca Raton, FL
Garetier M, Deloire L, Dédouit D, Dumousset E, Saccardy C, Ben SD (2017) Postmortem computed tomography findings in suicide victims. Diagn Interv Imaging 98(2):101–112
Gascho D, Heimer J, Tappero C, Schaerli S (2019) Relevant findings on postmortem CT and postmortem MRI in hanging, ligature strangulation and manual strangulation and their additional value compared to autopsy—a systematic review. Forensic Sci Med Pathol 15(1):84–92
Gluecker T, Capasso P, Schnyder P, Gudinchet F, Schaller MD, Revelly JP, Chiolero R, Vock P, Wicky S (1999) Clinical and radiologic features of pulmonary oedema. Radiographics 19:1507–1531
Grabherr S, Egger C, Vilarino R, Campana L, Jotterand M, Dedouit F (2017) Modern post-mortem imaging: an update on recent developments. Forensic Sci Res 2(2):52–64
Groenendaal F, de Vries LS (2017) Fifty years of brain imaging in neonatal encephalopathy following perinatal asphyxia. Pediatr Res 81(1–2):150–155
Hori A, Hirose G, Kataoka S, Tsukada K, Furui K, Tonami H (1991) Delayed postanoxic encephalopathy after strangulation. Serial neuroradiological and neurochemical studies. Arch Neurol 48(8):871–874
Imamura K, Akifuji Y, Kamitani H, Nakashima K (2010) Delayed postanoxic encephalopathy with visual field disturbance after strangulation: a case report. Brain Nerve 62(6):621–624
Jalalzadeh H, Giannakopoulos GF, Berger F, Fronczek J, van de Goot FR, Reijnders UJ, Zuidema WP (2015) Post-mortem imaging compared with autopsy in trauma victims—a systematic review. Forensic Sci Int 257:29–48
Jeffery AJ (2010) The role of computed tomography in adult post-mortem examinations: an overview. Diagn Histopathol 16:546–551
Kalita J, Mishra VN, Misra UK, Gupta RK (2002) Clinicoradiological observation in three patients with suicidal hanging. J Neurol Sci 198:21–24
Kawasumi Y, Kawabata T, Sugai Y, Usui A, Hosokai Y, Sato M, Saito H, Ishibashi T, Hayashizaki Y, Funayama M (2012) Assessment of the relationship between drowning and fluid accumulation in the paranasal sinuses on post mortem computed tomography. Eur J Radiol 81:3953–3955
Kawasumi Y, Kawabata T, Sugai Y, Usui A, Hosokai Y, Sato M, Saito H, Ishibashi T, Hayashizaki Y, Funayama M (2013) Diagnosis of drowning using post-mortem computed tomography based on the volume and density of fluid accumulation in the maxillary and sphenoid sinuses. Eur J Radiol 82:E562–E566
Kempter M, Ross S, Spendlove D, Flach PM, Preiss U, Thali MJ, Bolliger SA (2009) Post-mortem imaging of laryngohyoid fractures in strangulation incidents: first results. Leg Med (Tokyo) 11:267–271
Kiani SH, Simes DC (2000) Delayed bilateral internal carotid artery thrombosis following accidental strangulation. Br J Anaesth 84(4):521–524
Levy A, Harcke HT, Getz JM, Mallak CT, Caruso JL, Pearse L, Frazier AA, Galvin JR (2007) Virtual autopsy: two- and three-dimensional multidetector CT findings in drowning with autopsy comparison. Radiology 243:862–868
Maiese A, Gitto L, dell'Aquila M, Bolino G. (2014) When the hidden features become evident: the usefulness of PMCT in a strangulation-related death. Leg Med (Tokyo) 16(6):364–366
Malek AM, Higashida RT, Halbach VV, Dowd CF, Phatouros CC, Lempert TE, Meyers PM, Smith WS, Stoney R (2000) Patient presentation, angiographic features and treatment of strangulation-induced bilateral dissection of the cervical internal carotid artery. Report of three cases. J Neurosurg 92(3):481–487
Matsuyama T, Okuchi K, Seki T, Higuchi T, Ito S, Makita D, Watanabe T, Murao Y (2006) Magnetic resonance images in hanging. Resuscitation 69(2):343–345. Epub 2006 Feb
Miyamoto O, Auer RN (2000) Hypoxia, hyperoxia, ischemia, and brain necrosis. Neurology 54:362–371
Oesterhelweg L, Bolloger SA, Thalo MJ, Ross S (2009) Voirtopsy: post-mortem imaging of laryngeal foreign bodies. Arch Pathol Lab Med 133(5):806–810
Peschel O, Szeimies U, Vollmar C, Kirchhoff S (2013) Postmortem 3-D reconstruction of skull gunshot injuries. Forensic Sci Int 233:45–50
Plattner T, Bolliger S, Zollinger U (2005) Forensic assessment of survived strangulation. Forensic Sci Int 153(2-3):202–207
Poulsen K, Simonsen J (2007) Computed tomography as a routine connection with medico-legal autopsies. Forensic Sci Int 171:190–197
Raux C, Saval F, Rouge D, Telmon N, Dedouit F (2014) Diagnosis of drowning using post-mortem computed tomography—state of the art. Arch Med Sadowej Kryminol 64(2):59–75
Ruder TD, Thali MJ, Hatch GM (2013) Essentials of forensic post-mortem MR imaging in adults. Br J Radiol 87:20130567
Saukko P, Knight B (2004) Suffocation and asphyxia. In: Ueberberg A (ed) Knight's forensic pathology, 3rd edn. Arnold Publishers, London, pp 352–367
Schmitt-Sody M, Kurz S, Reiser M, Kanz KG, Kirchhoff C, Peschel O, Kirchhoff S (2016) Analysis of death

in major trauma: value of prompt post mortem computed tomography (pmCT) in comparison to office hour autopsy. Scand J Trauma Resusc Emerg Med 29:24–38

Sethi PK, Sethi NK, Torgovnick J, Arsura E (2012) Delayed left anterior and middle cerebral artery haemorrhagic infarctions after attempted strangulation: a case report. Am J Forensic Med Pathol 33(1):105–106

Spitz WU (2006) Asphyxia. In: Spitz WU, Spitz DJ (eds) Spitz and Fisher's medicolegal investigation of death: guidelines for the application of pathology to crime investigation, 4th edn. Charles CT, Springfield, IL, pp 783–845

Thali MJ, Viner MD, Brogdon BG (2010) Brogdon's forensic radiology, 2nd edn. CRC Press, Boca Raton, FL

Van Hoyweghen A, Jacobs W, Op de Beeck B, Parizel P. 2012. Can post mortem CT reliably distinguish between drowning and non-drowning asphyxiation? A prospective study. Abstract. 1st Congress of the International Society of Forensic Radiology and Imaging

Vilke GM, Chan TC (2011) Evaluation and management for carotid dissection in patients presenting after choking or strangulation. J Emerg Med 40(3):355–358. https://doi.org/10.1016/j.jemermed.2010.02.018. Epub 2010 Apr 3

Yen K, Thali MJ, Aghayev E, Jackowski C, Schweitzer W, Boesch C, Vock P, Dirnhofer R, Sonnenschein M (2005) Strangulation signs: initial correlation of MRI, MSCT, and forensic neck findings. J Magn Reson Imaging 22(4):501–510

Yen K, Vock P, Christe A, Scheurer E, Plattner T, Schön C, Aghayev E, Jackowski C, Beutler V, Thali MJ, Dirnhofer R (2007) Clinical forensic radiology in strangulation victims: forensic expertise based on magnetic resonance imaging (MRI) findings. Int J Legal Med 121(2):115–123

Zabel TA, Slomine B, Brady K, Christensen J (2005) Neuropsychological profile following suicide attempt by hanging: two adolescent case reports. Child Neuropsychol 11(4):373–388

Child Abuse, a Post-mortem Forensic Perspective

Rick R. van Rijn, Simon G. F. Robben, Judith Fronczek, and Willemijn M. Klein

Contents

R. R. van Rijn (✉)
Department of Radiology and Nuclear Medicine, Emma Children's Hospital—Amsterdam UMC, University of Amsterdam, Amsterdam, The Netherlands

Department of Forensic Medicine, Netherlands Forensic Institute, The Hague, The Netherlands
e-mail: r.r.vanrijn@amsterdamumc.nl

S. G. F. Robben
Department of Radiology, Maastricht University Medical Center, Maastricht, The Netherlands

J. Fronczek
Department of Forensic Medicine, Victorian Institute of Forensic Medicine Southbank, Southbank, Australia

W. M. Klein
Department of Medical Imaging, Radboud University Medical Center, Nijmegen, The Netherlands

© Springer Nature Switzerland AG 2022

F. Dedouit et al. (eds.), *Forensic Imaging*, Medical Radiology Diagnostic Imaging,
https://doi.org/10.1007/978-3-030-83352-7_9

1 Introduction

Child abuse is defined by the WHO as all forms of physical and/or emotional ill-treatment, sexual abuse, neglect or negligent treatment or commercial or other exploitation, resulting in actual or potential harm to the child's health, survival, development or dignity in the context of a relationship of responsibility, trust or power (World Health Organisation 2016). It is a world-wide problem that affects all societal levels and in its most severe form can result in the death of a child.

From a forensic radiological perspective both imaging in living and deceased children is of importance. In daily paediatric forensic radiological practice the mainstay of radiology deals with the living child. This chapter will, however, solely focus on post-mortem imaging in children and its relation to child abuse.

For the sake of clarity the chapter is divided into foetal, neonatal and infant/child post-mortem imaging. Part of this chapter is based on the newly developed evidence-based Dutch guideline for clinical post-mortem imaging. This clinical guideline was developed by a working group, consisting of radiologists, pathologists, and medical specialists, in collaboration with the Dutch knowledge institute of medical specialists (Klein et al. 2018). Although the guideline is dedicated to clinical post-mortem imaging, most aspects of it can be used in the field of forensic medicine and radiology as well.

2 Dutch Clinical Post-mortem Imaging Guideline

With the decline in clinical autopsies in the last decades in combination with the persisting urge to know the cause and manner of death, post-mortem radiology has found its place in both forensic and clinical post-mortem investigations. The diagnostic value of post-mortem radiology in adults in a forensic setting is known. However, scientific studies in the relatively new field of paediatric post-mortem radiology in the clinical setting are yet limited and thus the evidence for the diagnostic value of post-mortem radiology is limited as well (Thayyil et al. 2013; Arthurs et al. 2017; van Rijn et al. 2017; Sonnemans et al. 2018; Shelmerdine et al. 2019a, e). It seems that post-mortem MRI (PMMRI), as tested in a clinical setting, has a high diagnostic performance especially in foetuses and neonates and that in these cases PMMRI is superior to post-mortem CT (PMCT) scanning (Fig. 1a, b) (Thayyil et al. 2013). In older children PMCT seems to perform good, especially for cranial and musculoskeletal injuries and lesions, but less so in case of cardiac or abdominal diseases where autopsy clearly has higher diagnostic value (van Rijn et al. 2017; Shelmerdine et al. 2019a, b). The combination of post-mortem radiology and autopsy results in the highest diagnostic yield (Ampanozi et al. 2017).

Despite the use of post-mortem imaging there is a paucity of guidelines on when and how to use post-mortem imaging. To encourage and improve the implementation of clinical post-mortem radiology and to achieve a standard level of post-mortem care in the Netherlands, an evidence-based imaging guideline was developed. Although specifically developed with a clinical setting in mind, this guideline can be used for forensic imaging as well and therefore has served as the basis for this chapter (Klein et al. 2018). With respect to imaging protocols there is more literature available. For CT the European Society of Paediatric Radiology (ESPR) and International Society for Forensic Radiology and Imaging (ISFRI) have published a guideline (Table 1) for MRI the MaRIAS study has an extensive protocol (Table 2) (Thayyil et al. 2013; Shelmerdine et al. 2019d).

The guideline doesn't specify who should be in the lead in this process. However, in line with the statement joint statement of the British Neuropathological Society and International Society for Forensic and Radiology Imaging, which was solely focused on neuropathology, we feel that forensic pathologists should be in the lead of the case, i.e. they are responsible for post-mortem imaging referrals and assessing and integrating results of ancillary tests. In the final pathology report the cause of death should, based on all findings, be decided by the forensic pathologist.

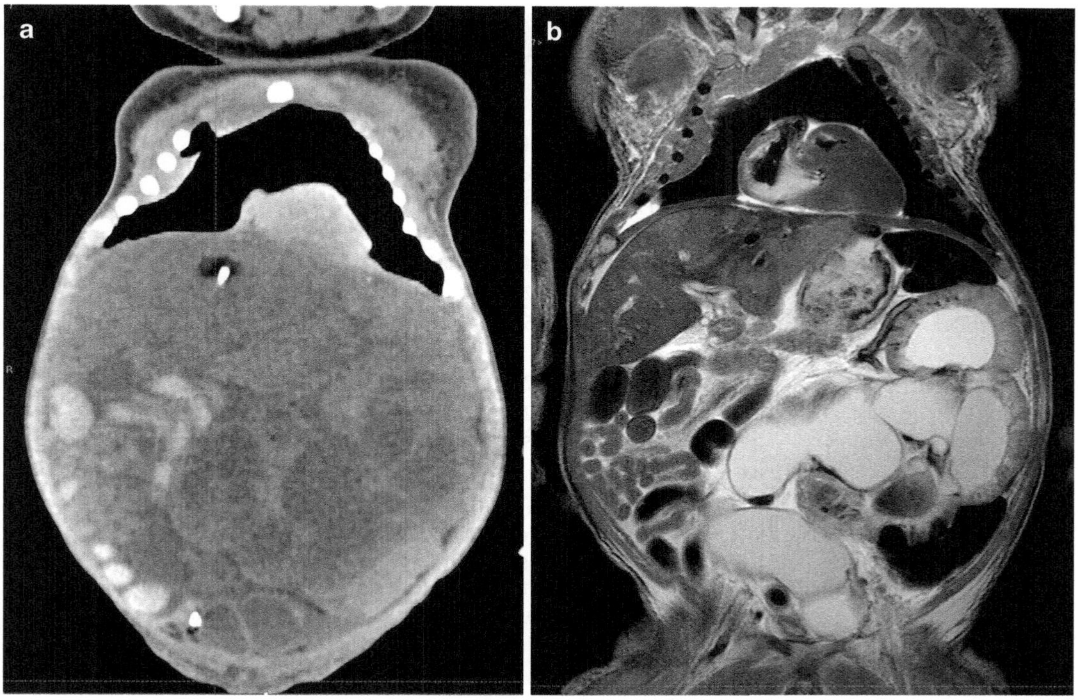

Fig. 1 Post-mortem foetal imaging. Coronal CT reconstruction (**a**) versus MRI (**b**) demonstrates the superiority of MRI in this child with massive dilatation of renal collecting system and ureter

Table 1 PMCT protocol as proposed by the European Society of Paediatric Radiology (ESPR) and International Society for Forensic Radiology and Imaging (ISFRI)

Image acquisition	
Coverage	Whole body (vertex to extremities)
Kilovoltage peak (kVp)	120
Milliampere seconds (mAs)	200–299
Pitch	0.5–0.8
Slice thickness (mm)	≤0.75
Energy source	Single source
Dose modulation	Off
Scan field of view (SFOV) (mm)	Adjust to patient size (small as possible)
Detector collimator (mm)	0.5–1.0
Rotation time (s)	1.0
Matrix	512 × 512
Kernel/filter/algorithm	Soft tissue and bone (whole body) Brain (brain coverage) Lung (thoracic coverage)
Reformats	Coronal, sagittal, volume rendering

3 Foetuses and Neonates

3.1 Post-mortem Imaging Guideline

In case of foetal demise in utero, termination of pregnancy, or perinatal demise, MRI is the modality of choice for non-invasive imaging of the head and body. PMMRI has a high diagnostic value for intracranial, spinal, thoracic, and abdominal structures. If skeletal abnormalities such as a skeletal dysplasia are suspected, a skeletal survey ('babygram') is the modality of choice in foetuses up to approximately 24 weeks of gestational age. Above this age a more extensive skeletal survey, where at least detailed imaging of the extremities should be achieved, is advised. Although there are several guidelines for skeletal surveys in general the guideline as specified by the Royal College of Radiology and the Society and College of Radiographers is advised;

Table 2 PMMRI protocol adapted from the MaRIAS protocol (Thayyil et al. 2011)

Sequence	Voxel size	TA (min)	TR (ms)	TE (ms)	Flip angle°	Averages
Brain imaging						
3 D CISS	0.6 × 0.6 × 0.06 mm	13.5	9.2	4.6	70	4
3D Flash T1W	**1 × 1 × 1 mm**	**5.4**	**11**	**4.9**	**15**	**3**
2D Destir T2W	**0.4 × 0.4 × 0.4 mm**	**13.5**	**5460**	**14,115**	**150**	**6**
GE (Haem)	0.5 × 0.4 × 4 mm	6.3	800	26	20	4
Spine						
2D T2-W TSE (children only)	**1 × 1 × 3 mm**	**5.43**	**3050**	**109**	**170**	**3**
3D CISS (foetus only)	**0.6 × 0.6 × 1 mm**	**4.2**	**9.1**	**4.5**	**70**	**8**
3D T1-W flash	0.6 × 0.6 × 1 mm	3.5	11	5.3	15	10
Body						
T2 W TSE	**0.8 × 0.8 × 0.8 mm**	**6.2**	**3500**	**276**		**2**
3D CISS	0.8 × 0.8 × 0.8 mm	5.2	5.2	2.3	54	3
3D T1W VIBE	0.8 × 0.8 × 0.8 mm	5.5	5.9	2.4	25	8
3D CISS (cardiac)	0.6 × 0.6 × 0.6 mm	29	5.6	2.5	54	10

TA time for acquisition, *TR* relaxation time, *TE* echo time, *ms* milli second, *min* minutes, *CISS* Constructive Interference Steady State, *GE* gradient echo, *TSE* turbo spin echo, DWI: diffusion-weighted imaging
With this protocol total scan time is about 90 min in foetuses and 60 min in children. In order to perform a PMMRI in a shorter time, we have highlighted in bold those sequences that we feel are essential for an adequate study. A gradient echo of the brain could be reserved for those cases where on antenatal ultrasound or on T1 and/or T2 sequences brain haemorrhages are seen

this guideline has been adopted by the European Society for Paediatric Radiology (Offiah et al. 2014; The Royal College of Radiologists (RCR) and the Society and College of Radiographers (SCoR) 2017; Wootton-Gorges et al. 2017; Born et al. 2020) (Table 3). In a forensic post-mortem setting high-quality detailed imaging is important; therefore we advise to obtain individual radiographs of the individual long bones. This is in contrast to the guideline which specifies that in young infants the whole extremity can be imaged on a single radiograph.

A PMCT scan is, compared to PMMRI, less diagnostic for the organs in foetuses and neonates due to the lack of intra-abdominal fat and organ contrast, but could be used for three-dimensional imaging of skeletal abnormalities such as dysplasia and fractures (Fig. 2a, b). There have been a few paediatric case reports but no large series; therefore there is little evidence for the use of post-mortem ultrasonography and PMCT angiography, although both could be advantageous in specific cases (Wozniak et al. 2015; Sarda-Quarello et al. 2016; Grabherr et al. 2018; Mokrane et al. 2018; Shelmerdine et al. 2019a, b, c).

Post-mortem ultrasonography (PMUS) is less expensive however more labour intensive.

Table 3 Adapted skeletal survey based on the guideline according to the Royal College of Radiology and the Society and College of Radiographers (The Royal College of Radiologists (RCR) and the Society and College of Radiographers (SCoR) 2017)

Skull	AP Lateral
Cervical spine	At this age, AP views of the cervical spine are hardly ever diagnostic and should only be made at the request of the radiologist.
Thorax	AP, to include the shoulders Both obliques (to include all the ribs, left and right) Lateral to include the whole spine
Abdomen, lumbosacral spine, pelvis	AP abdomen and pelvis
Upper extremities	AP humerus (including the shoulder and elbow) AP forearm (including the elbow and wrist) Coned lateral elbow Coned lateral wrist
Lower extremities	AP femur AP tibia and fibula AP knee Coned lateral knee AP ankle Coned lateral ankle
Hands	PA hand and wrist
Feet	AP/PA

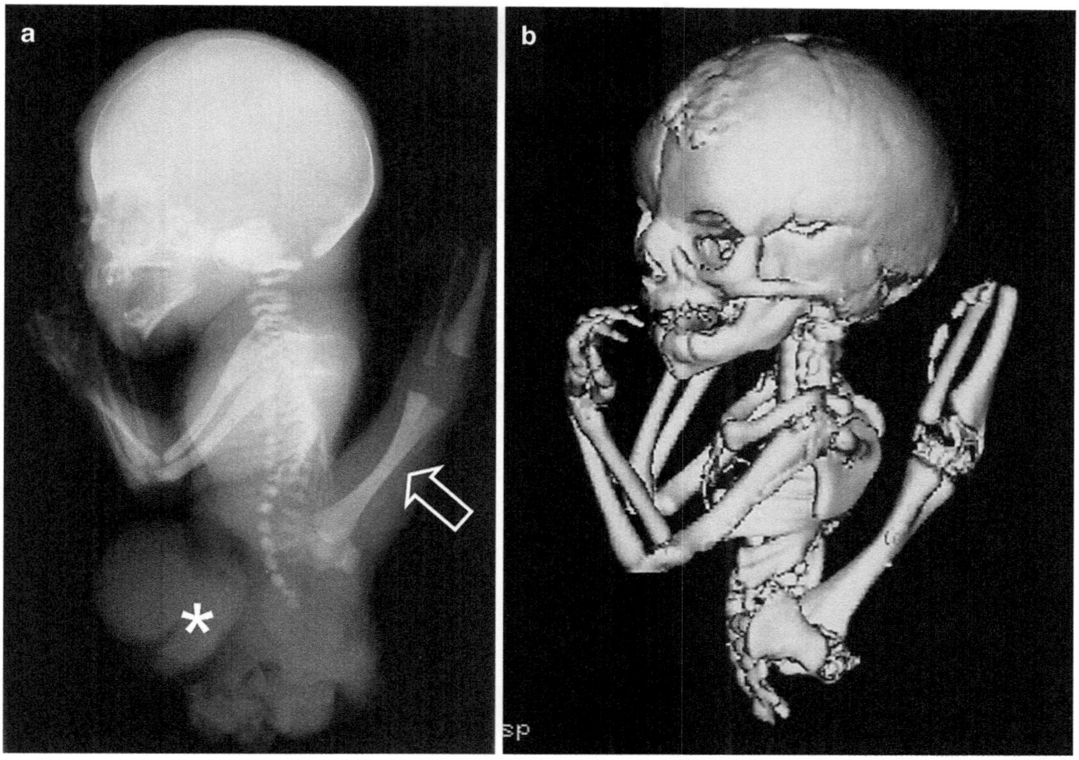

Fig. 2 Post-mortem lateral babygram of a foetus with complex deformation (limb body wall complex (asterisk) with sirenomelia (arrow)) (**a**). 3D-CT demonstrates the bony abnormalities to a better advantage (**b**)

Although not widely studied, there have been some publications regarding it as a tool for post-mortem imaging (Furness et al. 1989; Prodhomme et al. 2015). Given the small sample in both studies the level of evidence is low, and given the fact that the use in a forensic setting has not been studied, its use cannot be advocated in post-mortem forensic radiology (Charlier et al. 2013).

The Dutch guideline describes several scenarios and the corresponding most advantageous radiological imaging, taking into account the prenatal ultrasonography results and whether or not there is permission for autopsy of the body and brain. In the Dutch clinical guideline several categories of foetal demise were defined (Fig. 3a, b).

- Foetal demise prior to birth, with a normal antenatal US at 20 weeks and no structural anomalies detected during the ultrasound exam on which intrauterine death has been diagnosed. There is a limited value of a PMMRI.
- Foetal demise prior to birth, with an abnormal antenatal US at 20 weeks or structural anomalies detected during the ultrasound exam on which intrauterine death has been diagnosed. Autopsy is to be preferred and PMMRI should be advised, especially in case of brain/spine anomalies.
- Foetal demise during birth, without previously known or suspected abnormalities. In these cases a full workup consisting of an autopsy, PMMRI and skeletal survey should be performed.
- Termination of pregnancy, Autopsy is to be preferred and PMMRI should be advised. Especially in case of brain/spine anomalies. A babygram (up to a gestational age of 24 weeks) or skeletal survey should be performed in case of suspected skeletal abnormalities.

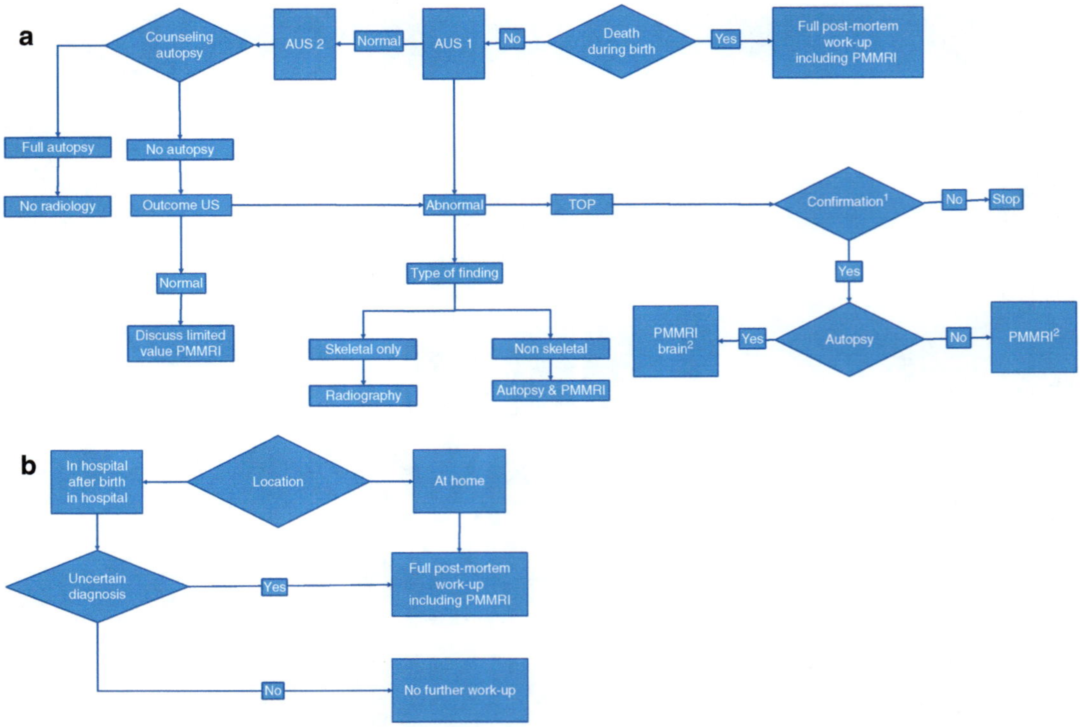

Fig. 3 (**a**) Flowchart of the Dutch clinical guideline for foetal post-mortem imaging (AUS 1 = antenatal US at 20 weeks, AUS 2 = antenatal US on which intrauterine death is diagnosed, [1] = Confirmation of AUS findings wanted by the parents, [2] = In case of skeletal anomalies also a skeletal survey or babygram). (**b**) Flowchart of the Dutch clinical guideline for neonatal post-mortem imaging (uncertain diagnosis includes uncertainty about impact of clinical treatment)

From a forensic perspective groups 1–3 are in rare cases relevant and the same accounts for group 4 in countries where termination of pregnancy is legalised. These cases will therefore not be discussed in depth in this chapter.

In case of neonatal demise there are two categories that were defined:

- Demise during hospital admission, with the baby born in the hospital.
  - In these cases only in case of an unclear diagnosis, questions related to medical treatment or the clinical course autopsy and PMMRI should be advised.
- Demise during hospital admission, with the baby born outside the hospital, or demise outside the hospital.
  - In these cases autopsy and PMMRI should be advised.

From a forensic perspective category 1, in cases where there is a question related to medical treatment, and category 2 are of relevance. In the first a medical error and in the second a potential non-natural cause of death could be an indication to perform a medico-legal autopsy with the relevant imaging. In the latter category PMCT could replace PMMRI, as a full legal autopsy, including brain and eye pathology, will be performed. There is no evidence that in these cases PMMRI will add significant medico-legal information.

3.2 Imaging Interpretation

As stated above forensic imaging is mainly limited to cases of neonaticide, i.e. the murder of a foetus/neonate within 24 h after birth (Resnick 1970). Although in rare cases the murder of a pregnant woman can lead to a subsequent forensic autopsy of the foetus.

3.3 Conventional Radiography

In all forensic cases radiography should be performed. This not only to rule out underlying diseases/disorders but also to rule out fractures and to assess gestational age (Fig. 4). With respect to gestational age the normal development, according to textbooks, can be assessed within certain limits. This however has a certain inter-observer variance and may therefore be of limited value in the forensic setting. A widely used method to assess gestational age is to measure the length of the femur; this can be done on calibrated radiographs of the femur. There are several methods and tables, based on different normative populations (Scheuer et al. 1980; Adalian et al. 2001; Johnsen et al. 2006; Okland et al. 2012; Choi et al. 2016). It is important to note that most normal values are specific for the geographic region and ethnicity for which the data was obtained. In reporting the estimated gestational age it is therefore important to specifically state which normal values were used. Assessing gestational age on a single parameter should be done with care as it can be difficult, if not impossible.

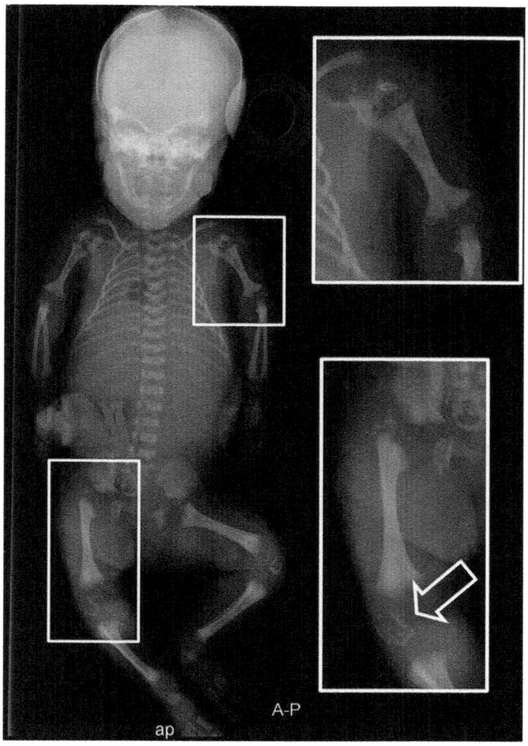

Fig. 4 Babygram of a termination of pregnancy due to skeletal anomalies seen on antenatal ultrasonography. The skeletal findings, shortening of the humerus and femora (see inserts) and stippling of the cartilage (arrow), are in keeping with rhizomelic chondrodysplasia punctata (OMIM #215100)

3.4 Post-mortem CT and MRI

In contrast to the clinical setting PMCT can play an important role in forensic foetal imaging, especially in those cases where a foetus is found long after demise and decomposition has begun (Fig. 5a, b) (Sieswerda-Hoogendoorn et al. 2013). In these cases post-mortem tissue decay can be so extensive that MRI of the soft tissues will not be of additional value. PMCT can be of aid in the assessment of skeletal development and consequently gestational age. The autopsy can, in these far decomposed cases and based on PMCT findings, be limited to rigorous external inspection and tissue sampling for DNA (Fig. 6a–c).

In all other cases PMMRI is preferred over PMCT. To date all studies into the value of PMMRI in foetuses (as in all age categories that will be discussed in this chapter) have been conducted in a clinical setting. The largest study is the Magnetic Resonance Imaging Autopsy Study (MaRIAS) which included 277 foetuses (185 foetuses 24 weeks gestation or less and 92 older foetuses) (Thayyil et al. 2011). In this study the value of PMMRI, read by a team of experienced and subspecialised paediatric radiologists, was compared to a complete autopsy, performed by experienced paediatric pathologists. There was also comparison to a limited autopsy but that is not relevant to a forensic setting, as a full autopsy will always be required. In this setting the concordance was, respectively, 42.7% ($N = 79$, 95% CI 35.8–49.9) and 63.0% ($N = 58$, 95% CI 52.8–72.2) (Table 4) (Thayyil et al. 2013). In the older foetuses only 4% of PMMRI studies were not diagnostic.

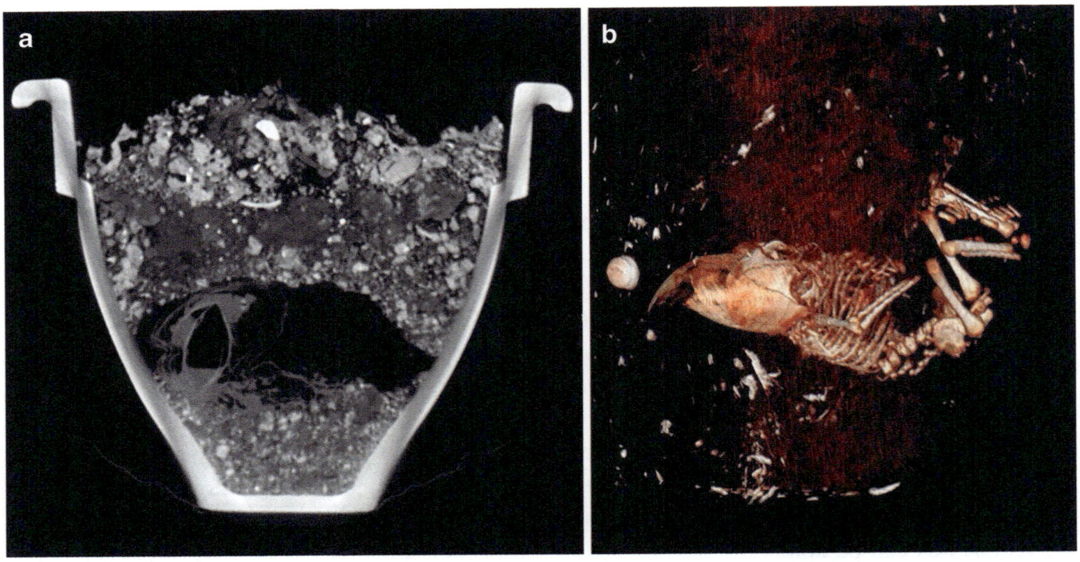

Fig. 5 Foetal body hidden in a pot covered with soil. High kV CT scan reveals the remains (**a**) and 3D reconstruction (**b**) discloses the bones for measurement and analysis

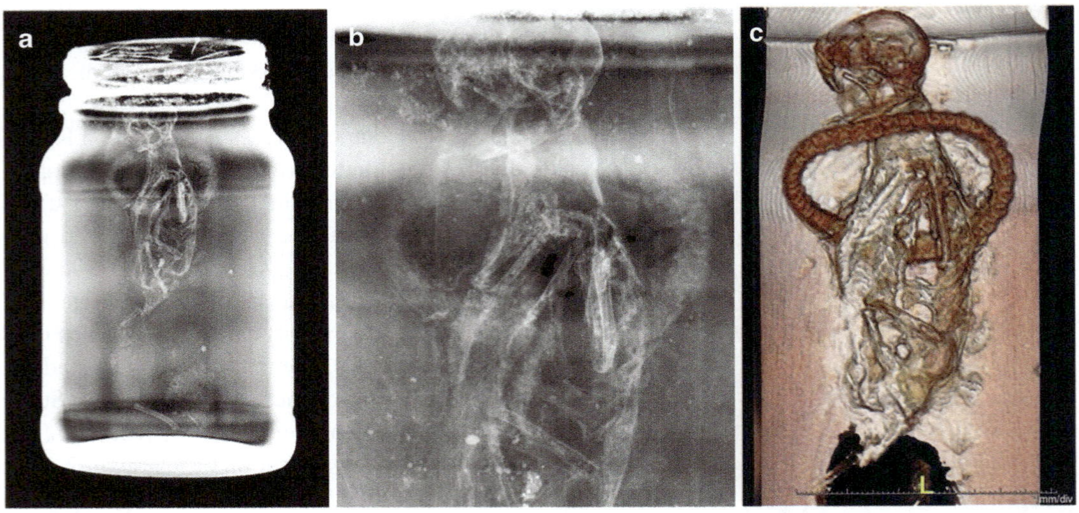

Fig. 6 Accidental finding on a playground. Suspected foetal remains in a sealed glass jar. Conventional radiograph with mammography technique (**a**) shows multiple bones and a skull, better seen on detail image (**b**). Analysis with 3DCT shows a non-human skeleton (**c**) (scan parameters: 140 kV, 212 mA, slice thickness 0.4 mm). Visual external inspection revealed it was a bird. Based on the imaging findings DNA analysis was cancelled

Table 4 PMMRI: comparison with full autopsy for detection of major pathological abnormalities related to death (Thayyil et al. 2013)

	≤24 weeks (*n* = 185)	>24 weeks (*n* = 92)
Concordant	79 (42.7%, 35.8–49.9)	58 (63.0%, 52.8–72.2)
Non-diagnostic	64 (35%)	4 (4%)
Apparent false-positives	2 (1%)	2 (2%)
Undetected abnormality	40 (22%)	28 (30%)

Table 5 Diagnostic accuracy in foetuses PMCT and PMMRI versus autopsy (Arthurs et al. 2016)

		ND	TP/FP	FN/TN	Sensitivity (%) (95%BI)	Specificity (%) (95%BI)
F < 24 weeks (*n* = 35)	PMCT	14	5/0	13/3	27,8 (12,5; 50,9)	100% (43,9; 100)
	PMMRI	4	10/0	15/6	40,0 (23,4; 59,3)	100% (61,0; 100)
F > 24 weeks (*n* = 18)	PMCT	4	4/0	4/6	50,0 (21,5; 78,5)	100% (61,0; 100)
	PMMRI	0	5/0	5/8	50,0 (27,3; 76,3)	100% (67,6; 100)

ND non-diagnostic, *TP* true-positive, *FP* false-positive, *FN* false-negative, *TN* true-negative

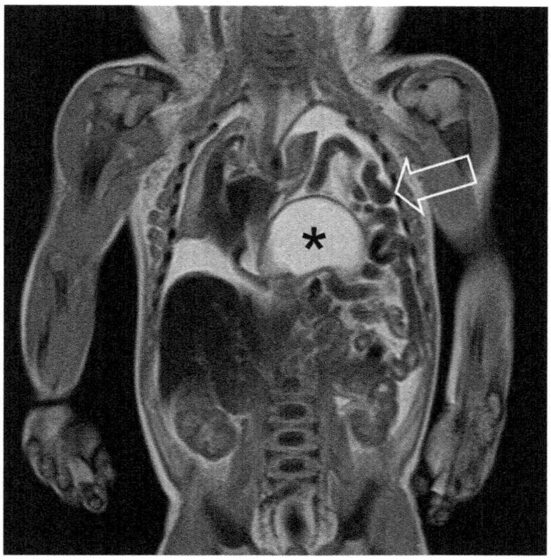

Fig. 7 Termination of pregnancy at a gestational age of 23 weeks. Prenatal ultrasonography showed a congenital diaphragmatic hernia. Post-mortem MRI confirmed this diagnosis. On the left side bowel loops (arrow) and the stomach (asterisk) are visible within the thorax

A sub-study (N=53) by Arthurs et al. where the PMCT of a foetal case was left to the decision of the reporting radiologist, showed a high concordance between PMCT to PMMRI (Table 5). Due to a selection bias it is unclear how PMCT would compare to PMMRI in a larger unselected or a forensic study population.

A major limitation of foetal studies into the value of PMCT and/or PMMRI is the fact that they have been validated for use in a clinical setting where, in this age group, the cause of death is often the result of major congenital anomalies (Fig. 7). These anomalies are readily diagnosed on PMMRI however, in none of the 277 included cases inflicted injury was a cause of death.

An important forensic question is whether or not a foetus or neonate was born alive or not, as this can influence the level of accountability and thus the potential level of a sentence. PMCT has been shown to be a valuable tool in these cases (Guddat et al. 2013; Baber et al. 2015; Phillips and Ong 2018). In the small studies that have been performed aerated lungs and air in the stomach and duodenum were present in children who were born alive in contrast to stillborn infants (Fig. 8).

4 Infants and Children

4.1 Post-mortem Imaging Guideline

To detect occult fractures in case of unexpected and unexplained death, it is strongly advised to perform a skeletal survey in all cases up to at least the age of 2 years but preferably up to 4 years of age (although the yield will be relatively low in this category). This skeletal survey should be in keeping with the guideline as specified by the Royal College of Radiology and the Society and College of Radiographers (The Royal College of Radiologists (RCR) and the Society and College of Radiographers (SCoR) 2017) (Table 2). In a forensic post-mortem setting high-quality detailed imaging is important; therefore it is advised to obtain individual radiographs of the individual long bones. This is in contrast to the guideline which specifies that in young infants the whole extremity can be imaged on a single radiograph. In children aged 5 years and older there is in general no indication for a skeletal survey, in cases with specific questions a focussed radiological examination could be performed.

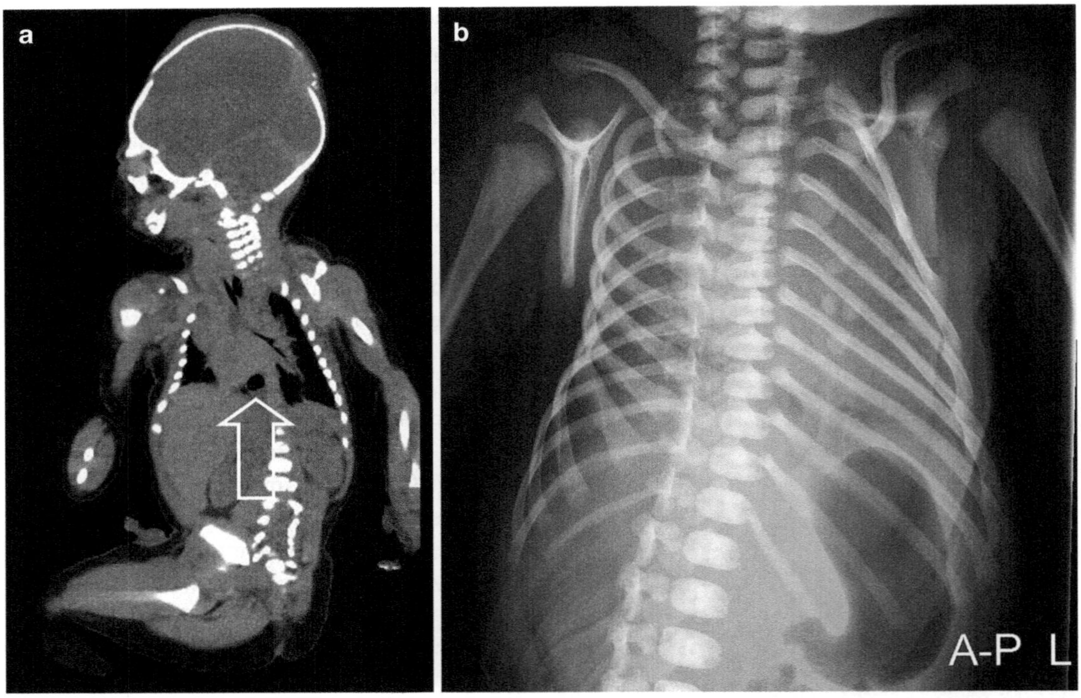

Fig. 8 In this found neonate PMCT clearly shows air in the lungs and digestive tract (arrow points towards air in the distal oesophagus) (**a**). This can of course also be seen on the conventional radiograph (**b**). Based on radiology and findings at autopsy it was decided that the baby was born alive

In case of death of an infant after the neonatal period up to 2 years, literature shows that PMMRI seems to be more beneficial than PMCT (Fig. 9a–d). This as PMMRI results in more detail due to higher contrast between the organs. Based on the literature between the ages of 2 and 4 years, MRI and CT seems equally valuable for the diagnosis of diseases or injuries that led to the patient's death. Therefore, both can be advised and the choice depends on the local situation, whether MRI or CT is available, and the preference of the radiologists. Even more important in the choice is the medical history of the child. CT images are better for the diagnoses of the osseous and aerated structures. MRI results in better contrast differentiation in the brain, heart and abdominal organs, and can be preferred for cases that are likely to have the cause of death in these areas. Still, autopsy is the most preferred method to find the cause of death and includes microbiological culturing (Fig. 10). Cardiac conductive disorders and metabolic diseases often are not diagnosed on radiology or autopsy, and need genetic examination.

In the Dutch clinical guideline three scenarios for post-mortem imaging in infants and young children are given:

- Up to the age of 2 years: in all cases a skeletal survey and a PMMRI should be obtained.
- Aged 2 up to and including 4 years: preferably a skeletal survey and PMMRI should be obtained. If PMMRI is not possible PMCT should be obtained.
- Aged 5 years and older: There is no indication for a skeletal survey. As there is insufficient evidence that PMMRI is superior to PMCT the latter is advised.

In contrast to a clinical setting in a forensic setting a full autopsy will always be performed.

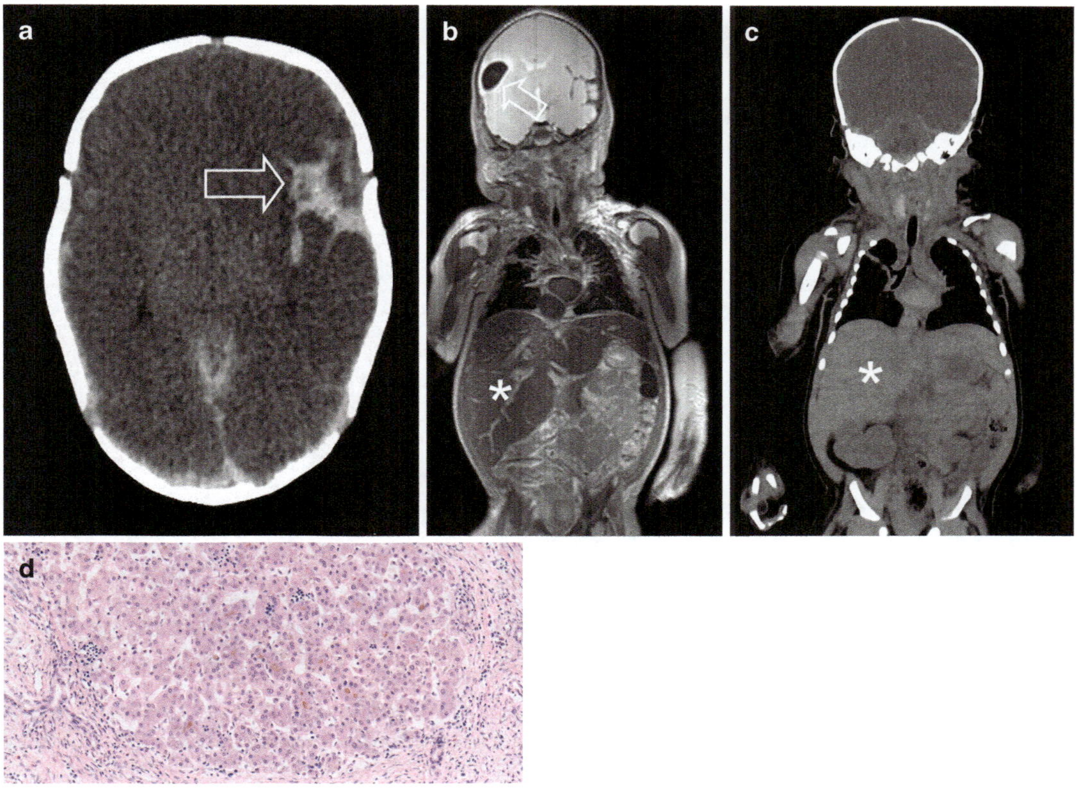

Fig. 9 One-month-old girl admitted with intracranial haemorrhage and retinal haemorrhages. Besides the haemorrhage (arrow) CT also showed absence of grey-white matter demarcation (**a**). PMMRI showed the haemorrhage (arrow) and also a homogeneously enlarged liver (asterisk) (**b**). On PMCT the haemorrhage isn't visible, in this setting, and the structure of the enlarged liver isn't discernible (asterisk) (**c**). Post-mortem US-guided biopsy yielded the diagnosis of biliary atresia (**d**), which has led to a bleeding diathesis. This case clearly shows the difference between the value of PMCT versus PMMRI

In this situation there is no evidence towards the additional value of PMMRI over PMCT and therefore in these cases PMCT can be the modality of choice.

5 Imaging Interpretation

5.1 Conventional Radiography

The focus of conventional radiology should be on the detection of fractures and the dating thereof. The conventional radiographs and/or the skeletal survey should preferably be reported by paediatric radiologists with experience in reporting and, within scientific limitations, dating fractures (Prosser et al. 2005, 2012; Drury and Cunningham 2018). This as it is of the utmost importance to be aware of normal variants and diseases/disorders that may simulate abuse (Fig. 11). If a paediatric radiologist is not available, it is advised to contact a paediatric radiologist who is willing and able to act as a co-reader or to find a centre of expertise to collaborate with. The final diagnosis should always be the result of multi-disciplinary collaboration in which a full differential diagnosis is considered (Wallace et al. 2007; Brink et al. 2015; Draus 2017; Teeuw et al. 2017).

When it comes to differentiating between accidental and non-accidental fractures in children, it is important to work in a structured manner. The most essential of all is a thorough clinical

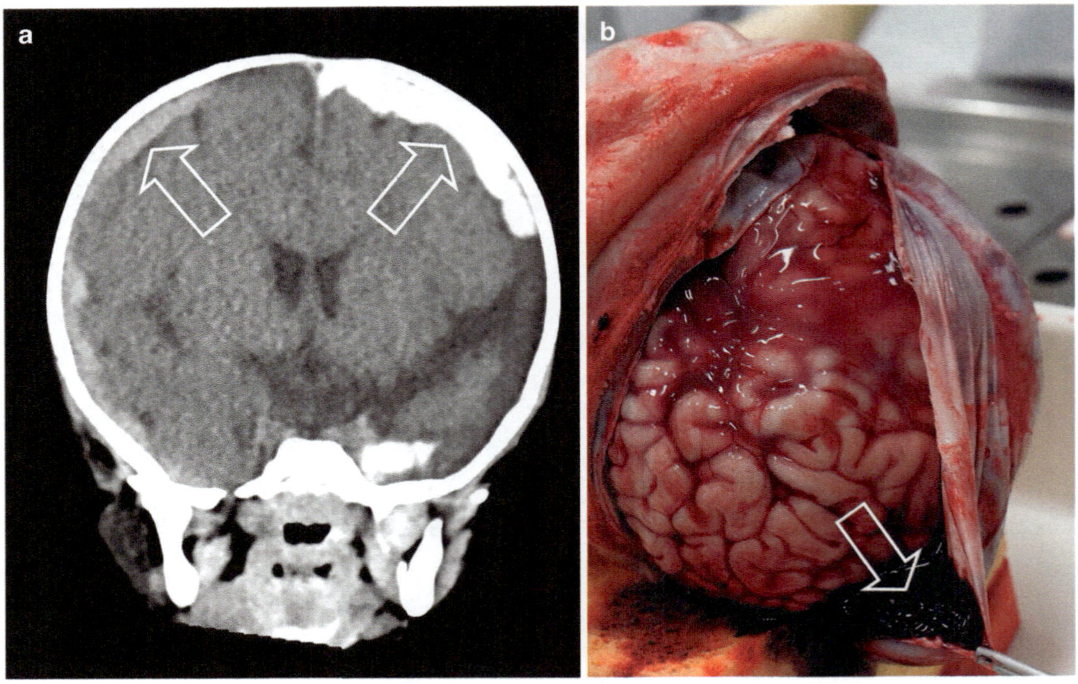

Fig. 10 Young child found dead in bed, during clinical post-mortem workup a lumbar puncture was performed which showed 'bloody tap'. As a result of this unexpected finding a legal autopsy and PMCT was requested. PMCT showed a bilateral subdural hematoma (arrows) (**a**). On autopsy the subdural hematoma (arrow) was confirmed and also subarachnoid blood was noted (**b**)

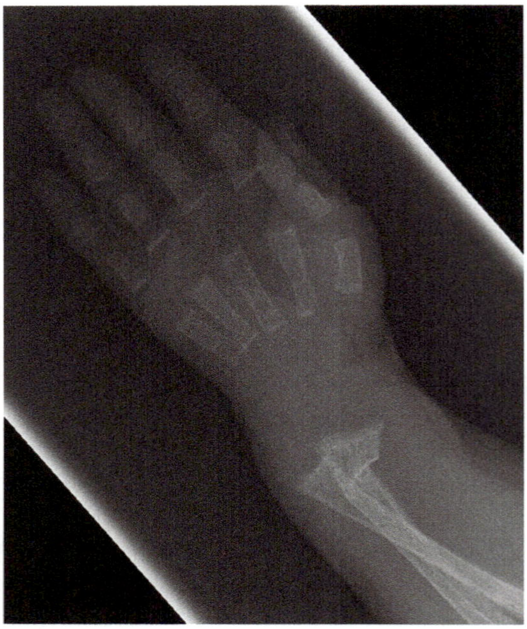

Fig. 11 Premature born baby (gestational age 24 6/7 weeks), seen at the NICU with a gestational age of 28 weeks with swollen wrist. Conventional radiography shows a distal radial fracture with signs of rickets of prematurity

examination, to check for other findings (e.g. bruises) and clinical history (e.g. underlying bone disorders or diseases), to get a good overview on the child's history, the overall development and achieved milestones, and the reported trauma mechanism or absence thereof. It speaks for itself that the younger the child is, and thus more limited in its mobility, the higher the chance that a fracture is the result of a non-accidental trauma.

An important factor to take into account is the location and distribution of fractures, as certain locations are more specific for non-accidental trauma (NAT) than others (Table 6). Of course even in fractures with a high specificity for NAT it is important to keep an open mind and go through the full differential diagnostic workup. It is outside the scope of this chapter to discuss the differential diagnosis in full and interested readers are referred to the corresponding chapters in this book or to existing textbooks on this topic (Kleinman 2015). Two fracture types will

Table 6 Specificity of skeletal injuries in child abuse, highest specificity applies in infants (Kleinman 2015)

Specificity	Type of fracture/skeletal lesion
High specificity	Classic metaphyseal lesion
	Rib fractures, especially posterior
	Scapular fractures
	Spinous processes fractures
	Sternal fractures
Moderate specificity	Multiple fractures, specifically bilateral
	Fractures of different ages
	Epiphyseal separation
	Vertebral body fractures and subluxations
	Digital fractures
	Complex skull fractures
Common but low specificity	Subperiosteal new bone formation
	Clavicular fractures
	Long bone shaft fractures
	Linear skull fractures

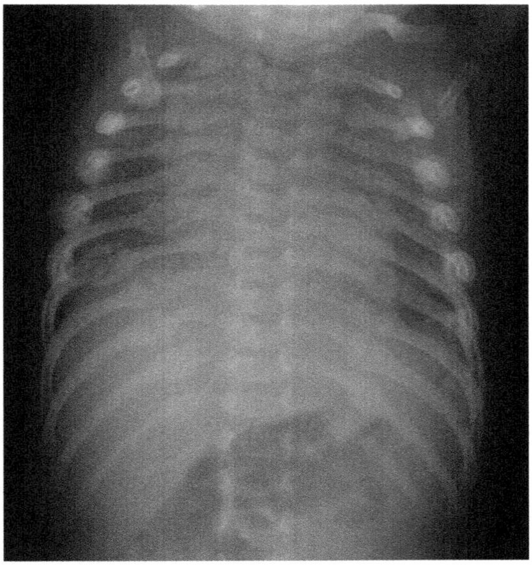

Fig. 12 Post-mortem chest radiograph showing multiple bilateral healing rib fractures

however be shortly discussed, as they are highly specific and relatively common in NAT cases. The first fracture is the posterior rib fracture; these fractures are the result of a compressive force on the chest. It is most often located posteriorly, paravertebral, or posterolateral (Fig. 12). They are also more often found on the left side of the chest, this as most adults are right handed and can exert more force with their dominant hand. Several studies have shown a high positive predictive value of posterior rib fractures for NAT (Table 7). This is supported by the common experience that posterior rib fractures are an exceptionally rare incidental finding in young children. A large retrospective study by Ruest et al. showed that in 7530 children aged 0–2 years who, during unique clinical encounters, underwent 9720 chest radiographs only five incidental rib fractures were diagnosed (Ruest et al. 2019). Of these in 3 cases there were concerns for NAT, 1 was a confirmed case of NAT, and in the last case radiographic findings consistent with osteopenia of prematurity were present. From this it must be concluded that in any child under the age of 2 years in whom a rib fracture is found, especially a posterior fracture, and in whom no known explanation is available, NAT should be considered.

The second fracture which should be discussed is the metaphyseal corner fracture, also known as the classic metaphyseal lesion. This specific fracture was first described by Caffey and later Kleinman introduced the term 'classical metaphyseal lesion' (CML) (Caffey 1957; Kleinman et al. 1986). These fractures are primarily seen in children under the age of 2 years and are found in 39%–50% of children of whom a skeletal survey was made because of suspected child abuse. They are most frequently found in the distal femur, the proximal and distal tibia (Figs. 13 and 14a–d) and the proximal humerus. Where the medial distal tibia is the most prevalent location (Tsai et al. 2018). Kleinman et al. have shown in a retrospective study that CMLs are exclusively found in children with a high risk of abuse and not in children with a low risk of abuse (Kleinman et al. 2011).

An important aspect of forensic radiology in children with fractures is dating of these fractures. After the acute stage in which soft tissue swelling can be seen, fracture healing follows a standard pattern consisting of subperiosteal new

Table 7 Predictive value of posterior rib fractures for non-accidental trauma in infants

Author	Number of cases (age)	Parameter	Percentage
Carty and Pierce (2002)	467 (425 < 2 years)	Specificity	100 (96–100)%
Bulloch et al. (2000)	39 (<12 months)	PPV	82 (66.5–82.5)%
Cadzow and Armstrong (2000)	18 (<2 years)	PPV	83 (58.6–96.4)%
Barsness et al. (2003)[a]	62 (< 3 years)	PPV	83.6%

[a]In the publication of Barsness et al. the authors inadequately calculated the PPV based on the number of fractures per group instead of the number of cases in each group. Based on their data, where 51 were identified as victims of abuse by the CAP team and the remaining 11 children had clinical or historical information causally related to 13 of the fractures, a corrected PPV was calculated

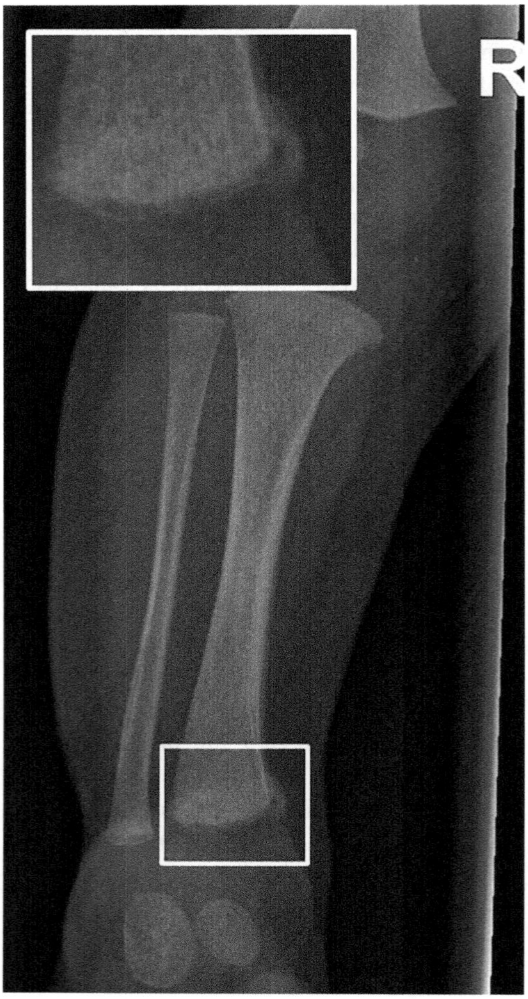

Fig. 13 Metaphyseal corner fracture of the right distal tibia (insert)

bone formation (SPNBF), soft callus formation, hard callus formation, bridging, and finally remodelling.

In one of the most recent studies Prosser et al. studied the healing pattern of 82 fractures in 63 children (mean age at first radiograph 4.8 years) on 228 radiographs (Prosser et al. 2012). In their study SPNBF was first seen at day 5 and seen in 62% of radiographs between days 15 and 35 and still visible in 33% of radiographs at day 36 onwards. Soft callus formation was first seen on day 12 and was visible in 26% of radiographs between days 15 and 21, in 41% of radiographs between days 22 and 35, after which the percentage declined sharply. Hard callus and bridging were first seen at day 19, was visible in 55% on day 22 and 38% on day 35, with increasing prevalence to 60% from day 36 onward.

With respect to dating it is important to be aware that all knowledge is obtained from clinical cases. In these cases, in contrast to child abuse, the fractures are treated and may not reflect the same healing as in forensic cases. Another limitation is the known inter-observer variance between radiologists; Halliday et al. have shown in a small study, consisting of 37 long bone fractures in 31 patients aged 0–44 months, that from all healing stages radiologists could only reliably assess SPNBF and the presence of callus (Halliday et al. 2011). Differentiation between soft and hard callus had low Kappa values varying between 0.17 (poor agreement) and 0.76 (substantial agreement). Between the different stages of callus formation and bridging the Kappa value was too low. From a forensic perspective we should remember the limitation of dating, in contrast to rib and long bone fractures CMLs cannot be dated, and in up to one-third of cases SPBNF is not seen (Tsai et al. 2019). And for skull fractures the lack of SPBNF and callus

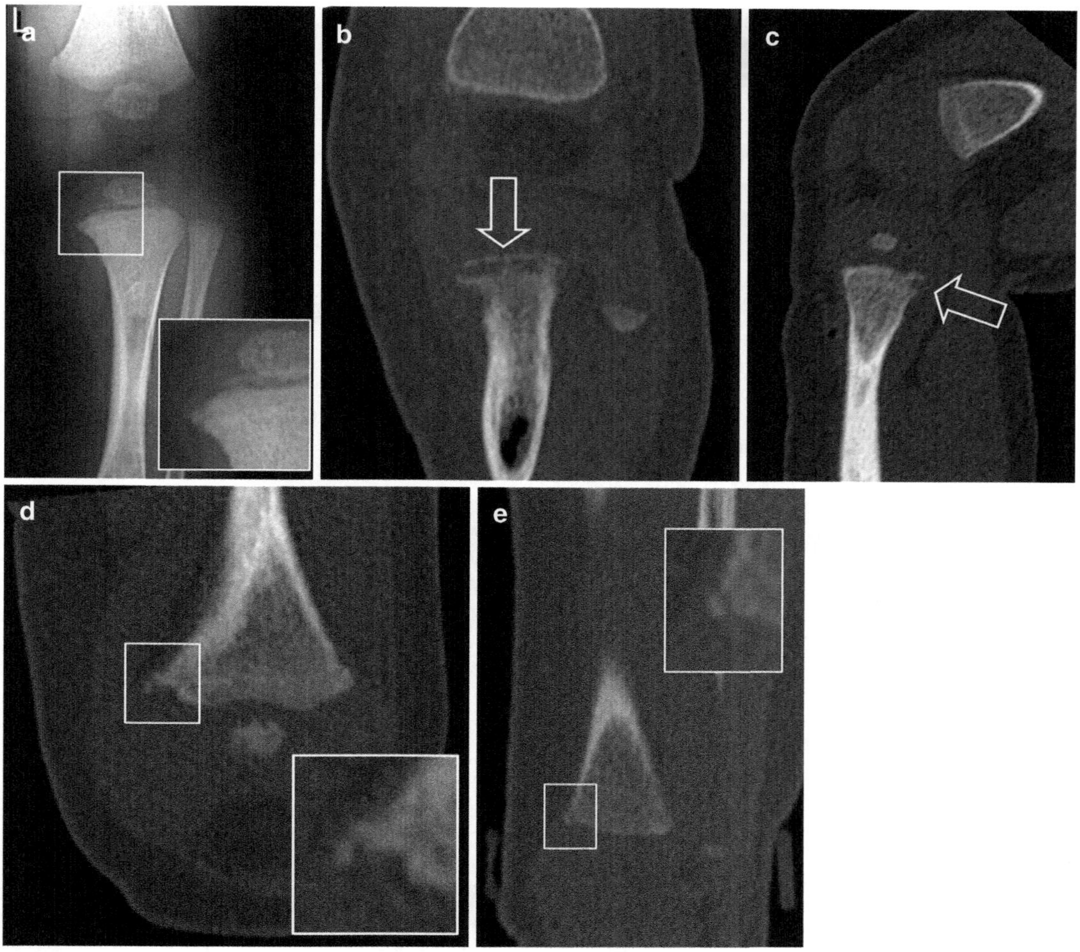

Fig. 14 Post-mortem skeletal survey (**a**) of a 3-month-old boy who died from NAT shows bucket handle type of CML at the proximal tibia and a corner fracture type of CML at the distal femur. PMCT also visualises the bucket handle fracture (**b** & **c**) and the corner fracture (**d**) to a good advantage. Additionally a small CML is seen at the distal tibia (**e**)

formation during the healing process makes it impossible to date skull fracture.

For rib fractures and long bone fractures dating is possible up to a certain level. Prosser et al. eloquently stated that 'Radiologic estimates of the time of injury are made in terms of weeks rather than days' but also that 'Radiologists can clearly differentiate recent from old fractures' (Prosser et al. 2005).

5.2 PMCT

There have been several studies into the value of PMCT in infants and children (Fig. 15a–c). Most studies have focused on younger children and all published studies have been done in relatively small populations. One of the first studies was performed by Proisy et al. In their study in 47 children of which 44 (93.6%) were younger than 2 years (Proisy et al. 2013), in 18 cases autopsy revealed a cause of death and in 15 cases (83.3%) PMCT showed concordant findings. The cause of death was unexplained in 29 cases (61.7%), of which in 27 cases (93.1%) PMCT showed no abnormal findings. In contrast to this study, van Rijn et al. showed that in a study in 54 children (median age 0.8 years) who died unexpectedly from a perceived natural cause of death in only 7 cases the cause of death could be identified on

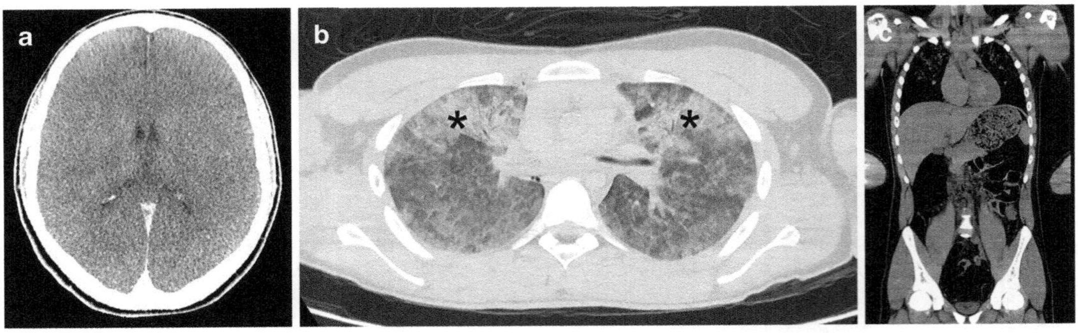

Fig. 15 PMCT scan of a teenager found dead sitting in bed. Because of this sudden unexpected death, a post-mortem investigation was initiated. On PMCT normal findings such as diminished grey-white matter differentiation (**a**), diffuse pulmonary consolidations (asterisk) (**b**), and normal abdominal findings (**c**) were found. Genetic testing showed a long QT type 3 gene, fitting the clinical history

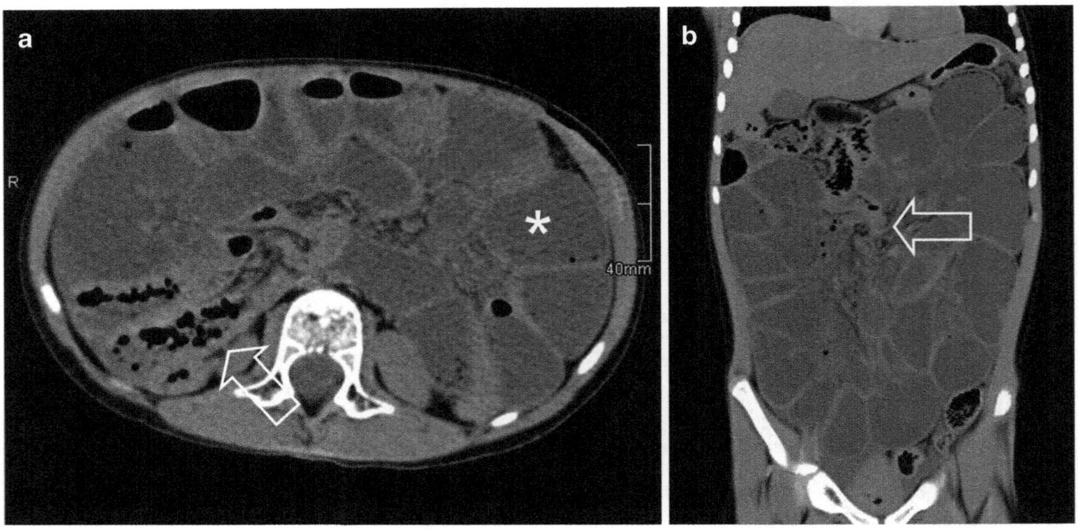

Fig. 16 PMCT shows segments of collapsed (arrow) and dilated bowel loops (asterisk) (**a**). Coronal reconstruction (**b**) shows a volvulus (arrow). Autopsy revealed necrosis of a segment of the small bowel secondary to volvulus

PMCT (van Rijn et al. 2017) (Figs. 16a, b and 17a, b). In 7 cases PMCT findings were clinically relevant but did not lead to a cause of death. In the remaining 40 cases PMCT did not add to the diagnostic workup. In a study into the value of PMCT in paediatric forensic cases Sieswerda et al. evaluated a series of 98 cases (median age was 1 year and 1 month, IQR 3 months to 6 years) (Sieswerda-Hoogendoorn et al. 2014). These were all cases referred to the Netherlands Forensic Institute, in 51 cases (52%) there was an unnatural cause of death, in 35 cases (36%) autopsy showed no cause of death, and in the remaining 12 cases (12%) a natural cause of death was found. Overall, PMCT and autopsy identified the same category for the cause of death in 69/98 cases (70%) (Fig. 18a, b). In all natural causes of death PMCT yielded no diagnosis. The authors state that 'The case mix of the patients seems to be an important predictor for the concordance between PMCT and autopsy'. In a retrospective study in 26 children (aged 0–12 years) who died of different causes, natural as well as non-natural, Krentz et al. (2016) compared autopsy and PMCT. They found that overall PMCT is less sensitive compared to con-

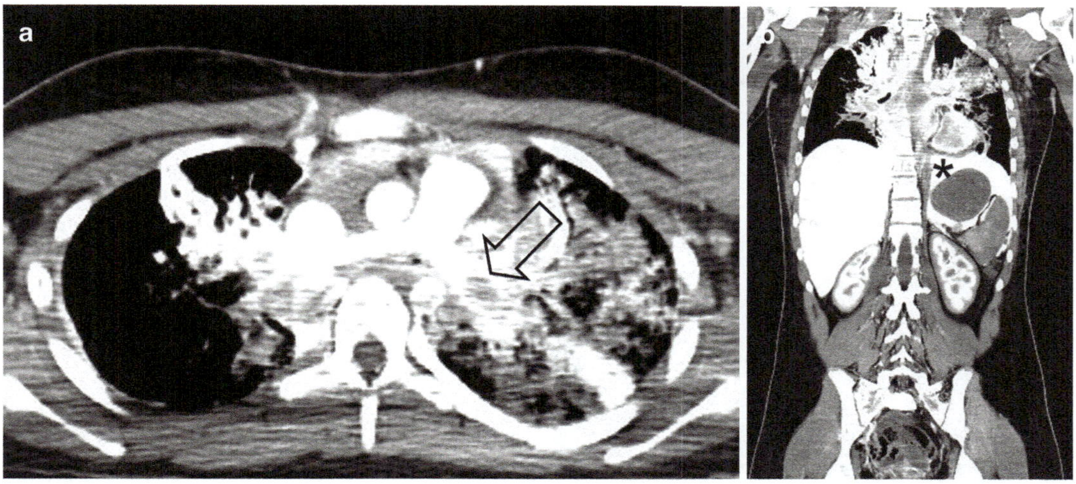

Fig. 17 PMCTA shows a pulmonary embolism (arrow) in the left pulmonary artery in a young girl using oral contraceptives (**a**). Also note the beam hardening artefacts due to the position of the arms during scanning. During PMCTA contrast extravasation (arrow) into the abdominal cavity occurred (**b**). As this was ruled a natural cause of death and the parents refused an autopsy, this finding could not be confirmed

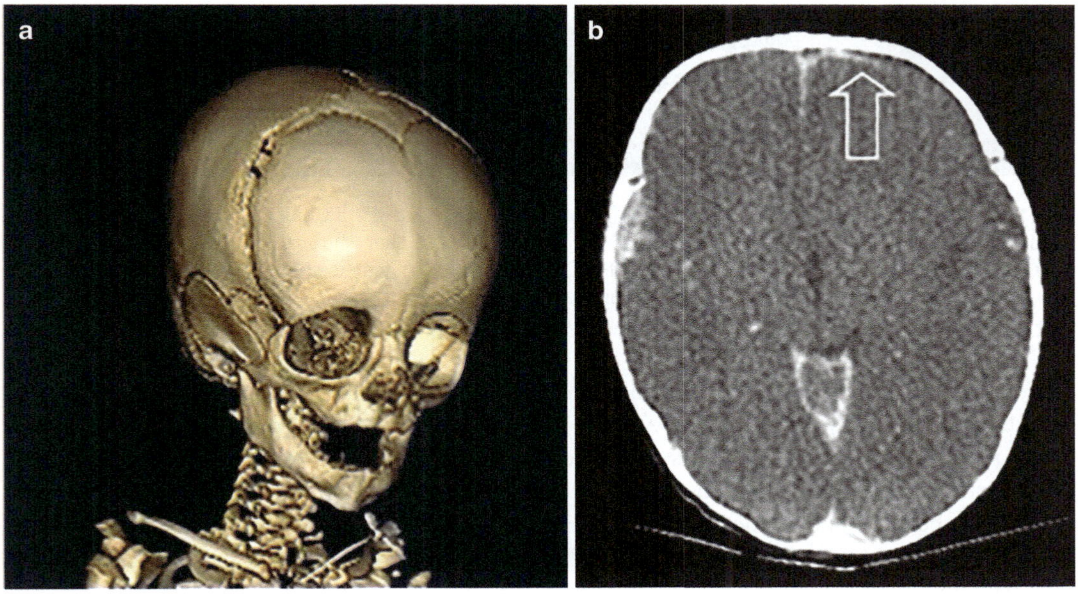

Fig. 18 PMCT of an infant shows a normal skull without fractures (**a**). Axial imaging shows a subdural hematoma (arrow) and diffuse subarachnoid blood (**b**). The cause of death on autopsy was ruled to be traumatic brain injury

ventional autopsy. But also that PMCT is superior to autopsy for the detection of bone lesions. The authors state that PMCT is indicated in cases of traumatic death, especially those with suspected bone lesions. Ishida et al. evaluated PMCT of 22 infants under the age of 3 years (mean age, 6.1 ± 8.2 months) who died in hospital due to non-traumatic causes of death (Ishida et al. 2020). They found a concordance of PMCT with autopsy in terms of the major underlying disease in 8/22 (36%) cases. The concordance of PMCT with autopsy in terms of the main organ–disease systems associated with the immediate causes of death in age-stratified paediatric cases was 5/16

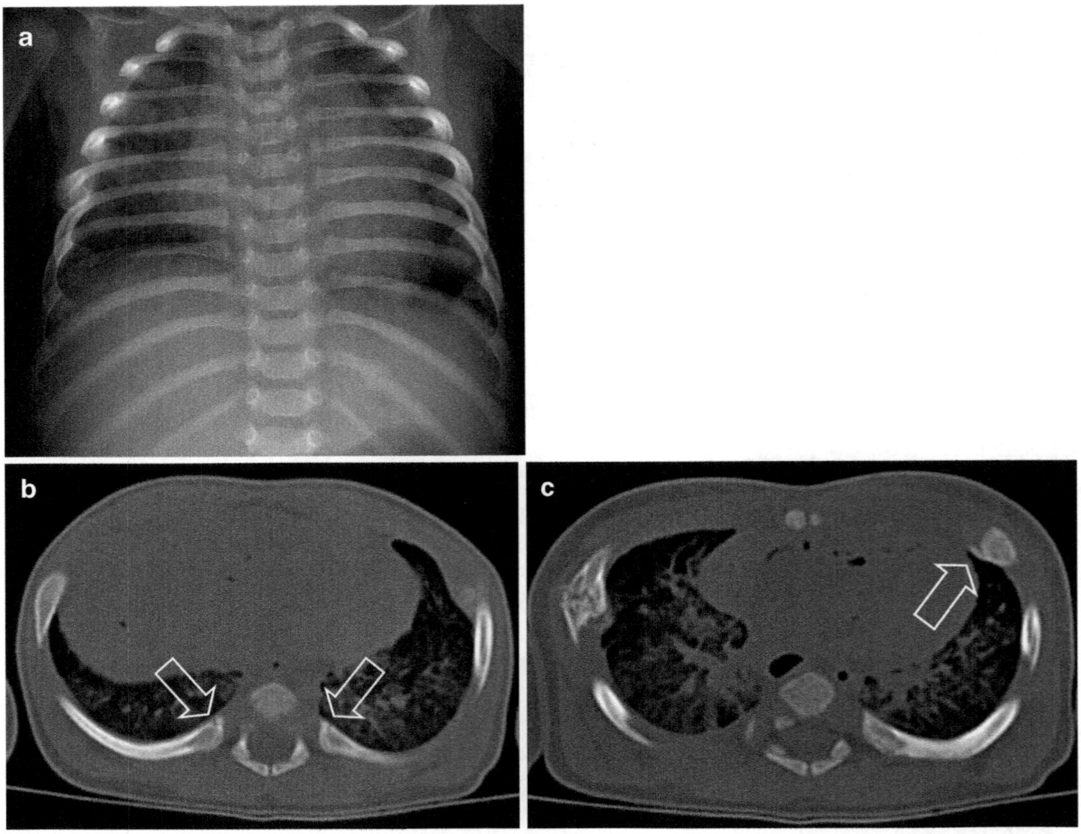

Fig. 19 Post-mortem chest radiograph of 3-month-old child. Healing fractures of lateral 5th right rib, posterior 11th left rib, anterior 6th and 7th left ribs (**a**). PMCT reveals additional fractures at the costovertebral junction of both 8th ribs (arrows) and 10th left rib (not shown) (**b**). In addition to the healing fracture of the 5th right rib, PMCT also shows unsuspected fractures at the ventral costochondral junction of the 4th (not shown) and 5th left ribs (arrow) (**c**)

(31%) for infants aged 0–1 year and 4/5 (80%) for infants aged >1–3 years.

An interesting aspect of PMCT is the detection of rib fractures (Figs. 19a–c and 20a–c). There have been several studies addressing the use of CT to detect fractures related to NAT. In 2011 Hong et al. reported on 13 cases and they found that radiography diagnosed rib fractures in 7/12 patients who had fractures found at autopsy, and on CT in 11/12 patients (Hong et al. 2011). On a fracture level 46% (38/83) of fractures were diagnosed on radiography, and 85% (86/101) on CT. In a study by Shelmerdine et al. an international group of 38 radiologists evaluated 25 cases (aged 1 month to 7 years), with 136 rib fractures diagnosed at autopsy (Shelmerdine et al. 2018). The radiologists diagnosed three times as many rib fractures on PMCT versus radiography (sensitivity 44.9% [95% CI 31.7–58.9] vs. 13.5% [8.1–21.5]). With respect to the correct location of rib fractures PMCT had a higher sensitivity compared to radiography (62.4% [95% CI 44.9–77.1] vs. 23.1% [12.9–37.8]; difference 39.3% [31.9–42.2; $p < 0.001$]). Although both studies have a relatively low number of included patients, the findings are in keeping with trauma studies, and confirm that PMCT is superior compared to radiography in diagnosing rib fractures (Fig. 17a, b).

Finally, PMCT can also be used in specific cases such as gunshot wounds, drowning, and severe burns although literature in these areas is mostly focussed on adults (Filograna et al. 2015;

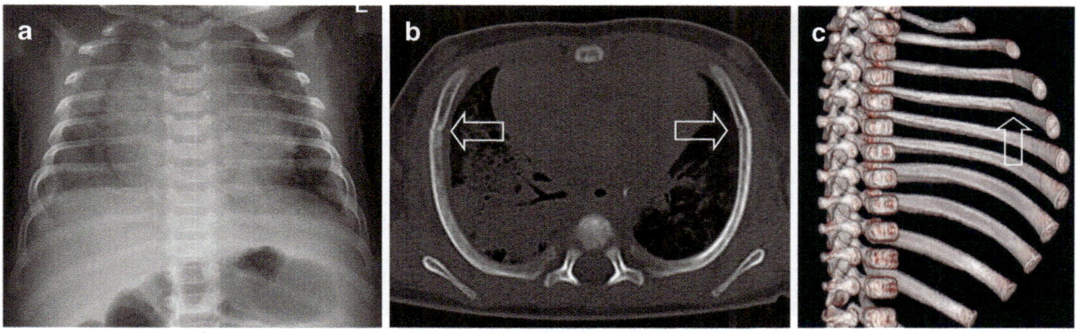

Fig. 20 A 10-week-old child with Influenza A infection. Post-mortem examination after unsuccessful prolonged cardiopulmonary resuscitation (CPR). Chest radiograph shows pulmonary abnormalities but no rib fractures (**a**). Reformatted CT slice reveals subtle fractures of both anterior 4th ribs caused by CPR (arrows) (**b**). 3D CT reconstruction shows subtle kinking of 2-4th left ribs (arrow) (**c**)

Vander Plaetsen et al. 2015; de Bakker et al. 2019; Del Fante et al. 2019).

5.3 PMMRI

There has been one major prospective paediatric PMMRI study, which has been referred to before in this chapter, the MaRIAS study (Thayyil et al. 2013). In this study in total 400 cases were included of which 53 were aged >1 month to ≤12 months and 28 > 12 months to ≤16 years. This study was skewed towards the younger infants and in the ensuing publications the data for the children aged >1 month and = < 16 years were grouped with neonatal cases (Taylor et al. 2014; Arthurs et al. 2014a, b; Arthurs et al. 2015a, c). Given the inclusion of neonates in these reported data sets the level of evidence for older children is therefore limited (Tables 8 and 9).

There are no studies with a sufficient number of older children to assess the impact of PMMRI on a forensic practice. There is therefore currently no strong indication to perform PMMRI in this population except for research purposes (Fig. 21a, b). One area in which PMMRI might be of value is in the workup of abusive head trauma (AHT) cases. Shelmerdine et al. have shown in an overview article that in a clinical setting PMMRI can identify brain lesions in foetuses and infants (Shelmerdine et al. 2017). In AHT there are several important findings that can be of importance in the diagnosis such as subdural haematomas, brain oedema, and hypoxic-ischaemic injury (Kemp et al. 2011). In the post-mortem setting the diagnostic value of PMMRI in brain oedema and hypoxic-ischaemic injury is limited. However, with respect to other findings PMMRI has a diagnostic value and can lead to a dedicated autopsy approach. In recent years more attention has been focussed on spinal lesions in AHT, such as spinal subdural haematomas, spinal epidural haematomas, and ligamentous injury (Kemp et al. 2010; Choudhary et al. 2012; Choudhary 2020). PMMRI can have a role in detecting ligamentous injuries, as these are difficult to detect at autopsy and in all spinal injuries if during the autopsy not the whole spine is dissected.

Table 8 Concordance for detection of major pathological abnormalities in infants and children on PMMRI (>1 month to = <16 years) related to death (Thayyil et al. 2013)

	Infants and children (n = 123)
Concordant	85 (69.1%, range 60.5–76.6)
Non-diagnostic	4 (3%)
Discordant	34 (27%)

5.4 Minimal Invasive Autopsy

Although in foetuses and neonates a minimal invasive autopsy (MIA) has been proven to be effective, in older children literature is lacking (Thayyil et al. 2010, 2013; Sebire et al. 2012;

Table 9 Overall diagnostic accuracy of PMMRI in neonates, infants and children

Organ system	*N*	FP/TP	FN/TN	Sensitivity (%)	Specificity (%)
Brain (Arthurs et al. 2015a)	118	13/49	1/55	98% (95% CI: 89.5–99.6)	80.9 (95% CI: 70–88.5)
Heart[a] (Taylor et al. 2014)	122	13/2	0/107	100% (95% CI: 77.2–100)	98.2% (95% CI: 93.6–99.5)
Thoracic[b] (Arthurs et al. 2014b)	123	24/28	34/37	45.2% (95% CI: 33.4–57.5)	60.7% (95% CI: 48.1–71.9)
Abdominal (Arthurs et al. 2015c)	123	14/12	5/92	70.6 (95% CI: 46.9–86.7)	86.8% (95% CI: 79.0–92.0)
Musculoskeletal (Arthurs et al. 2014a)	122	4/4	9/105	308.% (95% CI: 12.7–57.6)	96.3% (95% CI: 90.9–98.6)

[a]Non-cardiac thoracic anomalies
[b]For detection of any structural heart defect (major and minor)

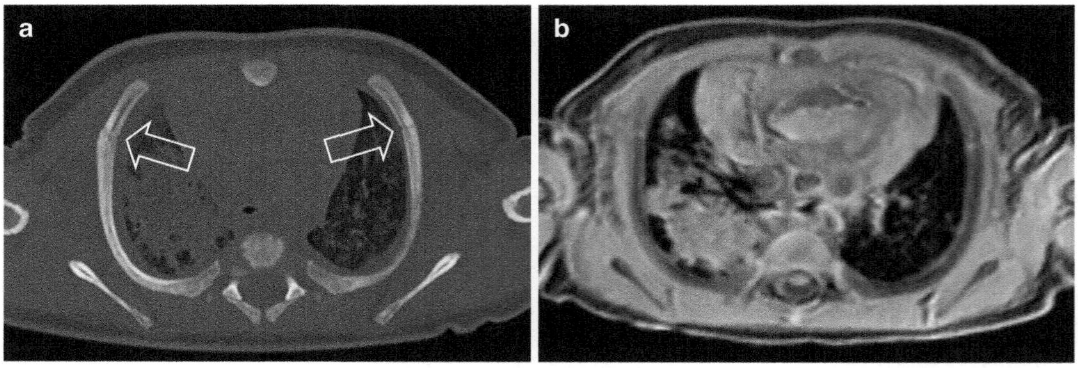

Fig. 21 Same patient as in Fig. 20. PMCT (Maximal Intensity Projection) clearly shows the subtle fractures of the anterior ribs (arrows) (**a**). They can easily be missed on PMMRI (T1 fatsat) (**b**)

Ben-Sasi et al. 2013). We therefore have to look at adult studies where MIA consists of a full review of the clinical history, if relevant genetic and metabolic tests (ante-mortem and post-mortem blood sampling), external examination, and post-mortem radiology and image-guided biopsies. These limited number of studies show somewhat conflicting results. Weustink et al. showed in a clinical study in 30 adult patients (age range, 46–79 years) that the minimal invasive autopsy and the conventional autopsy were in agreement in 23 patient (77%) (Weustink et al. 2009). Especially acute myocardial infarction as the cause of death ($N = 4$) was missed in all cases. In contrast Latten et al. concluded that in a MIA setting CT-guided post-mortem biopsies of the liver and lung have a mediocre predictive value and that conventional autopsy should still be preferred to biopsy-based post-mortem examination (Latten et al. 2019). From a forensics perspective it is clear that, at this moment in time, MIA cannot replace a conventional autopsy. And one could argue if this isn't the case for a clinical autopsy, in children, as well.

6 Autopsy Specimen

After the autopsy is concluded the pathologist can order specimen radiographs. Preferably these radiographs are obtained using a high-resolution radiography system. If the pathology department doesn't have access to dedicated self-contained, shielded cabinet specimen radiography systems, the use of mammography systems is advised. With its high resolution it is an ideal modality to image excision specimen (Fig. 22a–d). These high-resolution images can be used to guide the

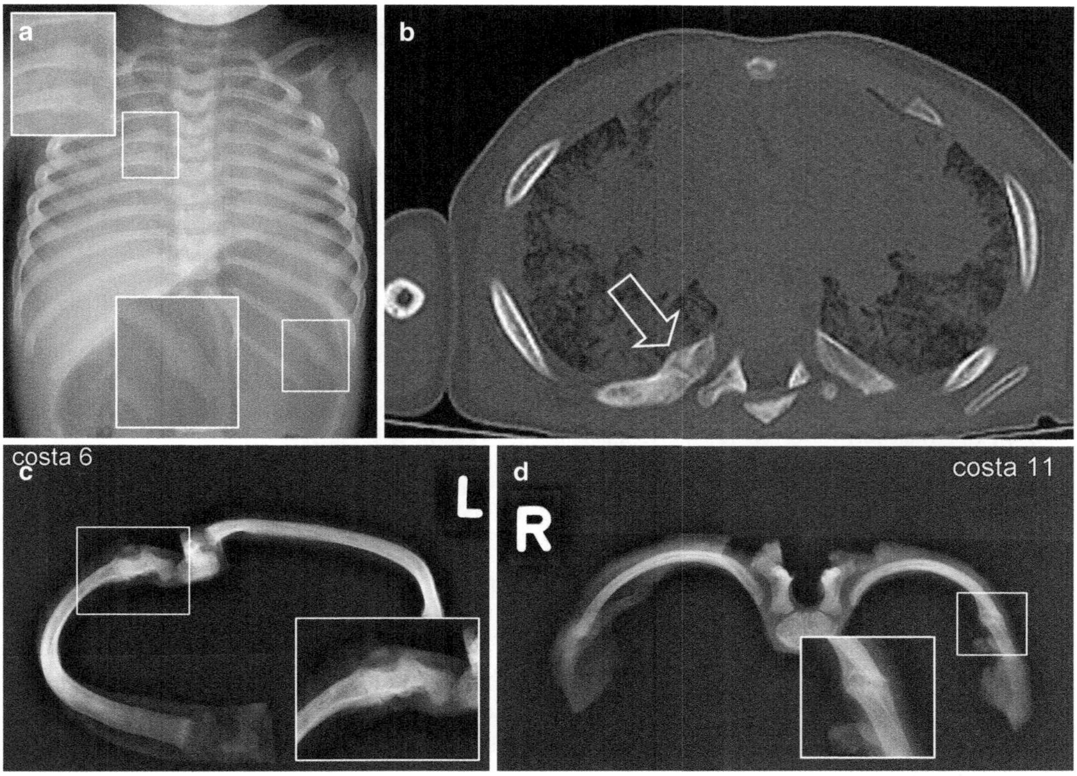

Fig. 22 Post-mortem chest radiographs showing multiple healing rib fractures (**a**). PMCT clearly shows the healing rib fracture (**b**). Specimen radiographs show healing rib fractures of the 6th rib on the right (**c**) and the 11th rib on the left (**d**)

pathologist in preparing the specimen for further histopathologic analysis.

7 Conclusion

Post-mortem imaging has developed into an important, if not vital, tool in the field of forensic paediatric medicine. From a radiologists perspective it requires specific knowledge and expertise in order to differentiate between normal post-mortem imaging findings and pathology (Klein et al. 2015; Sieswerda-Hoogendoorn et al. 2015; Arthurs et al. 2015b). Besides clinical radiological knowledge the radiologist should also have knowledge of forensic medicine and relevant legal guidelines and regulations of the country he or she is working in. It is also important to be aware of the potential barriers that can be encountered when starting a post-mortem paediatric radiology service (Cain 2015; Chapman 2015; Hatch 2015; Ruder 2015). Learning from experienced forensic/post-mortem radiologists is of the essence. This can be achieved by attending training courses or meetings such as organised by the International Society of Forensic Radiology and Imaging (www.isfri.org).

Finally we need to stress that until new scientific evidence becomes available forensic post-mortem imaging should be seen as complementary to the judicial autopsy. This in contrast to clinical studies where a MIA seems to be, in foetuses and neonates, a viable option. We would like to conclude our chapter with a quote from Flach et al. which describes the way forensic paediatric post-mortem imaging should be incorporated into the forensic workflow '*The most important part of the collaboration between radiologists and forensic pathologists is communication comparable to the relationship between the treating physician and the clinical radiologist in the clinical setting*' (Flach et al. 2014).

References

Adalian P, Piercecchi-Marti MD, Bourliere-Najean B, Panuel M, Fredouille C, Dutour O, Leonetti G (2001) Postmortem assessment of fetal diaphyseal femoral length: validation of a radiographic methodology. J Forensic Sci 46:215–219

Ampanozi G, Thali YA, Schweitzer W, Hatch GM, Ebert LC, Thali MJ, Ruder TD (2017) Accuracy of non-contrast PMCT for determining cause of death. Forensic Sci Med Pathol 13:284–292

Arthurs OJ, Barber JL, Taylor AM, Sebire NJ (2015b) Normal perinatal and paediatric postmortem magnetic resonance imaging appearances. Pediatr Radiol 45:527–535

Arthurs OJ, Guy A, Thayyil S, Wade A, Jones R, Norman W, Scott R, Robertson NJ, Jacques TS, Chong WK, Gunny R, Saunders D, Olsen OE, Owens CM, Offiah AC, Chitty LS, Taylor AM, Sebire NJ (2016) Comparison of diagnostic performance for perinatal and paediatric post-mortem imaging: CT versus MRI. Eur Radiol 26:2327–2336

Arthurs OJ, Hutchinson JC, Sebire NJ (2017) Current issues in postmortem imaging of perinatal and forensic childhood deaths. Forensic Sci Med Pathol 13:58–66

Arthurs OJ, Thayyil S, Addison S, Wade A, Jones R, Norman W, Scott R, Robertson NJ, Chitty LS, Taylor AM, Sebire NJ, Offiah AC (2014a) Diagnostic accuracy of post-mortem MRI for musculoskeletal abnormalities in fetuses and children. Prenat Diagn

Arthurs OJ, Thayyil S, Olsen OE, Addison S, Wade A, Jones R, Norman W, Scott RJ, Robertson NJ, Taylor AM, Chitty LS, Sebire NJ, Owens CM (2014b) Diagnostic accuracy of post-mortem MRI for thoracic abnormalities in fetuses and children. Eur Radiol 24:2876–2884

Arthurs OJ, Thayyil S, Owens CM, Olsen OE, Wade A, Addison S, Jones R, Norman W, Scott RJ, Robertson NJ, Taylor AM, Chitty LS, Sebire NJ (2015c) Diagnostic accuracy of post mortem MRI for abdominal abnormalities in foetuses and children. Eur J Radiol 84:474–481

Arthurs OJ, Thayyil S, Pauliah SS, Jacques TS, Chong WK, Gunny R, Saunders D, Addison S, Lally P, Cady E, Jones R, Norman W, Scott R, Robertson NJ, Wade A, Chitty L, Taylor AM, Sebire NJ (2015a) Diagnostic accuracy and limitations of post-mortem MRI for neurological abnormalities in fetuses and children. Clin Radiol 70:872–880

Baber Y, Iles L, O'Donnell C (2015) Determining live birth: an unusual case. Am J Forensic Med Pathol 36:262–264

de Bakker HM, Roelandt GHJ, Soerdjbalie-Maikoe V, van Rijn RR, de Bakker BS (2019) The value of post-mortem computed tomography of burned victims in a forensic setting. Eur Radiol 29:1912–1921

Barsness KA, Cha ES, Bensard DD, Calkins CM, Partrick DA, Karrer FM, Strain JD (2003) The positive predictive value of rib fractures as an indicator of nonaccidental trauma in children. J Trauma 54:1107–1110

Ben-Sasi K, Chitty LS, Franck LS, Thayyil S, Judge-Kronis L, Taylor AM, Sebire NJ (2013) Acceptability of a minimally invasive perinatal/paediatric autopsy: healthcare professionals' views and implications for practice. Prenat Diagn 33:307–312

Born M, Schwier F, Stoever B, Mentzel HJ, Freiberg J (2020) The German evidence-based child protection guideline—imaging in suspected child abuse. Rofo 192:343–348

Brink FW, Thackeray JD, Bridge JA, Letson MM, Scribano PV (2015) Child advocacy center multidisciplinary team decision and its association to child protective services outcomes. Child Abuse Negl 46:174–181

Bulloch B, Schubert CJ, Brophy PD, Johnson N, Reed MH, Shapiro RA (2000) Cause and clinical characteristics of rib fractures in infants. Pediatrics 105:E48

Cadzow SP, Armstrong KL (2000) Rib fractures in infants: red alert! The clinical features, investigations and child protection outcomes. J Paediatr Child Health 36:322–326

Caffey J (1957) Some traumatic lesions in growing bones other than fractures and dislocations: clinical and radiological features: the Mackenzie Davidson Memorial Lecture. Br J Radiol 30:225–238

Cain TM (2015) What are the greatest challenges or barriers to applying postmortem imaging in paediatric radiology? Pediatr Radiol 45:481

Carty H, Pierce A (2002) Non-accidental injury: a retrospective analysis of a large cohort. Eur Radiol 12:2919–2925

Chapman S (2015) What are the greatest challenges and/or barriers to applying postmortem imaging in paediatric radiology? Pediatr Radiol 45:478

Charlier P, Chaillot PF, Watier L, Menetrier M, Carlier R, Cavard S, Herve C, de la Grandmaison GL, Huynh-Charlier I (2013) Is post-mortem ultrasonography a useful tool for forensic purposes? Med Sci Law 53:227–234

Choi HY, Kim JH, Park JY, Jung EY, No JH, Oh KJ, Hong JS (2016) Simple mathematical formulae for estimation of median values of fetal biometry at each gestational age. Obstet Gynecol Sci 59:91–96

Choudhary AK (2020) Understanding the importance of spinal injury in abusive head trauma (AHT). Pediatr Radiol 50:15–16

Choudhary AK, Bradford RK, Dias MS, Moore GJ, Boal DK (2012) Spinal subdural hemorrhage in abusive head trauma: a retrospective study. Radiology 262:216–223

Del Fante Z, De Matteis A, Fazio V, Di Fazio N, Quattrocchi A, Romano S, Arcangeli M, dell'Aquila

M (2019) The importance of post mortem computed tomography (PMCT) in the reconstruction of the bullet trajectory. Clin Ter 170:e129–e133

Draus JM Jr (2017) A multidisciplinary child protection team improves the care of nonaccidental trauma patients. Am Surg 83:477–481

Drury A, Cunningham C (2018) Determining when a fracture occurred: does the method matter? Analysis of the similarity of three different methods for estimating time since fracture of juvenile long bones. J Forensic Legal Med 53:97–105

Filograna L, Tartaglione T, Vetrugno G, Guerra C, Fileni A, Bonomo L (2015) Freshwater drowning in a child: a case study demonstrating the role of post-mortem computed tomography. Med Sci Law 55:304–311

Flach PM, Thali MJ, Germerott T (2014) Times have changed! Forensic radiology--a new challenge for radiology and forensic pathology. AJR Am J Roentgenol 202:W325–W334

Furness ME, Weckert RC, Parker SA, Knowles S (1989) Ultrasound in the perinatal necropsy. J Med Genet 26:368–372

Grabherr S, Heinemann A, Vogel H, Rutty G, Morgan B, Wozniak K, Dedouit F, Fischer F, Lochner S, Wittig H, Guglielmi G, Eplinius F, Michaud K, Palmiere C, Chevallier C, Mangin P, Grimm JM (2018) Postmortem CT angiography compared with autopsy: a forensic multicenter study. Radiology 288:270–276

Guddat SS, Gapert R, Tsokos M, Oesterhelweg L (2013) Proof of live birth using postmortem multislice computed tomography (pmMSCT) in cases of suspected neonaticide: advantages of diagnostic imaging compared to conventional autopsy. Forensic Sci Med Pathol 9:3–12

Halliday KE, Broderick NJ, Somers JM, Hawkes R (2011) Dating fractures in infants. Clin Radiol 66:1049–1054

Hatch GM (2015) What are the greatest challenges or barriers to applying post-mortem imaging in pediatric radiology? Pediatr Radiol 45:480

Hong TS, Reyes JA, Moineddin R, Chiasson DA, Berdon WE, Babyn PS (2011) Value of postmortem thoracic CT over radiography in imaging of pediatric rib fractures. Pediatr Radiol 41(6):736–748

Ishida M, Gonoi W, Shirota G, Abe H, Shintani-Domoto Y, Ikemura M, Ushiku T, Abe O (2020) Utility of unenhanced postmortem computed tomography for investigation of in-hospital nontraumatic death in children up to 3 years of age at a single Japanese tertiary care hospital. Medicine (Baltimore) 99:e20130

Johnsen SL, Wilsgaard T, Rasmussen S, Sollien R, Kiserud T (2006) Longitudinal reference charts for growth of the fetal head, abdomen and femur. Eur J Obstet Gynecol Reprod Biol 127:172–185

Kemp AM, Jaspan T, Griffiths J, Stoodley N, Mann MK, Tempest V, Maguire SA (2011) Neuroimaging: what neuroradiological features distinguish abusive from non-abusive head trauma? A systematic review. Arch Dis Child 96:1103–1112

Kemp AM, Joshi AH, Mann M, Tempest V, Liu A, Holden S, Maguire S (2010) What are the clinical and radiological characteristics of spinal injuries from physical abuse: a systematic review. Arch Dis Child 95:355–360

Klein WM, Bosboom DG, Koopmanschap DH, Nievelstein RA, Nikkels PG, van Rijn RR (2015) Normal pediatric postmortem CT appearances. Pediatr Radiol 45:517–526

Klein WM, Duijst WLJM, Erwich JJHM, Hofman PAM, Kint PAM, Kroll JJF, Nikkels PGJ, Renken NS, Van Rijn RR, Rosier Y, Scheeren CIE, Stomp SJ, van der Valk P (2018) Klinische postmortem radiologie. Federatie Medisch Specialisten. https://richtlijnendatabase.nl/richtlijn/klinische_postmortem_radiologie

Kleinman PK (2015) Diagnostic imaging of child abuse. Cambridge University Press, Cambridge

Kleinman PK, Marks SC, Blackbourne B (1986) The metaphyseal lesion in abused infants: a radiologic-histopathologic study. AJR Am J Roentgenol 146:895–905

Kleinman PK, Perez-Rossello JM, Newton AW, Feldman HA, Kleinman PL (2011) Prevalence of the classic metaphyseal lesion in infants at low versus high risk for abuse. AJR Am J Roentgenol 197:1005–1008

Krentz BV, Alamo L, Grimm J, Dédouit F, Bruguier C, Chevallier C, Egger C, Da Silva LFF, Grabherr S (2016) Performance of post-mortem CT compared to autopsy in children. Int J Legal Med 130:1089–1099

Latten BGH, Bakers FCH, Hofman PAM, Zur Hausen A, Kubat B (2019) The needle in the haystack: histology of post-mortem computed tomography guided biopsies versus autopsy derived tissue. Forensic Sci Int 302:109882

Mokrane FZ, Dercle L, Meyrignac O, Crubézy É, Rousseau H, Telmon N, Dedouit F (2018) Towards multi-phase postmortem CT angiography in children: a study on a porcine model. Int J Legal Med 132:1391–1403

Offiah AC, Adamsbaum C, van Rijn RR (2014) ESPR adopts British guidelines for imaging in suspected non-accidental injury as the European standard. Pediatr Radiol 44:1338

Okland I, Nakling J, Gjessing HK, Grottum P, Eik-Nes SH (2012) Advantages of the population-based approach to pregnancy dating: results from 23,020 ultrasound examinations. Ultrasound Obstet Gynecol 39:563–568

Phillips B, Ong BB (2018) "Was the infant Born alive?" A review of postmortem techniques used to determine live birth in cases of suspected neonaticide. Acad Forensic Pathol 8:874–893

Prodhomme O, Baud C, Saguintaah M, Béchard-Sevette N, Bolivar J, David S, Taleb-Arrada DI, Couture A (2015) Principles of fetal post mortem ultrasound: a personal review. J Forensic Radiol Imaging 3:12–15

Proisy M, Marchand AJ, Loget P, Bouvet R, Roussey M, Pele F, Rozel C, Treguier C, Darnault P, Bruneau B (2013) Whole-body post-mortem computed tomography compared with autopsy in the investigation of unexpected death in infants and children. Eur Radiol 23:1711–1719

Prosser I, Lawson Z, Evans A, Harrison S, Morris S, Maguire S, Kemp AM (2012) A timetable for the

radiologic features of fracture healing in young children. AJR Am J Roentgenol 198:1014–1020
Prosser I, Maguire S, Harrison SK, Mann M, Sibert JR, Kemp AM (2005) How old is this fracture? Radiologic dating of fractures in children: a systematic review. AJR Am J Roentgenol 184:1282–1286
Resnick PJ (1970) Murder of the newborn: a psychiatric review of neonaticide. Psychiatry 126:1414–1420
van Rijn RR, Beek EJ, van de Putte EM, Teeuw AH, Nikkels PGJ, Duijst W, Nievelstein RA (2017) The value of postmortem computed tomography in paediatric natural cause of death: a Dutch observational study. Pediatr Radiol 47:1514–1522
Ruder TD (2015) What are the greatest challenges or barriers to applying post-mortem imaging in pediatric radiology? Pediatr Radiol 45:479
Ruest S, Kanaan G, Moore JL, Goldberg AP (2019) The prevalence of rib fractures incidentally identified by chest radiograph among infants and toddlers. J Pediatr 204:208–213
Sarda-Quarello L, Bartoli C, Laurent PE, Torrents J, Piercecchi-Marti MD, Sigaudy S, Ariey-Bonnet D, Gorincour G (2016) Whole body perinatal postmortem CT angiography. Diagn Interv Imaging 97:121–124
Scheuer JL, Musgrave JH, Evans SP (1980) The estimation of late fetal and perinatal age from limb bone length by linear and logarithmic regression. Ann Hum Biol 7:257–265
Sebire NJ, Weber MA, Thayyil S, Mushtaq I, Taylor A, Chitty LS (2012) Minimally invasive perinatal autopsies using magnetic resonance imaging and endoscopic postmortem examination ("keyhole autopsy"): feasibility and initial experience. J Matern Fetal Neonatal Med 25:513–518
Shelmerdine SC, Arthurs OJ, Gilpin I, Norman W, Jones R, Taylor AM, Sebire NJ, Chitty LS (2019c) Is traditional perinatal autopsy needed after detailed fetal ultrasound and post-mortem MRI? Prenat Diagn 39:818–829
Shelmerdine SC, Davendralingam N, Palm L, Minden T, Cary N, Sebire NJ, Arthurs OJ (2019a) Diagnostic accuracy of postmortem CT of children: a retrospective single-center study. AJR Am J Roentgenol:1–13
Shelmerdine SC, Gerrard CY, Rao P, Lynch M, Kroll J, Martin D, Miller E, Filograna L, Martinez RM, Ukpo O, Daly B, Hyodoh H, Johnson K, Watt A, Taranath A, Brown S, Perry D, Boel LWT, Borowska-Solonynko A, van Rijn R, Klein W, Whitby E, Arthurs OJ (2019d) Joint European Society of Paediatric Radiology (ESPR) and International Society for Forensic Radiology and Imaging (ISFRI) guidelines: paediatric postmortem computed tomography imaging protocol. Pediatr Radiol 49:694–701
Shelmerdine SC, Gerrard CY, Rao P, Lynch M, Kroll JJF, Martin D, Miller E, Filograna L, Martinez RM, Ukpo O, Daly B, Hyodoh H, Johnson K, Watt A, Taranath A, Brown SD, Perry DH, Thorup Boel LW, Borowska-Solonynko A, van Rijn RR, Klein WM, Whitby A, Arthurs OJ (2019e) Joint European Society of Paediatric Radiology (ESPR) and International Society for Forensic Radiology and Imaging (ISFRI) guidelines: paediatric post-mortem computed tomography (CT) imaging protocol. Pediatr Radiol 49(5):694–701
Shelmerdine SC, Hutchinson JC, Sebire NJ, Jacques TS, Arthurs OJ (2017) Post-mortem magnetic resonance (PMMR) imaging of the brain in fetuses and children with histopathological correlation. Clin Radiol 72:1025–1037
Shelmerdine SC, Langan D, Hutchinson JC, Hickson M, Pawley K, Suich J, Palm L, Sebire NJ, Wade A, Arthurs OJ (2018) Chest radiographs versus CT for the detection of rib fractures in children (DRIFT): a diagnostic accuracy observational study. Lancet Child Adolesc Health 2:802–811
Shelmerdine SC, Sebire NJ, Arthurs OJ (2019b) Perinatal post mortem ultrasound (PMUS): a practical approach. Insights Imaging 10:35
Sieswerda-Hoogendoorn T, Beenen LF, van Rijn RR (2015) Normal cranial postmortem CT findings in children. Forensic Sci Int 246:43–49
Sieswerda-Hoogendoorn T, Soerdjbalie-Maikoe V, de Bakker H, van Rijn RR (2014) Postmortem CT compared to autopsy in children; concordance in a forensic setting. Int J Legal Med 128(6):957–965
Sieswerda-Hoogendoorn T, Soerdjbalie-Maikoe V, Maes A, van Rijn RR (2013) The value of post-mortem CT in neonaticide in case of severe decomposition: description of 12 cases. Forensic Sci Int 233: 298–303
Sonnemans LJP, Vester MEM, Kolsteren EEM, Erwich J, Nikkels PGJ, Kint PAM, van Rijn RR, Klein WM (2018) Dutch guideline for clinical foetal-neonatal and paediatric post-mortem radiology, including a review of literature. Eur J Pediatr 177:791–803
Taylor AM, Sebire NJ, Ashworth MT, Schievano S, Scott RJ, Wade A, Chitty LS, Robertson N, Thayyil S (2014) Postmortem cardiovascular magnetic resonance imaging in fetuses and children: a masked comparison study with conventional autopsy. Circulation 129:1937–1944
Teeuw AH, Sieswerda-Hoogendoorn T, Aaftink D, Burgers IAV, Vrolijk-Bosschaart TF, Brilleslijper-Kater SN, Heymans HSA, van Rijn RR (2017) Assessments carried out by a child abuse and neglect team in an Amsterdam teaching hospital led to interventions in most of the reported cases. Acta Paediatr 106:1118–1127
Thayyil S, Chitty LS, Robertson NJ, Taylor AM, Sebire NJ (2010) Minimally invasive fetal postmortem examination using magnetic resonance imaging and computerised tomography: current evidence and practical issues. Prenat Diagn 30:713–718
Thayyil S, Sebire NJ, Chitty LS, Wade A, Chong W, Olsen O, Gunny RS, Offiah AC, Owens CM, Saunders DE, Scott RJ, Jones R, Norman W, Addison S, Bainbridge A, Cady EB, Vita ED, Robertson NJ, Taylor AM (2013) Post-mortem MRI versus conventional autopsy in fetuses and children: a prospective validation study. Lancet 382:223–233

Thayyil S, Sebire NJ, Chitty LS, Wade A, Olsen O, Gunny RS, Offiah A, Saunders DE, Owens CM, Chong WK, Robertson NJ, Taylor AM (2011) Post mortem magnetic resonance imaging in the fetus, infant and child: a comparative study with conventional autopsy (MaRIAS protocol). BMC Pediatr 11:120

The Royal College of Radiologists (RCR) and the Society and College of Radiographers (SCoR) (2017) The radiological investigation of suspected physical abuse in children. https://www.rcr.ac.uk/publication/radiological-investigation-suspected-physical-abuse-children

Tsai A, Connolly SA, Ecklund K, Johnston PR, Kleinman PK (2019) Subperiosteal new bone formation with the distal tibial classic metaphyseal lesion: prevalence on radiographic skeletal surveys. Pediatr Radiol 49(4):551–558

Tsai A, Johnston PR, Perez-Rossello JM, Breen MA, Kleinman PK (2018) The distal tibial classic metaphyseal lesion: medial versus lateral cortical injury. Pediatr Radiol 48:973–978

Vander Plaetsen S, De Letter E, Piette M, Van Parys G, Casselman JW, Verstraete K (2015) Post-mortem evaluation of drowning with whole body CT. Forensic Sci Int 249:35–41

Wallace GH, Makoroff KL, Malott HA, Shapiro RA (2007) Hospital-based multidisciplinary teams can prevent unnecessary child abuse reports and out-of-home placements. Child Abuse Negl 31:623–629

Weustink AC, Hunink MG, van Dijke CF, Renken NS, Krestin GP, Oosterhuis JW (2009) Minimally invasive autopsy: an alternative to conventional autopsy? Radiology 250:897–904

Wootton-Gorges SL, Soares BP, Alazraki AL, Anupindi SA, Blount JP, Booth TN, Dempsey ME, Falcone RA Jr, Hayes LL, Kulkarni AV, Partap S, Rigsby CK, Ryan ME, Safdar NM, Trout AT, Widmann RF, Karmazyn BK, Palasis S (2017) ACR appropriateness criteria(®) suspected physical abuse-child. J Am Coll Radiol 14:S338–s349

World Health Organisation (2016) Child maltreatment; fact sheet. http://www.who.int/mediacentre/factsheets/fs150/en/. Accessed 12 Jan 2018

Wozniak KJ, Moskala A, Kluza P, Romaszko K, Lopatin O, Rzepecka-Wozniak E (2015) Whole-body postmortem computed tomography angiography of a newborn revealing transposition of great arteries. Int J Legal Med 129:1253–1258

Post-mortem Computed Tomography of Charred Victims in Modern Forensic Medicine

Mehdi Gaha, Fabrice Dedouit, Mathilde Ducloyer, Eric Dumousset, Mathieu Auffret, Claire Saccardy, and Douraied Ben Salem

Contents

M. Gaha (✉)
Forensic Imaging Unit,
University Hospital of Brest,
Brest Cedex, France
e-mail: mehdi.gaha@chu-brest.fr

F. Dedouit
Department of Forensic Medicine, Hôpital Rangueil,
Toulouse Cedex 9, France
e-mail: dedouit.f@chu-toulouse.fr

M. Ducloyer
Department of Forensic Medicine, Department of Radiology, University Hospital of Nantes,
Nantes, France
e-mail: mathilde.ducloyer@chu-nantes.fr

E. Dumousset
Imaging Department,
CHU Gabriel Montpied,
Clermont-Ferrand, France
e-mail: e_dumousset@chu-clermontferrand.fr

M. Auffret
Imaging and Radiology Department,
Brittany Atlantic Hospital of Vannes, Vannes, France
e-mail: mathieu.auffret@ch-bretagne-atlantique.fr

C. Saccardy
Forensic Institute, University Hospital of Brest,
Brest Cedex, France
e-mail: claire.saccardy@chu-brest.fr

D. Ben Salem
Forensic Imaging Unit, University Hospital of Brest,
Brest Cedex, France

LaTIM, Inserm UMR 1101, UBO, Univ Brest,
Brest Cedex, France
e-mail: douraied.bensalem@chu-brest.fr

© Springer Nature Switzerland AG 2022

F. Dedouit et al. (eds.), *Forensic Imaging*, Medical Radiology Diagnostic Imaging,
https://doi.org/10.1007/978-3-030-83352-7_10

1 Background

The forensic pathologist can examine or perform an autopsy in cases with fatal and nonfatal exposures to heat and cold (causing thermal injuries as burns and scalds) in different forensic contexts: accidental or with a homicidal intent. In case of homicidal heat exposure, different scenarios are possible: an arson with the intention to cause the death of a person or an arson to conceal a recent homicide.

Hypothermic injuries, on the other hand, are rarely criminal (Reinhard et al. 2014). The identification of hypothermia as the cause of death might be difficult in forensic pathology because of unspecific, inconstant, or even negative macroscopic and microscopic findings. However the simultaneous presence for example of frost erythema, Wischnewski spots, hemorrhages into the synovial membrane, bloody discoloration of synovial fluid of the knee, and basal vacuolization of the renal tubular epithelial cells indicates fatal hypothermia, their absence does not allow the diagnosis of hypothermia to be ruled out (Rousseau et al. 2021). Post-mortem biochemical investigations are valuable in detecting adaptation responses to cold stress and metabolic changes that occur following cold exposure. Ethanol intoxication prevents appearance of adaptation responses to cold, rendering the diagnosis less obvious (Reinhard et al. 2014). Immunohistochemistry, post-mortem imaging, and molecular pathology have shown promising results, although at present they do not always provide pathognomonic signs of fatal hypothermia (Palmiere et al. 2014; Rousseau et al. 2021).

The forensic assessment of severely burned and charred bodies is challenging for the forensic pathologist because it is usually impossible to distinguish cutaneous and subcutaneous antemortem burns from post-mortem burns based on gross and microscopic examinations (Di Maio and Di Maio 2001; Levy et al. 2009). Consequently, the forensic pathologist relies upon the combination of classical findings such as:

- Physical signs of smoke inhalation such as soot in the deep airways which is a forensic vitality sign.
- Cherry red coloration of liver mortis, muscles, blood, and organs suggesting carbon monoxide intoxication (Levy et al. 2009).
- Toxicological samples analyses with the assessment of the percentage of serum carboxyhemoglobin (COHb) to determine whether death occurred before or during the fire, also including cyanide as well as full toxicology analyses to exclude an intoxication or unconsciousness during the start of the fire (Levy et al. 2009).

For cases with charring, the autopsy may be limited. It can be difficult or impossible for the forensic pathologist to detect subtle fractures and injuries secondary to antemortem traumatisms. Post-mortem Computed Tomography (PMCT) is a common and useful complementary exploration for autopsies performed on charred bodies. It allows the documentation of fractures and injuries, but also a localization of different foreign bodies, as metallic fragments, which can be found intra- or extra-corporal. PMCT can also permit a positive identification of the deceased when fingerprinting and DNA analysis cannot be performed (Levy 2009). To differentiate between antemortem traumatic injuries and those caused by the fire (Bohnert et al. 1998), the radiologist needs to understand the resulting findings of heat-induced changes on a body.

Through this pictorial review, the authors wish to give the radiologist some guidelines and an aid to obtain complete and accurate PMCT reports for burned or charred victims.

The radiologist will have to answer to the following relevant questions, in order to help the forensic pathologist:

- Are there any relevant elements that could permit a positive identification of the victim?
- Are there optimal sites for fluid sampling (for toxicological or genetic analysis)?
- Are there reliable vitality signs that can be detected on PMCT?
- What are the "typical findings" following heat exposure seen on PMCT?

2 The Role of PMCT and How to Proceed

2.1 The Role of PMCT

With the updating and improvement of cross-sectional imaging techniques, PMCT has in theory and praxis replaced conventional radiographies. PMCT provides an entire-body volumetric exploration, and consequently help forensic teams in their investigations (Dirnhofer et al. 2006).

The role of PMCT is to complement the autopsy and help to highlight injuries that autopsy doesn't "see", such as traumatic bone injuries and gas infiltration or collection. These elements can be difficult to diagnose during autopsy in charred bodies.

PMCT is accessible, affordable, reliable, reproducible and attainable in OECD (Organisation for Economic Cooperation and Development) countries (Coty et al. 2018). However, if PMCT is not available, radiographies must be performed in cases of putrefied or charred bodies (Fig. 1).

PMCT explorations show morphological changes of the bodies in heat-related death. Radiologists are able to detect damages, losses of soft tissues, bone damages, and also to localize gas collections and foreign bodies (Figs. 2a, $2b_1$, $2b_2$) (de Bakker et al. 2019).

Levy et al. showed a high correlation between PMCT and autopsies concerning charred bodies (Levy et al. 2009). PMCT and autopsies are able to document quite similarly:

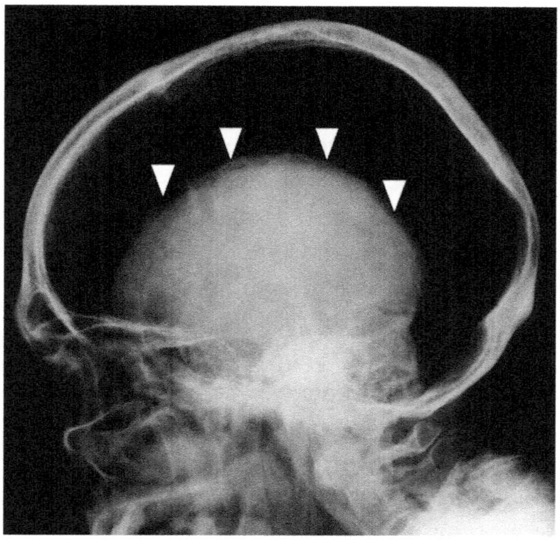

Fig. 1 Post-mortem sagittal view plain-film radiography showing retraction of cerebral hemispheres into the skull base (arrowheads) in a charred case

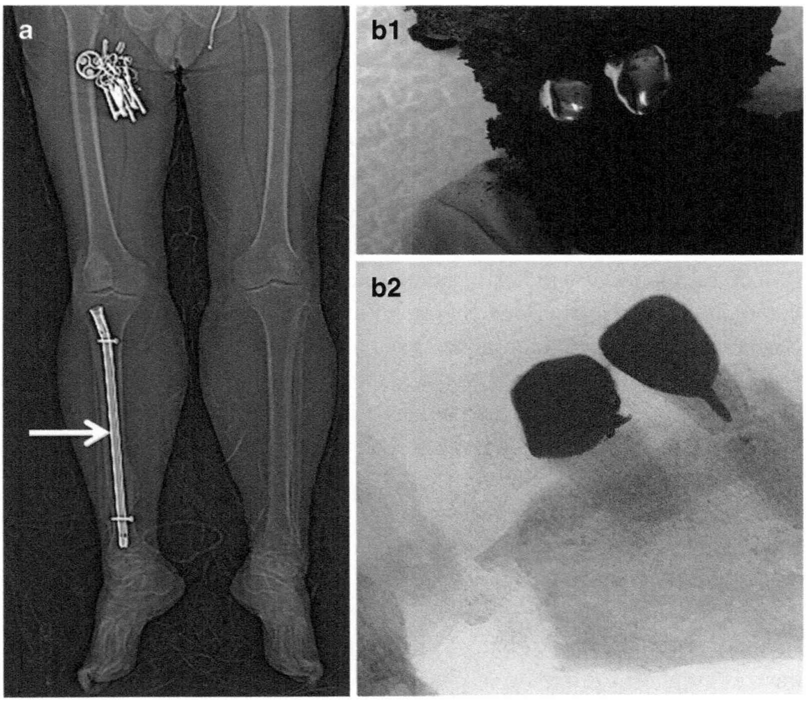

Fig. 2 (**a**) Scout view of a PMCT showing a centromedullary osteosynthesis in the right tibia (arrow). (**b**) Dental material: Macroscopic examination (**b1**); X-Ray (**b2**)

- The progressive thermal tissue loss: with a skin and subcutaneous fat loss, then an exposure of skeletal muscle, a skeletal muscle retraction, and finally an amputation.
- Thermal effects on the craniofacial region with: facial and scalp soft tissue loss, then a thermal destruction of the facial bones, a thermal peeling of the outer table of the calvarium, a brain retraction associated to thermal epidural hematoma, and different steps of destruction of the calvaria, first concerning the vertex and progressing to the skull base (Levy et al. 2009).

The brain itself shows a loss of liquid and becomes more dense and smaller.

Fractures of the skull base, spine, and pelvis are also easily detected in PMCT. In a general way, a complete dissection of these bone structures is fastidious, especially in charred bodies, and consequently rarely performed during autopsy. As complete dissection of such injuries in charred tissues is arduous and in some cases impossible, hence, detection and diagnosis of these fractures before the autopsy is useful for the forensic pathologist and may increase the accuracy rate of abnormalities detection during the autopsy (Levy et al. 2009).

2.2 Limitations of PMCT

The major thermal damages of the soft tissues are responsible for the main limitation of PMCT in charred bodies. The usual appearance of the internal organs is sometimes greatly modified by heat.

If antemortem injuries can be suspected by PMCT, the main cause of death, namely carboxyhemoglobin intoxication due to smoke and gas inhalation, is not visible on PMCT, as so as the presence of soot in the airways. Yet, these elements will be crucial to prove that the victim was alive when the fire began (de Bakker et al. 2019).

2.3 How to Proceed for PMCT Realization?

In contrast to other post-mortem circumstances, there is no place for the use of contrast media in PMCT scans of severely burned victims. The severe injuries of the skin and soft tissues make the use of contrast agents impossible (Coty et al. 2018).

The protocol of PMCT is a classical full body-exploration with no contrast media injection. Small technical difficulties concern the state of dilapidation or pugilistic posture of the charred body, which may practically complicate the transport and the moving of the deceased on the CT table (Coty et al. 2018).

The acquisition protocol is standard with a helical acquisition on the skull (in thin slices of 0.625 mm thickness for example) and the neck. The radiological analysis of the images will be done in soft tissue and bone windows.

A whole-body exploration is always mandatory. It consists of a first head-neck-chest-abdomino-pelvic helical acquisition (with mediastinal, pulmonary, abdominal and bone windows), and a secondary helical acquisition on the lower limbs (with bone and soft tissues windows). The presence of foreign bodies (e.g., house or vehicle's debris) in the tissues and the body or on its surface is a particularity to take into consideration (Fig. 3) (Gaha et al. 2019).

3 Guidelines for the Radiologist Concerning PMCT in Heat-Induced Deaths and His Radiological Report

3.1 Complete Description of Potential Identification Elements

Confirming the presumed identity of the victim constitutes one of the main issues of forensic investigations. The visual identification by close relatives can be attempted when burn injuries are minor and/or do not concern the face. Unfortunately, a corpse found in a fireplace will be generally extensively charred, preventing any visual identification. The alteration of tissues will further complicate the task of the pathologist in this goal (Coty et al. 2018).

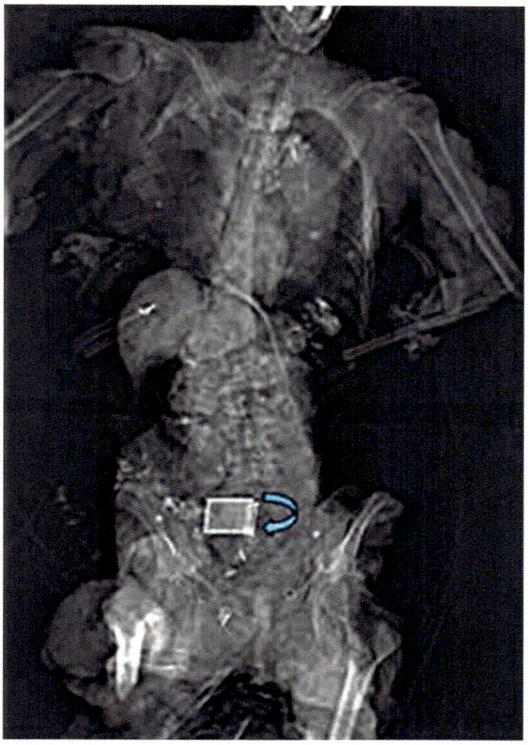

Fig. 3 Scout view of a PMCT showing incorporation (fusion) of external foreign bodies within the charred body (curved arrow)

Personnal effects of the victim may be present in the body bag and can be described easily if they are metallic, like jewelry or watches. Their description by the radiologist can facilitate the recognition by the pathologist among numerous burned fragments.

Internal medical devices such as dental fillings, osteosynthesis, vascular prosthesis, surgical clips, pacemaker, etc. must be noted to compare them with the medical records of the potentially identified person.

Sex determination: PMCT can provide a first determination of the sex of the victim. If the external examination of the genital organs is unreliable, internal sexual organs such as the uterus or the prostate are usually preserved from the heat, as the pelvic girdle is one of the last structures to be destroyed. The internal organs are easily seen on PMCT, which will be a precious tool to accelerate the identification process.

Biological samples: For extremely charred bodies, it may be difficult for the forensic team to collect bone samples suitable for further assessment. A fragment of femoral bone is classically sampled to proceed to DNA analyses (Butler 2005). When the body displays extensive thermal destructions, biological samples for genetics can be obtained from other bones such as the sternum or the petrous bone, or from soft tissues such as the psoas muscles, the spinal cord or the dura mater, known for its resistance to thermal injuries (Motani et al. 2006). The radiologist must keep in mind, that the description of unaltered bones or tissues can greatly facilitate bone sampling and the identification process.

3.2 Identification of the Collection Sites Available for Biological Samples Dedicated to Toxicology

Besides genetic purposes, PMCT can be helpful to detect the best localisation of biological samples such as blood or gastric content for the toxicological screening, which is mostly performed for two purposes. First, to determine the percentage of carboxyhemoglobine, and its role in the cause of death. If the rate of carboxhemoglobine is high, it will be a good indicator to confirm that the victim was alive in the fire. Secondly, it will provide further information about the circumstances: did the victim consume toxic substances which may have altered his attention? Was the deceased poisoned before the fire started? (Schwed and Schulz 1978).

The success of the procedure depends on the availability of biological fluids, the burning level of the body. The radiologist can provide a detailed imaging analysis of the PMCT, which can be very usuful in identifying possible collecting sites (Coty et al. 2018) (Fig. 4a, b).

3.3 Detection of Foreign Bodies, Especially Ballistic, and Traumatic Injuries

The main purpose of the forensic investigation is to establish the cause of death: whether death is due to a chemical asphyxia (meaning that the victim was alive when the fire began) or was he/she

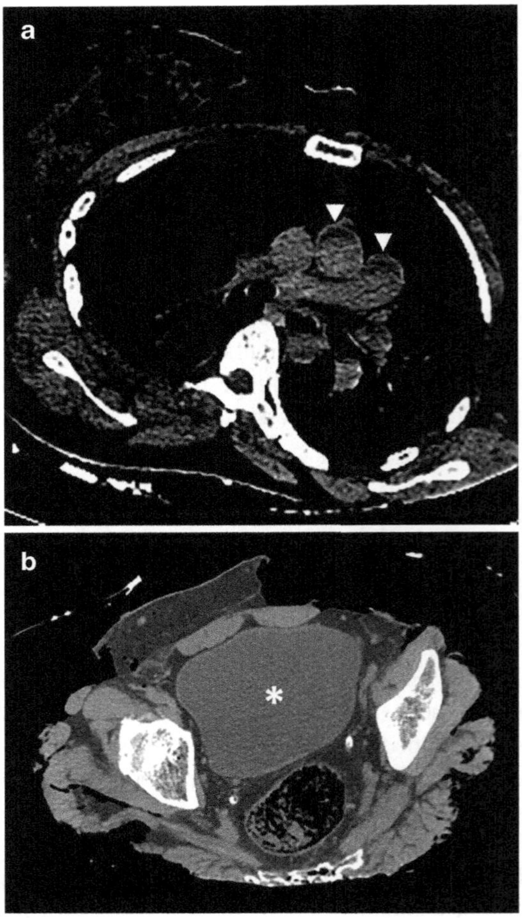

Fig. 4 (**a**) Axial plane, chest, PMCT: note the fluid-fluid level in the ascending aorta and the pulmonary artery (arrowhead), pointing out that non-coagulated blood is available for sampling and toxicological analysis. (**b**) Axial plane, pelvic, PMCT: presence of a full bladder suitable for urine sampling (asterisk)

already dead (maybe because of a homicidal or an accidental cause)? In this last situation, maybe a fire was set to conceal a homicide. Sometimes the cause of death can also be traumatic and the fire an incidential repercussion, for example, in motor vehicle accidents (car accidents).

The state of charring can complicate the autopsy. The soft tissues (skin, subcutaneous fat, muscles) are taut, retracted, and adhere to each other and to the bones, their dissection is difficult. In those cases, traumatic bone fractures and ballistic material as shrapnels, pellets or bullets can be remain undiagnosed.

Thanks to its high sensibility to metallic artifacts, PMCT is essential in gunshot trauma to detect and localize the ballistic foreign bodies. PMCT can help the forensic pathologist to characterize entry and exit bone wounds, the trajectory of the projectile and to determine the death mechanism (Fig. 5a, b) (Harcke et al. 2007). The body might contain many pellets in the case of lead shots or hunting rifles. The pellets must be counted in the radiological report.

Suspicious skin lesions identical to stab wounds must be examined. In such cases, in contrast to thermal skin damage, stab wounds have clean edges with signs of subcutaneous emphysema surrounding the linear cut lines on PMCT (Coty et al. 2018).

In different circumstances, like car accidents, death can occur from severe traumatic injuries first, and the vehicle may start to burn secondly. The PMCT in this case will show visceral and bone trauma injuries (with a radiological aspect different from bone thermal fractures) along with heat-induced lesions.

3.4 Characteristic Burn-Related Lesions

3.4.1 Overall State of Charred Bodies

The earliest effect of fire on a body is the loss of the skin and subcutaneous tissues, which exposes skeletal muscles.

The craniofacial area is the anatomic region that is usually directly exposed to the fire and often presents with severe soft tissue damages.

For the extremities, skeletal muscles contract and shrink because of the heat, giving some flexion deformity aspects. Muscle retractions predominate in the flexor muscles of the forearms and wrists as well as in the leg flexors. The muscle retraction results in a particular attitude of the upper limbs called “pugilistic attitude”, as it imitates the position of a boxer during a fight (Fig. 6a–c) (Reinhard et al. 2014). Thin linear superficial fractures of the cortical surface of bone are characteristic of thermal fractures. Thermal amputations occur when the distal extremities are completely consumed by fire.

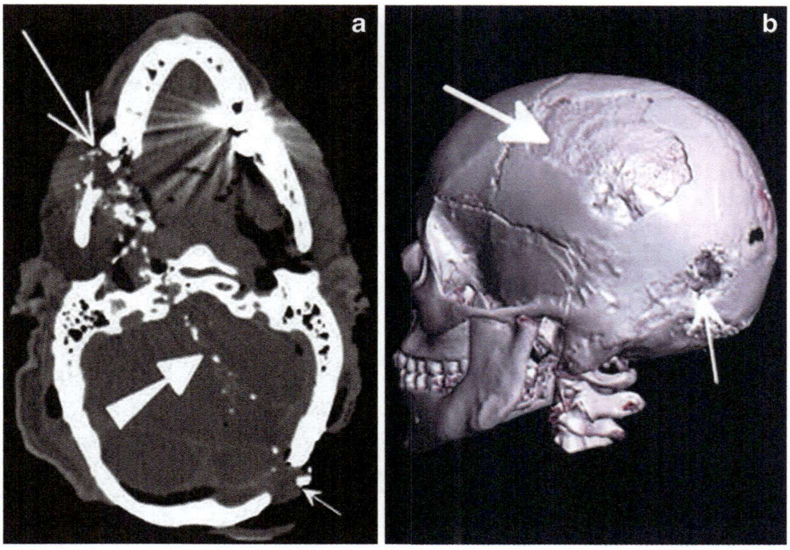

Fig. 5 Axial plane, skull, PMCT (Courtesy of G. Gorincour). (**a**) Presence of a ballistic trajectory (thick arrow) on a charred body. Bone entry (long thin arrow) and exit wounds (short thin arrow) may not be obvious at autopsy in a charred body. (**b**) 3D volume rendering reconstruction of the skull: typical heat-induced delamination of the external table of the left parietal bone (thick arrow). Bone exit wound (thin arrow)

The thermal changes in the skull vary gradually from thin cortical fractures of the outer table to the loss of the outer table, the development of a thermal epidural hematoma, and a potential progressive complete destruction of the cranium (from the vertex to the skull base) (Pope and Smith 2004; Levy et al. 2009).

Shrinkage of organs due to heat is a well-documented effect of thermal damages. De Bakker et al. described a typical dense border sign in situations where the liver, the lung, or the brain were exposed directly to the fire. The high temperature induces dehydration and shrinkage of the exposed tissues (de Bakker et al. 2019). In these situations, the forensic pathologist finds superficial black and stiff modifications of the damaged tissues and organs. Organs and muscular tissues do not burn easily, but will retract or shrink instead. Tissues such as skin, tendons, bones, and fat, however, are more vulnerable to thermal damage.

Levy et al. described the association of bone fractures and joint dislocations for thermal flexion deformities (Levy et al. 2009). The pugilistic posture seen in the upper extremities of severely burned bodies results from a flexion of the shoulder, elbow, and wrist joints. The authors observed that the combination of severe flexions and thermal tissue losses can create joint disarticulations as well as bone fractures (Levy et al. 2009). At the lower extremities, similar flexed deformities occur for the hips and knees, but the phenomenon is classically less pronounced. Flexion deformity of the feet and ankles is more pronounced, and can again generate bone fractures and joint disarticulations. Levy et al. hypothesized that these changes are due to mechanical forces associated with thermal muscular contraction and shrinkage, which create unbalanced forces on the joints. The sequence of flexion contracture and fracture/dislocation precedes the final thermal bone destruction leading to thermal amputations (Levy et al. 2009).

3.4.2 Head

The thinness of the subcutaneous tissues of the face and the scalp makes the cephalic extremity particularly vulnerable to thermal effects of a fire. The extent of head and neck degradation depends directly on the time of exposure to heat and different patterns are described in forensic medicine (Bohnert et al. 1998). The radiologist must know them and be able to make differences between heat-related injuries and other post-mortem changes. He also has to be able to identify antemortem trauma (Coty et al. 2018).

The soft tissues of the scalp and the face are the first to be effected and destroyed by the heat.

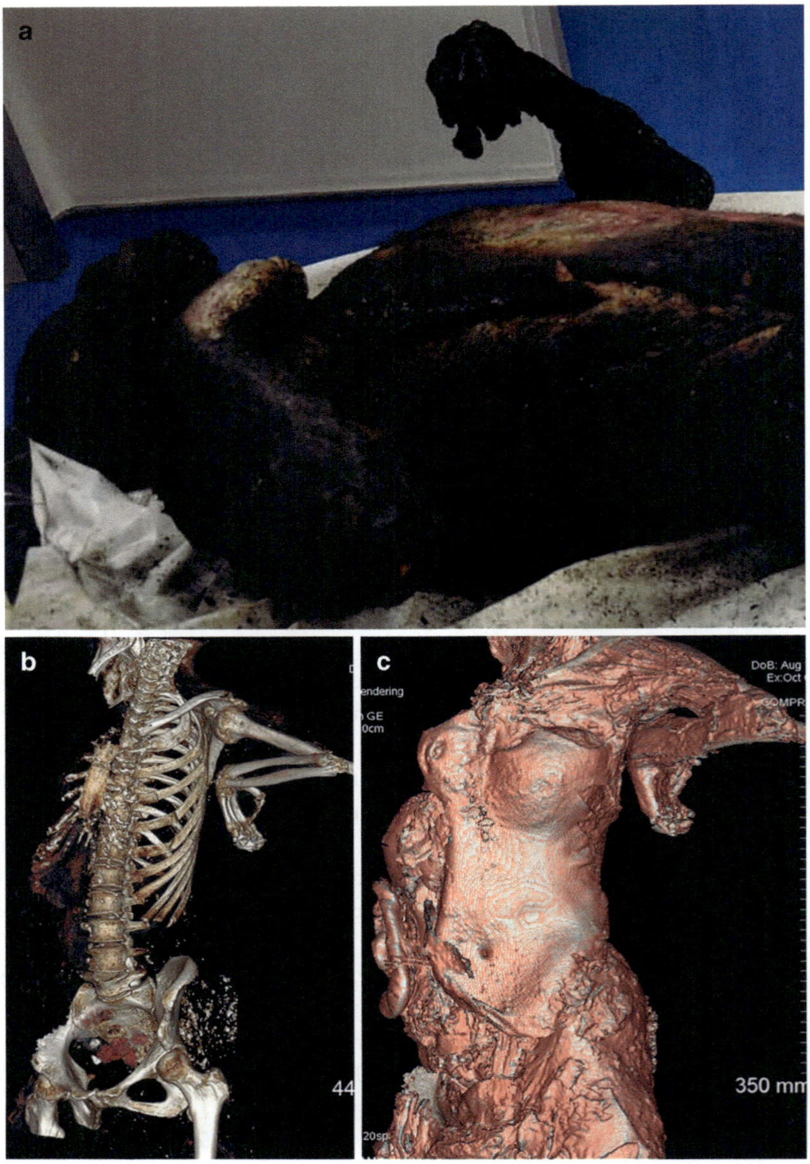

Fig. 6 Illustration of the pugilistic attitude. (**a**) Autopsy's picture: characteristic triple flexions of the left upper limb due to muscle thermal retraction. Pugilistic posture with an anteromedial flexion of the humerus on the body, flexion of the forearm on the arm, and flexion of the wrist on the forearm. (**b, c**) 3D volume rendering reconstructions of the whole body, PMCT (**b**: without soft tissues; **c**: with soft tissues) showing the characteristic pugilistic attitude

These defects are rarely visible on PMCT, unless a wide window is used.

Once soft tissues are consumed, the skull is rapidly exposed. Heat is then responsible for a progressive damage of the calvaria, with thin linear fracture lines of the outer table and following delamination of the outer table, with variable preservation of the inner table. PMCT as thin linear fracture lines of the outer table of the calvarium. First a partial, later on a complete delamination of the outer table into multiple fragments can be seen while the inner table remains intact (Fig. 7a, b).

In addition to the bone lesions, one can also witness changes in the cranial cavity due to the heat exposure. The high temperature within the skull induces dura mater retraction, leading to an exfoliation from the bone and to blood exudation from the venous sinuses within the epidural space. In case the heat process continues, the blood col-

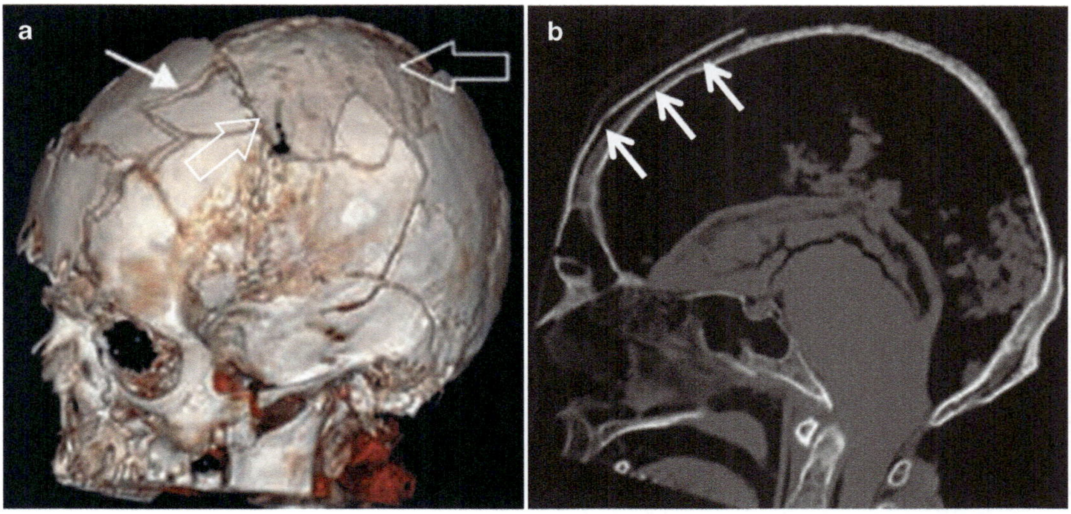

Fig. 7 Illustrations of the delamination of the outer table of the calvarium, with regular contours exposing the inner table. (**a**) volume rendering reconstruction, PMCT: delamination of the outer table of the calvarium (large arrows). Thin linear fracture line of the outer table of the calvarium (thin arrow). (**b**) Sagittal plane, PMCT: delamination of outer table of the calvarium (arrows)

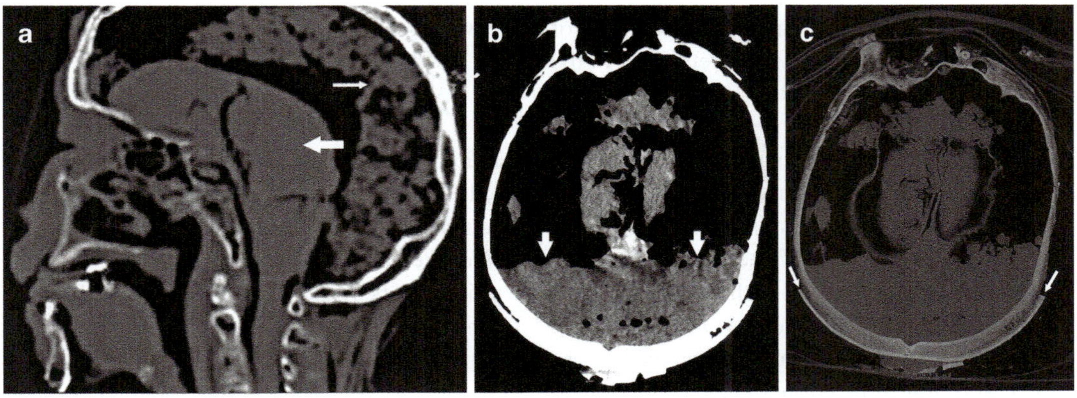

Fig. 8 Epidural thermal hematoma. (**a**) Sagittal plane, brain, PMCT: epidural thermal hematoma described as "cooked hematoma" at autopsy. Honeycomb appearance (thin arrow) and cerebral retraction (thick arrow). (**b**) Axial plane, brain, PMCT soft tissue window: epidural hematoma (arrows). (**c**) Axial plane, brain, PMCT bone window: delamination of the outer table (arrows)

lection coagulates and forms a heat epidural **hematoma** (Coty et al. 2018). The heat epidural hematoma is one of the most frequent heat-induced lesions found in burned bodies. The radiologist must distinguish this heat epidural hematoma from a traumatic one. The heat-hematoma exhibits low densities and is crescent shaped (with a "honeycomb appearance"). This crescent-shaped appearance is close to a subdural hematoma, frequently crosses the midline and detaches the venous sinus (Fig. 8a–c), unlike a traumatic epidural hematoma which is dense, convex, and lens shaped (de Bakker et al. 2019). The mechanisms responsible for these two types of intracranial collections easily explain their appearance and distribution: the pseudo hematoma due to heat is the result of transsudation of blood and liquid through the retracted pachymeninge, while an extra dural hematoma is resulting from the injury of an artery and/or vein of the skull, leading to an active bleeding.

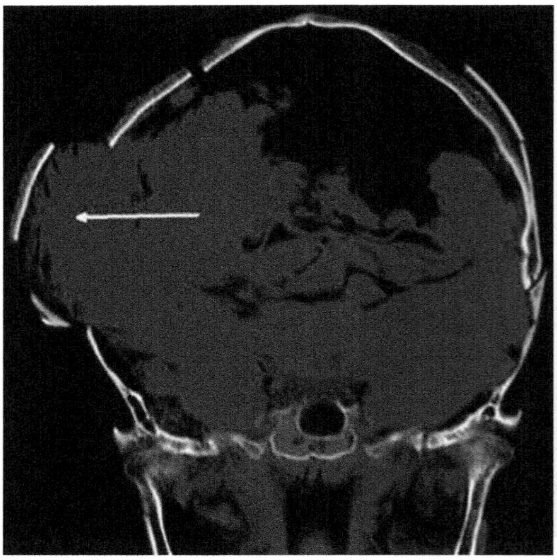

Fig. 9 Coronal plane, head level, PMCT: fracture of the inner table, gradual disappearance of the vault, extra-cranial cerebral herniation (arrow)

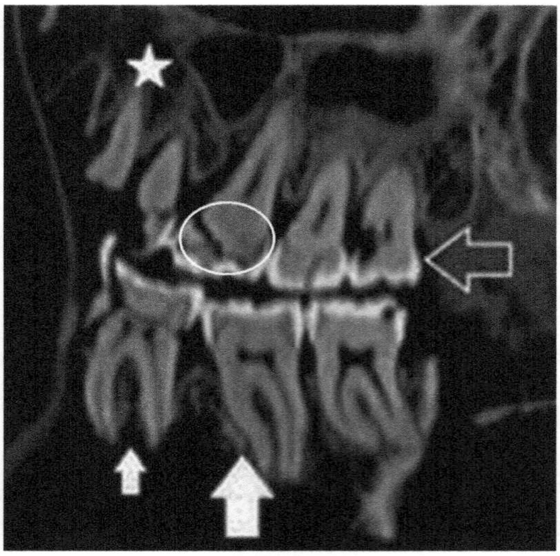

Fig. 10 Dental thermal injuries. Sagittal reconstruction, PMCT: anteroposterior severity gradient. The severity was higher in the front teeth region (at the left of the image), 18 seems normal, except for an carious lesion (empty arrow), 16 showed a fracture of the crown (circle) 47 showed small dentin fractures (big filled arrow), 46 showed severe fracture with beginning crown detachment (small filled arrow), and 14 lost its crown (star)

In extreme cases, a complete detachment of the dura mater of the skull with a retraction of the cerebral hemispheres towards the base of the skull can be observed.

The pathogenesis of this phenomenon is still unknown, but a boiling mechanism due to the local thermal effects is postulated for a pressure increase causing a split of the dura mater. The cerebral tissue can exit from the skull and burn under the heat effect (Kondo and Ohshima 1994). The forensic pathologist can observe the macroscopic appearance of the herniated brain, which then shows “cauliflower” or “mushroom” appearances. In areas where heat acted locally and severely on the skull, leading to bone destruction, the dura mater can however remain intact. Surprisingly a heat generated brain herniation in the epidural spaces can occur when the dura mater is disconnected, without being burned directly (Fig. 9).

Particular findings can be related to carbon monoxide exposure. Lapresle and Fardeau described in their autopsy findings necrosis in the globus pallidus, demyelination in the cerebral white matter, spondylotic changes in the cerebral cortex, and necrosis in the hippocampus (Lapresle and Fardeau 1967).

3.4.3 Dental Lesions

Teeth are quite vulnerable to the effects of heat. Their destruction may complicate the identification of the victim.

Fire may be responsible for thin tooth fissures, tooth fractures and tooth avulsion, especially when the alveolar bone is also damaged and presents fractures and resulting in enlargment of the alveolo dental space (Fig. 10) (Auffret et al. 2014). An attentive screening of the oral cavity and the oropharynx is also important, as teeth may have fallen out after their avulsion.

As for any unidentified body, the exhaustive description of dental filling material and implants is crucial.

PMCT can reveal thin tooth fissures, fractures (with displacement) and if more severely injured a crown detachment.

Alveolar bone can also be affected by the heat and present thermal fractures with an alveolo-dental space enlargement possible with tooth avulsion that can be complete or incomplete. Dental filling material, like all medical implants

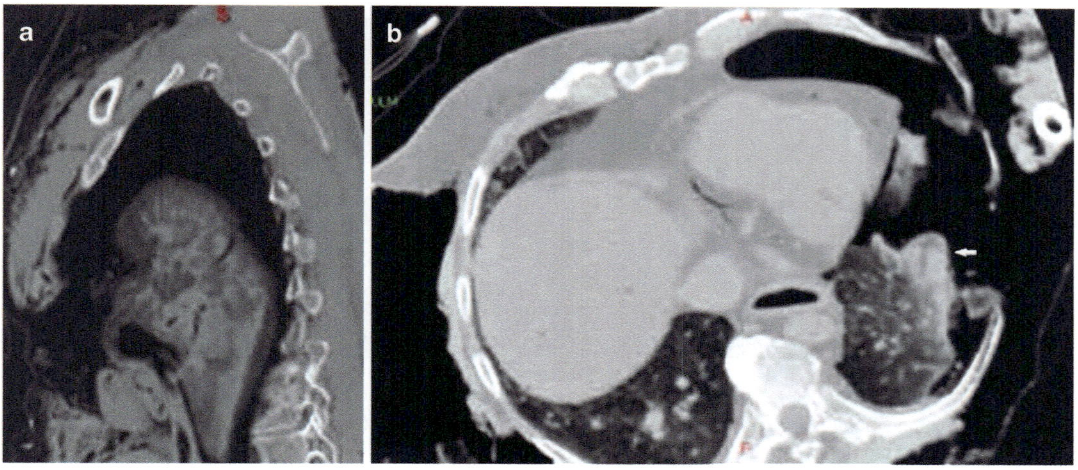

Fig. 11 Lung injuries (**a**) Sagittal plane, PMCT (lung window): retraction of the lung. (**b**) Axial plane, PMCT (lung window): retraction of the lung and increased density (arrow) of the parenchyma. Lack of chest parietal soft tissues and ribs due to the thermal injuries

should be reported in the PMCT final report for victim identification purposes.

3.4.4 Airways and Chest

The presence of soot in the respiratory tract and sometimes in the oesophagus is the direct sign of inhalation of smoke and soot, and proves that the victim was alive when the fire began. The detection of soot is particularly easy during autopsy, visible as black deposits on the trachea and bronchi mucous membrane, but remains undetectable on PMCT.

The inhalation of hot gases causes mucosal damage inducing pulmonary edema. This edema has the appearance of a classical pulmonary edema with diffuse ground glass opacities extended to all pulmonary lobes (Fig. 11a, b). The ground glass opacities are generally posterior and sloping, contiguous with the pulmonary fissures and sparing the upper areas. These density gradient lesions must be distinguished from hypostatic lividities (Ishida et al. 2015).

3.4.5 Abdomen

The abdominal content is generally rather preserved from the heat: the organs are protected by the adipose and muscular tissues of the abdominal wall, but also the intra abdominal fat and peritoneum. If they are exposed to heat, internal organs and vessels usually present major alterations such as shrinkage or retraction, which may prevent the detection of traumatic injuries or pre-existing desease (Levy et al. 2009).

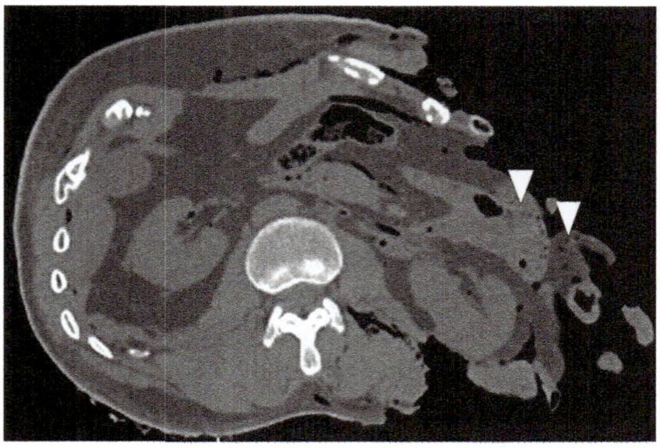

Fig. 12 Axial plane, abdomen: extensive soft tissue loss with evisceration (arrowheads)

The presence of an evisceration, most of the time with protrusion of the abdominal contents is the obvious sign of a peritoneal effraction (Fig. 12). The protrusion of the digestive tract through a dehiscence of the abdominal wall occurs approximately 30 min after the beginning to the exposure. The density of solid organs such as the liver are not modified by the heat (Coty

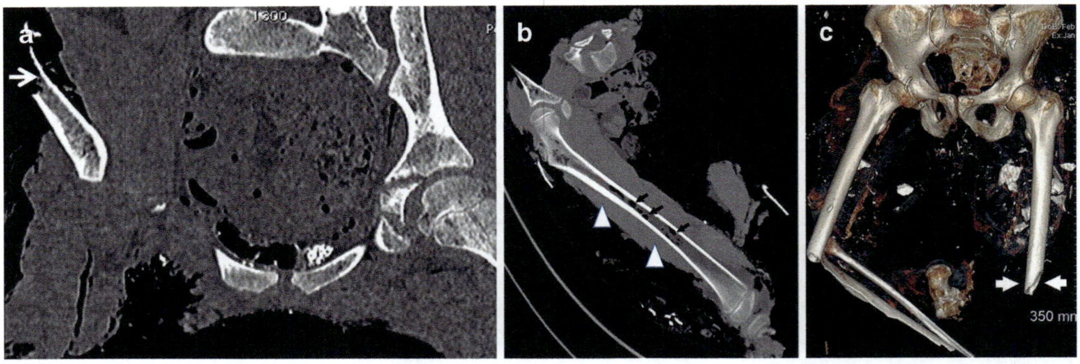

Fig. 13 PMCT. Bone injuries. (**a**) Coronal plane, pelvis: smooth-marginated fractures uncovered by skeletal muscle with a thermal amputation (arrow). (**b**) Sagittal plane, right femur: mottled lucencies of marrow spaces (arrows) with soft tissue retraction (arrowheads). (**c**) 3D volume rendering reconstruction, pelvis and lower limbs: typical appearance of "flute mouthpiece" fracture (arrows)

et al. 2018). Intestinal evisceration is a delayed heat induced consequence, taking place after approximately 30 minutes of fire exposure, depending on the temperatures. Otherwise, the abdominal organs, particularly the liver, don't show density changes, regardless of the burning state severity.

3.4.6 Long Bones

Limb extremities are particularly vunerable to fire. Skin, subcutaneous fat and muscles are the first to disappear as quickly as they are thin, like for the wrist, the fingers or the feet. It leads to thermal amputation, revealing the long bones below. Specific fractures of these long bones will appear then: transverse fractures, sometimes only concerning the cortical bone, uncovered by soft tissue; particular amputation of the extremity of the burned bone, described as a "flute mouthpiece" fracture (de Bakker et al. 2019). These fractures must be distinguished from ante mortem traumatic bone injuries, which concern bones still covered by soft tissues and appear like usual traumatic bone patterns (clean margins, both cortical concerned, comminution..). The bone marrow is also modified by the heat, as it can localy melt and be replaced by gas. This is only valid for bones exposed to fire.

The lucencies in the bone marrow spaces represent the thermal loss of the bone marrow elements and of the thin trabecula, with a preservation of the thicker bony trabecula. This finding is indicative of bone exposition to extreme heat and may therefore be useful when the position of the deceased relative to the fire has to be determined (Fig. 13a–c) (Levy et al. 2009).

Two factors are responsible for the acceleration of the dismemberment of the extremities. First, the pugilistic attitude, which worsens the exposition of the wrists and ankles to the heat. The destruction will be accelerated by their poor fat and water content; their distance to the body also allows for a better oxygenation around them (Symes et al. 2008). Second, the muscular retraction will increase the tension applied on the joints, wich are no longer supported by the soft tissues. Concerning the patella, the strength of muscular retraction can also cause a proximal dislocation of the patella. Another possible finding is that the patellar ligament burns through or ruptures because of the strength of the shrinking and retracting rectus femoris muscle (Ubelaker 2009).

4 Conclusion

Post-mortem computed tomography is nowadays fully integrated in forensic prodecures, because of its availability and its high added value to complete the autopsy. The aim of this pictorial review was to give an overview of the role of PMCT in the context of charred body, considering the technical approach and the guidelines for a complete study. The content of the report can be summarize as follows: identification elements, optimal sites for biological samples, and all the signs that could lead to the suspicion of homicide especially antemortem injuries, internal foreign bodies.

One benefit of PMCT is that when answers arise after forensic investigations, complementary radiological interpretations might be added to the autopsy results. CT findings enable the radiologist and the pathologist to look at post-mortem anatomy in two and three dimensions without dissection. The reconstructions are useful for demonstration during trial in court, based on non-bloody images.

PMCT also constitutes a precious tool to explore some of internal body parts, which are particularly difficult to examine during the autopsy, such as the face or the extermities. Some fractures found with PMCT can be omitted by the pathologist. It's usually subtle fractures which are difficult to see during autopsy, particularly on charred bodies.

Tiny radiopaque foreign bodies like metal splinters are easily diagnosed with PMCT. The informed pathologist can adapt the autopsy protocol to examine injuries previously detected PMCT, which could have been missed without radiology. As metal is well seen on PMCT, visualization of surgical material or dental implants has a great value in the process of victim identification (Bohnert et al. 1998).

PMCT has also a great importance in forensic investigation of burned bodies for the exploration of soft tissue, bones, identification localization of artifacts and gas collections. Besides, PMCT identifies typical aspects of body parts exposed to high heat: delamination of the outer table of the calvaria, intracranial heat-induced epidural hematoma, dense border sign of the brain, the liver and the lung, mottled lucencies in bones, joint luxations and others.

Some autopsy findings are however not detectable with PMCT, for example: superficial thermal injuries or the presence or absence of soot and thermal damages in the airways (de Bakker et al. 2019).

Consequently, the forensic autopsy together with histological and toxicological analysis is still essential to determine the cause of death and to evaluate signs of vitality of the abnormalities diagnosed. PMCT serves as a real added value for the post-mortem forensic investigation of burned victims.

Acknowledgments The authors are grateful to Taiseer Khalil for the English editing of this chapter.

References

Auffret M, Laurent PE, Saccardy C, Suply B, Diallo I, Piercecchi-Marti MD, Gorincour G, Ben Salem D (2014) Contribution of post-mortem multidetector computed tomography of the head and neck to the forensic evaluation of severely burned bodies. J Neuroradiol 41:15. https://doi.org/10.1016/j.neurad.2014.01.041

Bohnert M, Rost T, Pollak S (1998) The degree of destruction of human bodies in relation to the duration of the fire. Forensic Sci Int 95:11–21. https://doi.org/10.1016/s0379-0738(98)00076-0

Butler J (2005) Forensic DNA typing biology, technology, and genetics of STR markers, 2nd edn. Academic, Cambridge

Coty JB, Nedelcu C, Yahya S, Dupont V, Rougé-Maillart C, Verschoore M, Ridereau Zins C, Aubé C (2018) Burned bodies: post-mortem computed tomography, an essential tool for modern forensic medicine. Insights Imaging 9(5):731–743. https://doi.org/10.1007/s13244-018-0633-2

de Bakker HM, Roelandt GHJ, Soerdjbalie-Maikoe V, van Rijn RR, de Bakker BS (2019) The value of post-mortem computed tomography of burned victims in a forensic setting. Eur Radiol 29(4):1912–1921. https://doi.org/10.1007/s00330-018-5731-5

Di Maio DJ, Di Maio VJM (2001) Forensic pathology, 2nd edn. CRC, Boca Raton

Dirnhofer R, Jackowski C, Vock P, Potter K, Thali MJ (2006) Virtopsy: minimally invasive, imaging-guided virtual autopsy. Radiographics 26(5):1305–1333. https://doi.org/10.1148/rg.265065001

Gaha M, Auffret M, Hmandi O, Saccardy C, Gorincour G, Ben Salem D (2019) Post-mortem computed tomography of charred victims. In: Gorincour G et al (eds) Illustrated atlas of practical postmortem imaging. SFR, Paris, pp 72–79

Harcke HT, Levy AD, Abbott RM, Mallak CT, Getz JM, Champion HR, Pearse L (2007) Autopsy radiography: digital radiographs (DR) vs multidetector computed tomography (MDCT) in high-velocity gunshot-wound victims. Am J Forensic

Med Pathol 28(1):13–19. https://doi.org/10.1097/01.paf.0000257419.92109.ce

Ishida M, Gonoi W, Okuma H, Shirota G, Shintani Y, Abe H, Takazawa Y, Fukayama M, Ohtomo K (2015) Common postmortem computed tomography findings following atraumatic death: differentiation between normal postmortem changes and pathologic lesions. Korean J Radiol 16(4):798–809. https://doi.org/10.3348/kjr.2015.16.4.798

Kondo T, Ohshima T (1994) Epidural herniation of the cerebral tissue in a burned body: a case report. Forensic Sci Int 66(3):197–202. https://doi.org/10.1016/0379-0738(94)90344-1

Lapresle J, Fardeau M (1967) The central nervous system and carbon monoxide poisoning. II. Anatomical study of brain lesions following intoxication with carbon monixide (22 cases). Prog Brain Res 24:31–74. https://doi.org/10.1016/s0079-6123(08)60181-8

Levy AD, Harcke HT, Getz JM, Mallak CT (2009) Multidetector computed tomography findings in deaths with severe burns. Am J Forensic Med Pathol 30(2):137–141. https://doi.org/10.1097/PAF.0b013e3181879cc9

Motani H, Sakurada K, Akutsu T, Ikegaya H, Hayakawa M, Sato Y, Yajima D, Sato K, Kobayashi K, Iwase H (2006) Usefulness of dura mater in providing DNA samples for identifying cadavers. J Forensic Sci 51(4):888–892. https://doi.org/10.1111/j.1556-4029.2006.00157.x

Palmiere C, Teresiński G, Hejna P (2014) Postmortem diagnosis of hypothermia. Int J Legal Med 128(4):607–614. https://doi.org/10.1007/s00414-014-0977-1

Pope EJ, Smith OC (2004) Identification of traumatic injury in burned cranial bone: an experimental approach. J Forensic Sci 49(3):431–440

Reinhard B, Dettmeyer RB, Verhoff MA, Schütz HF (2014) Forensic medicine. Springer, Berlin. https://doi.org/10.1007/978-3-642-38818-7

Rousseau G, Chao de la Barca JM, Rougé-Maillart C, Teresiński G et al. (2021) Preliminary metabolomic profiling of the vitreous humor from hypothermia fatalities. J Proteome Res 20(5):2390–2396. https://doi.org/10.1021/acs.jproteome.0c00901

Schwed W, Schulz E (1978) Carboxyhaemoglobin and methaemoglobin findings in burnt bodies. Forensic Sci Int 12(3):233–235. https://doi.org/10.1016/0379-0738(78)90008-7

Symes SA, Rainwater CW, Chapman EN, Gipson DR, Piper AL (2008) Patterned thermal destruction of human remains in a forensic setting. In: Schmidt CW, Symes SA (eds) The analysis of burned human remains. Academic, London, pp 15–52

Ubelaker DH (2009) The forensic evaluation of burned skeletal remains: a synthesis. Forensic Sci Int 183(1–3):1–5. https://doi.org/10.1016/j.forsciint.2008.09.019

Part III

Examples for Typical Non Traumatic Forensic Cases

Natural Death

Heon Lee, Sookyoung Lee, Taehwa Baek,
Jang Gyu Cha, and Kyung-moo Yang

Contents

1 Introduction

Although there is still some debate, natural death refers to death from a naturally occurring disease process in contrast to non-natural type of death such as an accident, or violence (Oehmichen and Meissner 2000). For example, natural death is the end result of an illness or an internal failure of the body, which leads to death at some point. In cases of natural death, the person did not die from an intentional act, e.g., suicide or homicide, or an accident, such as a fatal fall, traffic crash, or drug overdose. The most common cause of natural death worldwide is ischemic heart disease, followed by stroke, chronic respiratory disease, and pneumonia (World Health Organization 2018). In contrast to the clinical setting, however, natural deaths investigated for forensic purposes mostly consist of sudden or unexpected events, especially in younger individuals. This is because death investigations and autopsy dissections are rarely performed in the majority of natural deaths, as death is already expected, especially in the elderly ones or in patients with known disease (Levy and Harcke

H. Lee (✉) · J. G. Cha
Department of Radiology, Soonchunhyang University Hospital Bucheon, Bucheon, Republic of Korea

Department of Forensic Medicine, National Forensic Service, Gangwon, Republic of Korea

S. Lee · T. Baek · K.-m. Yang
Department of Forensic Medicine, National Forensic Service, Gangwon, Republic of Korea

© Springer Nature Switzerland AG 2022
F. Dedouit et al. (eds.), *Forensic Imaging*, Medical Radiology Diagnostic Imaging,
https://doi.org/10.1007/978-3-030-83352-7_11

2011; Koehler 2016). Sudden death is an unexpected natural death occurring within 24 h after onset of symptoms, and sudden cardiac death (SCD) is defined clinically as cardiac death occurring within an hour following onset of acute symptoms (Biorck and Wikland 1972; Virmani et al. 2001; La Russa et al. 2019). The most frequent cause of sudden death is cardiovascular disease related to atherosclerotic coronary artery disease. Other types of cardiovascular disease that may cause sudden death include hypertrophic cardiomyopathy, coronary artery anomaly and dissection, ruptured aortic aneurysm, and aortic dissection (Virmani et al. 2001; Chugh et al. 2008; Michaud et al. 2012; McElwee et al. 2016; La Russa et al. 2019). Non-cardiac diseases, such as cerebrovascular disease, asthma, pulmonary embolism, and intra-abdominal hemorrhage, may also cause sudden death (Levy and Harcke 2011; Risgaard et al. 2015).

The main purpose of post-mortem imaging in cases of natural death is to identify the corresponding lethal pathologies for later confirmation at autopsy and to screen for non-natural manner of death. Recently, post-mortem imaging, particularly post-mortem computed tomography (PMCT), has proven to be a useful diagnostic tool in forensic practice and has become increasingly important in death investigations. PMCT scan is now part of the routine investigation process in many forensic institutions worldwide, with the goal of providing less-invasive, objective, and reproducible forensic investigations as a complement to autopsy. PMCT angiography (PMCTA) has been developed to address forensic questions raised regarding vascular pathologies, and has yielded promising results for exploring the vascular system, especially in cases of suspected natural death, by visualization of anatomic variation and detection of vascular rupture or occlusion that may lead to fatal consequences (Grabherr et al. 2014; Ross et al. 2014; Lee et al. 2019).

This chapter introduces the current roles of post-mortem imaging, especially with PMCT and PMCTA, in evaluation of natural death cases by describing various pathological conditions at different sites in the body.

2 Coronary Artery Disease and Ischemic Myocardium

As described above, cardiovascular diseases are the most common causes of natural death worldwide and SCD is mostly attributable to ischemic heart disease related to atherosclerotic coronary artery disease and its complications (La Russa et al. 2019) whereas, in athletes younger than 35, hypertrophic cardiomyopathy is a more prevalent cause of SCD (McElwee et al. 2016; Maron et al. 1986). Accordingly, the most frequent autopsy finding identified in 80% of SCD victims is atherosclerotic luminal stenosis of >75% in cross-sectional area (considered as critical or hemodynamically significant) in one or more coronary arteries (Virmani et al. 2001; Chugh et al. 2008; Michaud et al. 2012; Morgan et al. 2013; McElwee et al. 2016). Coronary thrombi and plaque rupture are reportedly detected in 20–70% of SCD cases (Virmani et al. 2001). The mechanism underlying SCD is fatal arrhythmia, such as tachyarrhythmia (ventricular fibrillation), bradyarrhythmia, or asystole (McElwee et al. 2016) caused by acute ischemia with or without myocardial infarction (Huikuri et al. 2001; Virmani et al. 2001; McElwee et al. 2016). Therefore, it is important to understand that SCD can be established in the absence of myocardial infarction, but in the presence of diffuse non-occlusive coronary artery disease when supported by rigorous exclusion of non-cardiac causes of death (Virmani et al. 2001; McElwee et al. 2016).

Post-mortem imaging evaluation of ischemic heart disease consists of examination of coronary arteries and myocardium (Polacco et al. 2015). In cases of suspected SCD, the determination of coronary artery morphology and luminal patency is obviously of greatest importance (Palmiere et al. 2013). PMCT can be used for detection and quantification of coronary artery calcification (calcified plaque), which has been recognized as an indicator of the presence of atherosclerotic plaques and is therefore a predictor of future adverse cardiovascular events in a clinical setting (Rumberger et al. 1995; Leontiev and Dubinsky 2007). However, without vascular contrast enhancement, the presence of atherosclerotic plaque or thromboembolic occlusion cannot be evaluated and the degree of consequent luminal stenosis cannot be assessed (Oudkerk et al. 2008; Michaud et al. 2012). Although it has traditionally been agreed that coronary calcium burden is grossly related to the atherosclerotic burden, it is not to the degree of luminal stenosis. Furthermore, the absence of coronary calcium on CT does not exclude the presence or rupture of noncalcified plaques and consequent thrombotic occlusion of coronary arteries (Rumberger et al. 1995; Leontiev and Dubinsky 2007). Recent studies focusing on PMCTA have yielded promising results; PMCTA enables investigation of coronary arteries and the cardiac structures, allowing excellent depiction of coronary plaques or thrombus, evaluation of coronary stenosis and occlusions (Fig. 1), and detection of myocardial damage such as rupture. The main advantage of PMCTA is the possibility of visualization of coronary arteries throughout their course in a minimally invasive manner (Fig. 2) even in severely decomposed cases (Fig. 3). Therefore, PMCTA allows to detect even short segments of critical stenosis that could be missed by dissecting the coronary artery at a relatively large interval (without preparation along its course) during autopsy (La Russa et al. 2019). There is only low risk of dislodging antemortem thrombus using lower perfusion pressure than in vivo (Michaud et al. 2012; Palmiere et al. 2013). Furthermore, using enough pressure to expand collapsed lumen, PMCTA has also been recognized as a better method of demonstrating the patency of calcified coronary vessels that would have otherwise been described as occluded at autopsy (La Russa et al. 2019).

Although PMCTA is an excellent tool for detection and quantification of coronary artery stenosis, it has limitations in its ability to describe the pathomorphological characteristics of the lesions that lead to stenosis, primarily due to its inherently low soft tissue resolution at least at the present time. The presence of hemorrhage, erosion, and

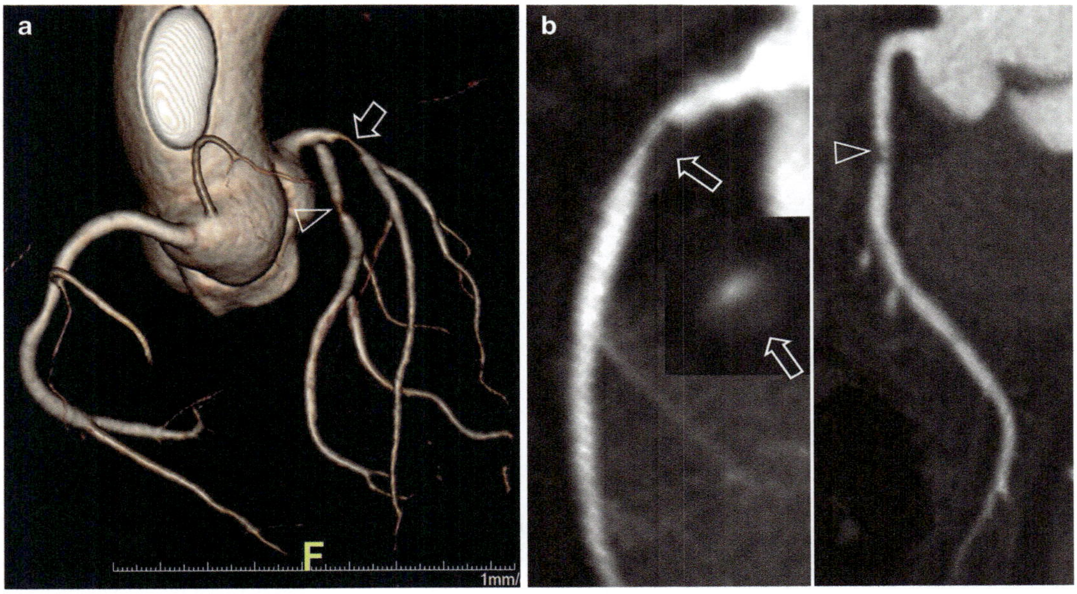

Fig. 1 Coronary artery disease in a 56-year-old male who collapsed shortly after complaining of chest pain following intense physical activity. Three-dimensional volume rendering image (**a**) shows focal stenosis of the left anterior descending artery (LAD, arrow) and left circumflex artery (LCX, arrowhead) coronary artery caused by noncalcified plaques of LAD (arrow) and LCX (arrowhead) demonstrated on curved multiplanar reformation images (**b**). A cross-sectional view of LAD in the box (**b**) shows noncalcified plaque (arrow) with a stenotic area >75%. A photograph of cut space of the LAD shows severe luminal narrowing caused by atherosclerotic plaques (arrows) (**c**) without gross morphological abnormalities of the myocardium (**d**)

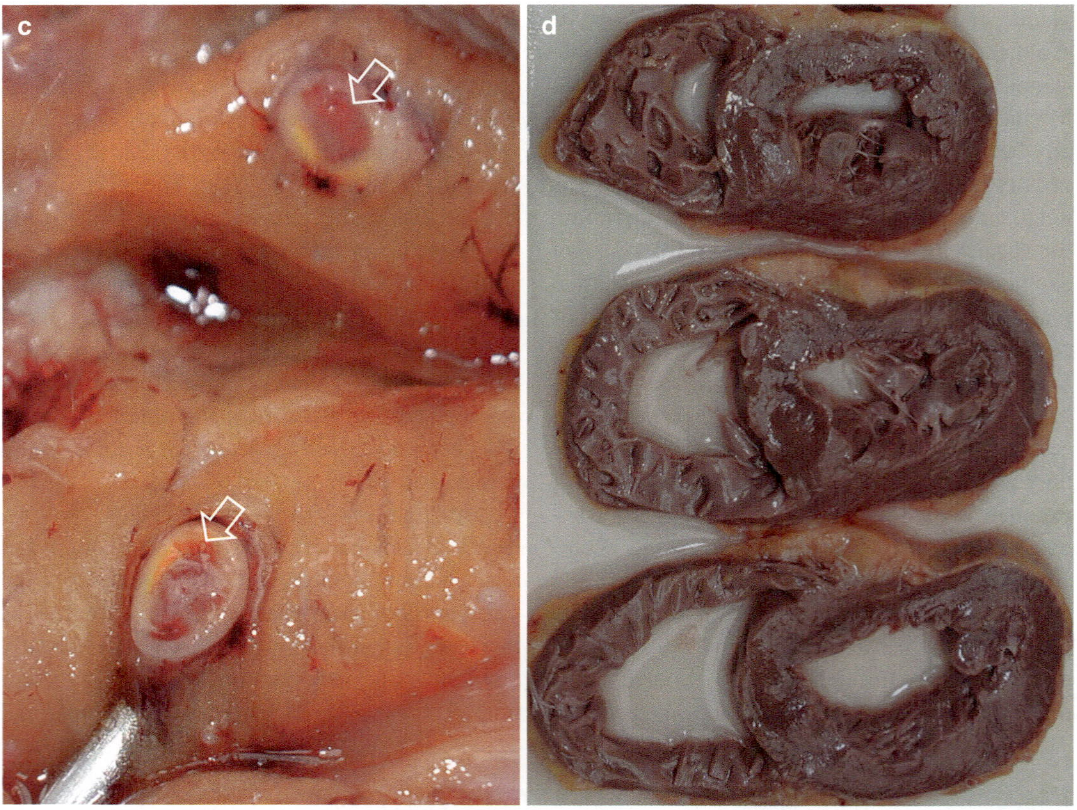

Fig. 1 (continued)

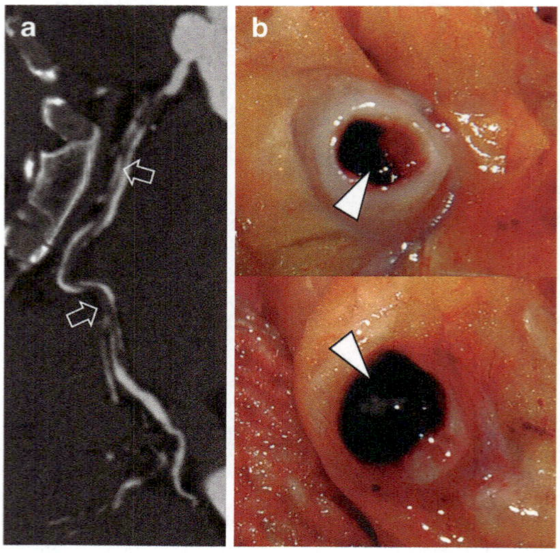

Fig. 2 Coronary artery dissection in a 69-year-old female. Post-mortem CT angiography image of right coronary artery (RCA) (**a**) shows dissection flap (arrows) from proximal to distal segment with multifocal thrombosis in the false lumen. Photographs of cross section of RCA (**b**) show coronary dissection and false lumen thrombosis (arrowheads)

rupture in plaques as well as thrombus formation should be confirmed on histological examination. In cases where coronary artery stenosis is identified by PMCTA, CT can also guide forensic pathologists to localization of the stenosis for histology sampling, facilitating the workflow in the autopsy procedure. On the other hand, PMCTA is a morphological imaging tool and does not provide functional information on the hemodynamic significance of the identified arterial stenosis as in a clinical setting (Michaud et al. 2012; La Russa et al. 2019). Luminal stenosis itself is often not sufficient to diagnose the exact cause of death. Even pronounced stenosis and atherosclerotic changes found on cardiac CT angiography alone do not reliably predict the presence of myocardial ischemia in a clinical setting. In much the same way in the field of post-mortem imaging, PMCTA has yet to be appropriately validated for diagnosis of ischemic myocardium (Polacco et al. 2015). Practically, however, detection of area stenosis

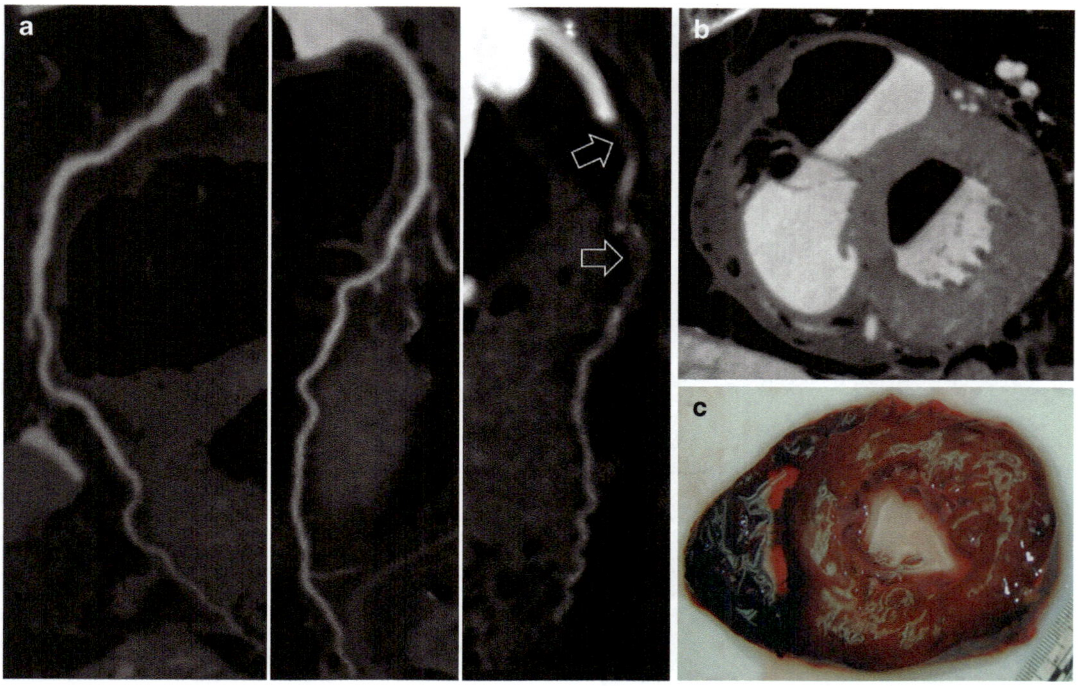

Fig. 3 A case of a 48-year-old male found decomposed in a park. Curved multiplanar image of post-mortem CT angiography (**a**) shows filling defects (arrows) in the middle segment of the left circumflex artery (right). Note normal contrast filling in the right (left) and the left anterior descending (middle) coronary artery. Short axis reformatted image (**b**) demonstrates multiple gas bubbles in the soft tissue and intraventricular gas filling the ventricular cavity, reflecting advanced putrefaction. Photograph of a cut section (**c**) of the left and right ventricle shows advanced putrefaction of myocardium

>75% with PMCTA represents a critical lesion with hemodynamic significance that may result in acute ischemia and SCD after exclusion of other lethal pathologies (Virmani et al. 2001; Michaud et al. 2012).

At present, histological investigation remains the reference to assess the time-dependent pattern of myocardial ischemia for the post-mortem diagnosis of ischemic heart disease (Michaud et al. 2012). Several recent articles have indicated that PMCTA may suggest the area of myocardial infarction by showing "pathological" enhancement as an indirect sign of ischemic necrosis, which is especially well correlated with the area of pathologically proven subacute and old infarction (Michaud et al. 2012; Palmiere et al. 2013; La Russa et al. 2019). However, the precise mechanism underlying this enhancement is not well understood and further research is required to establish the significance of this sign (Michaud et al. 2012; Polacco et al. 2015).

3 Heart and Aorta

Myocardial rupture is a complication of myocardial infarction, cardiac trauma, endocarditis, or even vigorous cardiopulmonary resuscitation. It has been reported to occur in 1–3% of cases with myocardial infarction and is the second most common cause of in-hospital death in ST-segment elevation myocardial infarction (Mantovani et al. 2002; Figueras et al. 2008) occurring mostly among those older than 55–60 and typically 1–7 days after infarction (Mantovani et al. 2002). Although myocardial rupture can be suspected on PMCT images indicating the presence of hemopericardium, the precise site of rupture can be determined by intravascular contrast injection. As shown in Fig. 4, PMCTA successfully demonstrated myocardial rupture together with corresponding coronary artery stenosis, raising strong suspicion of ischemic infarction as the cause of the rupture. In this way, post-mortem CT imaging

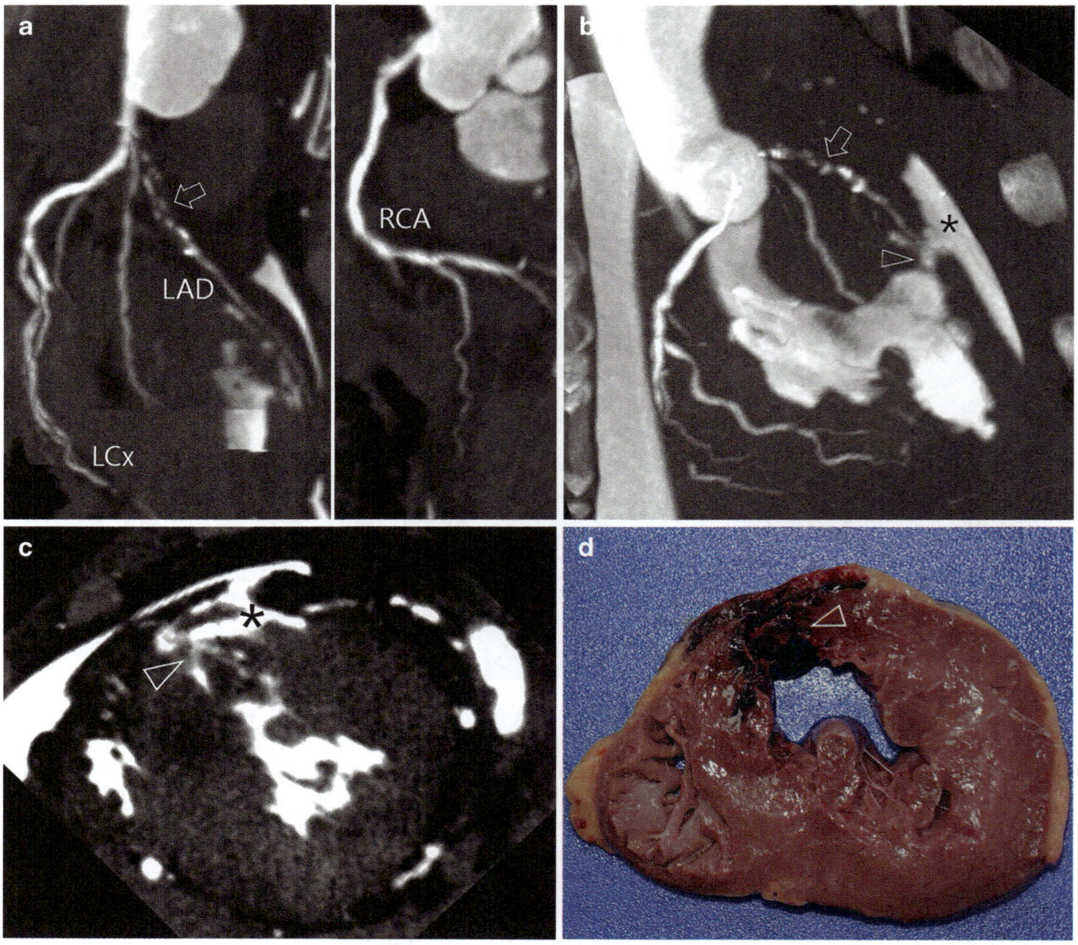

Fig. 4 Myocardial rupture in a 73-year-old male. Multiplanar (**a**) and maximum intensity reformation (**b**) images of coronary arteries from post-mortem CT angiography (PMCTA) show mixed calcified and noncalcified plaques leading to diffuse stenosis of the proximal to middle segment of the left anterior descending artery (arrow). PMCTA reveals a contrast leakage (arrowhead) into the pericardial cavity (*) from the left ventricular cavity, depicting irregular myocardial perforation as the cause of hemopericardium. Short axis (**c**) image of the left ventricle shows myocardial rupture with contrast leakage (arrowhead) and a connection between the left ventricle and pericardial cavity (*), which is confirmed in the cut surface of the resected myocardium (arrowhead in (**d**)). *LAD* left anterior descending artery; *LCX* left circumflex artery; *RCA* right coronary artery

can provide condensed information in a few images for intuitive understanding of disease mechanisms.

Aortic dissection and aneurysm are aortic diseases that may also result in natural death. Aortic dissection is defined as a longitudinal separation of the medial layer of the aortic wall caused by a tear in the aortic intima (Corvera 2016; Bossone et al. 2018). Blood enters the medial layer through the tear and creates two channels: a true lumen and a false lumen. The dissection can propagate in either direction, proximally or distally, into the aortic valve, coronary arteries, or branches of the thoracoabdominal aorta. A higher mean pressure in the false lumen can cause dynamic compression or static occlusion of the aortic branches, resulting in end-organ malperfusion and ischemia (Lempel et al. 2014; Corvera 2016; Bossone

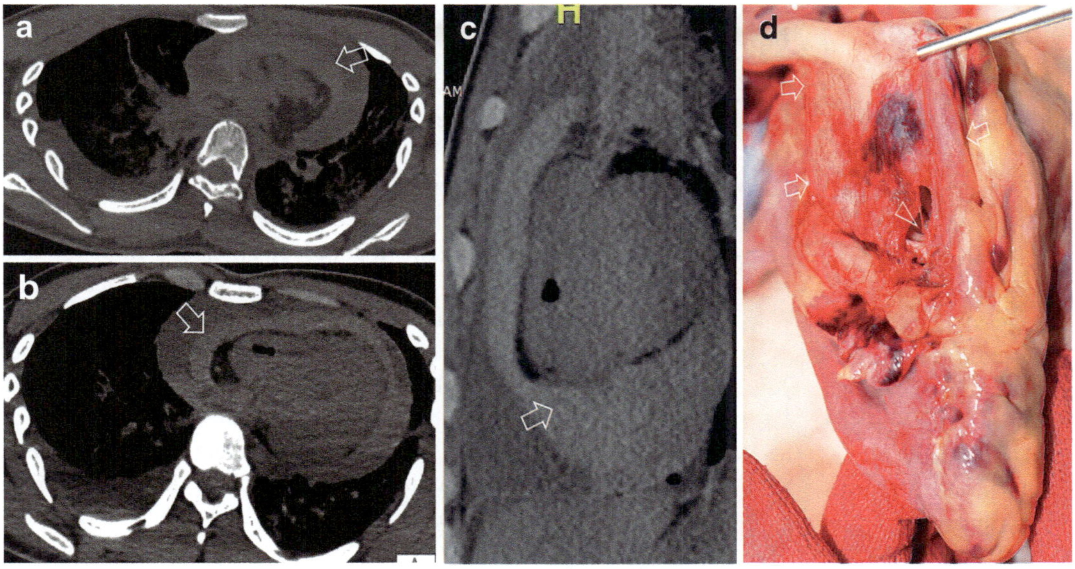

Fig. 5 An 18-year-old male with suspected Marfan syndrome collapsed during physical activity. PMCT demonstrates double concentric rings of intrapericardial hemorrhage, with an inner dense ring (arrows) originated from motion-induced selective coagulation of blood on the epicardial surface in axial (**a**, **b**) and sagittal (**c**) images. This finding provides forensic evidence of the heart beating at the initiation and for the duration of pericardial bleeding, suggesting cardiac tamponade as the cause of death. Photograph of gross specimen (**d**) showing a rupture (arrowhead) of dilated ascending aorta (outlined by arrows) as a cause of hemopericardium

et al. 2018). Death occurs as a result of malperfusion of aortic branches to vital organs or blood loss from the ruptured wall. In cases of dissection involving ascending aorta, malperfusion of coronary arteries, aortic insufficiency, or pericardial tamponade may be the causes of death. Aortic aneurysms are potentially life-threatening disease. By definition, an aortic aneurysm involves dilatation of the aorta to at least 1.5 times the expected normal diameter (Johnston et al. 1991). Although typical aortic aneurysms develop gradually, and such aneurysms rarely produce specific symptoms, they result in weakness in the wall of the aorta and their rupture can be lethal, mainly due to massive internal hemorrhage.

The nonenhanced PMCT findings in aortic dissection include deformity of the aortic contour and intramural hematoma or thrombosed false lumen. Hemopericardium is the most common fatal PMCT finding in cases of death from aortic dissection (Levy and Harcke 2011), and is characterized by double concentric layering with a hyperdense inner ring on the epicardial surface and hypodense outer ring (Fig. 5), so-called “armoured heart-sign” (Shiotani et al. 2004). However, contrast enhancement is required to identify true and false lumen with intervening dissection flaps. Nonenhanced PMCT may show free blood in body cavities in cases of ruptured aneurysm as well as large aortic aneurysm itself with or without wall calcifications, but the exact site of rupture cannot be determined. PMCTA allows visualization of the entire aorta including the ascending arch, enabling the diagnosis and characterization of dissection and aneurysm as well as depiction of their fatal complications such as rupture and hemopericardium (Lee et al. 2019). For example, PMCTA permits the localization of the entry tear and evaluation of the extension of intimomedial flap to the branch vessels in cases of dissection and it also provides information on the size, location, and extent of the lesion with its relation to branch vessels in aortic aneurysm, along with the presence of

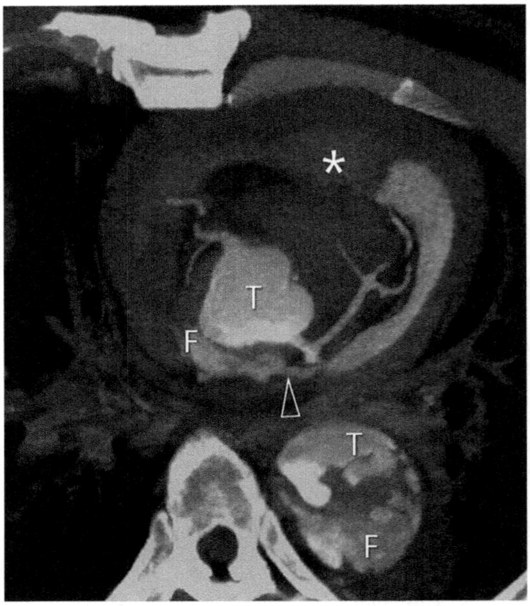

Fig. 6 Post-mortem CT angiography of a 43-year-old male with Stanford class A dissection. MIP image depicts dissection flaps and perforation (arrow head) through which contrast leaks from false lumen into the pericardial cavity. Note double concentric ring with a dense inner layer (*), indicative of cardiac tamponade. *T* true lumen; *F* false lumen

complications such as aortic wall rupture (Fig. 6) and end-organ ischemia. Therefore, determination of the cause of death may be feasible before autopsy in such cases if aneurysm and dissection are depicted with their fatal complications (Ross et al. 2014; Lee et al. 2019).

4 Cerebrovascular and Intracranial Disease

Stroke (cerebrovascular accidents) is the second leading cause of death (Johnson et al. 2016). The sudden death of brain cells due to oxygen deprivation occurs when the cerebral blood flow is cut off by arterial blockage or rupture (Owolabi et al. 2015).

There are two different types of stroke, i.e., hemorrhagic and ischemic, which account for 10–20% and 80–90% of cases, respectively (Lloyd-Jones et al. 2009; Runchey and McGee 2010; Musuka et al. 2015). Hemorrhagic stroke is caused by the rupture of weakened blood vessels or aneurysms within the brain parenchyma (intracerebral hemorrhage, ICH) or into the subarachnoid space (subarachnoid hemorrhage, SAH) (Lloyd-Jones et al. 2009; Runchey and McGee 2010). ICH is more common, accounting for approximately two thirds of cases of hemorrhagic strokes and is associated with a higher mortality rate (Dennis et al. 1993; Runchey and McGee 2010). Intracranial hemorrhage in or around the brain causes tissue edema and raises intracranial pressure, resulting in brain damage and death.

In comparison, ischemic stroke is caused by either embolic or thrombotic occlusion of an intracranial artery. Arterial obstruction in ischemic stroke is more commonly embolic—either cardioembolic from diseases such as atrial fibrillation, or artero-embolic (distal embolization of thrombus) from proximal atherosclerotic disease in the extracranial arteries. A less frequent cause of ischemic stroke is thrombotic; occlusion of intracranial artery due to rupture of atherosclerotic plaque and formation of on-site thrombus (Musuka et al. 2015).

Although less common, hemorrhagic stroke is associated with a higher mortality rate, with only 38% (ICH) and 52% (SAH) of affected patients surviving for 1 year in comparison to 77% of those with ischemic stroke, and is responsible for up to 40% of all stroke-related deaths (Sacco et al. 1982; Dennis et al. 1993; Andersen et al. 2009; Mansour et al. 2017).

Loss of gray-white matter differentiation and brain swelling, causing effacement of the ventricle and cisterns, are normal post-mortem changes in the brain detected on PMCT, commencing immediately after death (Smith et al. 2012; Ross et al. 2014; Ishida et al. 2015). These findings, however, may be understood differently based on individual characteristics, such as age, duration of agonal stage, or concurrent antemortem conditions (Ishida et al. 2015).

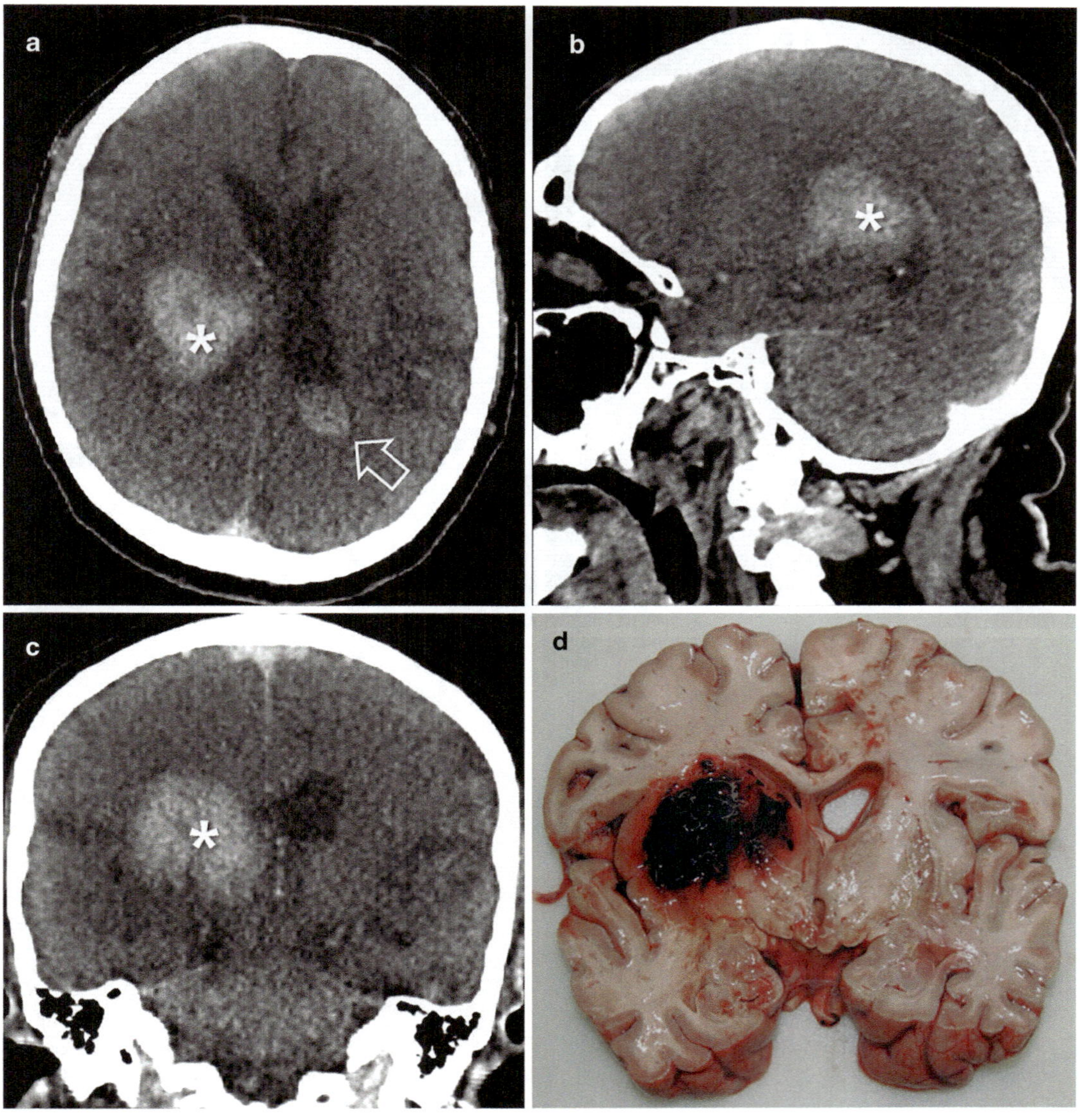

Fig. 7 Intracerebral hemorrhage in a 67-year-old male found dead sitting on his sofa. Axial (**a**), sagittal (**b**), and coronal (**c**) images of post-mortem CT show a high-density hemorrhage in the right basal ganglia (*) and in the left lateral ventricle (arrow). The autopsy photograph (**d**) shows hemorrhage in the right basal ganglia in the cut surface of the brain

Acute intracranial hemorrhage appears hyperdense compared to the brain parenchyma either on antemortem and post-mortem CT without contrast enhancement (Figs. 7 and 8) because of clotted blood with a high protein concentration (mainly globin). In clinical radiology, hemorrhage reaches its maximum density up to 80–100 HU at 120 kVp in the first few hours of bleeding due to clot formation and its retraction. If the patient survives beyond this acute phase, hemorrhage becomes isodense to the brain and difficult to identify over days to a few weeks, and it can be used to approximate the age of hemorrhage (Parizel et al. 2001; Ruder et al. 2013). In contrast, normal physiological breakdown of globin molecule seems to stop after death. Therefore, intracranial blood found on PMCT represents hemorrhage in a

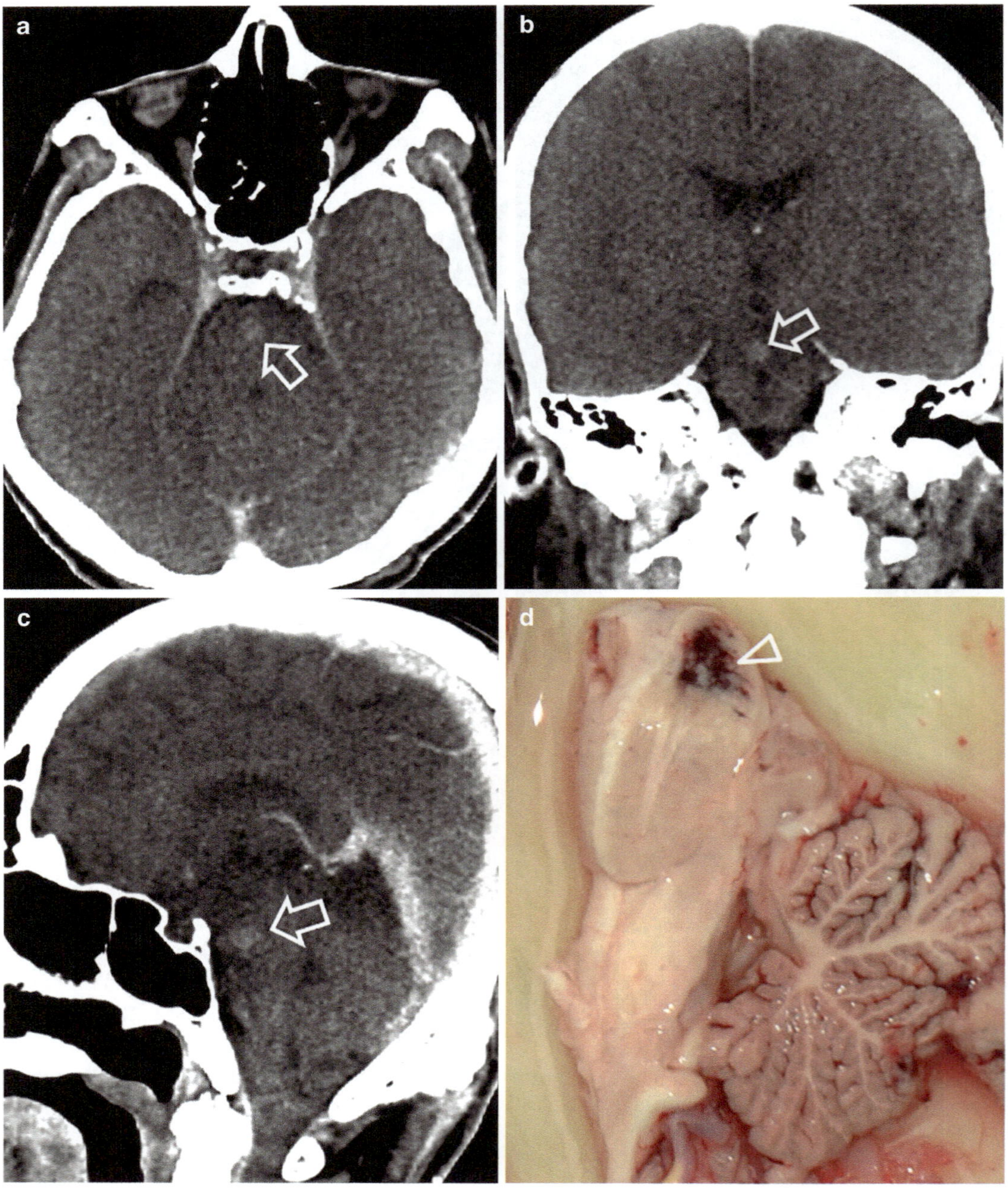

Fig. 8 A case of a 48-year-old male whose sudden collapse was observed. Post-mortem CT Images show a small area of high density in the pons (arrow) in axial (**a**), coronal (**b**), and sagittal (**c**) images. Autopsy photograph of the brainstem (**d**) shows a small hemorrhage (arrowhead) in the corresponding location of the pons

stage of evolution (age of hemorrhage) at the time of death (Fig. 9). This observation suggests that PMCT may be used to approximate the antemortem age of intracranial blood at the time of death and determine the cause of death even in cases of severe decomposition (Fig. 10) (Ruder et al. 2013).

PMCTA allows the noninvasive display of the entire cerebral vasculature in situ as well as better distinction of gray and white matter. Intravascular

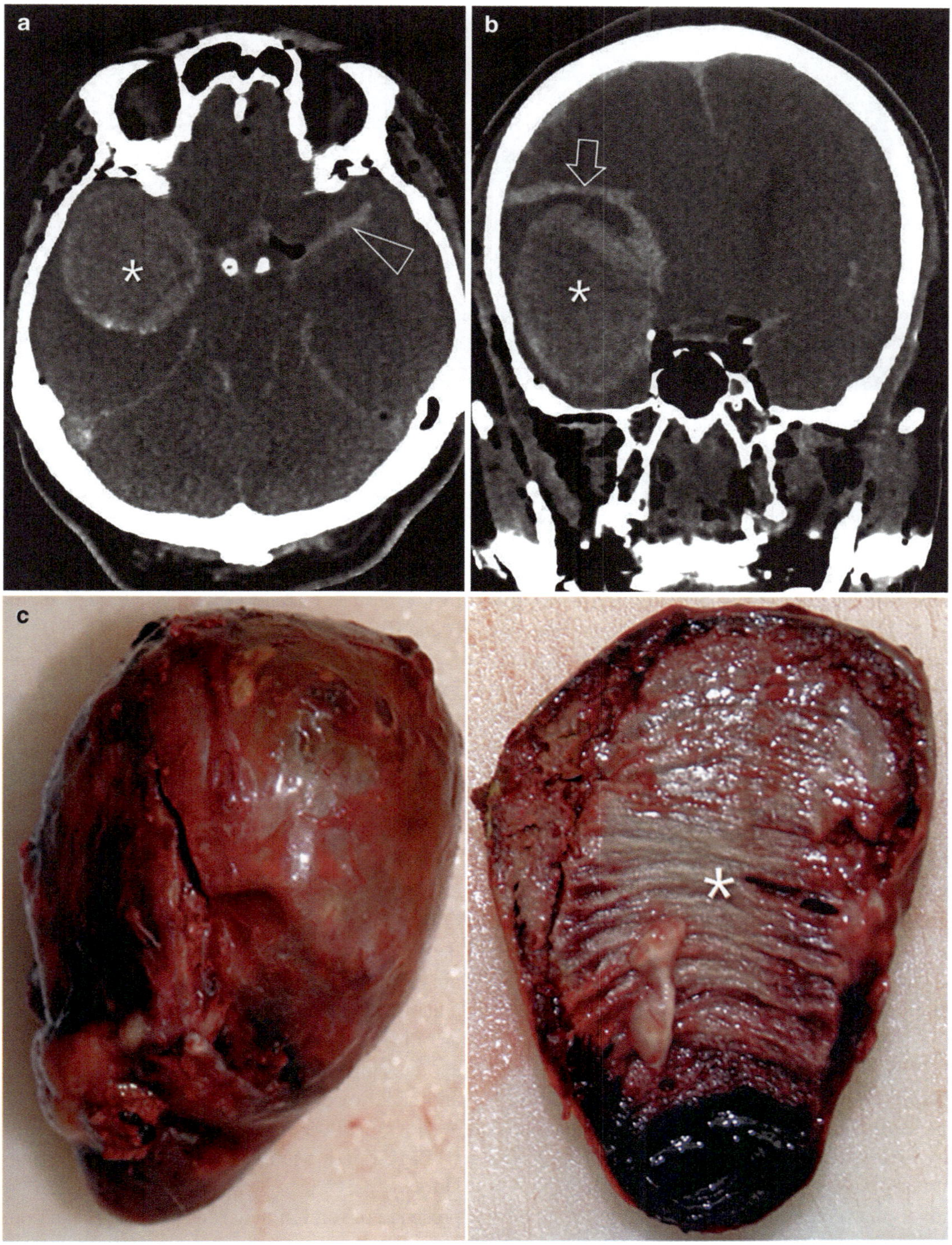

Fig. 9 A giant cerebral aneurysm in a 37-year-old male. Post-mortem CT demonstrates a well-defined, 9-cm large, hyperdense, and heterogenous extra-axial mass (*) in the right temporal fossa, combined with subarachnoid hemorrhage in basal cistern (arrowhead) and along the sylvian fissure (arrow) (**a**, **b**). These findings raise the suspicion of a giant aneurysm with different stage of thrombus formation and rupture. Autopsy photograph (**c**) of the resected aneurysm with its cut surface shows different stages of thrombus evolution including the organized thrombus (*) in the aneurysmal sac

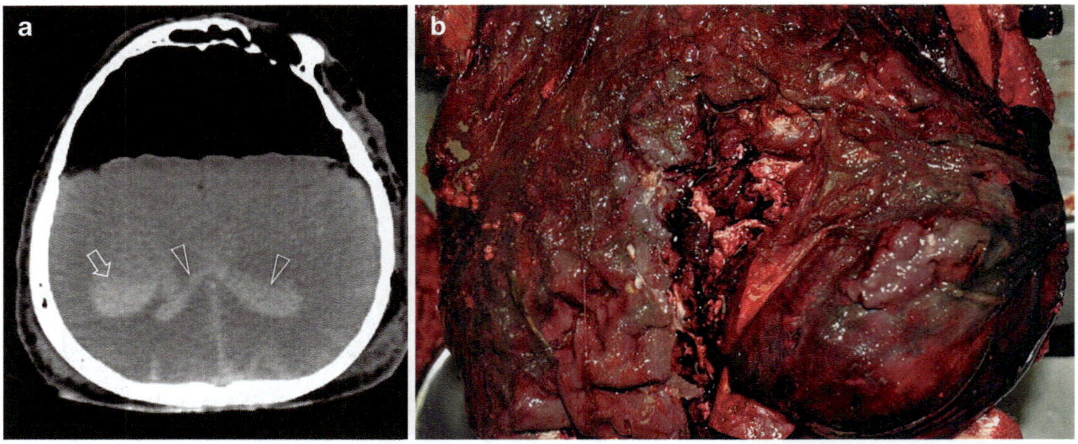

Fig. 10 A case of a 51-year-old male found decomposed. CT (**a**) shows intracerebral (arrow) and intraventricular (arrowheads) hemorrhage in the brain with moderate to advanced decomposition. Note the liquefaction and posterior settling of the brain with air-fluid level as well as putrefactive gas in the cranial cavity and soft tissue of the scalp. Autopsy photograph (**b**) shows softening and partial liquefaction of the brain with reddish discoloration. Identification and localization of hemorrhage is not easy at autopsy under these conditions

injection of contrast material expands the collapsed vascular lumen and thus allows detection of noncalcified plaques and estimation of luminal stenosis. With PMCTA, even small vascular abnormalities such as aneurysms of the circle of Willis (Fig. 11) or posterior circulation can be successfully depicted. In cases of vascular rupture, the localization of bleeding sources is possible in most cases, which would be time-consuming or even impossible in conventional autopsy dissection (Grabherr et al. 2014; Ross et al. 2014; Lee et al. 2019).

5 Airways and Respiratory Diseases

Asphyxia is defined as a condition that causes a lack of gas exchange, resulting in simultaneous hypoxia and hypercapnia. It occurs when oxygen transport is blocked at many different levels involving oxygen intake into the lungs, delivery to the tissues, and uptake across the cell membrane (Byard 2016).

Choking is a well-known example of mechanical asphyxia that may lead to non-natural death, typically occurring when food or foreign materials unintentionally block the passage of air to the lungs. However, chocking can be also caused by any mechanical obstruction of the airways that prevents normal breathing, including swelling and inflammation of the airway tissues, extrinsic compression in strangulation, and tumors in the oral cavity and upper airway. Although most deaths due to choking are accidental and involve airway obstruction by food, it is commonly associated with a variety of predisposing factors, such as old age, poor dentition, natural diseases, such as neurological disorders, alcohol consumption, and sedative drugs (Mittleman and Wetli 1982; Wick et al. 2006; Iino and O'Donnell 2010).

PMCT is a useful tool as it provides a preautopsy preview of the airway to inspect the presence of foreign materials prior to visual con-

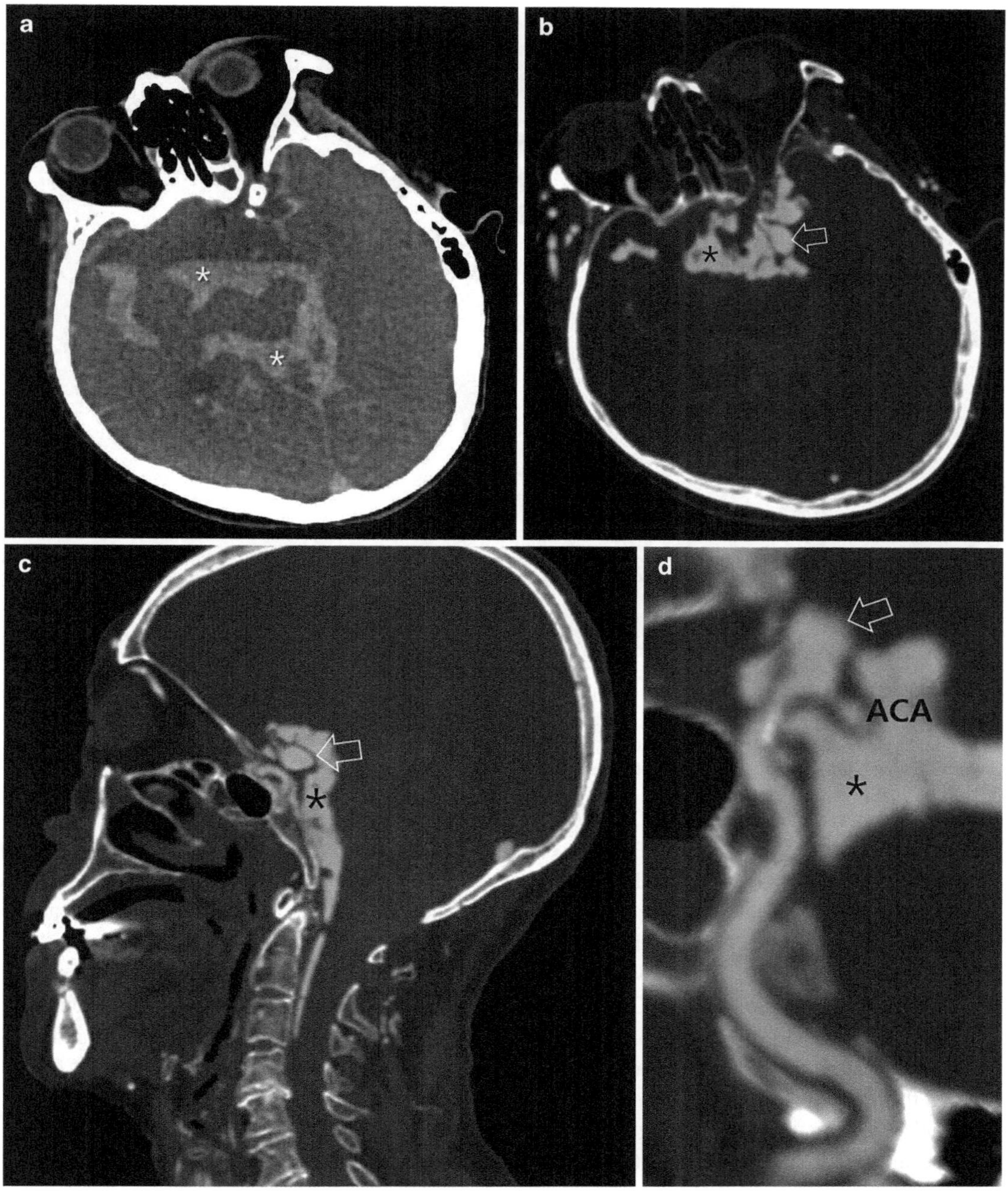

Fig. 11 Cerebral aneurysmal rupture in a 70-year-old female found dead on her bed. Basal subarachnoid hemorrhage (white *) was detected on axial image of post-mortem CT (**a**). With contrast injection (**b–d**), an aneurysmal sac (arrow) is demonstrated at the junction of the left middle and anterior cerebral artery and also contrast leakage (black *) into the basal cistern and cervical subarachnoid space

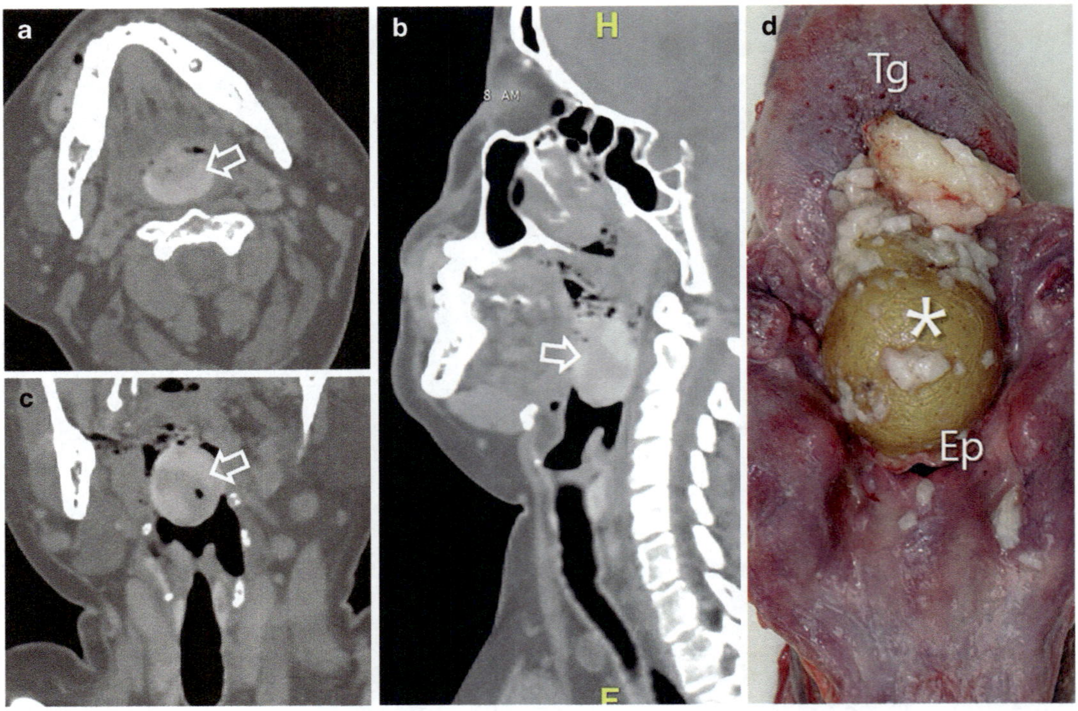

Fig. 12 A case of accidental death of a 50-year-old female with choking. Post-mortem CT images (**a–c**) shows an oval-shaped density (arrow) entirely blocking the oropharynx. Autopsy photograph (**d**) of the upper airway shows a potato (*) located between the root of the tongue and epiglottis, causing complete airway obstruction. *Tg* tongue; *Ep* epiglottis (note: manner of death: non-natural, accidental)

firmation. Moreover, pre-autopsy PMCT scanning assists the pathologists to tailor the dissection and prepare for unexpected findings in subsequent autopsy procedures (Lee et al. 2019; Iino and O'Donnell 2010). In cases in which airway obstruction is suspected on CT, PMCT can guide the identification and removal of foreign bodies (Fig. 12) in case of accidental deaths (not the topic of this chapter), or target the lesions for histological sampling (Fig. 13), thereby reducing the time and extent of autopsy dissection required (Grabherr et al. 2018; Lee et al. 2019).

Respiratory disease is an important cause of natural death worldwide. In 2016, lung infections (mostly pneumonia and tuberculosis, ranked 3rd), chronic obstructive pulmonary diseases (ranked 4th), and lung cancer (ranked 6th) together accounted for 16% (9.0 million deaths) of total deaths worldwide (World Health Organization 2018). Although sudden death is unusual in most patients with respiratory diseases, pulmonary thromboembolism, airway obstruction from asthma, and massive hemoptysis related to pneumonia, tuberculosis, and cancer can cause sudden death. Deaths from pneumonia are uncommon in medicolegal cases but are more frequently found in clinical settings. However, pneumonia can be a cause of unexpected death, particularly if the causative agent is highly pathogenic or if the individual's immune system is not functioning properly.

PMCT makes a small contribution to proposal of the possible cause of death when it originates from respiratory infection. Although focal

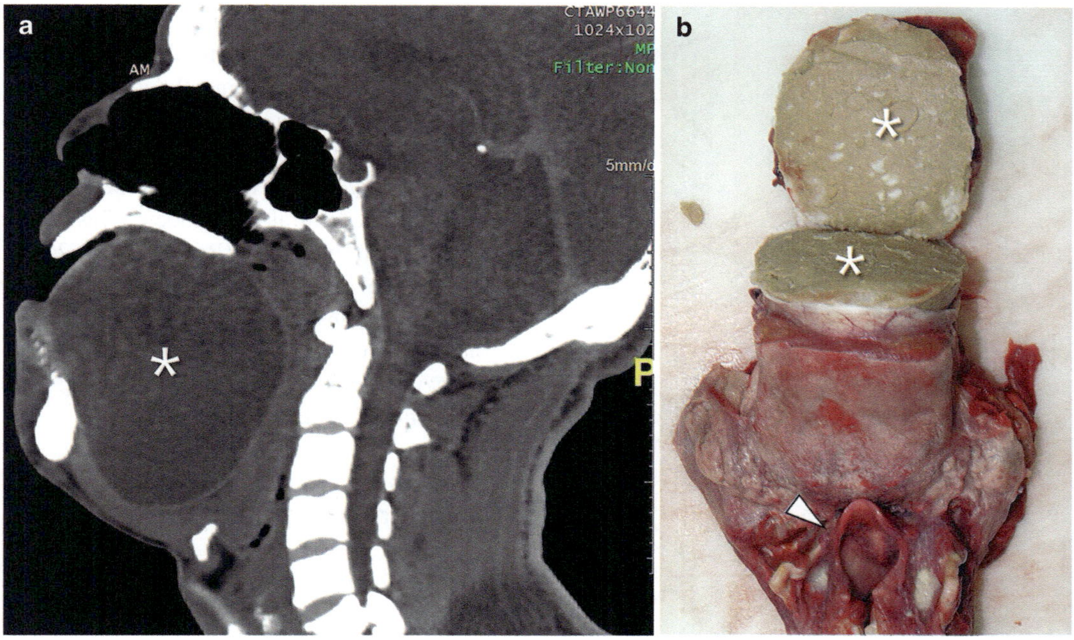

Fig. 13 A case of lingual epidermoid cyst. A 44-year-old male was found dead in his hotel room. Sagittal post-mortem CT image (**a**) shows a huge mass that entirely fills the oral cavity and may cause obstruction of the airway—oropharynx. Photograph of cut section (**b**) of the tongue indicates a cystic lesion filled with yellowish cheesy material (*), extending from the base of the tongue above the vestibule of the larynx and aryepiglottic fold (arrowhead) to the tip, which is histologically consistent with a diagnosis of epidermoid cyst

well-defined or patchy ill-defined consolidations with pleural effusions are the PMCT findings typical of lobar or bronchopneumonia (Fig. 14). In cases of fatal pneumonia, however, total or near-total opacification of the lungs may be present on PMCT (Fig. 15). Nevertheless, they should be confirmed histologically and microbiologically (Franquet 2011). It is sometimes difficult to differentiate hypostasis (livor mortis) in the dependent positions of the lungs from alveolar consolidation of an infectious or neoplastic origin. Hypostasis is the earliest post-mortem change and is characterized by gradually increasing density in the dependent location of organs, such as the skin and lungs. It is often bilaterally symmetrical and relatively homogenous, appearing as ground glass opacities with a horizontal, well-defined border in the dependent lung. In

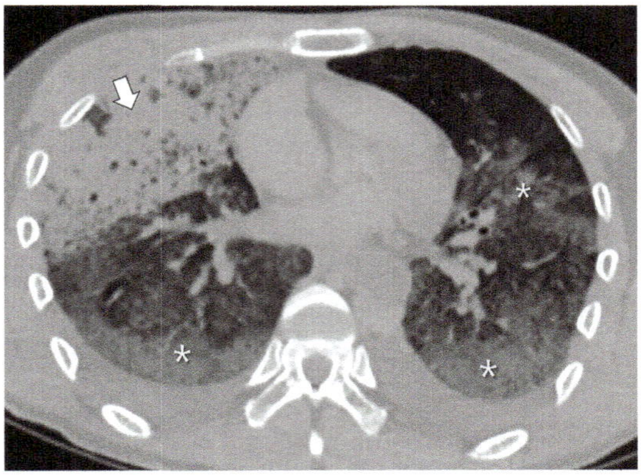

Fig. 14 A 40-year-old male with suppurative pneumonia. PMCT image in the lung window setting shows a lobar distribution of consolidation (arrow) in the right middle lobe. Note ground glass opacity with horizontal border (*) in the dependent position of both lungs in the lung window settings, indicative of post-mortem sedimentation (livor mortis)

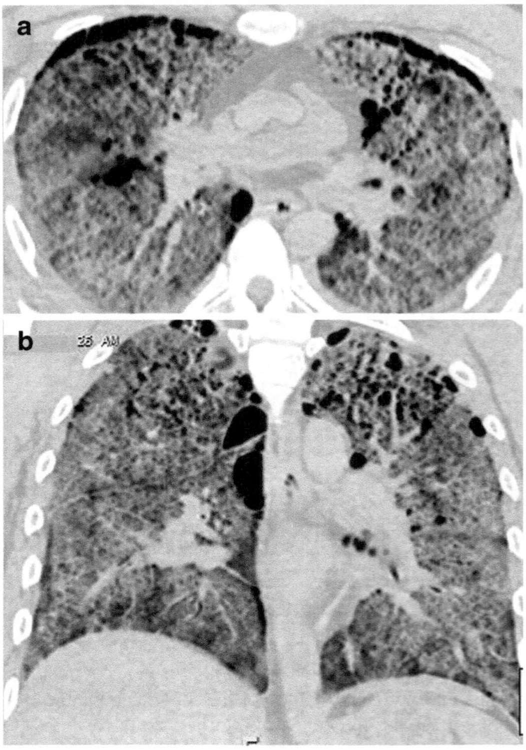

Fig. 15 A case of pneumocystis pneumonia in a 49-year-old male found dead in his seat during a flight without evidence of trauma. Post-mortem axial (**a**) and coronal (**b**) CT shows dense ground glass opacities in a diffuse, bilateral, and symmetric distribution and associated interlobular septal thickenings, multiple foci of consolidation, and variable-sized pneumatoceles, which are characteristic CT findings of pneumocystis pneumonia

contrast, patchy parenchymal consolidations with an asymmetrical, peribronchial distribution may indicate a pathological condition, such as pneumonia (Lee et al. 2019),

In investigation of death, pulmonary thromboembolism is an important cause of natural death frequently found in forensic autopsies but, generally, it cannot be identified by noncontrast PMCT. Pulmonary arteries are well demonstrated on PMCTA after contrast filling of the right cardiac chambers by antegrade contrast infusion through the femoral vein. However, post-mortem clotting is often present, especially in cases with a prolonged agonal period, and tends to be found on the segmental and subsegmental branches as filling defects on PMCTA (Ross et al. 2012; Bruguier et al. 2013). Therefore, any contrast defect in the pulmonary arteries could be related to an antemortem thromboembolus or post-mortem clot, which develops mostly in these locations. Nonetheless, these extended defects of contrast filling in the pulmonary trunk and the main pulmonary arteries have been reported to be indicative of a central thromboembolus rather than post-mortem clots (Ross et al. 2014). However, the final diagnosis of pulmonary thromboembolism should still be made based on histological analysis of the suspected thromboembolic materials (Bruguier et al. 2013; Ross et al. 2014; Lee et al. 2019).

6 Intra-abdominal Diseases

Natural deaths from intra-abdominal causes are rarely subject to forensic investigation. However, massive and uncontrolled hemorrhage of gastrointestinal intestinal tract, peritoneal cavity, and retroperitoneal space may lead to fatal consequence. Such life-threatening hemorrhage of the gastrointestinal tract is uncommon but results from peptic ulceration, ruptured esophageal varices, or malignancies, among other causes. In contrast, intra-abdominal hemorrhage may result from ruptured aneurysm of an aorta or smaller visceral artery, hepatic or splenic rupture secondary to an underlying infection, coagulopathy, or neoplasms, and gynecologic conditions, such as ectopic pregnancy and ruptured ovarian cyst in women of child-bearing age (Lubner et al. 2007). Therefore, cases with large hemoperitoneum and hemoretroperitoneum should undergo careful examination of the abdominal vasculature and visceral organs at autopsy dissection.

Acute intra-abdominal hemorrhage appears hyperdense on nonenhanced CT. In addition, independently of the time since death, high-density blood on PMCT also represents hemorrhage in the acute stage of evolution at the time of death (Fig. 16). Although intraperitoneal hemorrhage spreads into the dependent spaces of the peritoneal cavity—Morison's pouch (hepatorenal recess), paracolic gutters, and the pelvic space (retrouterine pouch of Douglas in women and retrovesical space in men)—it tends to collect near

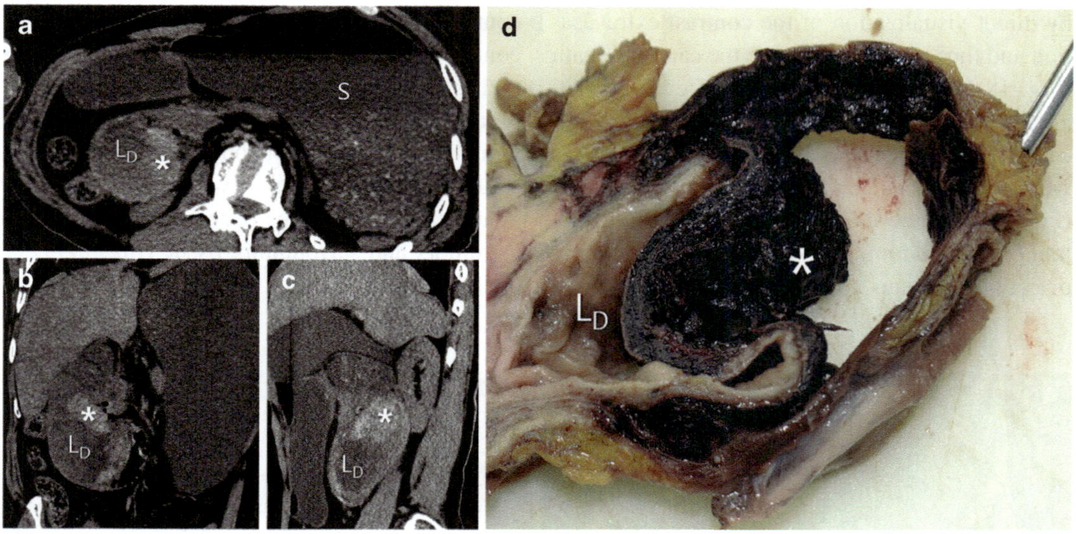

Fig. 16 A case of spontaneous intramural hematoma of the duodenum associated with pancreatitis in a 66-year-old male found dead in his office with vomitus around his body. Post-mortem axial (**a**), oblique coronal (**b**), and oblique sagittal (**c**) images demonstrate a high-density hematoma of the duodenal wall, located in the descending to horizontal portion, and severe dilatation of the stomach with fluid and food materials, indicative of gastric outlet obstruction. Photograph of pathologic specimen (**d**) shows the true lumen and intramural thrombus (*). L_D true duodenal lumen; *S* stomach

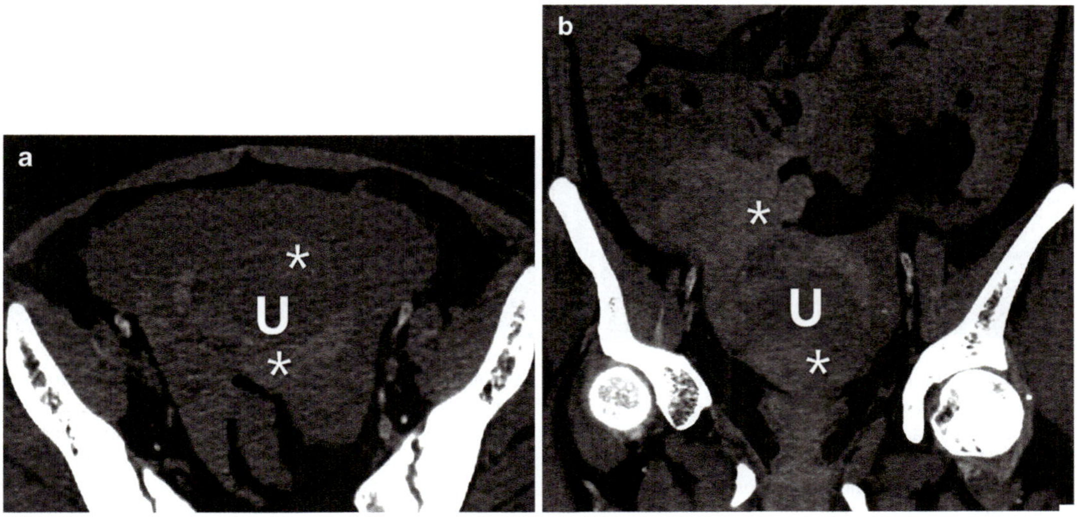

Fig. 17 A case of massive intraabdominal hemorrhage in a young female. Post-mortem axial (**a**) and coronal (**b**) images show a relatively highly attenuating hemorrhage (*) accumulating near the uterus (U) in the pelvic cavity, which raises suspicion of uterine injury as a source of hemorrhage (sentinel clot sign). Autopsy confirmed uterine rupture associated with angiomyoma of the uterus

the bleeding organ initially as a relatively highly attenuating fluid (sentinel clot) on nonenhanced CT (Fig. 17) (Orwig and Federle 1989). This sentinel clot sign has been used to identify potential sources of acute hemorrhage on PMCT as in clinical setting (O'Donnell et al. 2011). However, this is an indirect sign by which PMCT alone would raise only suspicions of bleeding from possible vascular rupture or organ injury. PMCTA allows the precise localization of vascular tear or rupture by direct visualization of the contrast extravasation and thus help to determine the cause of death (Fig. 18). On PMCT, collection of even a small amount of free gas can be easily documented in cases of hollow viscus perforation (Fig. 19) as well as gaseous distension of bowel loops (Fig. 20). However, without contrast enhancement, intra-abdominal solid organs are barely discernable because of inherently low soft tissue contrast of CT. After intravascular injection of contrast medium, variable degrees of parenchymal enhancement are observed in intra-abdominal organs, depending on the vascularity of the individual organ and type of contrast medium (water-soluble vs. lipid-soluble), which provide better contrast between space-occupying lesions such as tumors and surrounding tissue (Fig. 21) (Lee et al. 2019).

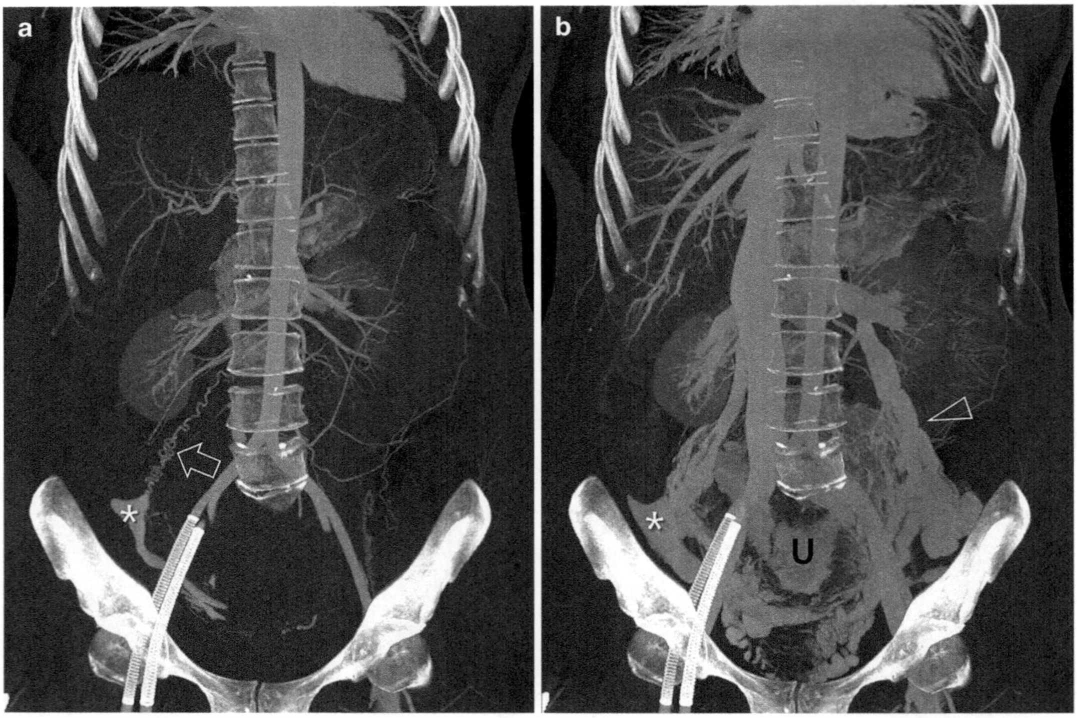

Fig. 18 Post-mortem CT angiography of a 33-year-old female who died of postpartum uterine hemorrhage after cesarean delivery. Coronal maximum intensity projection (**a**, **b**) and sagittal multiplanar reformation image (**c**, **d**) obtained after arterial injection of contrast medium shows a persistent bleeding from a tortuous ovarian artery (arrow) into the pelvic cavity (*) but no contrast enhancement of the uterus and cervix. CT images (**b**, **d**) with venous contrast injection demonstrates dilatation of venous structures of the uterine wall, which were not sufficiently compressed, and contrast extravasation into the uterine cavity and vagina (long arrowhead in **d**), indicative of active venous bleeding. Also, note dilatation of pelvic venous structures including ovarian veins (arrowhead in **b**) and pelvic bleeding (* in **b**) as well as uterine myoma (long arrow in **d**) *U* uterine cavity

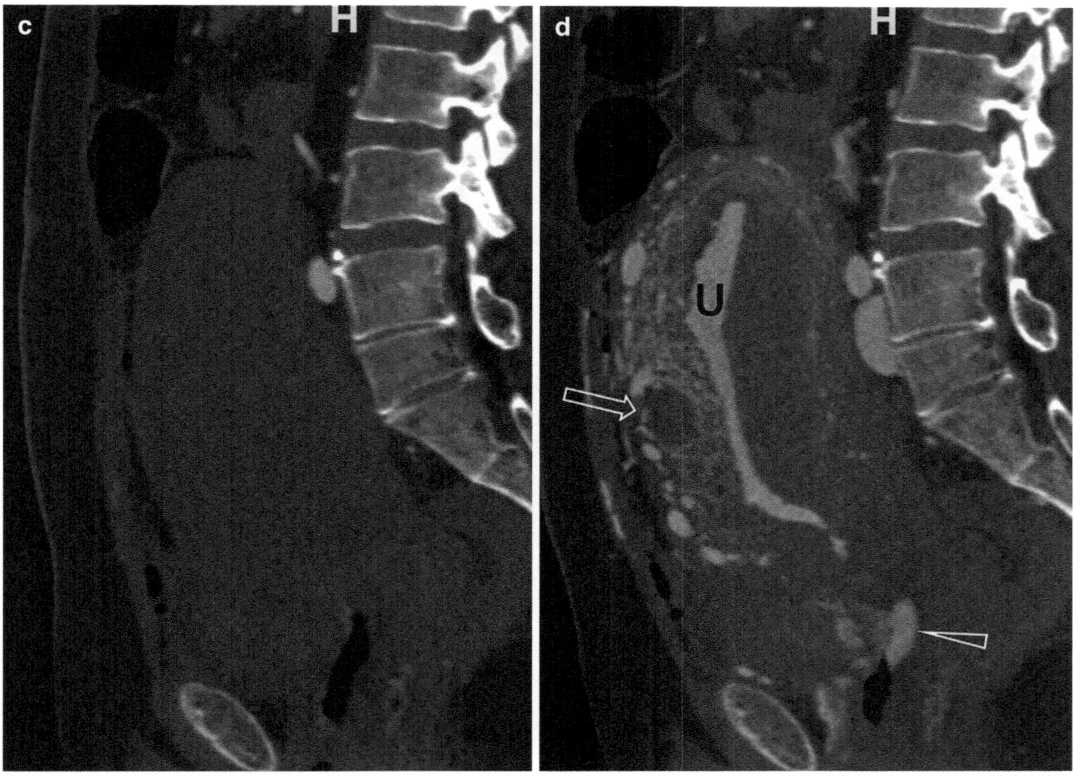

Fig. 18 (continued)

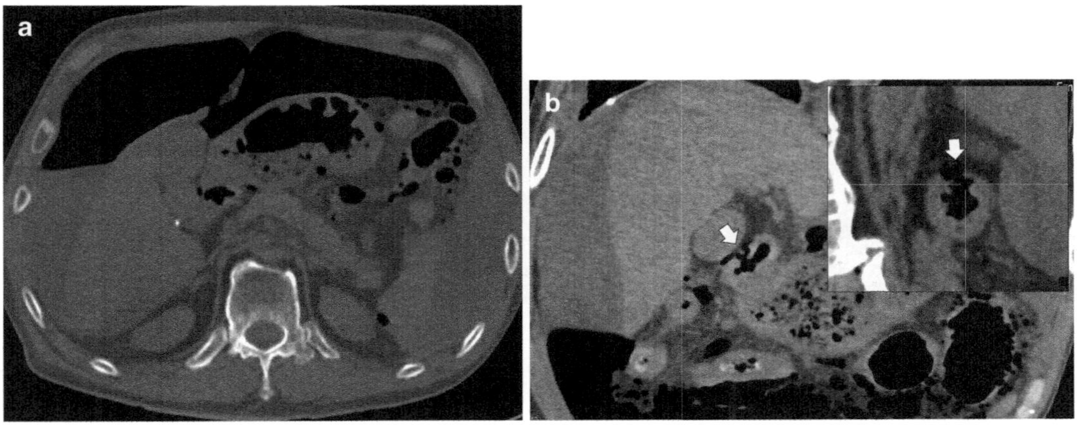

Fig. 19 A 62-year-old male found dead in a parking lot near his home. He was reported to have suffered from abdominal pain and to have taken some medicine to aid digestion. Post-mortem axial (**a**) and coronal (**b**) CT images show massive hydropneumoperitoneum and air leakage through perforation of the duodenal bulb (arrow in **b**)

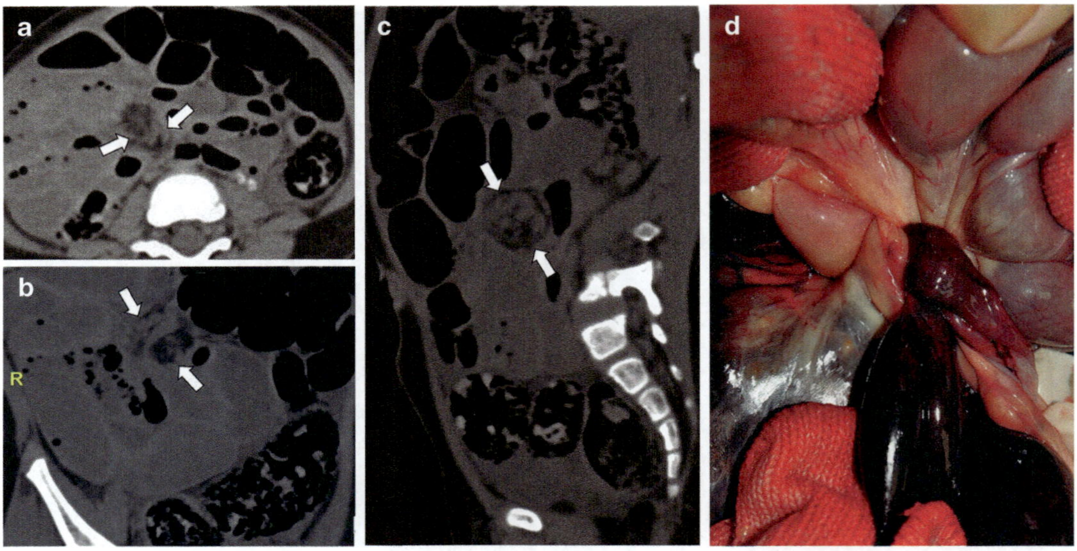

Fig. 20 A case of mesenteric volvulus in a 1-year-old baby. Axial (**a**), oblique coronal (**b**), and oblique sagittal (**c**) images from post-mortem CT depicts swirling (arrows) of mesenteric soft tissue, fat and vessels surrounded by adjacent dilated small bowel loops, which corresponds to small bowel obstruction due to mesenteric volvulus. Autopsy photograph (**d**) shows twisted bowel loops with severely ischemic or necrotic changes with dark purple discoloration

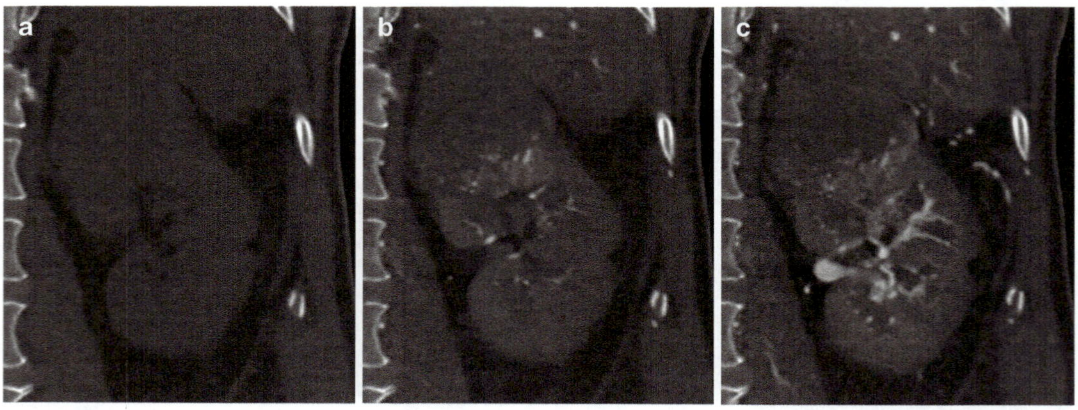

Fig. 21 A case of renal cell carcinoma with extensive systemic metastases. Coronal images of the left kidney from PMCT (**a**) after contrast injection into an artery (**b**) and then a vein (**c**). A renal mass is suspected on nonenhanced CT image (s) based only on external contour bulging resulting from its exophytic growth. After intravascular injection of contrast medium (**b**, **c**), variable degrees of enhancement are observed in the kidney, thus allowing easy detection of the mass by providing tissue contrast between the space-occupying lesion and background. Note crescentic enhancement (outlined by arrows) and low-density cystic area (*) of the tumor in the coronal oblique maximum intensity projection image (**d**), corresponding to solid component (outlined by arrows) and necrotic area (*) of the gross autopsy specimen (**e**), respectively.

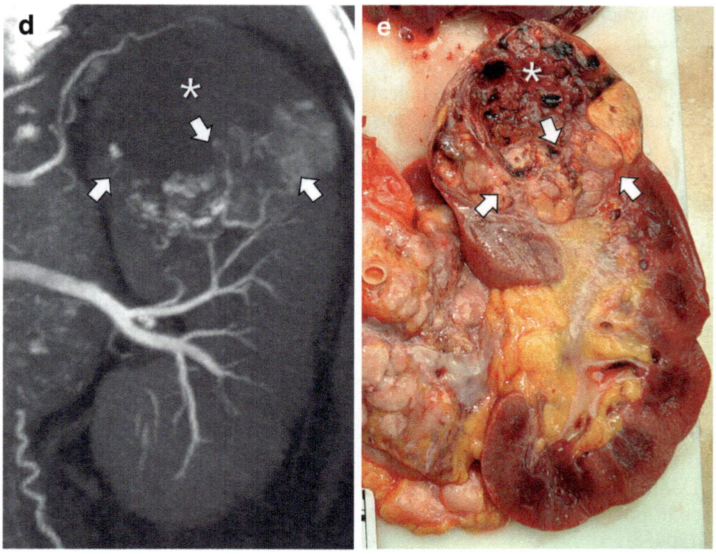

Fig. 21 (continued)

7 Conclusion

PMCT has shown to be useful in death investigation and has become a standard pre-autopsy procedure in many medicolegal institutions worldwide. Since its introduction into the forensic field, PMCT has been mostly used for the investigation of traumatic death due to its ability to demonstrate bone fractures, localize foreign materials, and identify abnormal air collections. In cases of suspected natural death, PMCT can also accurately detect fatal hemorrhages, such as intracerebral hemorrhage and hemopericardium, and easily depict abnormal gas collections, such as air embolism, free air in the body cavities, and soft tissue emphysema. PMCTA enables comprehensive visualization of the vascular system and precise localization of vascular rupture or occlusion in cases of unexpected natural death, such as aortic disease or SCD. Currently, these imaging techniques have been shown to play useful roles in screening for potential causes of natural death and guiding tailored dissection of the suspected area for visual demonstration, which would be sometimes difficult or time-consuming by standard dissection alone. However, in post-mortem setting, accurate image interpretation further requires knowledge and understanding of "normal" post-mortem tissue changes and iatrogenic artifacts secondary to vigorous perimortem resuscitation or medical interventions. Therefore, familiarity with these potential mimickers is important to avoid misinterpretation of the findings as true pathologies on imaging analyses of natural death cases.

Acknowledgment The authors would like to thank the medical examiners in NFS Korea for their advice and help in preparation of this chapter.

References

Andersen KK, Olsen TS, Dehlendorff C, Kammersgaard LP (2009) Hemorrhagic and ischemic strokes compared: stroke severity, mortality, and risk factors. Stroke 40:2068–2072

Biorck G, Wikland B (1972) "Sudden death"—what are we talking about? Circulation 45:256–258

Bossone E, LaBounty TM, Eagle KA (2018) Acute aortic syndromes: diagnosis and management, an update. Eur Heart J 39:739–749d

Bruguier C, Mosimann PJ, Vaucher P et al (2013) Multiphase postmortem CT angiography: recognizing technique-related artefacts and pitfalls. Int J Legal Med 127:639–652

Byard R (2016) Asphyxia: pathological features. In: Payne-James J, Byard R (eds) Encyclopedia of forensic and legal medicine, 2nd edn. Elsevier, Amsterdam, pp 252–260

Chugh SS, Reinier K, Teodorescu C et al (2008) Epidemiology of sudden cardiac death: clinical and research implications. Prog Cardiovasc Dis 51:213–228

Corvera JS (2016) Acute aortic syndrome. Ann Cardiothorac Surg 5:188–193

Dennis MS, Burn JP, Sandercock PA, Bamford JM, Wade DT, Warlow CP (1993) Long-term survival after first-ever stroke: the Oxfordshire Community Stroke Project. Stroke 24:796–800

Figueras J, Alcalde O, Barrabes JA et al (2008) Changes in hospital mortality rates in 425 patients with acute ST-elevation myocardial infarction and cardiac rupture over a 30-year period. Circulation 118:2783–2789

Franquet T (2011) Imaging of pulmonary viral pneumonia. Radiology 260:18–39

Grabherr S, Grimm J, Dominguez A, Vanhaebost J, Mangin P (2014) Advances in post-mortem CT-angiography. Br J Radiol 87:20130488

Grabherr S, Heinemann A, Vogel H et al (2018) Postmortem CT angiography compared with autopsy: a forensic multicenter study. Radiology 288:270–276

Huikuri HV, Castellanos A, Myerburg RJ (2001) Sudden death due to cardiac arrhythmias. N Engl J Med 345:1473–1482

Iino M, O'Donnell C (2010) Postmortem computed tomography findings of upper airway obstruction by food. J Forensic Sci 55:1251–1258

Ishida M, Gonoi W, Okuma H et al (2015) Common Postmortem computed tomography findings following atraumatic death: differentiation between Normal Postmortem changes and pathologic lesions. Korean J Radiol 16:798–809

Johnson W, Onuma O, Owolabi M, Sachdev S (2016) Stroke: a global response is needed. Bull World Health Organ 94:634–634a

Johnston KW, Rutherford RB, Tilson MD, Shah DM, Hollier L, Stanley JC (1991) Suggested standards for reporting on arterial aneurysms. Subcommittee on reporting standards for arterial aneurysms, ad hoc committee on reporting standards, Society for Vascular Surgery and North American Chapter, International Society for Cardiovascular Surgery. J Vasc Surg 13:452–458

Koehler S (2016) Death investigation. In: Freeman M, Zeegers M (eds) Forensic epidemiology principles and practice. Elsevier, London, pp 179–199

La Russa R, Catalano C, Di Sanzo M et al (2019) Postmortem computed tomography angiography (PMCTA) and traditional autopsy in cases of sudden cardiac death due to coronary artery disease: a systematic review and meta-analysis. Radiol Med 124:109–117

Lee H, Lee S, Cha JG, Baek T, Yang KM (2019) Postmortem computed tomography and computed tomography angiography: cardiothoracic imaging applications in forensic medicine. J Thorac Imaging 34(5):286–298

Lempel JK, Frazier AA, Jeudy J et al (2014) Aortic arch dissection: a controversy of classification. Radiology 271:848–855

Leontiev O, Dubinsky TJ (2007) CT-based calcium scoring to screen for coronary artery disease: why aren't we there yet? AJR Am J Roentgenol 189:1061–1063

Levy A, Harcke HJ (2011) Natural death. In: Levy AD, Theodore Harcke H (eds) Essentials of forensic imaging: a text atlas. CRC, Boca Raton, pp 217–234

Lloyd-Jones D, Adams R, Carnethon M et al (2009) Heart disease and stroke statistics—2009 update: a report from the American Heart Association Statistics Committee and Stroke Statistics Subcommittee. Circulation 119:480–486

Lubner M, Menias C, Rucker C et al (2007) Blood in the belly: CT findings of hemoperitoneum. Radiographics 27:109–125

Mansour TR, Alam Y, Dahbour L, Alnemari A, Jumaa M, Schroeder JL (2017) Streptococcus Mutans: a potential risk factor in recurrent Hemorrhagic stroke. Cureus 9:e1264

Mantovani V, Vanoli D, Chelazzi P, Lepore V, Ferrarese S, Sala A (2002) Post-infarction cardiac rupture: surgical treatment. Eur J Cardiothorac Surg 22:777–780

Maron BJ, Epstein SE, Roberts WC (1986) Causes of sudden death in competitive athletes. J Am Coll Cardiol 7:204–214

McElwee SK, Velasco A, Doppalapudi H (2016) Mechanisms of sudden cardiac death. J Nucl Cardiol 23:1368–1379

Michaud K, Grabherr S, Doenz F, Mangin P (2012) Evaluation of postmortem MDCT and MDCT-angiography for the investigation of sudden cardiac death related to atherosclerotic coronary artery disease. Int J Cardiovasc Imaging 28:1807–1822

Mittleman RE, Wetli CV (1982) The fatal cafe coronary. Foreign-body airway obstruction. JAMA 247:1285–1288

Morgan B, Biggs MJ, Barber J et al (2013) Accuracy of targeted post-mortem computed tomography coronary angiography compared to assessment of serial histological sections. Int J Legal Med 127:809–817

Musuka TD, Wilton SB, Traboulsi M, Hill MD (2015) Diagnosis and management of acute ischemic stroke: speed is critical. CMAJ 187:887–893

O'Donnell C, Bedford P, Burke M (2011) Massive hemoperitoneum due to ruptured ectopic gestation: postmortem CT findings in a deeply frozen deceased person. Leg Med (Tokyo) 13:245–249

Oehmichen M, Meissner C (2000) Natural death. Gerontology 46:105–110

Orwig D, Federle MP (1989) Localized clotted blood as evidence of visceral trauma on CT: the sentinel clot sign. AJR Am J Roentgenol 153:747–749

Oudkerk M, Stillman AE, Halliburton SS et al (2008) Coronary artery calcium screening: current status and recommendations from the European Society of Cardiac Radiology and North American Society for cardiovascular imaging. Int J Cardiovasc Imaging 24:645–671

Owolabi MO, Akarolo-Anthony S, Akinyemi R et al (2015) The burden of stroke in Africa: a glance at the present and a glimpse into the future. Cardiovasc J Afr 26:S27–S38

Palmiere C, Lobrinus JA, Mangin P, Grabherr S (2013) Detection of coronary thrombosis after multi-phase postmortem CT-angiography. Legal Med (Tokyo) 15:12–18

Parizel PM, Makkat S, Van Miert E, Van Goethem JW, van den Hauwe L, De Schepper AM (2001) Intracranial hemorrhage: principles of CT and MRI interpretation. Eur Radiol 11:1770–1783

Polacco M, Sedati P, Arena V et al (2015) Visualization of myocardial infarction by post-mortem single-organ coronary computed tomography: a feasibility study. Int J Legal Med 129:517–524

Risgaard B, Lynge TH, Wissenberg M et al (2015) Risk factors and causes of sudden noncardiac death: a nationwide cohort study in Denmark. Heart Rhythm 12:968–974

Ross SG, Bolliger SA, Ampanozi G, Oesterhelweg L, Thali MJ, Flach PM (2014) Postmortem CT angiography: capabilities and limitations in traumatic and natural causes of death. Radiographics 34:830–846

Ross SG, Thali MJ, Bolliger S, Germerott T, Ruder TD, Flach PM (2012) Sudden death after chest pain: feasibility of virtual autopsy with postmortem CT angiography and biopsy. Radiology 264:250–259

Ruder TD, Zech W-D, Hatch GM, Ross S, Ampanozi G, Thali MJ, Flach PM (2013) Still frame from the hour of death—acute intracerebral hemorrhage on post-mortem computed tomography in a decomposed corpse. J Forensic Radiol Imaging 1:73–76

Rumberger JA, Simons DB, Fitzpatrick LA, Sheedy PF, Schwartz RS (1995) Coronary artery calcium area by electron-beam computed tomography and coronary atherosclerotic plaque area. A histopathologic correlative study. Circulation 92:2157–2162

Runchey S, McGee S (2010) Does this patient have a hemorrhagic stroke?: clinical findings distinguishing hemorrhagic stroke from ischemic stroke. JAMA 303:2280–2286

Sacco RL, Wolf PA, Kannel WB, McNamara PM (1982) Survival and recurrence following stroke. The Framingham study. Stroke 13:290–295

Shiotani S, Watanabe K, Kohno M, Ohashi N, Yamazaki K, Nakayama H (2004) Postmortem computed tomographic (PMCT) findings of pericardial effusion due to acute aortic dissection. Radiat Med 22:405–407

Smith AB, Lattin GE Jr, Berran P, Harcke HT (2012) Common and expected postmortem CT observations involving the brain: mimics of antemortem pathology. AJNR Am J Neuroradiol 33:1387–1391

Virmani R, Burke AP, Farb A (2001) Sudden cardiac death. Cardiovasc Pathol 10:211–218

Wick R, Gilbert JD, Byard RW (2006) Cafe coronary syndrome-fatal choking on food: an autopsy approach. J Clin Forensic Med 13:135–138

World Health Organization 2018 The top 10 causes of death

Death at Hospital and Medical Liability: Investigation of Medical Interventions with Fatal Outcome by Post-mortem Computed Tomography

Axel Heinemann

Contents

1 Introduction

The use of imaging for the detection of errors in treatment dates back to 1895, when it was first accepted as evidence in court (Brogdon 1998).

There is a rising number of reports about the advantages of post-mortem imaging in cases with fatal outcome after medical intervention (Palmiere et al. 2012; Wichmann et al. 2012, 2014; Zerlauth et al. 2013; Vogel et al. 2013a, b; Westphal et al. 2014). Autopsy can be guided and complemented by PMCT in these cases by typical features resulting in fatal complications after medical treatment which can be exemplified by the following categories:

- Confirmation of the appropriate site of applied medical devices (Figs. 1a, b and 2a, b)
- Documentation of the misplacement of
  - Central lines (Fig. 3a, b)
  - Drainages (pleural (Fig. 4a, b), pericardial, abdominal)

In memoriam Prof. Hermann Vogel

A. Heinemann (✉)
Institute of Legal Medicine, University Medical Center Hamburg-Eppendorf, Hamburg, Germany
e-mail: heinemann@uke.de

© Springer Nature Switzerland AG 2022
F. Dedouit et al. (eds.), *Forensic Imaging*, Medical Radiology Diagnostic Imaging,
https://doi.org/10.1007/978-3-030-83352-7_12

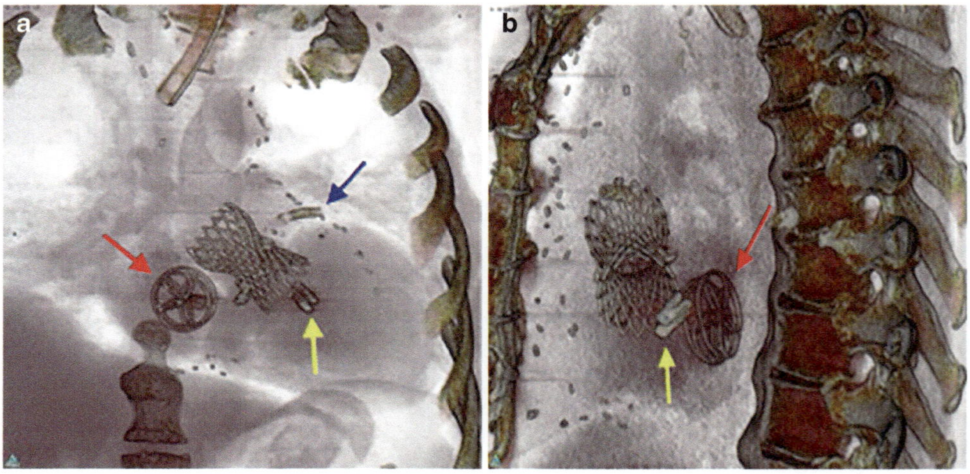

Fig. 1 (**a**) Severe cardiac disease with a variety of cardiac interventions/surgery (no indication for inappropriate positions): TAVI in aortic valve position, mitral valve clips (yellow arrow), left atrial appendage occluder (red arrow), coronary stent in the LCA (blue arrow), bypass surgery with staples along typical pathways for LIMA and RIMA bypass surgery. PMCT, 3D Rendering of left thorax, frontal view. (**b**) See 1a. 3D Rendering. View from left side

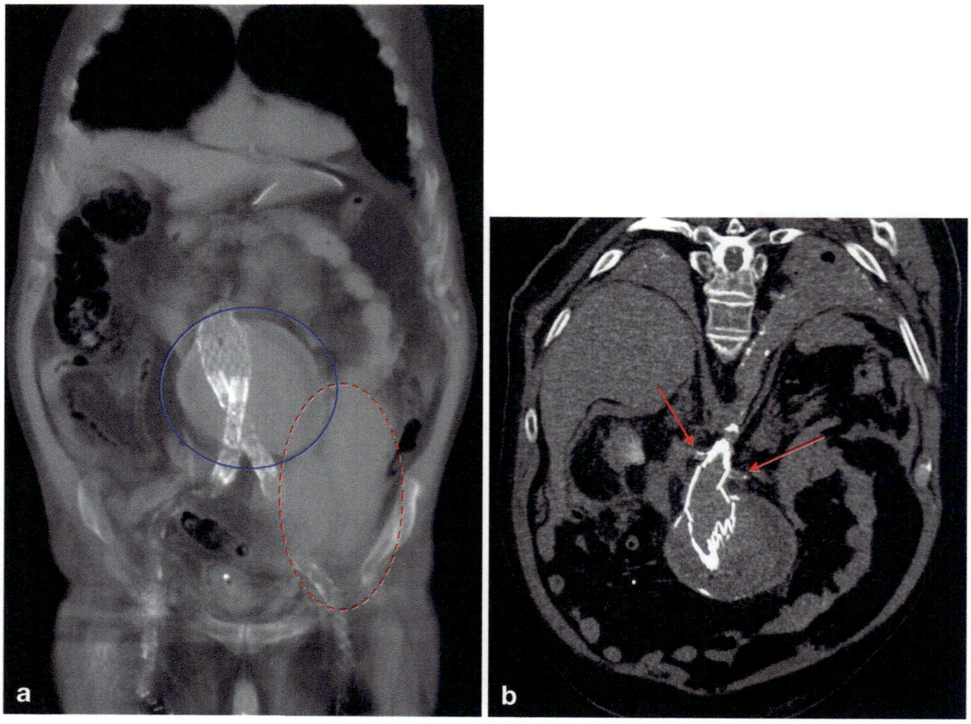

Fig. 2 (**a**) Aneurysm of the abdominal infrarenal aorta (blue circle, max. Diameter 11,1 cm), Endovascular aneurysm repair (EVAR) with multiple sequential stents. Twisted iliac artery stents following kinking vessels without sign of displacement at the attachment site to aortic stent. Acute retroperitoneal hemorrhage to the left side (dotted circle). The patient died of hemorrhagic shock. Unenhanced PMCT, frontal plane, mean intensity projection. (**b**) See 2a. Level of renal artery branching with fenestrated stents. Aneurysm bulge starts well 1.8 cm after branch arteries, stents here attached to parallel aortic walls. Oblique frontal plane, VR intensity projection

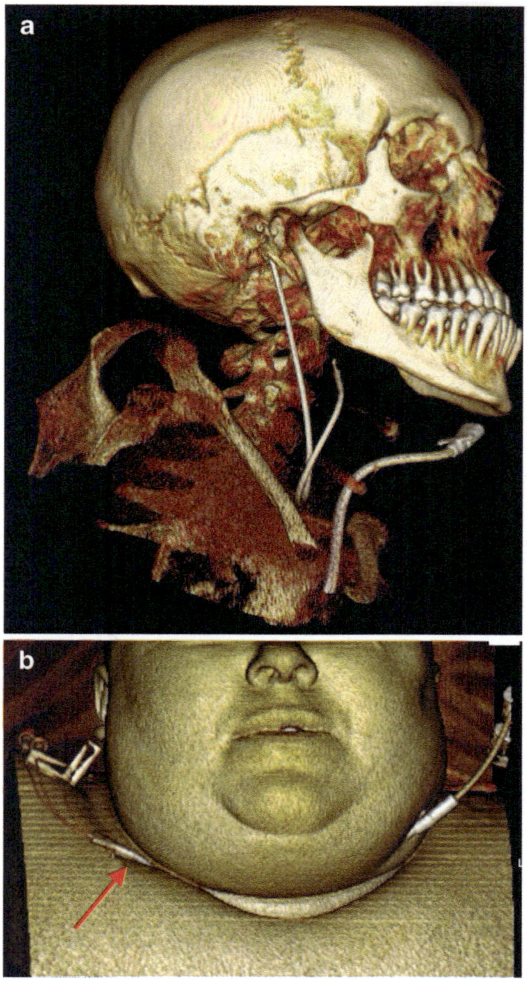

Fig. 3 (**a**) Female, 47 years. Multi-organ failure by acute myeloid leukemia. Jugular central venous line, suddenly going into reverse upwards reaching the level of the jugular foramen. Left side subclavian catheter in standard position. PMCT, 3D volume rendering, bone window. View from below right side. (**b**) See 3a. Note the remarkable short-necked and stout neck configuration which elevated the risk for misguided puncture. The site of entry was above the level of the clavicula but still apart from the neck base which predisposed for misguided catheter placement. Volume surface rendering of the anterior neck region

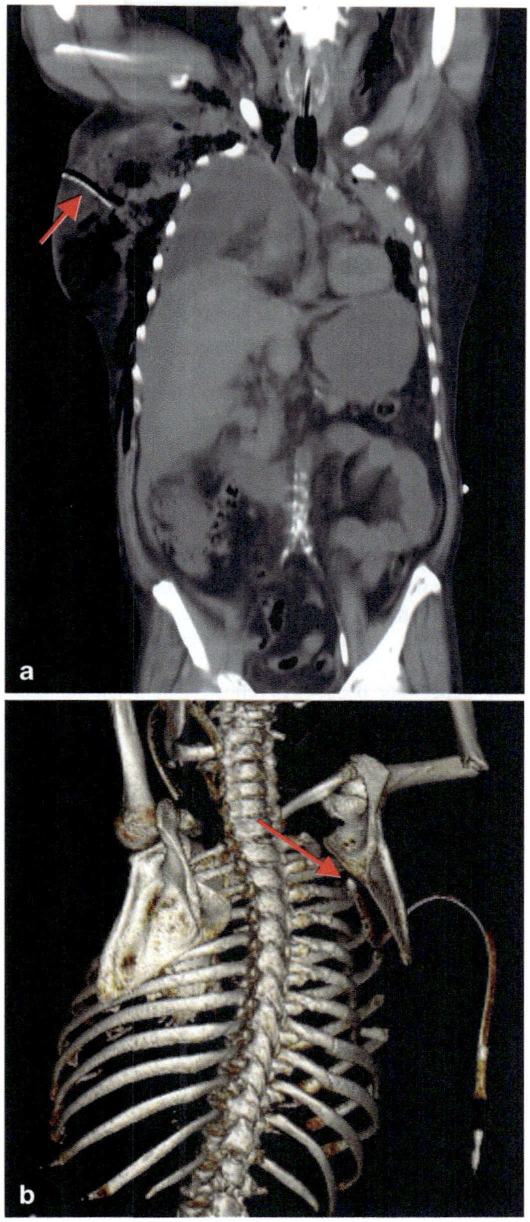

Fig. 4 (**a**) Male child, 8 years. Fall from second floor window to the ground. Severely dislocated multiple fractures of second to tenth rib on the right side with flail chest and hematopneumothorax. Soft tissue emphysema on the right upper thorax in the region of the access for the pleura drainage (arrow). PMCT, frontal reconstruction, mean intensity projection. (**b**) See 4a. The pleura drainage did not reach intrathoracic level, its tip (arrow) remains in the subscapular soft tissues, facilitated by the massive dislodgement of several ribs. Volume rendering with view from backside

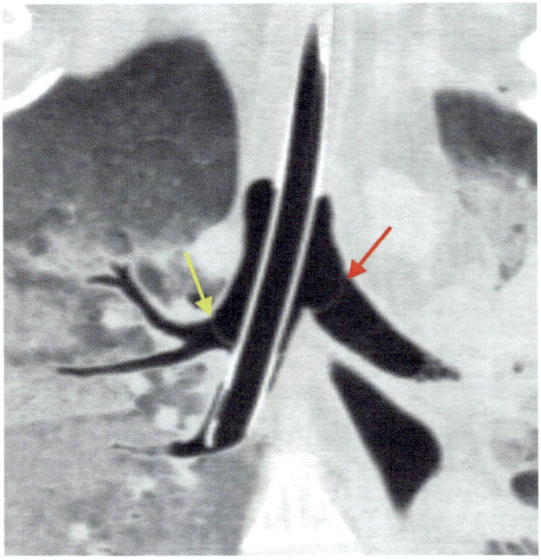

Fig. 5 Failed resuscitation attempt. Endotracheal tube with non-preferred placement of the tip in the right medial lobe bronchus. The cuff blocks ventilation of the left main bronchus (note the bulged cuff wall, red arrow) and the right upper lobe bronchus (yellow arrow). The fenestrations and the tip openings seem to be covered by bronchial mucosa. PMCT, frontal reconstruction

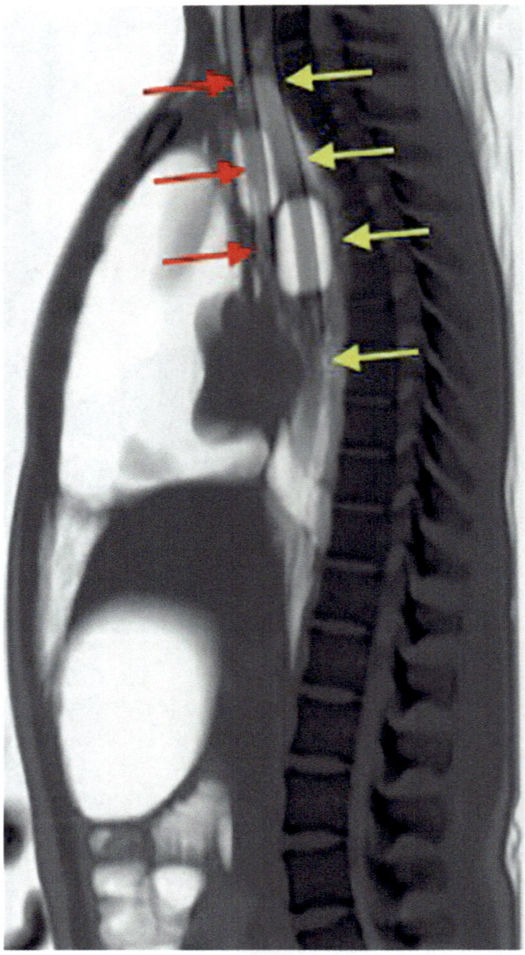

Fig. 6 Emergency case due to acute coronary syndrome: Failed primary cuffed intubation of the esophagus (yellow arrows) which had not been removed before second intubation with finally correct endotracheal position (red arrows). Sagittal plane, mean intensity projection. PMCT, sagittal reconstruction, mean intensity projection

  - Breathing tubes (endotracheal or tracheostoma tubes) (Figs. 5 and 6)
  - Catheters or cuffs accessing hollow organs (particularly urinary catheters) (Figs. 7a, b and 8a, b) or stomach tubes (Figs. 9b, c, 10a, b, and 11a, b),
  - Guide wires (Fig. 12a, b)
- Sources of intervention-related hemorrhages (Figs. 13a, b, 14a, b, 15a, b, and 16)
- Evidence for regular or for impaired perfusion after vascular interventions (Fig. 17a, b, 18a, b, and 19a, b)
- Gas at inappropriate places as soft tissues or body cavities, gas embolism (Figs. 18a–d and 20a–c)
- General indications for underlying fatal pathologies potentially independent from antemortem medical procedures in question (Figs. 2a, b, 17a, b, and 22a–c)

PMCT is a valuable diagnostic tool that adds further information after fatal or unexpected deaths following medical treatment, particularly if an autopsy diagnosis is not achievable due to refusal of patient's/family consent (Thali 2011; Westphal et al. 2014; Heinemann et al. 2015), biological hazards or lack of time before burial under the framework of religious/ethnic doctrines (Patriquin et al. 2001; Shojania and Burton 2008; Friedrich 2012). Post-mortem imaging has the potential to be acknowledged as a tool for quality control in hospitals. On the other hand, the interdisciplinary cooperation between radiologists and clinical pathologists has not reached a significant level in many countries. Forensic

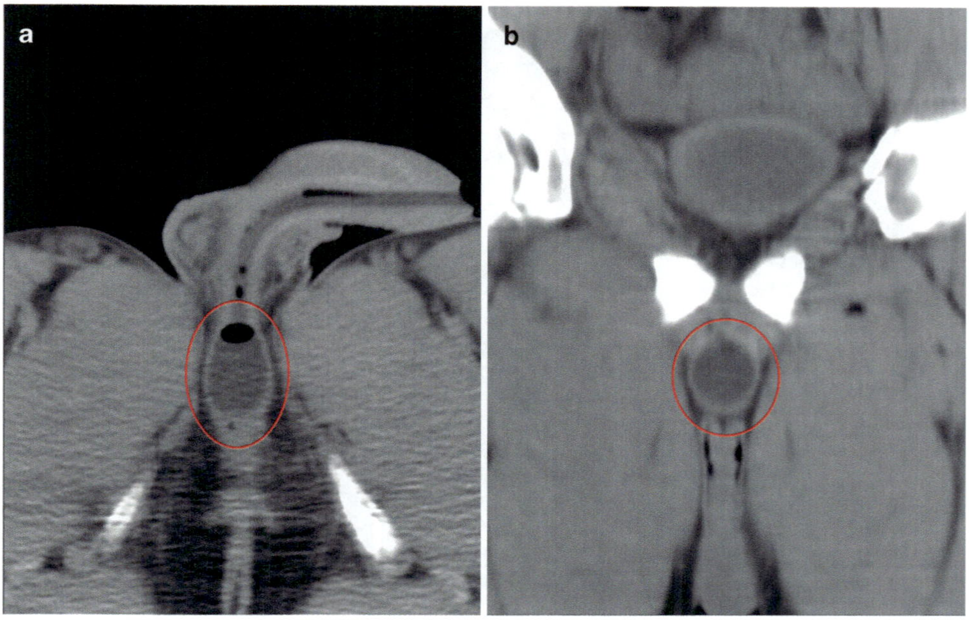

Fig. 7 (**a**) Displaced blocker cuff (red circles) of a urinary catheter in the urethra of a male who had a short intensive care treatment after an accidental fall with deceleration trauma in an indoor ski hall resulting in a rupture of the aortic arch with hemopericardium. PMCT, axial reconstruction, mean intensity projection. (**b**) See 7a: Frontal reconstruction, mean intensity projection

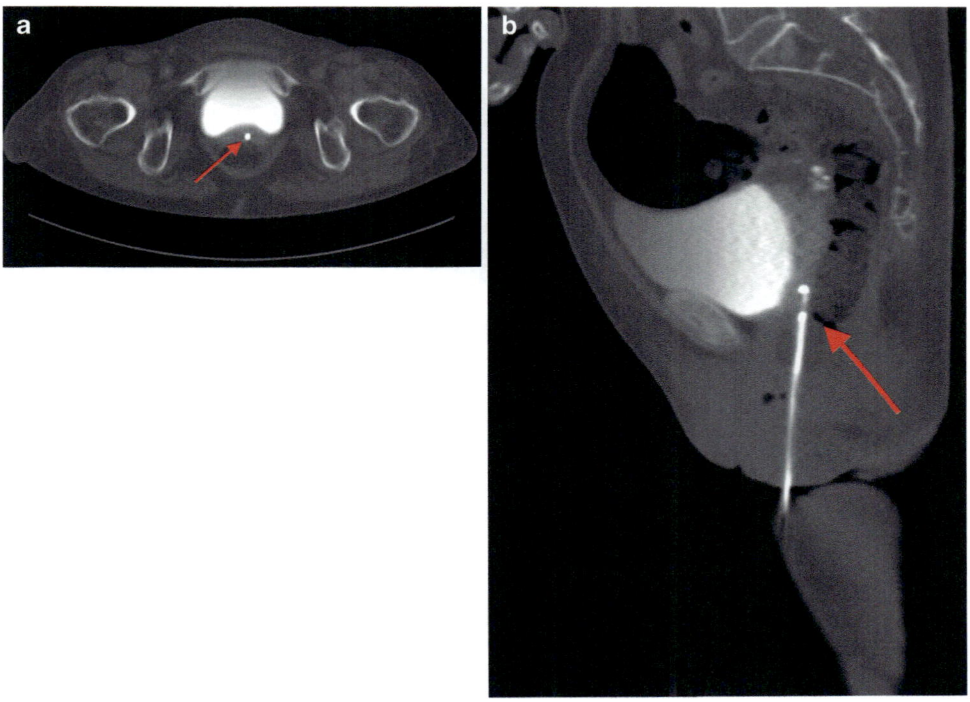

Fig. 8 (**a**) Female, 49 years. Craniocerebral trauma, intensive care treatment. Urinary catheter (arrows) displaced in the fornix vaginae (Urinary bladder enhanced by antemortem contrast agent). Axial reconstruction, mean intensity projection (PMCT). (**b**) See 8a: Sagittal reconstruction, mean intensity projection

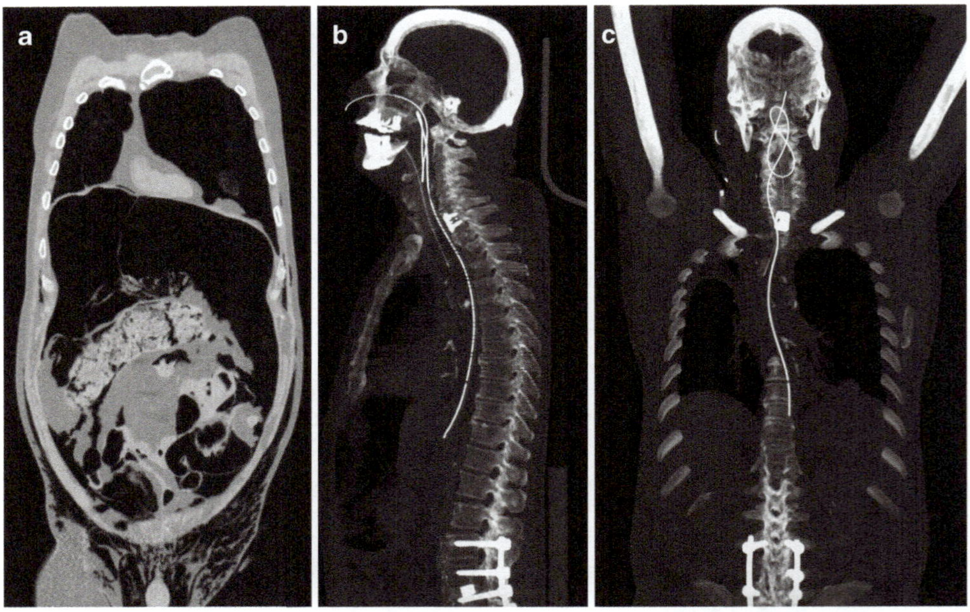

Fig. 9 (**a**) Male, 63 years. Severe chronic lung disease with high-grade pulmonary emphysema and myocardial infarction. Resuscitation, complicated by tension pneumothorax on the left side, small pneumothorax on the right side and massive pneumoperitoneum. No rib fractures. PMCT, frontal reconstruction, anterior plane. (**b**) See 9a. Gastric tube with a loop in the hypo- and epipharynx, the tip does not reach stomach level. The loop indicated a potential cause for tension pneumothorax which was ruled out by autopsy. During resuscitation, a chest compression system had been applied. A pleural rupture caused pneumothorax and massive gas emphysema expanded below the diaphragm level. Sagittal reconstruction. (**c**) Same as before. Gastric tube with a loop in the upper trachea and larynx. Frontal reconstruction

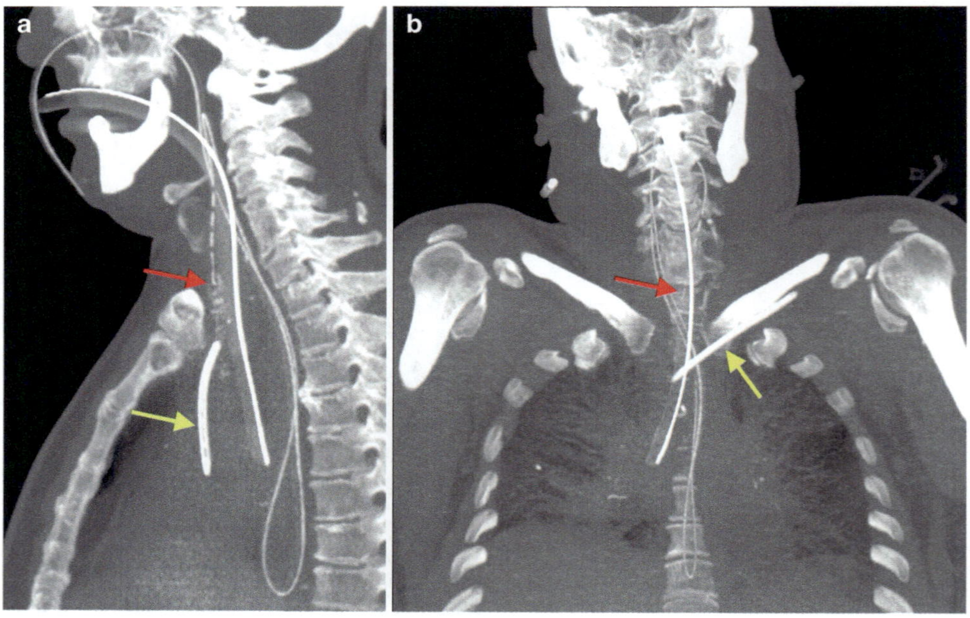

Fig. 10 (**a**) Male, 54 years. Stab wound in the right thigh. Emergency treatment with intubation (misplacement in the right main bronchus). Naso-gastroduodenal tube with first loop in the esophagus, then looping again in the epipharynx, the tip (red arrow) finally ending in the trachea just below the larynx. (Yellow arrow: Subclavian central venous line). PMCT, sagittal reconstruction. Maximum intensity projection. (**b**) See 10a. Frontal reconstruction. Maximum intensity projection

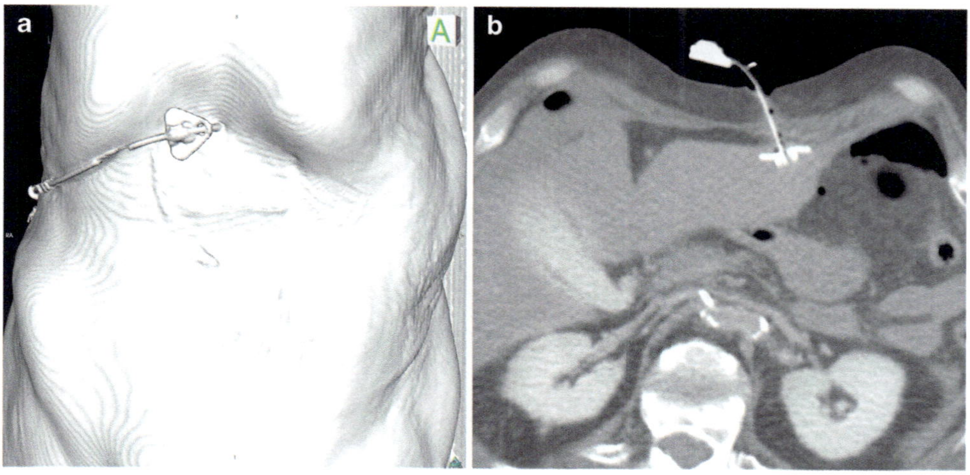

Fig. 11 (**a**) Female, 75 years, hospitalized 4 days after percutaneous endoscopic gastrostomy. Diagnosis of a rupture of the gastric wall in emergency CT. The patient died before a decision on surgical intervention had been finalized. A misplacement of the PEG tube was suspected. 3D rendering of the trunk of the patient with view on the PEG entering the abdominal wall near the midline. PMCT, 3D surface reconstruction, frontal view. (**b**) See 11a. Misplaced percutaneous endoscopic gastrostomy (PEG) tube, ending in the left lobe of the liver (misplacement and peritonitis as cause of death confirmed by autopsy). Axial plane at the level of the epigastrium, MIP

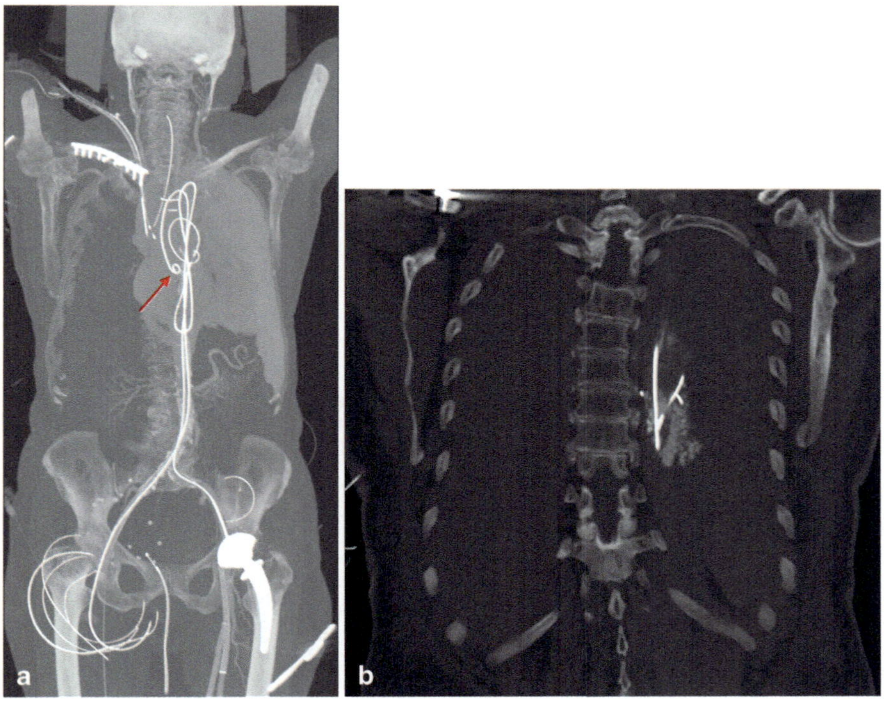

Fig. 12 (**a**) Female, 76 years. Aortic valve stenosis. Attempt for a transcatheter aortic valve implantation (TAVI). During advancement of the guidewire, double looping happened in the thoracic aorta and the aortic wall was perforated, the tip of the wire getting trapped in the prevertebral mediastinum (red arrow). Intraprocedural death by hemorrhagic shock. Hemomediastinum and hemothorax on the left side. Arterial phase 1200 ml of multiphase post-mortem CT angiography. Frontal reconstruction, maximum intensity projection. (**b**) See 12a. Early arterial phase with 250 ml contrast agent applied to the femoral artery, demonstrating the localization of the perforation at 6th/7th thoracic vertebra level by limited extravasation of contrast medium

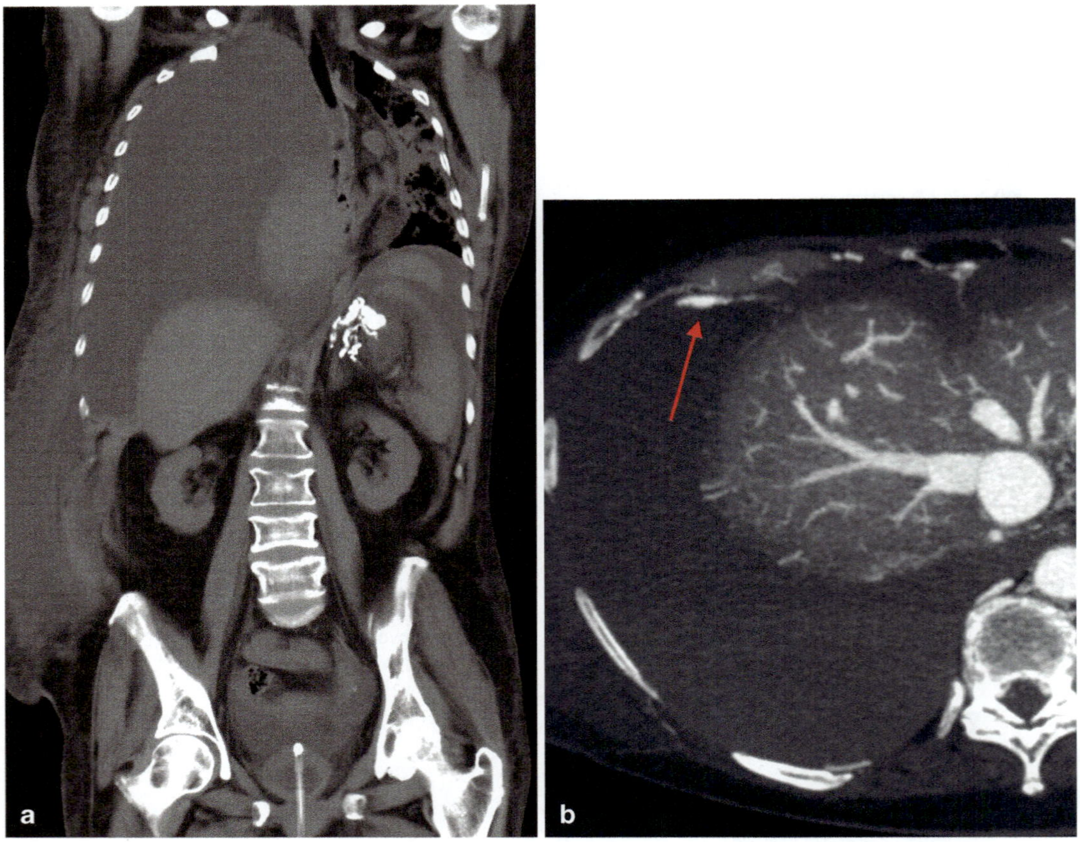

Fig. 13 (**a**) 58 years, female. Decompensated alcoholic liver disease. Post-mortem identification of hematothorax on the right side after pleurocentesis the day before and sclerozitation of gastric varicoceles (see hyperdense structure in the center) had been reported. Autopsy revealed that the hematothorax was due to prolonged resuscitation with multiple rib fractures. Death due to purulent pancreatitis. PMCT, frontal plane. (**b**) See 13a. Fracture of the right seventh rib with extravasation of contrast agent (arrow). Axial plane, MIP, arterial phase of MPMCTA

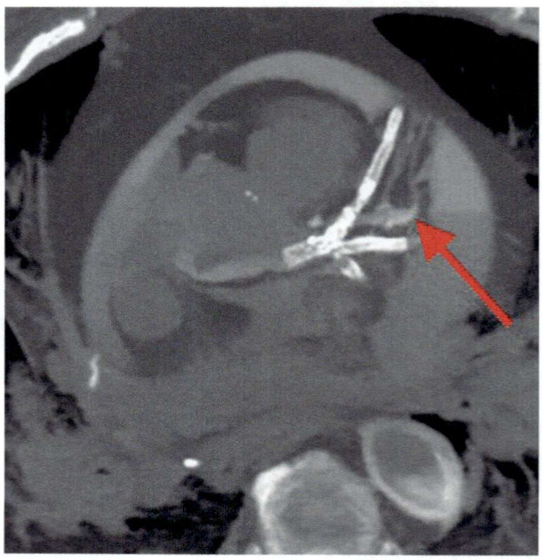

Fig. 14 Perforation of the LAD during percutaneous coronary intervention with multiple stenting of the left coronary artery branches, antemortem extravasation of contrast agent beneath epicardium and perforation into the pericardial sac with sedimentation of contrast agent (red arrow). PMCT, axial view

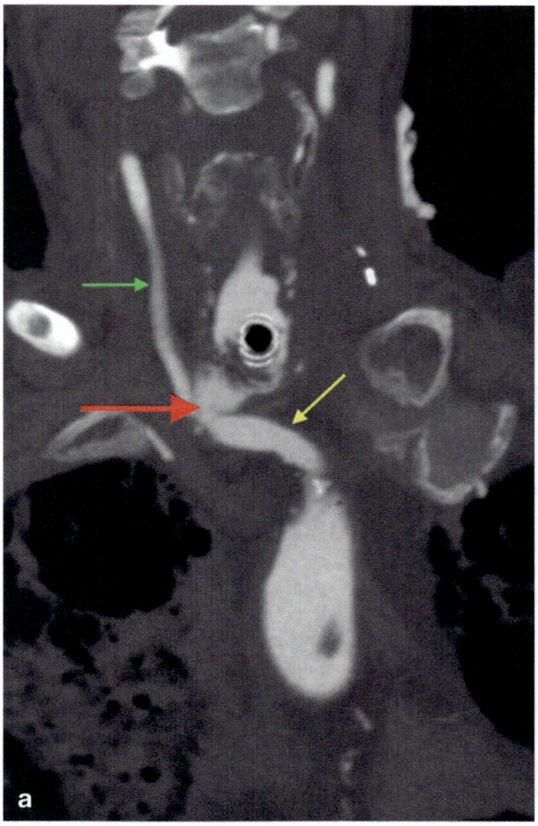

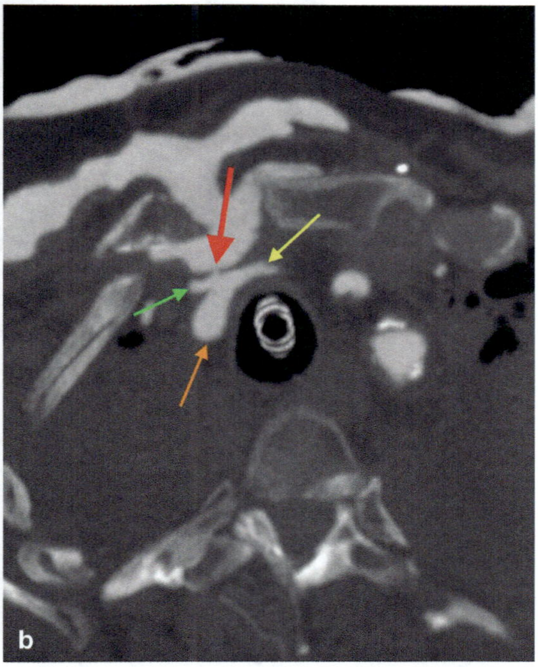

Fig. 15 (**a**) Male, 65 years, hypopharyngeal carcinoma after surgical resection, tracheostomy, radiation treatment, and necrosis of soft tissues in the anterior neck region; Failed attempt to close soft tissue defects by a pectoralis flap, secondary wound infection, removal and second attempt with an anterolateral thigh (ALT) flap which had been inverted into the wound opening close to the tracheostomy cannula. On the day after the ALT flap procedure, sudden fatal hemorrhage was observed resulting in severe bleeding from the flap margins and the cannula region. Arterial phase of MPMCTA shows contrast agent leakage at the site of the inflammatory erosion (red arrow, *middle and left*) of the right common carotid artery (green arrow) at its branching from the innominate artery (yellow arrow). Extravasation of contrast agent into the soft tissues around the flap, into the trachea perforation for the tracheostomy cannula and upper parts of the trachea (*right*) and to the anterior chest wall. PMCT, slightly oblique frontal reconstruction, MIP. (**b**) See 15a. Slightly oblique axial reconstruction, MIP

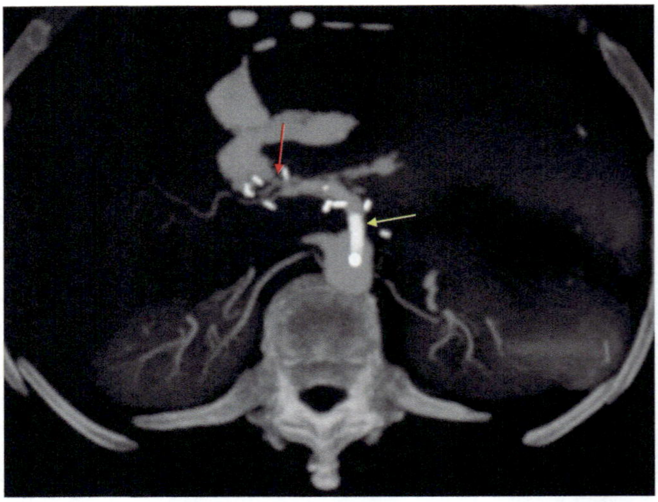

Fig. 16 Male, 57 years. Tumor of the Treitz´ band, surgical removal of pancreatic tail, parts of the duodenum and descending colon. Hepatic ischemia revealed a thrombosis of the celiac trunk. Catheter-guided embolectomy and stenting of the celiac trunk. Placement of the catheter tip in the common hepatic artery at the level of the branching of the gastroduodenal artery. Application of negative pressure and withdrawal of the catheter. Indication for vessel perforation in CT and attempt to overstent the hepatic artery where the leakage was suspected. Circulatory failure during the emergency stent procedure. MPMCTA shows the stent in the celiac trunk (yellow arrow) and multiple clips for branches of common hepatic artery. Leakage at the branching of the clipped gastroduodenal artery (red arrow). PMCT, axial reconstruction, early arterial phase with 250 ml contrast agent

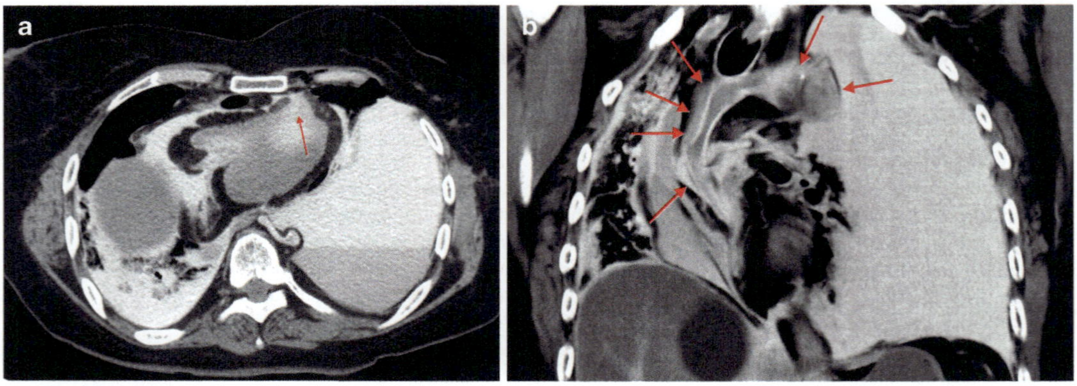

Fig. 17 (**a**) Thoracic aortic dissection (Stanford A) during percutaneous coronary intervention: Hemopericardium with indication of ventricular perforation at cardiac apex (arrow). Myocardial enhancement of the apex by antemortem contrast agent. Bilateral hematothorax, sedimentation of blood and contrast agent on the left side. Collapse of descending aorta. PMCT, axial reconstruction at cardiac ventricular level. (**b**) See 17a. Aortic dissection including ascending and aortic arch (red arrows). An autopsy was waived in this case. Suspected ventricular rupture due to myocardial infarction, combined with intraprocedural aortic complication. Oblique frontal reconstruction, mean intensity projection

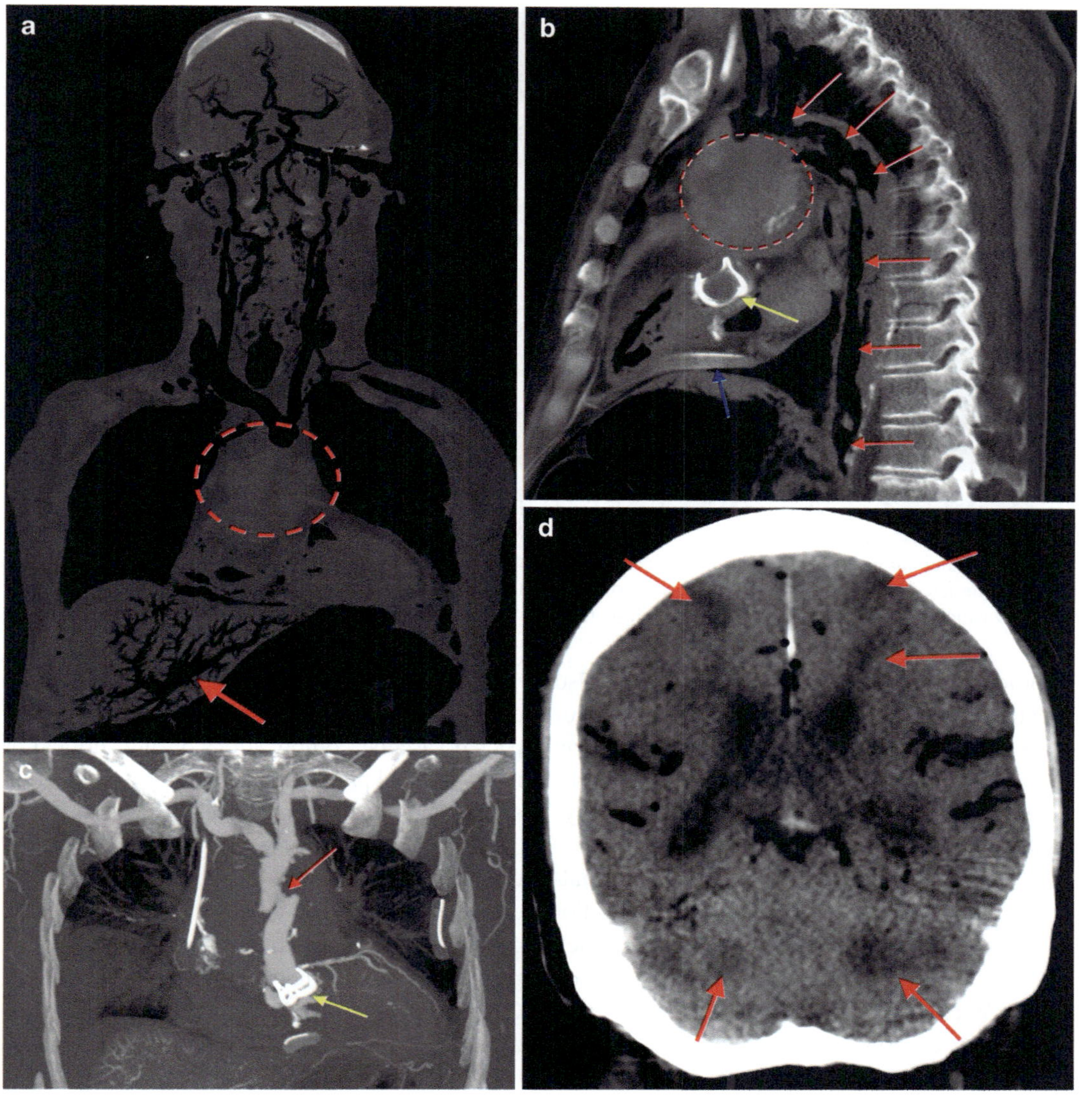

Fig. 18 (**a**) Ruptured aneurysm (dotted circle) of the ascending aorta and aortic arch. Recent cardiothoracic intervention with application of a heart-lung-machine replaced the aortic valve and ascending aorta after a thoracic endovascular repair had failed. The patient died shortly after surgical intervention, a multi-organ failure was certified. There was no major bleeding at the time of death apparent in the body but a hemopericardium (treated with a pericardial drainage) and limited mediastinal hemorrhage; central jugular lines on both sides had been left in place. There was abundant gas detection in the arterial system of the aorta and major branches, including the cerebral arteries (see also cerebral lesions in 4d), but also in jugular veins and the portal system (red arrow). Unenhanced PMCT, 20 h post-mortem interval, frontal plane, minimum intensity projection. (**b**) See 18a. Aneurysm (dotted circle). Gas content in the aortic arch and descending aorta (red arrows) and in both cardiac ventricles. Aortic valve prosthesis (yellow arrow). Pericardial drainage (blue arrow). Oblique sagittal plane, minimum intensity projection. (**c**) See 18a. Arterial phase of MPMCTA. Narrowing at the level of anastomosis between prosthesis of ascending aorta and aneurysm section of aortic arch (red arrow). Narrowings also at the origin of major branches from aortic arch. Frontal plane, maximum intensity projection. (**d**) See 18a. Unenhanced PMCT: Multiple hypodense parietal and cerebellar (ischemic) lesions (examples indicated by red arrows). Oblique frontal plane, mean intensity projection

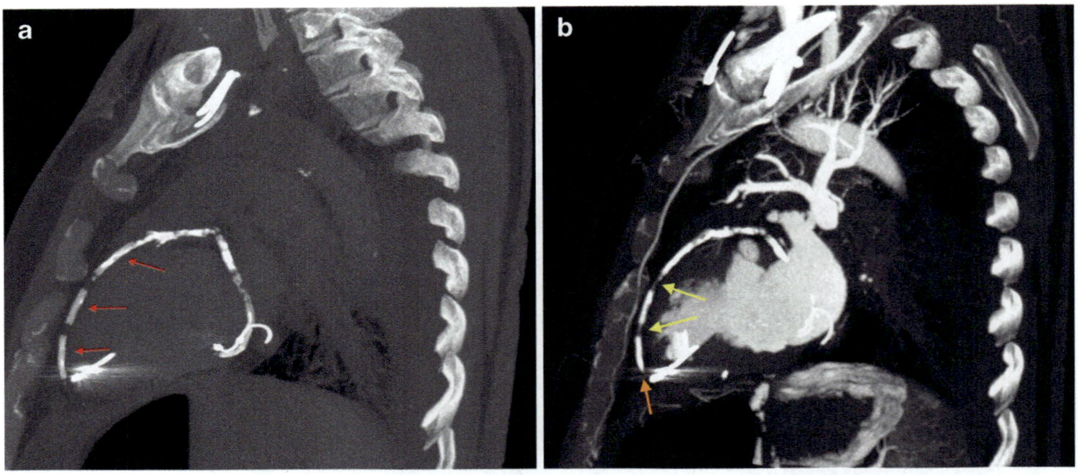

Fig. 19 (**a**) Male, 67 years. After 6 weeks in hospital and cardiac pacemaker intervention sudden cardiac failure with myocardial infarction; Multiple stents in all three main coronaries. Note three sequential stents (arrows) in the LAD which is highly calcified in its proximal section. PMCT, sagittal plane, MIP. (**b**) See 19a. Arterial phase of MPMCTA, MIP. Threadlike contrast media opacification distal from first and second stents (yellow arrows), but missing (orange arrow) behind third stent. Autopsy revealed in- stent thromboses in LAD and RCA

pathologists and forensic radiologists do also experience a range of suspected medical error cases but reports to hospital quality control may be considerably delayed after expert opinions have been primarily used for criminal or liability-related jurisdictions.

In the assessment of suspected medical malpractice, PMCT has established its role for radiological access of morphological findings which are indicative for or against an iatrogenic caused injury (Wichmann et al. 2012; Heinemann et al. 2015). Key criteria for the decision to perform post-mortem imaging and for its interpretation can be obtained from the preliminary inspection of the medical history of a deceased patient (Vogel et al. 2013b).

The verification of bleeding sources (Palmiere et al. 2012; Heinemann et al. 2015) after suspected vascular complications during surgical or interventional procedures justifies the application of post-mortem CT angiography (PMCTA).

The post-mortem evaluation of in-hospital deaths by imaging relies on the availability of CT examinations in the radiology, accident and emergency department or—if available—in or near to a pathology unit/morgue. Depending on the country CT examinations may be done on request by clinical colleagues and—if required—consented by next of kin in cases of naturally certified deaths. Furthermore, this is possible in cases in which public prosecution decides to stop further investigations in primarily certified unclear manner of death.

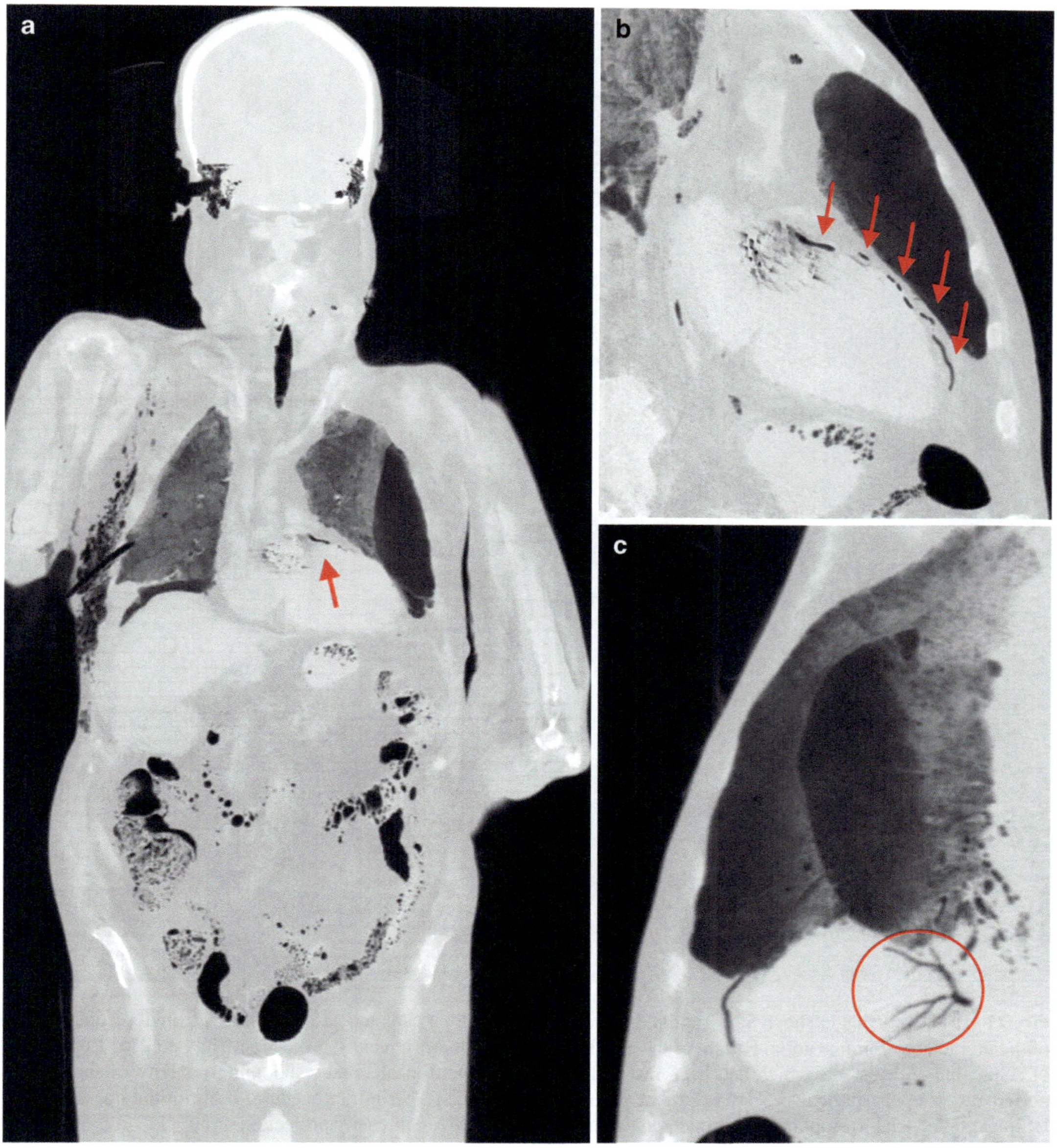

Fig. 20 (**a**) PMCT in a case with sudden cardiac failure during coronary angiography, prolonged resuscitation. Patient with transcatheter aortic valve implantation (TAVI), pleural drainage, central venous catheters. Catheters had been removed. Note that there is no gas in the vessel system including liver but in the LAD (arrow). Frontal plane, MiniP. (**b**) See 20a. LAD with sequential gas contents down to the cardiac apex (arrows). Oblique plane, MiniP. (**c**) See 20a. Further sequential gas contents in distal branches of the RCX (red circle). Oblique plane, MiniP

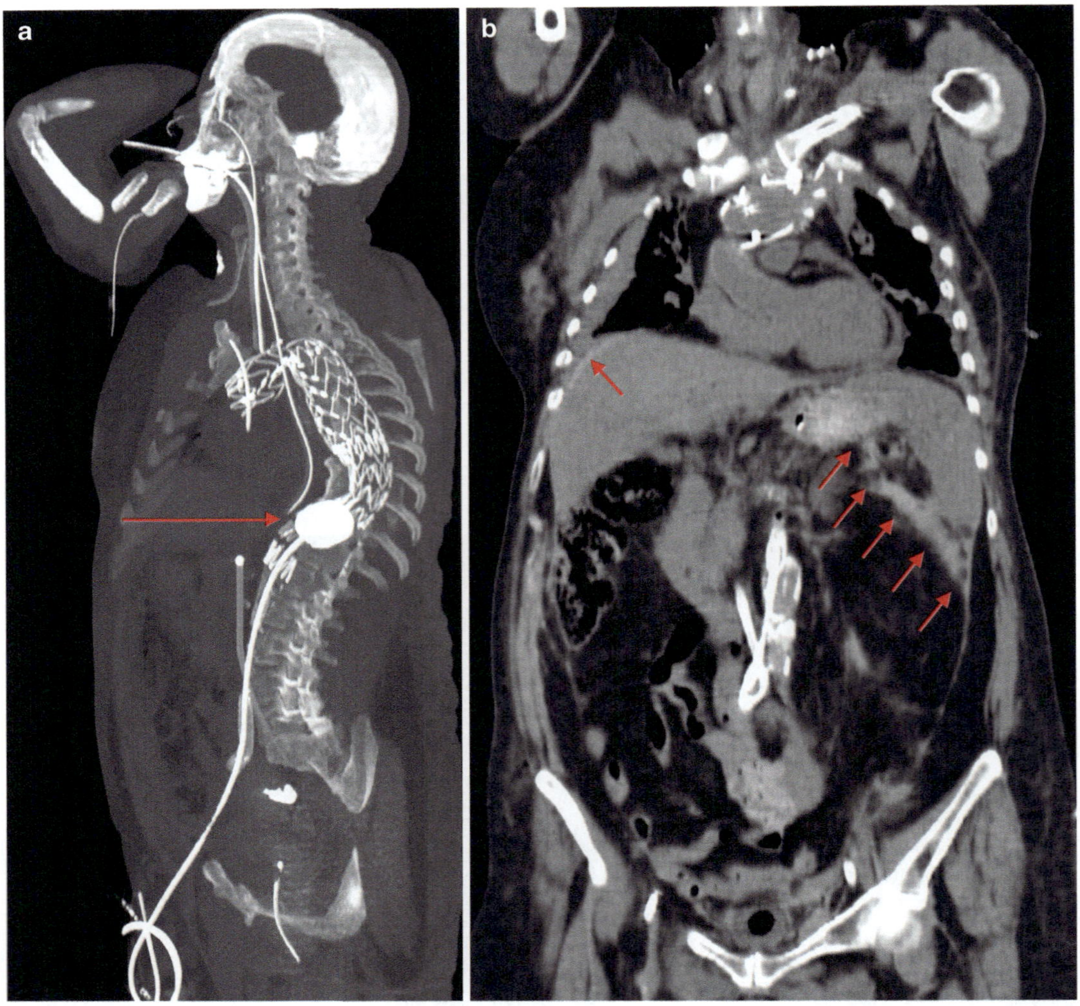

Fig. 21 (**a**) Hemorrhagic shock after ruptured dissection of the thoracicoabdominal aorta. Failure of the attachment of sequential aortic stents which had been inserted, supported by an open surgical procedure after laparotomy. Ultimate failed trial to stop the abdominal hemorrhage by a balloon catheter (arrow). PMCT, frontal reconstruction, maximum intensity projection. (**b**) See 21a. Remains of retroperitoneal and abdominal cavity hemorrhages (arrows) after intraprocedural death in the operating theater. Mean intensity projection

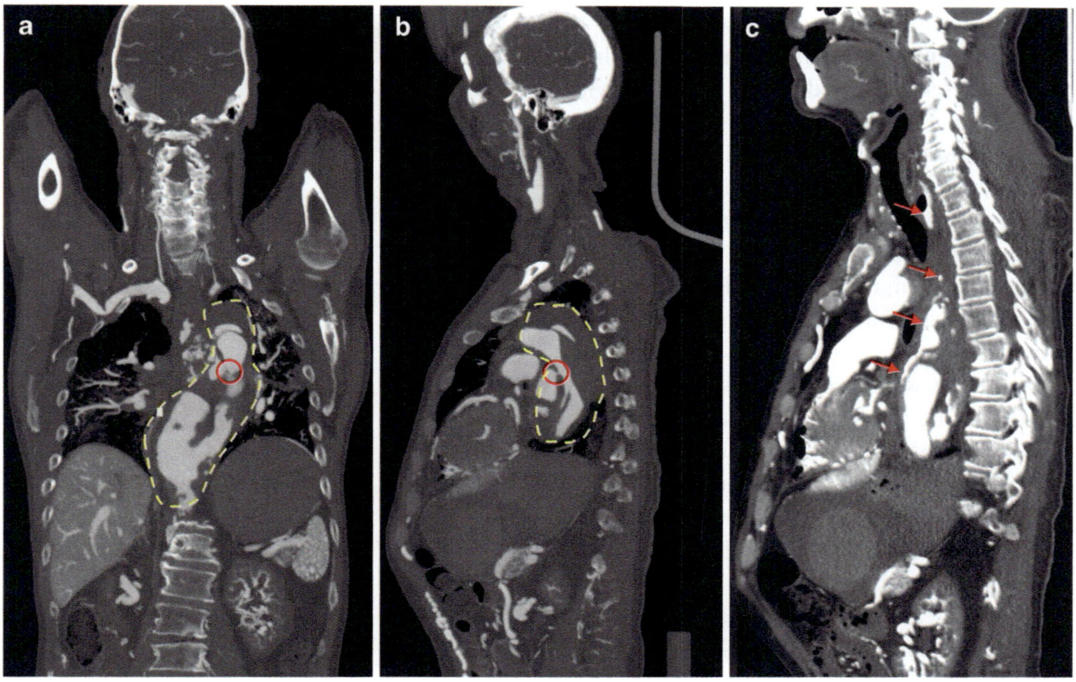

Fig. 22 (a) Male, 61 years, with large aneurysm of the descendent thoracic aorta (yellow dashed frame) with putrid inflammation. Thoracic surgeons decided to implant a pericardium patch around the ascending aorta in a first step, then to wait for a stabilized medical condition for an aortic replacement operation. Before the second step was initiated, the patient died suddenly by gastrointestinal hemorrhage. Arterial phase of MPMCTA shows an esophago- aortic fistula (red circle). PMCT, frontal projection. (**b**) See 22a: Sagittal projection (**c**) See 22a. Trait of contrast medium leakage (arrows) into the esophagus which had been shifted forward at the level of the aortic aneurysm. Note hyperdense content in the stomach (1.2 l blood). Sagittal projection centrally to that of Fig. 21a on the right

2 Fatal Outcome in Preclinical and Clinical Settings: Common Case groups

2.1 Emergency Medicine and Intensive Care

Autopsy procedures are at risk to artificially displace foreign materials before documentation of their original position in the body at the time of death. PMCT allows to perpetuate evidence of their position (Heinemann et al. 2015).

Airway management-related complications in pre-hospital metropolitan emergency cases are seen in a relevant number of cases (Colwell et al. 2009; Cobas et al. 2009). They include esophageal positioning of a tube, bronchial intubation, esophageal or tracheal perforation but also disconnection or dislodgement of the tracheal tube. Figure 6 demonstrates a doubled intubation after correction of a displaced endotracheal tube still observable in the esophagus.

Pneumothoraces may result from thoracic trauma or iatrogenically from subclavian puncture or thoracentesis (Ault et al. 2015); often, a small pneumothorax or the extent of the mediastinal shift due to tension pneumothorax can be depicted by PMCT in a better quality than at autopsy. In a similar way, insufficient pleural drainage can be localized, whereby a post-mortem shift has to be checked (Fig. 4a, b). Thoracic hemorrhages after pleurocentesis (Fig. 13a, b) or abdominal hemorrhages after paracentesis are well-known complications particularly in patients with coagulation disorders.

3D reconstructions illustrate very well the transvenous placement of central support lines, gastric tubes and electrodes from medical devices with irregular loops and bending as well as the placement of different kinds of drainages.

Figure 3a, b illustrates the misplacement of a jugular venous central line going suddenly in the opposite direction up to the level of the right jugular foramen. Figures 9a–c and 10a, b demonstrate the malposition of gastric tubes, which loop in an uncontrolled manner.

In patients with cardiac or respiratory failure, Intensive Care Units use more and more aortic balloon pumps, ventricular assist devices, and extracorporal membrane oxygenation (ECMO) as a bridge for recovery, transplantation, or as an ultima ratio. PMCT easily identifies the position of the incoming and outgoing components as well as the location of pump systems (Vogel et al. 2013a, b; Heinemann and Vogel 2016). Gas accumulation in vascular tissues may point to an air embolism (see Fig. 18a–d) or massive blood loss, gas accumulations in soft tissues of the neck and upper trunk regions are occasionally observed after misplaced tracheotomy or coniotomy. It remains challenging in PMCT to detect the point of origin of gas/air leakage but at least PMCT allows comprehensive detection of gas, even in minimum amounts, as well as demonstration of its distribution when spreading out from a suspected source.

2.2 Transvascular Interventions

Following *percutaneous coronary intervention* (PCI), sometimes contrast enhancement of the myocardium might be seen, which seems caused by contrast agent deposits that have not been completely washed out (Figs. 17a and 23). The correspondence to the supply area of a coronary artery may be taken as an indication for sudden interruption of coronary perfusion before death or immediate cardiac arrest after contrast medium application.

The patency of the vessel, calcifications of the vessel wall as well as implanted stents are illustrated by PMCTA. The indication for thrombotic occlusion after stent implantation can be visualized (Fig. 19a, b). The detection of gas bubbles in a coronary artery after fatal outcome during a PCI procedure (Fig. 20a–c) arises the question if a gas embolism could have happened. Postmortem gas formation is a very unlikely explanation when gas detection is restricted to the coronary arteries. Another differential diagnosis is the replacement of blood by gas via unlocked catheters which had not been removed from the body immediately after the procedure (Heinemann et al. 2015).

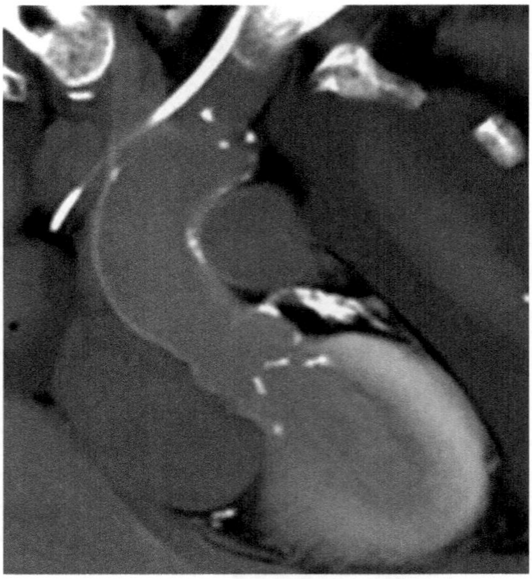

Fig. 23 Enhancement of large areas of the left ventricular myocardium by antemortem contrast agent which has not been washed out before death. Sudden fatal cardiac arrhythmia during contrast agent injection for coronary angiography. PMCT, frontal plane, mean intensity projection

Coronary perforations with cardiac tamponade (Fig. 14) and dissections are rare fatal complications after transvascular cardiac interventions, sometimes resulting in aortic dissections (Fig. 17a, b). Perforations result from balloon expansions of the arterial wall or stent expansion, at times directly from a catheter tip in a vulnerable vessel wall (Vogel et al. 2013b; Vogel and Heinemann, 2016). PMCTA might fail to detect the leakage site of a vessel in cases of emergency treatment with covered stents in the position of the ruptured vessel wall.

Furthermore, but very rarely seen, PMCTA may fail to demonstrate the exact lesion of the vessel wall in cases of cardiac tamponade if the pressure in the pericardial sac prevents contrast medium from leaking out of a rupture due to the adherence of blood clots to the surface of the traumatized tissue.

Transvascular valve placement refers predominantly to the transcatheter aortic valve implantation (TAVI; bovine pericardium bioprosthesis mounted on a ballon expandable stainless steel or cobalt chromium stent) (Fig. 1a, b). The advancement of the guide wire or a delivery system carries the risk of iliac or aortic perforation (Fig. 12a, b). The positioning of the valve, a potential coronary obstruction (Ribeiro et al. 2013) as well as signs of incompatibility of the aortic diameter and the expanded frame with the risk of valve insufficiency can be visualized by PMCTA.

During the last couple of years, *endovascular aneurysm repair* (EVAR) has been widely adopted for abdominal aneurysms—extendable into the iliac arteries—as well as thoracic (TEVAR: thoracic EVAR) aortic aneurysms even in emergency situations with ongoing aneurysm ruptures (Fig. 2a, b) and aortic dissections (Fig. 21a, b). The endograft represents an artificial lumen reducing the pressure in the aneurysm.

A major cause of complications in abdominal EVAR is the failure of the seal between the proximal, infrarenal aneurysm neck and the endovascular graft; an unsuitable fit between the aortic wall and the graft with compromised seal and an instable anatomy may elevate the risk (Greenhalgh et al. 2010; Becquemin et al. 2011). Advanced technologies introduced enlargements of the grafts including branched EVAR combined with fenestrations [FEVAR, see Fig. 2b] to maintain the patency of visceral and thoracic arteries, chimneys, snorkels, or direct fixation. PMCTA allows the analysis of the patency of indispensable aortic branches or surgical bypasses and visualizes endoleaks between device and original or false aortic wall, which may result in a reperfusion of aneurysms or dislocation of the prosthesis (Heinemann et al. 2015; Vogel and Heinemann 2016).

2.3 General and Cardiothoracic Surgery

The diagnostic efficiency of PMCT(A) after fatal outcome *of open surgical interventions* is raised with the detailed knowledge of the preexisting morbidity, the sequence of antemortem interventions and preceding complications to the last operation (Heinemann et al. 2015).

A typical scenario of suspected medical error is a challenged decision to wait and see instead of starting surgical exploration in case of abdominal pain. Sometimes, the intervention risk appears to be inadequate if the patient is already in a prefinal state at admission. Figure 11a, b illustrates a case with fatal outcome after gastric wall rupture due to dislocation of an epigastric percutaneous endoscopic gastrostomy tube.

A range of laparotomy-related complications can be illustrated by PMCTA as well. Examples are postoperative ischemia of the bowel with indirect radiological signs as in the living, a paralytic ileus with bowel distension and the presence of multiple gas-fluid levels. On the other hand, PMCT is of limited value for peritonitis from suture insufficiency after bowel resection, postoperative respiratory failure with pneumonia, wound infections with abscess formation or pyelonephritis which are suspected reasons for a sepsis/SIRS-related multi-organ dysfunction syndrome.

General soft tissue edema, fluid in the peritoneal and pleural cavities are indicative signs of heart, kidney, and liver failure. Maximum pulmonary edema without major post-mortem change and pleural effusions demonstrate respiratory failure and sometimes overhydration. An extravascular distribution of contrast agent deposits in the kidneys or in the uro-genital-tract indicates antemortem contrast-enhanced imaging in excretion-dependent short-term intervals before death. Hemorrhages from dehiscent vessel anastomoses or ligatures after resections of abdominal organs are visualized; however, a collapse of major vessels such as vena cava as a sign of hemorrhagic shock is usually missing because of massive transfusion or hyperhydration. In PMCTA liver failure is associated with a general elevated tissue enhancement.

Whereas, simultaneous enhancement of arterial and portal structures on the arterial-phase images is indicating the presence of open arterio-portal shunts in the post-mortem setting.

Sudden fatal hemorrhages may also result from erosion of arterial or venous vessels due to inflammation or necrosis of surrounding tissues after surgical and radiation treatment (Fig. 15a, b). A different issue concerns the question if surgeons did act in time before a fatal complication could happen, regarding the sequence of events of minimal invasive and ultimate open surgical procedures (Fig. 21a, b).

Coronary bypass surgery includes aortocoronary venous bypasses, LIMA (Left Internal Mammary Artery) and RIMA (Right Internal Mammary Artery) bypasses which are identified in PMCT by clips in characteristic formation (Fig. 1a) (Vogel et al. 2013a). PMCTA illustrates the patency of the vessel as well as of calcifications and stents in the graft.

Surgical repair with prosthesis for the aortic arch or further major vessels should be examined for their patency. Sometimes, hemorrhages under surgery or the application of support systems like heart lung machines may rise questions when extensive gas appearances in the vasculature system suggest air embolism (Fig. 18a–d).

The diagnosis of gastrointestinal hemorrhage sources is facilitated by PMCTA. Forensic questions may arise on the question how successful a hemorrhage had been stopped by endoscopic intervention. PMCTA helps to identify the sufficiency of vessel closure if not hindered by unspecific contrast extravasation due to post-mortem gastric mucosal destruction. Bleeding sources in the esophagus can be easily detected (Fig. 22a–c) as well as the success of sclerotization of esophageal varicoceles (Fig. 13a).

Figure 16 illustrates specific complications following abdominal tumor surgery after hepatic ischemia and detection of a thrombosis in the celiac trunk. The catheter-guided embolectomy of the common hepatic artery resulted in a perforation of the clipped gastroduodenal artery. This source of hemorrhage could be proven by means of MPMCTA.

3 Conclusions

Medical malpractice allegations after deaths were between 1990 and 2000 in Germany occasion for approximately 4.4% of the judicial autopsies; the trend is likely to be increasing since then (Madea and Preuß 2009). Usually in these cases a forensic autopsy in combination with preliminary information from the medical files of the deceased is needed to decide whether a peer review for the final evaluation of the case in question is needed.

If the patient dies from the effects of treatment failure, negligent physical injury with fatal consequences or even manslaughter have to be considered. Typical medical error categories are the omission or delay of necessary diagnostic or therapeutic procedures and negligent causation of and/or delayed response to periinterventional complications (Madea and Preuß 2009). The forensic clarification of medical malpractice allegations frequently ends up in exculpation of accused clinicians. Nevertheless, this process has an acknowledged effect with regard to secondary medical error prevention (Dettmeyer et al. 2004).

Frequent risk factors of medical errors are missing open-mindedness for an error culture, insufficient prevention of mistakes (drugs, right-left confusion, mistake of patients), communication errors among those administering treatment, heavy workload, lack of clarity about the responsibilities and inadequate patient monitoring and a mismatch between low estimated risk and fatal outcome (Heinemann et al. 2015). A potential added value of a multimodal post-mortem analysis including imaging methods should always be considered in periinterventional/post-surgical complications. However, the investigation of allergic reactions to different agents or under-/overdosage of medical drugs, which necessiate toxicological investigations, will be based mainly on medical history and laboratory markers.

A decline of clinical autopsies results in an overestimation of the sensitivity of clinical antemortem diagnosis (Shojania and Burton 2008). Clinicopathological studies with PMMRI have been reported (Weustink et al. 2009), some with special respect to pediatric pathology (Thayyil et al. 2010; Arthurs et al. 2014). The application of PMCT in case of deceased patients from an Intensive Care Unit at a University Medical Center shows a high accordance rate of clinical "major"—and "minor"—diagnoses between imaging and autopsy results and PMCT and PMCTA which has become a highly standardized and evaluated methodology (Grabherr et al. 2011, 2014, 2018) may supplement clinical diagnoses in cases of missing autopsy (Wichmann et al. 2012; Wichmann et al. 2014; Heinemann et al. 2015). There was a high accordance even in the subcategory of cardiovascular diagnoses—however, a major limitation was still that myocardial infarctions were confirmed by potential coronary culprit lesions in PMCTA only (Wichmann et al. 2014)—PMMRT has been proven to be less compromised in the diagnosis of myocardial ischemia (Jackowski et al. 2013; Guidi et al. 2018).

PMCTA detects hemorrhage sources even in cases in which autopsy fails (Zerlauth et al. 2013; Grabherr et al. 2014). Blood coagulation disorders are a frequent condition in the case group of hemorrhage complications under suspicion of medical error. Post-surgical suspected medical error often challenge the forensic pathologist at autopsy with the preponderance of

- Discrete bleeding sources in small arterial branches.
- Venous leakages without recognizable lacerations of small veins/venules, which is typical for the renal bed, mesenteric veins and venous plexus in the pelvic region.
- Bleedings through minuscule defects caused by perforations with tiny instruments such as catheter tips.
- Multiple bleeding sources which succeed each other at various time points.
- Coagulopathy as a frequent condition in these cases (Heinemann et al., 2015).

Due to the reluctance of medical doctors concerning informed autopsy consent and inadequate prioritization by the legislature (Burton and Mossa-Basha 2012) post-mortem imaging presents an alternative. Furthermore, it could serve as a screening tool guiding the discussion on how to decide about a more detailed forensic or clinic-pathological examination (Dirnhofer et al. 2006). This could apply for unexpected deaths in the context of medical treatment—however, standardization of protocols for PMCT and post-mortem magnetic resonance imaging (MRI) is still pending (Shojania and Burton 2008).

Limitations refer primarily to thromboembolic complications as post-mortem imaging is restricted to probabilistic approaches concerning the quality of obliterating material in a vessel.

Another obstacle is the early post-mortem change (Christe et al. 2010) with hypostatic fluid transgression between different anatomic compartments resulting in diagnostic pitfalls in the radiological assessment of the lung (Heinemann et al. 2015).

In cases in which antemortem imaging can be compared with post-mortem imaging , this might help in the expert's delimitation of ex-ante and ex-post judgements by clarification of situational conditions in the very moment of a challenged medical action or decision.

The combination of imaging and autopsy, histology and toxicology could enhance the cost efficiency of criminal proceedings by accelerated setting the course and avoidance of costly follow-up assessments (Zerlauth et al. 2013). Furthermore, multimodal post-mortem examinations place an emphasis on clinical mortality analysis as a stimulus for continuous improvement of clinical outcomes.

References

Arthurs OJ, Thayyil S, Owens CM et al (2014) Diagnostic accuracy of post mortem MRI for abdominal abnormalities in foetuses and children. Eur J Radiol 84(3):474–481

Ault MJ, Rosen BT, Scher J et al (2015) Thoracentesis outcomes: a 12-year experience. Thorax 70(2):127–132

Becquemin JP, Pillet JC, Lescalie F et al (2011) A randomized controlled trial of endovascular aneurysm repair versus open surgery for abdominal aortic aneurysms in low- to moderate-risk patients. J Vasc Surg 53(5):1167–1173

Brogdon BG (1998) Forensic radiology. CRC, Boca Raton

Burton E, Mossa-Basha M (2012) To image or to autopsy? Editorial. Ann Intern Med 156(2):158–159

Christe A, Flach P, Ross S et al (2010) Clinical radiology and postmortem imaging (Virtopsy) are not the same: specific and unspecific signs. Legal Med 12(5):215–222
Cobas MA, De la Pena MA, Alejandra M et al (2009) Prehospital intubations and mortality: a level 1 trauma center perspective. Anesth Analg 109(2):489–493
Colwell CB, Cusick JM, Hawkes AP et al (2009) A prospective multicenter evaluation of prehospital airway management performance in a large metropolitan region. Prehosp Emerg Care 13(3):304–310
Dettmeyer R, Preuß J, Madea B (2004) Malpractice—role of the forensic pathologist in Germany. Forensic Sci Int 144(2–3):265–267
Dirnhofer R, Jackowski C, Vock P et al (2006) VIRTOPSY: minimally invasive, imaging-guided virtual autopsy. Radiographics 26(5):1305–1333
Friedrich MJ (2012) Can imaging help revive the autopsy? JAMA 307(14):1471
Grabherr S, Doenz F, Steger B et al (2011) Multi-phase post-mortem CT angiography: development of a standardized protocol. Int J Legal Med 125(6):791–802
Grabherr S, Grimm J, Dominguez A et al (2014) Advances in post-mortem CT-angiography. Br J Radiol 87(1036):20130488
Grabherr S, Heinemann A, Vogel H et al (2018) Postmortem CT angiography compared with autopsy: a forensic multicenter study. Radiology 288(1):270–276
Greenhalgh RM, Brown LC, Powell JT et al (2010) Endovascular versus open repair of abdominal aortic aneurysm. United Kingdom EVAR Trial Investigators. N Engl J Med 362(20):1863–1871
Guidi B, Aquaro GD, Gesi M et al (2018) Postmortem cardiac magnetic resonance in sudden cardiac death. Heart Fail Rev 23(5):651–665
Heinemann A, Vogel H (2016) Postmortem angiography after invasive surgery. In: Grabherr S, Grimm J, Heinemann A (eds) Atlas of postmortem angiography. Springer International Publishing, Cham, pp 327–344
Heinemann A, Vogel H, Heller M et al (2015) Investigation of medical intervention with fatal outcome: the impact of post-mortem CT and CT angiography. Radiol Med 120(9):835–845
Jackowski C, Schwendener N, Grabherr S et al (2013) Post-mortem cardiac 3-T magnetic resonance imaging: visualization of sudden cardiac death? J Am Coll Cardiol 62(7):617–629
Madea B, Preuß J (2009) Medical malpractice as reflected by the forensic evaluation of 4450 autopsies. Forensic Sci Int 190(1–3):58–66
Palmiere C, Binaghi S, Doenz F et al (2012) Detection of hemorrhage source: the diagnostic value of post-mortem CT-angiography. Forensic Sci Int 222(1–3):33–39
Patriquin L, Kassarjian A, O'Brien M et al (2001) Postmortem whole-body magnetic resonance imaging as an adjunct to autopsy: preliminary clinical experience. J Magn Reson Imaging 13(2):277–287
Ribeiro HB, Webb JG, Makkar RR et al (2013) Predictive factors, management, and clinical outcomes of coronary obstruction following transcatheter aortic valve implantation: insights from a large multicenter registry. J Am Coll Cardiol 62(17):1552–1562
Shojania KG, Burton EC (2008) The vanishing nonforensic autopsy. N Engl J Med 358(9):873–875
Thali M (2011) Virtual autopsy (virtopsy) in forensic science: from the scalpel to the scanner. Pathologe 2011(32 Suppl 2):292–295
Thayyil S, Chandrasekaran M, Chitty LS et al (2010) Diagnostic accuracy of post-mortem magnetic resonance imaging in fetuses, children and adults: a systematic review. Eur J Radiol 75(1):142
Vogel H, Heinemann A (2016) Postmortem angiography and clinical pathology. In: Grabherr S, Grimm J, Heinemann A (eds) Atlas of postmortem angiography. Springer International Publishing, Cham, pp 311–326
Vogel B, Heinemann A, Gehl A et al (2013a) Postmortem computed tomography (PMCT) and PMCT-angiography after transvascular cardiac interventions. Arch Med Sadowej Kryminol 63(3):255–266
Vogel B, Heinemann A, Tzikas A et al (2013b) Post mortem computed tomography (PMCT) and PMCT-angiography after cardiac surgery. Possibilities and limits. Arch Med Sadowej Kryminol 63(3):155–171
Westphal SE, Apitzsch JC, Penzkofer T et al (2014) Contrast-enhanced postmortem computed tomography in clinical pathology: enhanced value of 20 clinical autopsies. Hum Pathol 45(9):1813–1823
Weustink AC, Hunink MG, van Dijke CF et al (2009) Minimally invasive autopsy: an alternative to conventional autopsy? Radiology 250:897–904
Wichmann D, Heinemann A, Weinberg C et al (2014) Virtual autopsy with multiphase postmortem computed tomographic angiography versus traditional medical autopsy to investigate unexpected deaths of hospitalized patients. Ann Intern Med 160:534–541
Wichmann D, Obbelode F, Vogel H et al (2012) Virtual autopsy as an alternative to traditional medical autopsy in the intensive care unit. A prospective cohort study. Ann Intern Med 156:123–130
Zerlauth JB, Doenz F, Dominguez A et al (2013) Surgical interventions with fatal outcome: utility of multiphase postmortem CT angiography. Forensic Sci Int 225(1–3):32–41

GPSR Compliance

The European Union's (EU) General Product Safety Regulation (GPSR) is a set of rules that requires consumer products to be safe and our obligations to ensure this.

If you have any concerns about our products, you can contact us on ProductSafety@springernature.com

In case Publisher is established outside the EU, the EU authorized representative is:

Springer Nature Customer Service Center GmbH
Europaplatz 3
69115 Heidelberg, Germany

Batch number: 10732801

Printed by Printforce, the Netherlands